THINKING ABOUT MANAGEMENT

THINKING ABOUT MANAGEMENT

Implications of Organizational
Debates for Practice

Randal Cullen
Graduate School of Business.
UQ
August 2002

IAN PALMER and CYNTHIA HARDY

SAGE Publications
London · Thousand Oaks · New Delhi

SAGE Publications Ltd
6 Bonhill Street
London EC2A 4PU

SAGE Publications Inc
2455 Teller Road
Thousand Oaks, California 91320

SAGE Publications India Pvt Ltd
32, M-Block Market
Greater Kailash – I
New Delhi 110 048

British Library Cataloguing in Publication data

A catalogue record for this book is
available from the British Library

ISBN 0 7619 5535 6
ISBN 0 7619 5536 4 (pbk)

Library of Congress catalog card number 99-71354

Typeset by Type Study, Scarborough
Printed in Great Britain by Redwood Books, Trowbridge, Wiltshire

For Dianne, Matthew and Michelle
Ian

For Imad
Cynthia

CONTENTS

1 MANAGEMENT AND ORGANIZATIONAL DEBATES

There's nothing so practical as a good theory?

This conventional wisdom has a nice ring to it but it ignores two important facts. First, the management literature is replete with many good theories (and some not so good). So how do managers choose among them? Second, within the management literature what constitutes a 'good' theory is a matter of considerable debate. Debate is often something that we prefer to do without – it is associated with confusion, disagreement and conflict. However, debate is central to the development of academic theory because it helps to make assumptions explicit, to review logics, to explore implications and to assess directions. It is through debate that academics refine, reject and replace theories and theorizing. In this way, over the last thirty years, management thought has grown away from a relatively narrow emphasis on quantitative methods, scientific research and functionalist approaches to embrace a diversity of new and alternative ways of viewing organizations.[1] Today, while there may be less agreement on what management thought comprises, there are far more resources and insights on which we can draw in our attempts to understand and reflect on management.

The value of debate is not confined only to the academic arena, it also influences management practice. For example, understanding the assumptions that underlie their thinking helps managers to assess whether their actions are appropriate. By challenging those assumptions, managers may identify alternative options and possibilities that they would not otherwise have seen. By reviewing the logic underpinning a course of action, managers are able to assess the coherence, consistency and integration of these actions. They may find that their logic is 'faulty' – that what they are doing is likely to lead to a very different outcome to the one they had envisaged. Exploring the implications of their ideas and actions alerts managers to unanticipated consequences, warning them of events further down the road. Assessing possible future directions encourages managers to consider the big picture – to put their decisions and actions in context. In this way, managers may uncover discontinuities between what they are doing and where the organization is supposed to be going. By engaging in debate, then, managers are able to bring more insight to bear on their ideas, decisions and actions. Consequently, we would argue that there is nothing so practical as a good debate.

FROM THOUGHT TO PRACTICE

This book aims to engage managers in debate, specifically to involve them in some of the important debates that preoccupy contemporary management thought and to do so in ways that have relevance for management practice. The challenge lies in how to translate debates that are primarily embedded in academic discourse, and make them accessible to management practice. A number of different approaches to this problem of translating management theory in ways that have meaning for management practice have been adopted by other writers. They include avoidance, simplification and the use of multiple lenses.

Avoiding the problem?

Some academic writers simply avoid the problem of translation altogether by developing theories that are 'uncontaminated' by management practice. This is the ivory tower approach. Hardy and Clegg[2] note an inherent propensity among all forms of academic research to distance the act of research from the actions of the subjects under study. In the case of management and organization theory, this can mean ignoring managers and other organizational members as research becomes increasingly self-referential and divorced from everyday management experience. Some researchers would not see this as a problem, believing that theory and practice should be clearly demarcated activities in order to facilitate academic endeavours. As Zald[3] notes, it makes it easier for these distanced researchers to write 'because the subjects do not read your work any more. You are not worried about your audience, which is purely academic'.

While there are advantages to such an isolated existence, researchers risk marginalization by refusing to engage with the object of their theoretical study.[4] This is a particular problem as universities come under increasing pressure to engage with the communities of which they are a part and, in particular, to be more accessible, relevant and 'managerial'. While we acknowledge that there are problems with the increasing pressures to 'corporatize' universities, we also believe that there is a role for researchers to engage with the subjects they study – in this case, engaging with the people who populate organizations – through research and teaching. Further, such 'cross-fertilization' offers opportunities to inform both research and practice in ways that are intellectually interesting and practically stimulating. Consequently, we reject the idea that no translation between managerial thought and practice is necessary.

All things simple?

Some writers have confronted the issue of translation head on and have taken great pains to ensure that the outputs of academic discourse make their way directly to managers and employees. In the context of organization and management theory, this often means that simplification is the mode of translation. How many books have we seen on the 'one best way', the five steps to success, or the most recent managerial 'fad'?

There are, however, a number of problems with this mode of translation. First, while the presentation of simplicity may initially be comforting to managers, its effects rarely last. Most managers face organizational problems that are 'wicked'[5] – complex, multi-causal and multi-layered, and rarely solved by simple solutions. Consequently, as many times as we read about the 'one best way', we also hear about yet another organization that has tried restructuring, empowering, networking, downsizing and re-engineering, and still things are not working properly. Second, there is a risk with this approach that an agenda of consultancy determines research work. For example, Barley et al.[6] note how organization theorists' accounts of culture have been progressively influenced by concerns relating to practitioners and consultants. The problem with the search for quick and simple fixes that cater to managers' most pressing needs is that research agendas are concomitantly 'dumbed down'. In the longer term, this approach is likely to frustrate rather than facilitate attempts to translate management thought into practice – as managers become increasingly frustrated with simplistic 'solutions' that do not work, they are less likely to consider research and researchers as useful sources of insight into management practice.

Multiplicity?

A more recent development adopted by writers trying to translate the complexity of academic discourse in ways that are accessible to managers is by the use of multiple lenses through which issues and problems can be viewed. For example, managers may be invited to think of the organization as if it is a machine, an organism, a brain or some other metaphor.[7] Different theoretical perspectives may be used to analyse particular organizational activities.[8] Managers might be exhorted to apply different frames to explore problems and generate different solutions.[9] While not all these frameworks have been targeted directly at managers, advocates argue that different lenses help individuals to interpret problems in different ways, to gain insight into different aspects of the problem in question, to generate alternative possibilities for action, and to secure an appreciation for complexity.

There are, however, a number of problems with this mode of translation from theory to practice. First, individual perspectives are presented as self-contained 'compartments', each of which is unitarist in nature – there is little debate about the object of study once viewed through a particular lens.

Applying an individual lens removes much of the complexity that multiple frameworks attempt to make visible. Second, the integration or aggregation of different lenses is problematic because it is not clear how managers should amalgamate lenses that represent fundamentally different assumptions. In fact, the ability to combine different lenses or 'paradigms' has been a matter of intense debate among researchers for several years.[10] Consequently, we have little sense of how to combine perspectives in ways that are enlightening rather than simply confusing. So, while adding some appreciation of complexity, this mode of translation fails to capture an important source of it, namely the clash that occurs between different lenses.

Third, the source of multiplicity stems from a theoretical abstraction, i.e. a metaphor, a frame, a theoretical perspective, rather than from a practice-based issue confronting the manager. While we do not deny that there are benefits to be derived from asking an individual to think in political, structural and then humanistic terms, or to conceive of the organization as a brain and then a machine, management practice does not operate at this level of abstraction. Rather, management practice revolves around more concrete activities like how to manage a change programme, whether to implement downsizing, which new compensation scheme to consider, whether to reorganize the board of directors, how to go about changing the culture of a department. Managers and other organizational members have a need for translations that are more readily grounded in aspects of practice. In other words, while an appreciable improvement on other forms of translation, multiple approaches still do not take the translation far enough. This is why the mode of translation adopted in this book is one that focuses on debates.

A MATTER OF DEBATE

The basic premise of this book is that management thought is 'a contestable and contested network of concepts and theories which are engaged in a struggle to impose certain meanings rather than others on our shared understanding of organizational life'.[11] In other words, academic discourse is about debate and we believe that this debate can usefully be translated for managers in ways that are transferable into the realm of management practice.

One of the problems with debates, however, is that they often become polarized as the researchers of one genre or tradition develop their ideas in direct opposition to others.[12] As Van Maanen argues, the aim of engaging in debate is often 'to overwhelm or obliterate one's opponents: to prune, pare and discard'.[13] Combatants often use esoteric jargon or obscure statistics through which they speak to other researchers of the same persuasion. This form of debate is of little relevance to managers, who are relegated to the role of mere spectators and left wondering, at best, which side to choose and, at worst, whether the debate has any relevance to their experiences at all.

We suggest that there is a role for managers as consumers of academic debates and not helpless spectators. By this we mean that managers can learn from debates in ways that inform management practice by enhancing their understanding of and ability to deal with organizational complexity. In taking this position we suggest that managers can use debates to take stock of the competing logics and arguments, the assumptions behind them, and the different directions they suggest for practice. To consume debates in this manner and to make them relevant and accessible, debates must be translated in particular ways – they must be presented in context, relate to experience, encourage reflection, make connections, make sense and accommodate ambiguity.

Debates in context

As we have already argued, many academic debates are presented in theoretical, abstract terms that are divorced from any practical context,[14] while managers are typically forced to focus on practical issues. The debates in this book are linked to specific issues relating to management practice. The following chapters reflect broad arenas that are found in most texts on organizations and which are readily familiar to managers – structure, people, power, culture, strategy, change, learning and leadership. Within each of these chapters, we focus on more specific issues. So, for example, we talk about downsizing, and outsourcing in Chapter 2 on structure. Chapter 4 on power mentions empowerment, diversity, ethics and the board of directors. In our discussion of strategy (Chapter 6), we explore planning, strategic change, global and collaborative strategy and so on. In each section on a particular issue, we use debates to frame the discussion of activities that are familiar to managers. Accordingly, while we briefly review traditional academic debates relevant to each chapter, we concentrate on contemporary, issue-based debates that are of direct relevance to management practice. In this way, our approach differs from work that presents theories without embedding them in specific processes and practices.

The one exception to this model is the final chapter on postmodern approaches. Postmodernism represents a theoretical perspective, not a managerial activity or aspect of management practice. The inclusion of this chapter is important because it integrates the practical context with the contemporary academic context – and increasing interest in postmodernism has radically changed the contemporary academic context. Any translation that does not bring more recent academic developments to the attention of managers is incomplete. Chapter 10 on postmodernism is, then, an important (and particularly challenging) translation because it reflects a direct attempt to bring to bear some of the recent and more fundamental debates in the academic arena on specific issues of management practice.

Experiencing debates

The key to translation is not only to put debates into context but to do so in a way that allows readers to draw on their own experience and to use that experience to inform their engagement with debates. If we neglect experience, managers lose the opportunity to 'fine-tune' their engagement with debates in ways that address their priorities. Consequently, this book has been designed to enable readers to engage in debates using their own experience and, in so doing, translate debates into a more useful resource for practice.

Each chapter contains a variety of exercises that enable the reader to ground the debates experientially. The exercises have been designed to allow readers to refer to their own experiences or, in the case of less experienced readers, to use the experience of other managers by drawing upon literature searches, the media and other public presentations of this experience. Consequently, even readers who have only limited organizational experience are provided with the means through which they can assess the practical relevance of debates. The aim of these exercises is not to dispel debate but to raise awareness of the conflicting currents that constitute particular debates. We suggest that readers should not try to resolve debates – to come up with the right 'answer' – but instead should try to understand the complexities and nuances associated with the debate. In this way, we hope to enable readers both to draw on and to move beyond their experience – avoiding becoming enslaved by experience which, at the same time, is necessary.[15]

Reflecting on debate

Assessing the relevance of debates, in terms of experience and context, encourages the reader to engage in reflection. Reflection heightens awareness and encourages individuals to look more closely at what they think they know and the assumptions on which this 'knowledge' is based. The call for reflection has been heard frequently in the recent academic literature, [16] but the benefits of reflection are not confined to academics. The capacity for critical self-understanding[17] also provides managers with the ability to question the continuing relevance of their assumptions in situations where organizations and 'best practice' are constantly changing.

We encourage reflection in two ways. First, through the issue-based debates presented in the individual chapters, we explicitly ask managers to think carefully about taken for granted assumptions and conventional wisdom. For example, a common assumption is that new organizational forms are needed to respond effectively to the fast-changing business environment. However, knowledge of the debate about the relationship between traditional and new organizational structures alerts managers to the possibility that both new and old forms may be necessary. Reflecting on the assumptions that underpin both bodies of theory opens up new alternatives that can be tailored to varying circumstances and needs, rather than simply replacing old structures with new ones. Similarly, reflecting on the different assumptions that underpin agency theory and stewardship theory in the context of corporate governance helps to provide different alternatives regarding board reorganization, as well as identifying their potential pitfalls. Agency theory argues that managers are opportunistic and are best held accountable to a strong, independent board that is needed to monitor managers and their decisions. Stewardship theory argues that managers are good stewards of the corporation and allowing 'amateur' outsiders access to the board is detrimental because it compromises sound managerial decisions and hampers strong leadership.

A second means of reflection is encouraged through Chapter 10 on post-modernism. Postmodern approaches have had a major impact on management theory and organization studies by challenging some of our most basic assumptions regarding the definition of organizations, the status of the researcher and the nature of 'knowledge'. In this regard, this body of work has generated considerable debate and, in so doing, encouraged far more reflection than has often been the case. While most of its impact has so far been felt primarily in the academic arena, by translating some key aspects of this body of work we believe it can also help to encourage reflection in the arena of practice.

Connecting the debates

We have already talked about how managers can connect academic debates to specific contexts of management practice and to their own experience. Other connections must also be made – among different debates and among different issues.

First, individual debates are rarely self contained – even in relation to a particular issue, different debates have implications for each other. To help the reader to make links among different debates, we make connections within individual chapters. For example, in Chapter 6 on strategy we explore a debate regarding the nature of strategy and present different views of strategy. We then link this debate regarding the nature of strategy to four interconnected issue-based debates regarding the relationship of strategy and structure, the value of planning, the nature of strategic change and the contribution of research. The 'answers' to these more specific debates are influenced by the broader debate. In other words, depending on your view of strategy, you will probably form different views about whether structure should follow strategy, whether planning is a useful activity, how strategic change should be orchestrated and whether research has anything useful to say about strategy making. Similarly, the debate about whether organizational learning is an individual, structural or interpretive phenomenon will connect to many other debates about how (and whether) to organize for learning. Managers who make these connections are likely to derive a broader, deeper understanding about management practice.

Second, while we frame our debates in the context of specific issues, we recognize that connections must be made among issues (and chapters) if debates are to inform management practice. Issues rarely exist in isolation and attempts at managing or resolving issues inevitably have implications for other aspects of managing the organization. We use the last two chapters to make these connections. For example, we frame the debates discussed in Chapter 9 on leadership in terms of their relevance to managing structure, people, power, culture, strategy, change and organizational learning. In this way, we systematically review the earlier chapters, making connections among different issues and showing how managers can connect debates and their implications to all aspects of the organization. More generally, we also show how structure is not separate from people, but constituted by them; culture is not divorced from power; strategy and learning have consequences for change; action goes hand in hand with reflection; and theory and practice inform each other. Similarly, in using Chapter 10 on postmodernism to reflect on basic assumptions concerning 'organizations' and 'individuals', we revisit many of the issues raised in earlier chapters.

Making sense of debates

While the translation of debates means that some connections are made for readers, they will inevitably make their own connections too. 'Readers are interpreters: to read is an active sense-making process. Through texts such as this, the reader has an opportunity to rethink his or her own conversational practices as an organizational member.'[18] In this way, the debates open up new interpretations whereby individuals add to, shape and change their understanding and the understanding of others. They hold the potential for reinvigorating practice by adding new meaning to complex situations. For example, making sense of debates about downsizing differs depending on the interpretation placed upon the practice. From the vantagepoint of Chapter 2 on structure, one managerial interpretation of downsizing is that it is a mechanism for achieving structural realignment and cost cutting. From the point of view of Chapter 6 on strategy, additional meaning is created by questioning whether downsizing is accompanied by growth strategies. From the perspective of Chapter 3 on people, interpretations concerning issues of survivor trauma, morale and 'best practice' alert managers to the effects of downsizing on employees. Chapter 5 on culture points to the importance of what downsizing symbolizes and the extent to which it causes disruption in the informal organization. Chapter 10 on postmodernism challenges whether there is any 'rational' need for downsizing at all and, instead, would promote the idea that it has become embedded in managerial discourse and practice in ways that are extremely difficult to dislodge.

Making sense of the debates in this book widens the interpretations available to managers for understanding the complexities of the organizational world that confront them. It also turns them from mere spectators to consumers of the translation process – by reading the text, they add to it, change it, refute it, use it, ignore it. Without the reader, our translation of management thought will never get anywhere near management practice.

Living with the ambiguity of debate

It is through debates that we recognize that the organizational world is typically complex and ambiguous. Past management education has not helped in this regard. This is because the 'smooth, planned and programmatic image of rational organization that inhabits the textbooks is typically at odds with the muddle and conflict that is the meat of work experience'.[19] Reducing management to a series of simple solutions reflects neither managers' lived experiences nor the wealth of research about management. Attempting to sweep ambiguity under the organizational carpet in the name of producing neat explanations and clean solutions is unlikely to be an effective long-term strategy since paradoxes are difficult to resolve and simplistic solutions have a short shelf-life.

For this reason, at the start of each chapter, we point to the multiple definitions of each topic that abound. How should we deal with this complexity? Simply taking one definition ignores the wider range of issues raised by other definitions; attempting to adopt all definitions is likely to paralyse action. Somewhere between the two lies the path of the effective manager who is able to engage in the debates in ways that accommodate complexity and generate action, while recognizing the limitations and boundaries associated with any action.

In summary, the basic premise of this book is that debates are not only inevitable but also helpful to both research and practice. Our commitment to debate represents an acknowledgement of the diversity and plurality that exists in theorizing.[20] If theorizing is open to multiple, contradictory and contested interpretations, so too is practice. And it is in this 'struggle that we learn . . . from the diversity and ambiguity of meaning, not through the recitation of a presumed uniformity, consensus, and unity, given in a way that requires unquestioning acceptance'.[21] By engaging in debate, we can link management thought and practice in ways that 'plant, nurture and cultivate'[22] new ideas.

A FINAL WORD

The book has been designed with flexibility in mind. For this reason, each of the following chapters has been developed as a self-contained component allowing readers the choice between using all the chapters to provide a broad overview of management and selecting a small number to explore particular issues to suit their needs. By using the exercises and the supplementary reading indicated at the beginning of each chapter, readers can decide the level, depth and nature of their engagement with the debates. In addition, the Appendix provides the management educator with ideas on how to use this book in more traditional educational settings, such as universities.

Finally, it is important to remember that debates are constantly changing and emerging. Yet not all issues are open to debate, nor does everyone have equal access to debates. For example, it is only in recent years that debates about gender and race, the environment and the underemployed have emerged in the management literature. There are countless other potential debates that we have not presented and many more marginalized voices that we have been unable to include. We acknowledge that the debates in this book are a selection of possible debates, and we readily admit that we do not and cannot cover them all. There are also debates of which we are not yet even aware, but which may become vital to management theory and practice in the next few years.

Rethinking organizational debates is a process – a way of thinking and reflecting – that does not just hold for the particular issues covered in this book. It is a way of approaching both academic endeavour and management practice in general. We therefore encourage managers and researchers to be open to debates – new and old – as a way to approach management thought and management practice now and in the future.

NOTES

(See Bibliography at the end of the book for full references)

1 Clegg and Hardy, 1996
2 Hardy and Clegg, 1997
3 Zald, 1994: 520
4 Hardy and Clegg, 1997
5 Rittel and Webber, 1973
6 Barley et al. 1988
7 Morgan, 1986, 1993
8 Martin, 1992; Hatch, 1997
9 Bolman and Deal, 1997
10 Clegg and Hardy, 1996
11 Reed, 1996: 45
12 Van Maanen, 1995
13 Van Maanen, 1995: 140
14 Hardy and Clegg, 1997
15 Thomas and Anthony 1996
16 Hardy and Clegg, 1997
17 Roberts, 1996
18 Clegg and Hardy, 1996: 5
19 Roberts 1996: 67
20 Hardy and Clegg, 1997
21 Clegg and Hardy, 1996: 8
22 Van Maanen, 1995: 140

2 MANAGING STRUCTURE

A New World Dawning or an Old World Yawning?

Recent interest in various new organizational forms has meant that managers today are bombarded with a plethora of design solutions that purportedly solve a host of organizational problems.[1] They are told to de-layer and downsize; to re-engineer, restructure and right size; to be fast and flexible; to empower and collaborate; and to dismantle hierarchy, bureaucracy and boundaries. For some, this list is evidence that contemporary organizations are 'poised on the edge of order and chaos';[2] for others, it merely represents a continuation of challenges encountered back in the turbulent 1970s.[3] Either way, a renewed interest of both scholars and practitioners in organizational structure is evident (see Supplementary Reading box).[4] Organizational structure is acknowledged to be a key strategic variable[5] and problem-solving device[6] in meeting contemporary management challenges.

This chapter takes the reader into the labyrinth of debates that concern these new organizational forms. First, we describe the core themes that characterize new organizational forms and examine one of the main reasons posited for the resurgence of interest in organizational structure – the existence of a new era that necessitates new forms of organizing. Second, we revisit traditional assumptions about organizational structure in the light of these new forms. Third, we identify key areas of debate concerning new forms of organizing. Finally, we conclude with what we believe to be an important contribution of the work on new organizational forms – expanding managers' and researchers' mental models of organizing. In this way, we critically examine the extent to which new organizational forms are, indeed, new or whether they simply represent a re-hash of old ideas.

NEW ORGANIZATIONAL FORMS: PLETHORA, PRACTICE AND PURPOSE

There has been an explosion of labels for new organizational forms including: intelligent, chaotic, improvisational, boundaryless, collaborative, empowered, horizontal, self-designed and minimalist organizations; clusters,

STRUCTURE: SUPPLEMENTARY READING

- Dess G.G. et al. (1995) 'The new corporate architecture', *Academy of Management Executive*, 9 (3): 7–20.

- Donaldson, L. (1985) *In Defence of Organisation Theory*. Cambridge: Cambridge University Press.

- Eccles, R.G. and Nohria, N. (1992) *Beyond the Hype: Rediscovering the Essence of Management*. Boston, MA: Harvard Business School Press.

- Ghoshal, S. and Bartlett, C.A. (1995) 'Changing the role of top management: beyond structure to process', *Harvard Business Review* (Jan–Feb): 86–96.

- Hilmer, F.G. and Donaldson, L. (1996) *Management Redeemed: Debunking the Fads that Undermine Corporate Performance*. New York: Free Press.

- Hirschhorn, L. and Gilmore, T. (1992) 'The new boundaries of the "boundaryless" company', *Harvard Business Review* (May–June): 104–15.

- Jaques, E. (1990) 'In praise of hierarchy', *Harvard Business Review* (Jan–Feb): 127–33.

- Kiedel, R.W. (1994) 'Rethinking organisational design', *Academy of Management Executive*, 8 (4): 12–30.

- Lawler, E.E. (1997) 'Rethinking organization size', *Organizational Dynamics*, 26 (2): 24–35.

- Limerick, D. and Cunnington, B. (1993) *Managing the New Organisation: A Blueprint for Networks and Strategic Alliances*. San Francisco: Jossey-Bass.

- Miles, R.E. and Snow, C.C. (1992) 'Causes of failure in network organisations', *California Management Review*, 34 (4): 53–72.

- Miles, R.E., Snow, C.C., Mathews, J.A., Miles, G. and Coleman, H.J. (1997) 'Organizing in the knowledge age: anticipating the cellular form', *Academy of Management Executive*, 11 (4): 7–24.

- Mills, D.Q. (1993) *Rebirth of the Corporation*. New York: John Wiley.

- Mintzberg, H. (1983 1993) *Structure in Fives: Designing Effective Organisations*. Englewood Cliffs, NJ: Prentice-Hall.

- Morgan, G. (1993) *Imaginization: The Art Of Creative Management*. Newbury Park, CA: Sage.

- Nadler, D.A. and Tushman, M.L. (1997) *Competing by Design: The Power of Organizational Architecture*. Oxford: Oxford University Press.

- Powell, W.W. (1987) 'Hybrid organisational arrangements: new form or transitional development', *California Management Review*, 30 (1): 67–89.

shamrocks, spiders' webs, starbursts and consortia; circular, front/back, cyclical, and modular organizations; spherical, stable, internal and dynamic networks; organizations that are spun out, intersected, infinitely flat, inverted, fuzzy, fractal, federalist and virtual organizations.[7] While there are many new labels, they do not all represent separate new forms – many terms describe similar structures. For this reason, the term network organization is often used as a generic category to describe all non-classic forms of organizing.[8] Despite this overlap and confusion,these forms differ from the 'classic' organizational structures described in Table 2.1.

In particular, new organizational forms converge around three key characteristics (Table 2.2). In general, new organizational forms revolve around a *flat* structure with minimal hierarchical levels and small corporate headquarters. Their boundaries are *fuzzy* since traditional barriers are permeated by *collaboration* and *alliances* inside and outside the organization, and by *outsourcing* those activities in which the organization has no distinct competitive advantage. *Disaggregation* breaks the organization into small operational units, while the *empowerment* of staff enables them to act more quickly, especially in response to customer requirements. Flexible *teams* are established to achieve specific purposes; and employees are viewed as *mobile* resources whose careers take them to many different organizations.[9]

Since the classic designs have been with us for some considerable time, why are researchers and managers currently promoting and experimenting with the new organizational forms? One reason concerns new challenges associated with the current business environment[10] which are summarized in Table 2.3. Classic organizational structures, which emphasize issues like size, role clarity, formalization, specialization and control, offer little help in addressing these challenges. The new structural 'paradigm', on the other hand, emphasizes the importance of speed, flexibility, innovation and

TABLE 2.1 *Classic organizational designs*

- **Simple design** – flat structure, little or no middle management, direct reporting to CEO as found in many small businesses
- **Functional design** – structure is divided into units based upon the separate functions they perform such as production, marketing, sales, etc. Sometimes referred to as an 'inputs' model since the structure is based upon the skills that people bring 'into' the organization.
- **Product design** – also known as divisional, this structure is based upon dividing the organization into separate business units each of which is focused on producing a particular product (alternatively, each division may be focused on a geographic area).
- **Hybrid design** – combines functional and product structures. Some 'functions' are centralized in corporate headquarters; others are decentralized back to divisions or business units.
- **Matrix design** – teams are composed of individuals 'borrowed' from functional managers by account or product managers. These individuals therefore have two bosses (functional manager and product manager) and can be shifted into new projects as required.

TABLE 2.2   *Common characteristics of new organizational forms*

Flattened: to achieve empowerment	• At the extreme, this organization is virtually limitless, consisting of 'nodes' of individuals or 'brokerages' operating relatively independently of each other, dependent on a central authority for information and co-ordination, and connected to the centre through computers or other information-based technologies. Flattening may also involve a reduction of hierarchy to delegate power and responsibility to lower levels and to allow increased exposure and response to customers. • Problems include a lack of hierarchy and career progression; a loss of control; inadequate training to support new activities; a lack of rewards to compensate for new responsibilities.
Networked: in the light of core competencies	• Independent organizations are linked together at different points along the value chain to produce a particular product or service. Individual firms continually reappraise their core competencies to add value to current and potential network arrangements. Networks can respond to short product cycles as old products and services are dissolved and new ones brought on line, changing the network over time. • Problems include overspecialization in a particular product or market; excessive legal formalization of inter-organizational relationships making it difficult to change the network.
Clustered: around team-building	• Clusters of people are drawn from different disciplines to work together on a semi-permanent basis. The cluster handles administrative functions; develops expertise; expresses a strong customer orientation; pushes decision-making towards action; shares information; and is accountable for business results. Clusters traverse traditional hierarchical and departmental boundaries without requiring top management approval. • Problems arise when people lack the skills and motivation to work in teams; where the organization is based upon high volume, repetitive activities; where managers are unwilling to let go of top-down management practices.

Sources: Adapted from Quinn et al. 1996; Miles and Snow, 1992; Mills, 1993

integration across functional and other boundaries.[11] It assumes that organizations should be designed with 'survival of the fastest' in mind;[12] that 'bureaucratic fetters' must be 'chopped',[13] with flatter hierarchies and larger spans of control;[14] and, inside this new organizational form, new work practices must be introduced (Table 2.4).

In summary, the wide variety of new organizational forms is associated with flattened, networked and clustered organizational arrangements that are assumed to offer managers more scope and flexibility in dealing with what many consider to be a radically different and far more demanding environment.

TABLE 2.3 *New environmental challenges*

Hypercompetition	Increased competition is eroding traditional sources of competitive advantage such as cost, quality, timing and know-how. Deregulation is placing even more emphasis on market mechanisms.
Globalization	International geographic boundaries are becoming more permeable and change the nature of economic transactions.
Short product life cycles	Shorter life cycles result from technological advances combined with a proliferation of marketable products.
Technological change	Sophisticated information technology is becoming cheaper and creating new opportunities for products, services and markets.
Turbulence	Customer demands and the structure of markets are more rapid and unpredictable.
Corporate responsibility	Organizations are being made more accountable for a range of 'citizenship' responsibilities including diversity, worklife quality, the environment and professional standards.
Customization	Satisfying the customer requires an increased tailoring of products and services.

Sources: Adapted from Dunford and Palmer, 1996; Quinn et al. 1996: 350

TABLE 2.4 *Old and new work practices*

The old way	The new way
• Low trust	• High trust
• Hiding errors	• Uncovering errors
• Managers design work	• Employees design work
• Hierarchical, top down	• Lateral, collaborative
• Attention to cost	• Attention to adding value
• Individual training courses	• Continuous learning
• Internal competition	• Internal alliances

Source: Adapted from Nilson, 1993: 145

TRADITIONAL ASSUMPTIONS: FORCING A FIT?

Classic forms of organizing have been predicated on a number of key assumptions associated, primarily, with a contingency view of structure – the idea that the 'right' structure is contingent upon other factors such as size, environment, technology and strategy. Research and practice in new forms of organizing has led, however, to a reconsideration of these traditional assumptions, as we discuss below.

Size: is growth natural or do we call weight watchers?

Traditionally, much of the work on organizational structure has been premised on the 'life cycle' view where organizations start off as simple structures; then, as they grow, change into functional structures and, as they diversify, into multi-divisional structures.[15] The metaphor of the organization as a 'body' has underpinned this process: growth, birth, development and death are seen as natural.[16]

Underlying the work on new organizational forms is the contrary principle that 'smaller is better than large'.[17] We are in the midst of an era where downsizing and de-layering has led to the shedding of large numbers of staff from organizations. Organizations have been told to get smaller in order to get innovative.[18] Commentators have argued that fat, bloated, overweight, flabby, corpulent organizations are diseased, sick, ill, ailing, slothful, sluggish and lumbering. Their clogged up corporate arteries require radical surgery where the surgeon's scalpel will pare the organization to the bone and unclog blocked arteries. Somewhat less drastic solutions might involve putting the organization on a crash diet to trim the fat.[19]

A second challenge to the idea that growth is natural concerns the incidence of acquisitions and mergers that have historically been an important means of growth, especially for multi-divisional organizations. At the turn of the century, many companies acquired competitors in order to grow; the 1920s saw vertical growth through the acquisition of suppliers or buyers; the 1960s brought about diversification, where entire related and unrelated businesses were acquired to add to the firm's portfolio. During the 1980s, however, there was a wave of de-conglomerations and 'bust-up take-overs' where corporate 'raiders bought conglomerates and financed the deal through the post-acquisition sale of their separated parts.'[20] For these raiders, bigger was not better and the idea of an organization as a body which grows was replaced by a Lego view of organizations as 'financial tinker toys' to be broken up and rearranged at will.[21]

Another challenge to the idea that bigger is better comes from the small and medium size organizations that are prevalent in many societies – even Western industrial 'super powers' are numerically dominated by small organizations. These organizations, at some point, stop growing and never pass through all the life cycle phases. Indeed, a British study suggested that many small business owners actively resist the growth of their organizations beyond the point at which they lose personal control. For them, growth detracts from their reasons for forming the small business in the first place.[22]

This work suggests that we have seen the end of the concept of organizational growth as being natural and are, perhaps, witnessing the decline of the large organization in a number of ways. Networks promote the idea of scaling down the size of constituent organizations. Organizations are encouraged to get smaller by 'sticking to their knitting';[23] by identifying and honing their 'core competence' and divesting themselves of businesses outside their area of expertise. De-mergers encourage a move away from the firm as a portfolio of businesses.[24] The prevalence of downsizing suggests that 'small is beautiful'.

On the other hand, there are warning signals from those who worry that organizations are pursuing downsizing so vigorously that they are becoming too thin, anorexic, anaemic and losing muscle as well as fat.[25] Moreover, growth through mergers may be back on the business menu: mergers in the first quarter of 1995 were 36 per cent higher than 1994 which, itself, was a record high.[26] This trend has continued, with one writer labelling 1998 as 'the unofficial year of the merger'[27] and another writer arguing that America is now caught 'in the grip of merger mania'.[28] One study documents that in 1997 there were worldwide merger activities entailing $1.6 trillion, and in the first half of 1998 alone this figure was $1.3 trillion.[29] While some commentators argue that mergers and acquisitions in the 1990s are different – more strategic, synergistic and equity driven rather than debt driven – others[30] maintain they are still driven by traditional beliefs that businesses should reduce risk by diversifying into unrelated business domains; create value by 'milking' mature 'cash cows' products; and purchase, rather than develop, expertise. It may, then, be premature to report the demise of the large organization. There may be life – and growth – in the old organizational body yet.

The environment: survival of the fittest or figment of our imagination?

The structural contingency framework[31] argues that the environment is a major factor affecting which type of structure is likely to be successful. Stable environments are best suited to functional structures; diversified environments need divisionalized forms; while unstable and turbulent environments call for more flexible, agile structures like the matrix and adhocracy. The population ecology framework, which also examines the link between environment and structure, argues that the environment will select out inappropriate organizational structures in a Darwinian, 'survival of the fittest' manner.[32] In both these cases, the environment is considered to play a strong, influential role vis-à-vis structure.

Common to these positions is an assumption that the environment is knowable and concrete. But is the environment simply something we can objectively discover or 'unearth'; or is it 'constructed' from the perceptions which individuals have of it?[33] Smircich and Stubbart[34] argue for an 'enacted' view in which the environment does not exist independently of the mental frameworks through which individuals perceive it. What is taken as the environment becomes reinforced by the actions taken in relation to it which, in turn, emanate from individuals' perceptions. For example, many managers saw the piano industry as mature and looked to other fields for investment opportunities; managers in Yamaha had a different perception and saw it as a field of growth. Redefining it as the 'keyboard industry', they took corresponding actions which, in turn, helped to constitute a growing and profitable environment.[35] This market was enacted through different perceptions and actions and did not exist independently of them.

The debate about the relationship between organization structures and their environments also exists in the literature on new organizational forms. For some writers, new organizational forms are advocated as a way to create new environments by rewriting industry rules and transforming the competitive profile, using such mechanisms as strategic alliances, collaboration, networks and outsourcing to forge new relationships with suppliers, competitors, buyers, government and other organizations.[36] An alternative position is one which argues that because of the turbulent environment organizations need to adopt new organizational forms if they are to survive. Such a position takes a more objectivist view of the environment and assumes a relatively deterministic link between environment and structure.

Technology: puppet master or co-production?

Classic organization designs also assume a relatively deterministic relationship between technology and structure: for example, certain types of manufacturing technology are presumed to be instrumental in producing particular organizational structures. Other writers have suggested that size acts as a mediating factor in this relationship and is not unilaterally deterministic. Either way, these arguments suggest that managers need to choose the type of structure that best suits the type and complexity of technology, possibly within certain size parameters, to achieve optimal organizational efficiency.[37] Thus, certain structures are contingent upon particular technologies.

More recent theorizing, under the rubric of a 'structuration' approach, challenges the underlying assumption of contingency arguments that technology and structure can be treated as two separate entities, and that the one needs to 'fit' the other. Any distinction between structure and technology is an artificial 'duality and, in fact, structure is both a cause and effect of technology'. In other words, technology and structure enable and constrain each other; they bring each other into being in a process that is related both to the actions of individuals and to the historical period in which the actions occur.[38] The structuration approach also questions a common view that the development of new information technology has enabled new organizational forms to evolve, i.e. that new organizational forms are contingent upon the availability of certain types of information technology. Instead, it argues that:

> Information technology creates new options for organization design; and new organizational forms, in turn, provide new opportunities for technology design . . . The articulation of technology and organization recognizes that neither is fixed but that both are changing in relation to each other, and that technological users play active roles in shaping the design of this articulation.[39]

The structuration perspective challenges the idea that managers are puppets of an uncontrollable technological monster which controls their actions and dictates their decisions regarding organizational structure. Instead, it sees managers and other organizational actors as collaborators in the co-production and reproduction of both technology and structure, by engaging in actions that, by occurring in a particular time and place, are also shaped by broader influences, traditions and patterns of which they may not be totally aware.

Strategy–structure: chicken or egg?

Chandler[40] left a legacy in the form of an ongoing saga about which comes first: does strategy follow structure or does structure follow strategy?[41] He opted for the latter, although researchers continue to debate the question.[42] Regardless of the direction of causality, much of the discussion of the link between strategy and structure has been appropriated by the structural contingency view, couched in terms of achieving the best 'fit' between structure and strategy.

The assumptions underlying the idea of a fit between strategy and structure are also being questioned by the interest in new organizational forms. Ghoshal and Bartlett[43] argue that, by breaking down boundaries in organizations, managers have opened up the way towards viewing organizations not as structures but as processes, including entrepreneurial competency building and renewal processes. It is these processes – not formal structures – that must be managed. These authors argue that we must shift from a 'strategy–structure–systems' doctrine to a 'purpose–process–people' mindset. The latter focuses attention on how to 'shape the behaviours of people and create an environment that enables them to take initiative, to co-operate, and to learn.'[44] The managerial aim is framed as ensuring either that the strategy fits the structure or, alternatively, that the structure is designed to fit the strategy. Both views are too limited and too static. Instead, managers should consider how individuals can be enabled to achieve the organization's purposes through the design of processes that facilitate appropriate entrepreneurial behaviours and actions.

In summarizing this section, we can say that the traditional contingency view is based on the idea of 'fit' – organizational structure must fit with size, environment, technology and strategy. The insights that have arisen from the practice and study of new organizational forms suggest that we should jettison, or at least modify, the idea of 'fit'. They call into question many of the theoretical assumptions on which traditional approaches to organizational design are built, in particular, the relatively deterministic effect of size, environment, technology and strategy on structure. Instead, these variables are less clearly demarcated and influence each other in more complex, less discernible ways. Managers appear more likely to succeed, not by finding the right fit or combination of structural components for a particular situation, but by being aware of the fluidity of the processes that make up technology, environment, strategy and structure; and by developing skills to manage those processes more effectively. This is not to say, however, that we have reached the final word so far as organizational structure is concerned. Far from it: new forms of organizing are themselves the subject of intense scrutiny and debate, as we discuss in the next section.

DEBATING THE NEW ASSUMPTIONS

In this section, several 'new' debates are explored concerning the reaction against bureaucracy. We then examine a number of particular techniques associated with new organizational forms. Finally, we question whether these new organizational forms really are new. Elements of these debates are often found in traditional approaches to structure, but they are treated here separately on the grounds that they are predominantly associated with assumptions underlying the new organizational forms.

Desperately seeking flexibility?

In what has become almost a mantra within the new organizational forms literature, hierarchy and bureaucracy are treated with disdain. The 'intelligent enterprise' sets out to destroy hierarchy.[45] The 'minimalist organization' seeks to overcome the intrinsic dysfunctions of the bureaucratic form.[46] 'Enterprise' replaces 'hierarchy', which is 'too cumbersome' to be effective in 'a complex environment'.[47] Vertical hierarchy is jettisoned in favour of horizontal collaboration.[48] Rules, regulations and procedures are condemned for inhibiting flexibility and standardization and centralization berated for inhibiting responsiveness to diverse and fragmented markets.[49] In general, it is argued that 'today's hierarchical structure supported by highly sophisticated management systems no longer delivers competitive results'[50] to the extent that, within a decade or so, 'the notion of hierarchy may seem as archaic as the medieval belief in the divine right of kings'.[51] But such unequivocal dismissal of traditional structures is being questioned. Three particular arguments suggest that a blanket attempt to dismantle bureaucracy may be misguided: the need for reliability, the role of enabling rules and the creation of healthy hierarchies.

High reliability
One argument concerns the need for reliability especially since many managers neglect the potential impact of their decisions on both their organization and the environment. Organizational disasters such as Bhopal, Three Mile Island, the sinking of the *Herald of Free Enterprise* ferry, the *Exxon Valdez*, and the *Challenger* are well-known examples of inefficient organizational control systems. Roberts and Lihuser [52] suggest that not only are many organizations capable of causing great harm, but that their managers are often blind to this possibility. For example, a lack of internal

organizational monitoring of the trading decisions of Nick Leeson brought down the Barings Bank in 1994, resulting in huge financial losses. These authors suggest that a hierarchical loan approval system, with checks and balances would have ensured that such high-risk loans were not made. They conclude that, while many see rules and procedures as wasteful and bureaucratic, they represent ways to reduce risk, if properly followed and enforced.

In other words, managers should not unthinkingly dispense with rules in their rush to be responsive to a turbulent environment. Rather, they need to assess the requirement for *appropriate rules* to ensure that the 'high reliability' aspects of an organization's operations are protected. Even Tom Peters, who has argued strongly in favour of getting rid of 'verticallyoriented, staff-driven, thick-headed corporate structures',[53] has moderated this position. He acknowledges that he may have been 'thriving a little bit too much on chaos' – we dismiss Max Weber 'at our peril' since there remains an important role for organizing and regularity (Exercise 2.1).[54]

Enabling rules

Those with a negative view of bureaucracy see rules and regulations as lowering creativity, satisfaction, motivation and innovation; those who maintain a more positive view argue that it 'provides needed guidance and clarifies responsibilities, thereby easing role stress and helping individuals be and feel more effective'.[55] Studies have found support for a positive relationship between formalization and innovation, when rules formalize lessons learned from the past, facilitate large-scale co-ordination of projects, or free up individuals from having to concentrate on the 'routine' aspects of their jobs.[56] We need, then, to differentiate between 'coercive' and 'enabling' organizational rules. It is not formalization, rules and procedures per se that inhibit innovation, employee commitment and the like, but 'coercive' or 'constraining' rules. Rules can be designed either to enable employees to

---

EXERCISE 2.1 CAN WE RELY ON YOU?

Select an organization with which you are familiar, either from experience or from the business literature, that needs to ensure high reliability. Answer the following questions:

- Describe the organization.
- Explain why high reliability is important.
- What sorts of rules would be used to ensure high reliability in this organization?
- What would happen if those rules were relaxed?

perform their work more efficiently and innovatively, or to coerce individuals into 'controlled' behaviours over which they have little discretion (Table 2.5; Exercise 2.2).

Managers may, then, need to pay attention to different types of rules in their organization. Where tasks are routine or when reliability is important, they should address the extent to which rules are established by users and are seen by them as sensible. Where managers wish to facilitate innovative work, they must address the extent to which rules free up staff from having to spend time on the routine aspects of their work; incorporate an organizational memory of past experiences and best practices; and facilitate innovation without employees continually having to reinvent the wheel.[57]

TABLE 2.5 *Enabling and coercive rules*

Enabling rules	Coercive rules
• Provide organizational memory	• Force reluctant compliance
• Capture lessons learned from experience	• Extract recalcitrant effort
• Codify best practice	• More likely to be designed top down
• Diffuse new organizational capabilities	• Do not involve those to whom they apply
• More likely to have employee involvement in their formulation	• Deviation from rules is seen as intransigence by managers
• Seen as sensible by those to whom they apply	• Adherence to rules seen as repressive, pointless by employees

Source: Adapted from Adler and Borys, 1996

EXERCISE 2.2 RULE BOUND?

Select an organization with which you are familiar, either from experience or from the business literature, and answer the following questions:

- Identify six different rules, policies or procedures and briefly describe them.
- To what extent is each 'coercive' or 'enabling'? Explain your answer.
- Can the coercive ones be transformed into enabling ones? Explain how this might be done.
- What advantages and disadvantages follow from these changes?
- Consider your answers to the above three questions from the perspective of those *subjected* to these rules, policies or procedures and contrast them with the perspective of those *responsible* for implementing and monitoring them.

Healthy hierarchy

According to this view it is not hierarchy that is the problem, but 'unhealthy' hierarchies. Ashkenas et al. maintain that 'hierarchies are necessary, inevitable, and desired fixtures for organizational life. As long as organizations have limited resources and contain multiple perspectives, there will be a need for some people to be leaders and make decisions for others.'[58] Hierarchies are natural and effective as long as key 'switches' are used to prevent them from becoming slow, rigid and alienating.[59] By creating permeable vertical boundaries, managers are able to achieve a balance between control and hierarchical 'looseness' (Table 2.6).

TABLE 2.6   *Switches to create a healthy hierarchy*

Switch	Traditional hierarchy	Permeable hierarchy
Information	Flows upward; tightly controlled by top management	Widely shared; common goals; hologram form where staff can set goals consistent with organizational goals
Competencies	Leaders have know-how; lower level people have narrow technical skills	Competence deployed throughout organization; 'it's not my job' does not exist
Authority	Decisions made at top	Decisions made by persons closest to the issue
Rewards	Based on position	Based on accomplishment

Source: Adapted from Ashkenas et al. 1995: 43–51

Jaques[60] also argues in favour of hierarchies which, when properly structured, 'release energy and creativity, rationalize productivity, and actually improve morale'. The problem lies in the way hierarchies have been utilized in organizations 'to accommodate pay brackets and facilitate career development . . . If work happens to get done as well, we consider that a useful bonus'.[61] The solution is to distinguish between hierarchical layers and pay grades. The trouble is that companies use two or three times as many pay grades as they need working layers and, as a result, produce more layers than needed to carry out the work effectively (Exercise 2.3).

What is common to all these arguments concerning reliability, rules and hierarchy is that managers should not unthinkingly purge organizations of their hierarchy and bureaucracy in a relentless pursuit of flexibility. Rather, they should question the underlying logic of the existing hierarchical and bureaucratic structures with a view to achieving necessary reliability, instituting enabling rules and safeguarding healthy hierarchy.

It's all in the technique

In this section, we examine the debates that surround a number of management techniques in terms of their impact on organizational structure. We explore the intersection of total quality management and employee involvement; downsizing and retrenchment; outsourcing; and, finally, issues related to interorganizational collaboration and trust.

EXERCISE 2.3 HOW'S YOUR HEALTH?

Select an organization with which you are familiar, either from experience or from the business literature, and answer the following questions:

• Briefly describe the hierarchy.
• Explain whether it is unhealthy – and if so why?
• What specific actions would you take to use the switches identified in Table 2.6 to transform it into a healthy hierarchy?
• What outcomes would you expect to encounter if you took these actions?

Getting involved?

Employee involvement and empowerment is part of the 'new strategic architecture' to help organizations compete in the twenty-first century.[62] As organizations reduce management layers, employees are needed to move into decision-making areas that were once the sole domain of management; more delegation is needed to reduce product cycle times and to respond to changing market conditions.[63] In this way, employee involvement and enhanced quality processes are argued to have positive bottom line effects, as in organizations like Nissan, Hitachi and Honda. [64]

However, managers introducing employee involvement practices can be faced with two structure-related dilemmas. First, a dilemma occurs where such practices are introduced in conjunction with other programmes. For example, while some see employee involvement and total quality management (TQM) as going hand in hand, Lawler[65] suggests that each is underpinned by fundamentally different logics (Table 2.7). He argues that employee involvement programmes undermine organizational hierarchy. They rely on a flat organizational structure, with little hierarchy, in which self-managed teams are responsible for bottom line performance, including decisions about the design of work methods and procedures, the pace of work, team membership, and interactions with customers and suppliers. By contrast, TQM programmes 'typically accept the existing hierarchy and try to use it to produce system improvement'.[66] Less emphasis is placed on redesigning work and, where it does occur, tasks are more likely to be simplified than enriched. De-layering is not a major focus of TQM and the use of parallel techniques, such as quality circles, may even add support staff. Consequently Lawler argues that while employee involvement programmes and TQM have been shown, independently, to provide improvements over traditional bureaucratic management, it does not mean 'that they are necessarily interchangeable or even compatible'.[67]

A second structure-related dilemma in introducing empowerment practices arises when managers assume that teams will facilitate involvement and

TABLE 2.7 *Different logics of TQM and employee involvement*

TQM	Employee involvement
• Quality improvement	• Organizational effectiveness
• Management control	• Self-management
• Process improvement	• Organization design
• Work simplification	• Enrichment/work teams
• Work process codification	• Employee discretion
• Quality circles	• Work teams
• Internal customers	• Feedback
• Recognition rewards	• Financial rewards

Source: Adapted from Lawler, 1994: 71

increase performance. Teams are part and parcel of new organizational forms in breaking down the 'silo' nature of functional organizations and facilitating more permeable organizational boundaries.[68] An assumption is that teams will empower their participants, producing better decisions than those taken by senior managers who are removed from the action. Some writers, however, question the effectiveness of such teams. Morgan suggests that, in reality, many teams are 'pseudo-teams that are only capable of dealing with relatively minor issues'[69] because the team structure is grafted on to the old hierarchy without allocating any real decision-making power to the teams. In these situations, team meetings are often ritualistic, with a great deal of 'wheel spinning' and members 'sitting in' to report back to their functions on potential problems that might require counter-action.[70] Team members may also engage in 'self-limiting' behaviours, effectively withdrawing their participation, especially when experts are present; when members lack confidence; when decisions are seen as unimportant or meaningless; or when other team members exert pressures for conformity.[71] While steps can be taken to reduce the impact of such factors, managers can never be sure that they are enlisting the full, creative input of all team members (Exercise 2.4).

The conclusion to be drawn from this discussion is that managers need to move beyond glib pronouncements concerning the introduction of empowerment processes. Otherwise not only will they be disappointed with the results of TQM and cross-functional teams, but they are likely also to leave their staff cynical and disillusioned by the experience.[72]

Lean or mean?

As noted above, managers are under pressure to downsize to restore organizational health. Downsizing involves the intentional 'elimination of positions or jobs' and is portrayed as a technique to lower overheads, simplify bureaucracy, speed up decision-making, and enhance communication, entrepreneurship and productivity.[73] It remains popular today, with record numbers of organizations using it,[74] despite the fact that the promised benefits are not always delivered[75] and that a range of problems have come to

---

EXERCISE 2.4 ARE YOU INVOLVED?

Select an organization with which you are familiar, either from experience or from the business literature, and answer the following questions:

- Briefly describe a situation involving TQM or teams.
- What results were expected from the initiative?
- Were they achieved? Explain why or why not.
- What were the major challenges in implementing this initiative?
- What recommendations would you make for the successful implementation of such initiatives?

---

be associated with it, including damage to staff morale, to commitment, to productivity, to innovation, to risk taking, and to responsiveness to customers.[76]

Of interest here is how downsizing has been used to facilitate the emergence of new organizational forms. A major assumption underlying its use is that when the organization was smaller there was less bureaucracy, greater communication and more innovation. On these grounds, then, it stands to reason that to return the organization to its former days of glory requires de-layering and downsizing.[77] McKinley,[78] however, challenges this view for a variety of reasons. First, as the workforce is decreased, managerial time is soaked up in co-ordinating transition benefits, outplacement programmes and dealing with morale and inequity problems. Second, with the decrease in size comes the need to develop new administrative procedures, to introduce new services and to manage organizational politics. Third, when organizations decrease their size and engage in more interorganizational linkages, managers are needed to co-ordinate new and different areas of organizational activities. Ashkenas et al. point out that removing layers does not mean that information, competence, decision-making and rewards necessarily spread to lower levels, or that the old habits of top down, hierarchical management are removed.[79] As Morgan ironically concludes, when you downsize a bureaucracy, you still end up with a bureaucracy, it's just a smaller one.[80]

Managers employing downsizing measures need, then, to question whether it will simplify their organization and move it towards a new, streamlined, flexible organizational form. Often the work is not reduced, simply the number of people attending to it. Where they do engage in downsizing, managers need to identify 'best practices' in implementing it;[81] and, rather than employing it as a knee-jerk, cost-reduction technique, they should consider how it fits in with a broader strategic reorientation, that includes growth (Exercise 2.5).[82]

Outward bound?

Collaboration or 'collaborative advantage'[83] is a technique common to new forms of organizing and can entail the use of alliances, networks and outsourcing. It raises a number of questions, however, concerning the risks that come with handing over aspects of the business to outsiders.

While some commentators see collaboration in the form of partnerships and outsourcing as a source of competitive strength, others suggest that it 'hollows out' the organization.[84] In other words, while the idea behind outsourcing, networks and alliances is that organizations retain their core competencies in-house and hand over only those areas of their business where they cannot add value, actual practice does not always achieve the ideal. One problem is that organizations may not know exactly where and how they do add value and may, therefore, enter into collaborative arrangements that are based on a faulty assessment of their core competencies. Even where firms do make accurate assessments, market changes may lead to the need to develop new competencies. Organizations that farm out a large part of their business may lack a viable base on which to develop the new skills, rendering them particularly vulnerable to competition. Table 2.8 differentiates between offensive and defensive outsourcing, which illustrates some of the problems that companies can face if they make mistakes in forging collaborative relationships (Exercise 2.6).

Can we trust you?

With the new emphasis on collaboration, whether through networks, alliances or outsourcing, it is clear that new skills are required to manage it. A recurring theme is that managers need to develop competencies in building relationships. This involves developing trust.[85] While it is difficult to dismiss the importance of trust, some writers have labelled it as 'more American woolly-headedness' that evaporates when faced with issues of organizational self-preservation.[86] In fact, we know relatively little about

---

EXERCISE 2.5 DOWNSIZING DILEMMAS?

Select an organization engaged in downsizing with which you are familiar, either from experience or from the business literature, and answer the following questions:

- Identify and briefly describe the different methods of managing downsizing and the numbers and levels of the people affected.
- Describe the advantages and disadvantages of each method.
- What considerations in implementing downsizing are important if the organization is employing it as part of an initiative to become more flexible and responsive?

EXERCISE 2.6 DEFENSIVE POSTURE

Select an organization involved in an outsourcing arrangement with one or more other organizations with which you are familiar, either from experience or from the business literature, and answer the following questions:

- Briefly describe the outsourcing arrangement.
- To what extent can you categorize it as 'defensive' or 'offensive'? Explain your answer.
- What was the impact of this outsourcing arrangement on the organization?
- What lessons does it suggest for future ventures for this organization?

TABLE 2.8   *Offensive and defensive uses of outsourcing*

Defensive	Offensive
• The priority is to reduce costs. • A spiral is created as cost accounting systems bias the reallocation of overhead savings, lowering the apparent cost performance of these components and products and making them candidates for future outsourcing. • A score-keeping mindset prevails emphasizing reduced costs, improved returns, increased brand share. • Difficult problems are outsourced to make life easier for managers. • Competitive advantage of the core firm is unclear. • Competencies and skills are lost to supplier organizations, learning abilities of core organization are lowered, and initiative for future developments is lost.	• Skills and competencies to ensure sustained competitive advantage are retained; outsourcing is mainly used for functions away from core competencies. • Financial savings from outsourcing are redeployed to enhance core competencies. • The extent to which potential suppliers are likely to leverage their relationship to undermine the organization's long run core competencies is assessed. • Conditions under which an outsourcing relationship should be changed or ended are monitored. • Outsourcing is not used to fix a strategically sick business; it may provide a mechanism for a phased withdrawal from a business once a strategic exit decision has been made.

Source: Adapted from Bettis et al. 1992: 11–20

how to create trust between members of different organizations.[87] Writers have tended to assume that partners will collaborate voluntarily, share common goals and redistribute power. Such conditions may characterize some collaborative ventures but certainly not all, and certainly not all over time. Another issue concerning trust is the argument that effective inter-organizational collaboration cannot depend simply on a trusting relationship between particular individuals, one from each organization, who happen to like and trust each other. The new organizational forms rest on a multiplicity of connecting relationships in which many different employees from the two organizations must be able to work effectively together.

A further issue associated with trust is the argument that many of the complexities of interorganizational interactions are resolved not by trust but through implicit or explicit power relations among firms.[88] As Fox points out, 'We've got to trust them' often means 'We don't trust them but feel constrained to submit to their discretion'.[89] Such 'spurious' trust[90] may ensure co-operation and is certainly convenient from the dominant partner's point of view but it is unlikely to produce the synergy, creativity and innovation that more reciprocal collaboration is hoped to promote (Exercise 2.7). As one manager engaged in a 'collaboration' stated: 'They call it strategic partnership. We call it statutory rape.'[91]

In summary, the collaboration underlying the new interorganizational relationships involves certain risks and difficulties. Organizations must make an accurate strategic assessment not only of their strengths and weaknesses before contracting out parts of their business; they must also have

---

EXERCISE 2.7 WORKING TOGETHER?

Eaton's, a large Canadian department store, has 500 suppliers hooked into a new electronic data interchange (EDI) system. One of these suppliers is Grand National Apparel (GNA) which manufactures men's suits and sells them to Eaton's. Eaton's orders from GNA electronically – its software automatically reorders goods as they are sold to fill the 'model' inventory. The software notes changes in buying patterns and reorders accordingly. Eaton's shares sales data, product development information and marketing plans with GNA, which sells to other retailers although Eaton's is its largest customer. GNA is expected to invest time and money in building a relationship and a system to produce cost savings that can be passed on to Eaton's. GNA's performance is measured in terms of the time taken to fill an order and how completely it is filled.

To manage this new relationship, Grand National and Eaton's have formed cross-functional teams. In the past, all the information flowed through the Eaton's menswear buyer and the GNA sales representative. In the event of an invoicing discrepancy, for example, the accountant at GNA would phone the GNA sales representative who would phone Eaton's buyer, who would phone the accounting department in Eaton's to fix the problem. Now, accountants from both companies are members of the cross-functional team, as are members of distribution, information systems, marketing and other functions. The team has not been formed simply to fix problems; it is also supposed to innovate in product development, merchandizing, marketing and technology, which may produce savings but will also require considerable investment.

The jobs of both salespeople at GNA and buyers at Eaton's have changed significantly. The sales representatives no longer travel with samples to retail companies or lunch with buyers so much. Instead they help set up cross-functional teams and then step aside to take on a consulting role. Buyers used to have one of the most powerful jobs in retail: they decided what the store stocked and from whom it was bought. Whereas they used to know the whole system, now they can rely on others to work on finance, logistics, systems, etc.

Questions

- What new skills will be needed to manage this collaborative relationship?
- How can trust be built?
- What issues need to be formally negotiated?
- What scope is there for power to be used and what effect will it have?

Source: Adapted from Stevenson, 1993: 23

some idea of where the business is likely to go in the future to sustain viable core competencies. In addition, managers need to develop new skills to move from traditional relationships between organizations to new collaborative arrangements. In so doing, they need to confront the dilemmas associated with the development of trust.

What goes around comes around

In this section, we examine the 'newness' of new organizational forms. There is no doubt that the literature is replete with descriptions of new forms of organization. Some commentators suggest, however, that this evangelism has glorified – and overstated – the extent to which the environment is 'turbulent' and organizational forms are 'new'. Eccles and Nohria[92] suggest that contemporary researchers and managers tend to contrast a turbulent present with a stable past. But they point out that authors in the 1940s and 1950s also identified their period in history as one of great change. In fact, 'every generation of management discourse portrays the present as especially challenging, stereotypes the past, and then paints a vision of the future that is sharply contrasted with it'.[93] Consequently, there remains a question as to whether radical changes in organizational form are needed.

The 'newness' of these forms is also suspect. For example, features of the 'network organization' are similar to what Kanter referred to, in 1983, as the 'integrative organization'; and to what Burns and Stalker labelled as 'organic' in 1961.[94] It is also difficult to establish exactly how pervasive these new forms really are since much of the literature is based on case studies with little systematic evidence to assess how widespread are new organizational practices. Even systematic studies might find it difficult to identify these new, fluid forms which, by their nature, are difficult to track because 'they do not have stable boundaries and are composed of shifting arrays of specialized elements'; they cannot be identified in the same way as more traditional organizations.[95] In the following sections, we explore whether new forms are displacing old ones and some of the cyclical trends in organizational structure.

Off with the old and on with the new

Much of the literature suggests that the old structures are being thrown out and replaced, wholesale, by the new forms. For example, Seabright and Delacroix's description of the 'minimalist' organization as 'postbureaucratic' portrays it 'as the antithesis of the bureaucratic construct'.[96] As large, well-established organizations purportedly adopt new forms of organizing, the indications of a radical break from past practice in the heart of the business world appear clear. An alternative interpretation, however, is that these new forms are not replacing the old structures so much as being incorporated into them.[97] In other words, new arrangements may overlay more traditional structures and most employees continue to work in organizations with extensive formal procedures.[98]

The incorporation of new forms into existing structures raises issues that do not receive a high profile in the literature on new organizational forms. For example, what is the impact of incorporating new styles of organizing into old structures? Can parallel or competing logics exist within the one organization? What are the implications for managers in modifying old structures? What are the most appropriate modifications if both the old and new forms are to be successfully integrated?

The pendulum swings

The need for organizations to decentralize to provide operating flexibility and customer responsiveness has become an established principle in the new organizational forms literature. But it is not without its detractors. One view is that managers are being misled about the ability of decentralized operations to deliver innovative management. Chesbrough and Teece argue that, while some smaller networked organizations outperform large, supposedly cumbersome organizations operating in the same industry, many more fail – and we hear very little about these failures. They maintain that 'the virtues of being virtual have been oversold. The new conventional wisdom ignores

the distinctive role that large integrated companies can play in the innovation process. Those rushing to form alliances instead of nurturing and
guarding their own capabilities may be risking their future.'[99] These authors
differentiate between 'autonomous' and 'systemic' innovations. Autonomous innovations are added on to other developments and can be pursued
independently. For example, designing a turbocharger does not involve
redesigning the whole engine or car. By contrast, systemic innovations
involve fundamental, interrelated changes to product designs and production. Autonomous innovations can be fruitfully pursued through a
decentralized structure, but systemic innovations require centralized strategic co-ordination and sufficient scale to defray research and development
costs.

Another view seeks to dispense with the whole centralization–decentralization debate. It has become a 'faddish game, in which organizations swing
back and forth like pendulums'[100] as solutions to 'new problems' overturn
solutions to the old problems in a never-ending cycle. Ashkenas et al.[101]
suggest that managers should view the organization 'not as a set of functional boxes but as a set of shared resources and competencies', and ask how
their organization can create processes to ensure that all the resources and
competencies arrayed across the horizontal spectrum create value. 'Loosening horizontal boundaries . . . calls for integration, not decentralization;
process, not function; and teamwork, not individual effort.' However, it
becomes more difficult to dispose of the centralization vs. decentralization
debate in this way if new forms are only added on to traditional structures.
In this case, a process view is unlikely to pervade the entire organization.
Consequently, the pendulum will probably continue to swing between centralization and decentralization (Exercise 2.8).

These arguments alert managers to take a more informed historical view
of the new forms literature. Rather than be taken in by the prevalent evangelism, managers need to distinguish between hard evidence and rhetoric in
the messages presented to them about the environmental imperatives they
confront and the structures, which they should implement.

CONCLUSIONS: EXPANDING MENTAL MODELS OF STRUCTURE

The aim of this chapter has been to bring together a diverse set of writings
which, in different ways, impact upon issues relevant to managers who are
considering new forms of organizing. Rather than reviewing the merits of
particular new organizational forms, this chapter has mapped out a range
of debates that await the manager at different points along the road in order
to assist them in making more informed decisions.

Perhaps one of the most important contributions that the quest for new,
flexible forms of organizing can make is in helping managers – and
researchers – to expand their mental models to consider organizing in different ways. Kiedel argues that managers need to engage in 'rethinking' their

approach to restructuring.[102] For example, Morgan has used metaphors to help managers to 'imaginize' new options by thinking of organizations as spider plants, strategic termites and tubs of yoghurt (Exercise 2.9).[103] An 'action' or 'process' view of organizations moves mental models away from organizational charts that limit thinking and actions to the confines of pre-defined boxes (Exercise 2.10).[104] Organization charts may serve as static representations that 'thingify' organizational action, 'leading one to forget that organizations are really grounded in a network of ongoing conversations'.[105]

EXERCISE 2.8 TRADING IN THE OLD FOR THE NEW?

Select an organization with which you are familiar, either from experience or from the business literature, and answer the following questions:

- What evidence do you find of the classic organizational designs described in Table 2.1? Explain your answer.
- What evidence do you find of the new organizational forms described in Table 2.2 and the new work practices described in Table 2.4? Explain your answer.
- In what way do old and new structures co-exist? What are the advantages and disadvantages of such co-existence?
- If you find no co-existence (i.e. either only old or only new structures are to be found), what benefits might arise from mixing old and new? What would be the costs?
- What lessons do you learn from this analysis concerning organizational design?

EXERCISE 2.9 IMAGINE A METAPHOR?

Select an organization with which you are familiar, either from experience or from the business literature, and answer the following questions:

- 'My organization's structure is like a . . .' Complete the metaphor.
- What strengths and weaknesses are revealed by this metaphor?
- Would there be widespread agreement in this organization with this view of its structure? Explain your answer.
- If you were to address the 'problems', how could you redesign the structure without losing its strengths?

EXERCISE 2.10 LET'S TALK?

Select an organization with which you are familiar, either from experience or from the business literature, and answer the following questions:

- Draw a formal chart of the organization's structure.
- Consider the metaphor: 'My organization is made up of different conversations' and now draw your organization's structure.
- How does this metaphor change your view of your organization?
- What new information does it reveal? What aspects does it obscure?
- How does it add to your understanding of your organization?

As this chapter shows, the appropriateness of specific organizational structures is open to debate. The interest in new organizational forms has not resolved the debate – it has added new debates to the more traditional disputes surrounding contingency theories of organizational structure. The fact is that we are still not sure whether organizations should grow or stay small; whether they should develop healthy hierarchies or raze them to the ground; whether they should collaborate or compete. We do not attempt to answer these questions but sensitize readers to these debates with a view to learning more about the nuances and complexities of organizational structures.

NOTES

(See Bibliography at the end of the book for full references)

1 Keidel, 1994
2 Berquist, 1993: 11
3 Lucas, 1996
4 Victor and Stephens, 1994
5 Daft and Lewin, 1993; Bohl et al. 1996
6 Eccles and Nohria, 1992: 133
7 Crossan et al. 1996; Quinn et al. 1996; Romme, 1996; Seabright and Delacroix, 1996; Ashkenas et al. 1995
8 Quinn et al. 1996: 350
9 Palmer and Dunford, 1997
10 Neal and Tromley, 1995: 50
11 Ashkenas et al. 1995: 6–7
12 Vinton, 1992: 7
13 Gross, 1995: 130
14 Neal and Tromley, 1995: 43
15 Bolman and Deal, 1991
16 Davis et al. 1994: 551
17 Eccles and Nohria, 1992: 18
18 Peters, 1992: 14
19 Dunford and Palmer, 1996
20 Davis et al. 1994: 548
21 Davis et al. 1994
22 Scase and Goffee, 1987
23 Peters and Waterman, 1982; Goold and Luchs, 1993: 14
24 Davis et al. 1994: 566
25 Dunford and Palmer, 1996
26 Lubatkin and Lane, 1996: 21
27 Desmarescaux, 1998: 44
28 Walker, 1998: 83
29 Reported in Solomon, 1998
30 Lubatkin and Lane, 1996
31 Robbins, 1983
32 Robbins, 1983
33 Boyd et al. 1993
34 Smircich and Stubbart, 1985
35 Lubatkin and Lane, 1996: 27
36 Hamel and Prahalad, 1994
37 Donaldson, 1996: 58–62; more generally on these debates see Robbins, 1983.
38 Roberts and Grabowski, 1996: 417

39 Fulk and DeSanctis, 1995: 338. In making this argument they cite Beniger, 1986, 1990; Lucas and Baroudi, 1994
40 Chandler, 1962
41 Robbins, 1983
42 Amburgey and Dacin, 1994
43 Ghoshal and Bartlett, 1995: 88–9
44 Ghoshal and Bartlett, 1995: 96
45 Arthur et al. 1995: 7
46 Seabright and Delacroix, 1996: 141
47 Halal, 1994: 69
48 Mintzberg et al. 1996: 64, 70
49 Palmer and Dunford, 1997
50 Ghoshal and Bartlett, 1995: 87
51 Halal, 1994: 69
52 Roberts and Libuser, 1993
53 Peters, 1992: 13
54 Peters, 1996: 30
55 Adler and Borys, 1996: 61
56 Adler and Borys, 1996: 64–5
57 See the chapter on organizational learning.
58 Ashkenas et al. 1995: 33
59 Ashkenas et al. 1995: 41–2
60 Jaques, 1990: 127
61 Jaques, 1990: 129
62 Kiernan, 1993
63 McCaffrey et al. 1995: 608
64 Kiernan, 1993: 14
65 Lawler, 1994
66 Lawler, 1994: 72
67 Lawler, 1994: 73
68 Semler, 1994; Taylor, 1994; Jacob, 1995; Aughton, 1996
69 Morgan, 1993: 162
70 Morgan, 1993: 162–3
71 Mulvey et al. 1996: 42–4
72 Leiba and Hardy, 1994
73 Cascio, 1993: 96–7
74 McKinley et al. 1998
75 Cascio, 1993
76 O'Neill and Lenn, 1995; Schneier et al. 1992; Cascio, 1993; McKinley et al. 1995; Dougherty and Bowman, 1995
77 McKinley, 1992: 113–19
78 McKinley, 1992: 113–19
79 Ashkenas et al. 1995: 51–2
80 Morgan, 1993: 7
81 Cameron et al. 1991
82 Hamel and Prahalad, 1994; see also Bruton et al. 1996
83 Kanter, 1994
84 Bettis et al. 1992: 7
85 Palmer and Dunford, 1997; see also Handy, 1995; Jarillo, 1993; Gin, 1995
86 Bergstrom, 1994
87 Hardy and Phillips, 1998
88 Granovetter, 1985: 502; see also Bleeke and Ernst, 1995: 103; Hardy and Phillips, 1998
89 Fox, 1974: 95
90 Fox, 1974
91 President of D.G. Jewellry of Canada Ltd, quoted in Stevenson, 1993: 23
92 Eccles and Nohria, 1992
93 Eccles and Nohria, 1992: 25
94 Eccles and Nohria, 1992
95 Davis et al. 1994: 564
96 Seabright and Delacroix, 1996: 141
97 Palmer and Dunford, 1997
98 Adler and Borys, 1996: 61 draw upon Marsden et al. 1994 to argue that over 74 per cent of employees have written job descriptions, and 80 per cent have rules and procedures manuals.
99 Chesbrough and Teece, 1996: 65
100 Ashkenas et al. 1995: 124
101 Ashkenas et al. 1995: 127
102 Keidel, 1994
103 Morgan, 1993
104 Mills, 1991: 192
105 Eccles and Nohria, 1992: 55

3 MANAGING PEOPLE

Can't Manage With 'Em; Can't Manage Without?

Organizations clearly comprise more than their organization charts. In particular, they are made up of people. Managing people is a key challenge of contemporary organizational life. We are repeatedly told that 'people are our most important asset'. Such words ring hollow in the ears of many[1] since such statements are often made at the same time that organizations undertake massive corporate restructuring with traumatic consequences for victims and 'survivors' alike. The divergence between such public pronouncements and current practice has been attributed to a number of causes. Some observers suggest that such statements simply reflect political correctness,[2] while actions continue to reflect traditional views that staff is a cost which should be reduced, rather than a source of value creation.[3] Another view suggests that human resource executives simply do not know how to communicate to senior management that effective human resource management is important to the successful achievement of an organization's strategy.[4] A third view suggests that, while a small subset of individuals may be treated as organizational assets, less considerate people management strategies are imposed on the majority of the workforce.[5] Finally, some writers argue that the management of human resources is, and always has been, nothing more than a set of disciplinary practices designed to govern and control the activities and behaviours of employees.[6]

Clearly, then, the management of human resource entails an inherent debate regarding the worth of people in the organization and how they should be managed. Managers are placed in the situation of having to treat staff 'as both expendable and the key to future success'.[7] Even managers who do view their staff as an asset to the organization are faced with the reality that, unlike an oil field or a new plant, people can quit and move to a competing firm; demand higher wages; reject the firm's authority; and repudiate advancement opportunities. 'The most obvious problem is that the firm's assets walk out the door each day, leading to some questions about whether they will return.'[8] For a variety of reasons, then, the management of people is a source of great uncertainty for the organization and, when the commitment of an organization to its people is in question because of restructuring, so too is the reciprocal commitment of highly valued human assets.

In this chapter we investigate key debates concerning the management of people, which we have narrowed down to four main areas (see Supplementary Reading box). In the first section, we look at debates around the nature and role of human resource management (HRM) itself. We then explore some of the debates associated with a variety of HRM practices. In the third

PEOPLE: SUPPLEMENTARY READING

- Blyton, P. and Turnbull, P. (eds) (1992) *Reassessing Human Resource Management*. London: Sage.

- Boxall, P.F. (1993) 'The significance of human resource management: a reconsideration of the evidence', *International Journal of Human Resource Management*, 4 (3): 645–64.

- Brousseau, K.R., Driver, M.J., Eneroth, K. and Larsson, R. (1996) 'Career pandemonium: realigning organisations and individuals', *Academy of Management Executive*, 10 (4): 52–66.

- Davis, T.R.V. (1997) 'Open book management: its promise and pitfalls', *Organizational Dynamics*, 25 (3): 7–20.

- Limerick, D. (1992) 'The shape of the new Organisation: implications for human resource management', *Asia Pacific Journal of Human Resources*, 30 (1): 38–52.

- Mantz, C.C. (1992) 'Self-leading work teams: moving beyond self-management myths', *Human Relations*, 45 (11): 1119–40.

- Mirvis, P.H. (1997) 'Human resource management: leaders, laggards, and followers', *Academy of Management Executive*, 11 (2): 43–56.

- Mueller, F. (1994) 'Teams between hierarchy and commitment: change strategies and the "internal environment"', *Journal of Management Studies*, 31 (3): 383–401.

- Pfeffer, J. (1995) 'Producing sustainable competitive advantage through the effective management of people', *Academy of Management Executive*, 9 (1): 55–72.

- Pucik, V. (1988) 'Strategic alliances, organisational learning and competitive advantage: the HRM agenda', *Human Resource Management*, 27 (1): 77–93.

- Semler, R. (1994) 'Why my former employees still work for me', *Harvard Business Review* (Jan–Feb): 64–74.

- Von Hippel, C., Mangum, S.L., Greenberger, D.B., Heneman, R.L. and Skoglind, J.D. (1997) 'Temporary employment: can organisations and employees both win?', *Academy of Management Executive* 11 (1): 93–104.

section, we focus on some of the new contexts in which people are managed, specifically networked organizations, the outsourcing of human resource practices and the internationalization of organizational operations. In the fourth section we investigate managing people at the boundaries – between work and family and between diverse types of people.

TROUBLE IN PARADISE? TENSIONS IN DEFINING HRM

While the management of people is most commonly associated with the field of HRM, its parameters and nature are contested in terms of the dimensions of this field and the role and contribution of HRM as a set of management practices. In this section, we explore some of the different attempts to define the field of HRM.

Warmed over personnel management or nouvelle cuisine?

Some writers argue that the field of HRM emerged during the early 1980s and is substantively different to the old field of personnel management. Consequently, it is still 'in its infancy'.[9] Other writers dispute this, suggesting that there is little substantive difference between the concepts used in personnel management and HRM.[10] Some writers have attempted to differentiate HRM from personnel management in terms of its emphasis on a strategic approach, high commitment and the responsibility of line managers for people management.[11] Still other writers, however, argue that there is a difference between HRM and strategic HRM. HRM consists of a variety of organizational practices including recruiting, rewarding, training, appraising and planning which are treated as essentially separate tasks and which lack integration. Strategic HRM, on the other hand, is more integrative by aligning HRM practices with organizational goals and the broader strategic management process.[12] Legge[13] differentiates between soft and hard versions of HRM. The hard version stresses a more bottom-line, calculative view of HRM and focuses more on the 'resource management' side. The soft version draws upon assumptions of developmental humanism and stresses the 'human' part of managing people. This distinction has been attributed to fundamentally different understandings of human nature – so much so that 'they cannot both properly be incorporated within a single model of human resource management'.[14] Others argue that the two versions are simply ideal types, neither of which is found in a pure form: although organizations may embrace the rhetoric of the soft version – training, development and commitment – while practising the hard version – improvements in the bottom line.[15]

Another debate concerning the dimensions of the field of HRM relates to its theoretical underpinning. Some critics have defined it as 'culture-bound, atheoretical, idealistic and over-simplistic, often with little or no empirical evidence supporting the broad generalizations of the concepts and processes advanced'.[16] Other writers have set out to counteract the view that the field constitutes 'an atheoretical wasteland'.[17] Guest[18] argues that these debates have 'become rather introspective and boring'. Nevertheless, Kane is optimistic that the increasing diversity of theoretical perspectives provides a way to move beyond a consideration of 'dreary lists' of techniques that make up the heart of most HRM texts towards more exciting and relevant ways of considering people's roles in organizations. He suggests that practitioners will also benefit from these perspectives by widening their understanding of HRM issues which, in turn, will help them to implement more 'productive HRM policies and practices'.[19] (See Table 3.1.)

Finally, a debate exists concerning whether HRM practices are primarily found in large organizations and generally ignored by smaller organizations. Most studies focus on larger organizations, although others argue that small businesses have taken up a range of HRM practices including participation, teamwork, flexibility and cultural change.[20] New approaches to managing people in small businesses are likely to follow changes in ownership, the introduction of professional management standards and participation in management development programmes. However, it is often difficult for small businesses to pursue new modes of managing people since 'they lack resources, management expertise and are less likely to be aware of developments in other companies'.[21]

Just props and cops?

If there is a debate about what constitutes HRM as a field, there is also a debate concerning the role of HRM as a management function. In this section, we explore some of the different views of the HRM function found in the literature.

In the *hierarchical* model, human resource (HR) managers simply support top management teams in making strategic decisions. They provide advice

TABLE 3.1   *Different theoretical perspectives found in human resource management*

Guest (1997)	Kane (1996)	Delery and Doty (1996)	Swiercz (1995)	Wright and McMahan (1992)
• Strategic	• Unitarist	• Universalistic/ best	• Fit	• Behavioural
• Descriptive	• Resource-based	practices	• Functional	• Cybernetic
• Normative	• Best practices	• Contingency/ best fit	• Economic	• Agency/ transaction
	• Partnership	• Configurational	• Typological	cost
	• Customer service			• Resource-based
	• Multiple constituency			• Power/resource
	• Exploitation			dependency
	• Multicultural			• Institutional
	• Inherently limited			
	• Strategic			

Sources: Adapted from Wright and McMahan, 1992; Swiercz, 1995; Delery and Doty, 1996; Kane, 1996; Guest, 1997

and help oversee a range of people-related administrative activities. In the *professional* model, HR professionals manage relationships between the organization and external groups such as unions, governments and regulatory agencies. Organizations that use these two models are often characterized by mistrust on the part of line managers regarding the HRM function. HR executives are often recruited from outside a company and, therefore, their allegiance to the company is in question. HR managers are often viewed simply as 'props' and 'cops'. Props help senior line managers who are unable to deal with difficult human resource issues on their own; while cops are charged with enforcing compliance with corporate and regulatory policies and procedures.[22] In the *service business* model, the HRM function works with both divisions and customers to help them benchmark the performance of divisions and groups. However, difficulties arise for HR managers in trying to please customers associated with specific functional areas of the organization while, at the same time, taking decisions and actions to benefit the overall organization.[23] Given the difficulties with these three models, Eisenstat argues in favour of a *partnership*, where HR managers serve as catalysts and facilitators in a 'line-driven process that aligns the organization with its business strategy'.[24] He argues that this can be achieved by gaining organizational consensus on human resource tasks and implementing learning across organizational units.

Another model is that of *ombudsman* in which HR managers are charged with implementing fairness and justice, particularly in an era when fewer employees are members of unions. Distributive justice – how resources get allocated – has changed in recent times with an increasing disparity between employee wages, executive remuneration and returns to stockholders. Procedural justice – organizational rules – and corrective justice – correcting problems and mistakes – have also suffered with fewer employees having union protection. In this case, rather than performing a strategic function and contributing only to the bottom line of the organization, the HRM department tries to protect individuals from unfair organizational processes.[25] Finally in the *nodal* model, human resources management is depicted as a 'virtual' department – a node in a network of HRM suppliers and users.[26] In this instance, the HR department acts as a co-ordinator within a larger network.

These roles are not mutually exclusive and within any one organization a number may apply, to varying degrees, at one and the same time. Regardless of the model, the HRM function continues to face a disadvantage in being taken seriously by other managers who still view the HR department as composed of people who 'brought the watermelon to the picnic, and screwed you at increase time'.[27] In addition, while HRM managers are continually told that people management is an important part of achieving bottom-line productivity, HR departments are also being pressured into becoming smaller and more strategic. As one manager said: 'We decided that we could no longer afford two personnel managers at $35,000 each – we could only afford one at $70,000!'[28] Some organizations have even outsourced their entire HRM department, as we discuss later in this chapter. Such changes are predicated on the view that the management of people is not a task that can be allocated to a particular section of an organization but, rather, an integral part of all managerial positions. Such different views of the HRM function raise questions concerning the legitimacy of HRM within the larger organization, as well as the training and career development of HRM staff (Exercise 3.1).

Straight to the bottom line?

The impact of 'human resource management on performance has become *the* dominant research issue in the field'.[29] Managers will invest in HRM only if human resource practices, such as developing staff, communicating openly and honestly with them and allowing them access to the organization's books, can be shown to result in greater profits, lower operating costs and more satisfied customers. In the absence of such evidence, the HRM function will continue to struggle with its legitimacy and be consigned to 'altruistic fluff' in the eyes of line managers.[30] Unfortunately for HR managers, the link has proved difficult to establish.

Some support for the link between HRM practices and organizational performance has been found. Becker and Gerhart[31] argue that research evidence consistently points to the positive bottom-line performance which human resource policies can have for organizations. Similarly, Huselid et al. point out that recent empirical research suggests that firm performance is

---

EXERCISE 3.1 SHOULD WE REFLECT ON THIS?

Select an organization with which you are familiar, either from experience or from the business literature, reflect on the role of the HR department and answer the following questions:

- Of the six roles of HR departments identified in the text – hierarchical, professional, service business, partnership, ombudsman and nodal – which one(s) best describes the human resource department in the organization?
- Assess the advantages/disadvantages associated with this model. Relate your answers to concrete examples.
- What are the implications for individuals pursuing a career in HRM in this organization?
- Is there an alternative model that would be of greater benefit to the organization in the next five years? Explain your answer. What are the key issues that would need to be addressed in order to achieve this model?

affected by the HRM practices that are in place. Their research, which drew on 293 US firms, supports 'the decade-old argument that investments in human resources are a potential source of competitive advantage'.[32]

The problem is that nobody agrees on why this might be the case.[33] Guest[34] argues that the field has been more concerned with 'statistical sophistication' at the expense of 'theoretical rigour'. As a result, the studies are 'non-additive, except in a very general way' and there is still no clear theoretical understanding of the link between HRM and performance. Some researchers suggest that performance is enhanced when HRM practices are linked to the organization's external strategy. Others argue that performance relates to the employment of an ideal set of HRM practices. A third approach suggests that performance is linked to the use of specific configurations or bundles of HRM practices.[35] While Guest suggests there is some support to the view that particular HRM practices are related to higher performance, writers differ as to which are the relevant high performing practices. For example, some researchers place a low emphasis on the importance of variable pay, while others accord a high priority to this practice.[36]

Another approach to performance suggests that the external reputation of the firm as a 'good HRM employer' has a positive effect on share price. Pfeffer[37] suggests that announcements of the adoption of certain best practices signal that an organization is well managed. Consequently, financial markets perceive the organization as able to attract value-added employees. Wright et al. found that announcements of quality affirmative action programmes were associated with significant, positive stock price changes, while announcements of discrimination settlements, which signalled discriminatory corporate practices, were associated with significant, negative stock price changes.[38] In contrast, Hannon and Milkovich[39] found only limited support for this hypothesis.

Barney and Wright[40] propose a completely different way to examine the economic effects of managing people and of specific HRM practices by drawing upon the resource-based view of the firm. It entails examining the extent to which human resources constitute a competitive advantage for the organization by assessing the extent to which specific HR practices affect value, are rare, can be imitated by competitors and can be easily adopted by the organization (Exercise 3.2).

In summary, there are a number of debates that surround the fundamental nature of HRM as an area of research, a management practice and its impact on organizational performance.

PRACTICE MAKES PERFECT

In this section we examine a series of debates around the practice of HRM. We first explore what HRM practices involve. We then focus in more detail on managing competencies, managing temporary employees, managing with an open book, managing careers and managing motivation and commitment.

EXERCISE 3.2 ARE WE WELL RESOURCED?

Select an organization with which you are familiar, either from experience or from the business literature. For each area of its human resource policies and practices assess the extent to which each constitutes a competitive advantage for the organization. Use the following grid to conduct the audit.

HR Policy/practice	Value: does it help to decrease costs or increase revenue?	Rareness: is it commonly found in competing firms?	Imitability: is it able to be easily imitated by competitors?	Organization: is the firm organized to exploit its advantages?
Recruitment				
Training				
Compensation				
Appraisal				
Grievance				
Job design				
Involvement				

What are your overall conclusions about the distinctiveness of the human resource systems and their contribution to the competitive advantage of the organization?

Source: Adapted from Barney and Wright, 1998

The first question concerns what do HRM practices involve? As alluded to above, this debate revolves around whether it comprises a series of *individual* practices or whether it involves a package or configuration of *related* practices. Some authors urge managers to adopt one best set of people management practices. Blackburn and Rosen,[41] in their analysis of winners of the Malcolm Baldrige National Quality Award, present fourteen practices that constitute an 'ideal' profile of human resource strategies. Jeffrey Pfeffer[42] identifies thirteen best practices for managing people (Table 3.2) which, more recently, he has condensed into a list of seven: employment security, selective hiring, decentralized self-managed teams, high performance related pay, training, reduction in social and economic differences within the organization, and information sharing.[43] He argues that successful firms such as Plenum Publishing, Tyson Foods, Wal-Mart, Circuit City and Southwest Airlines have achieved a sustained competitive advantage by relying 'not on technology, patents, or strategic position, but on how they manage their workforce'.[44] These practices cannot easily be imitated because they are less visible and hard to comprehend from the outside (Exercise 3.3).

Critics of the best practice approach suggest that there is a lack of consistency in terms of which practices are cited as best.[45] Others are critical on the grounds that the best practice approach does not focus on which specific practices are most important to managing specific management dilemmas.[46] These writers suggest that specific *groupings* of practices are effective in different strategic situations. Within this contingency or fit approach, there are differences of opinion regarding whether the HRM practices should be formulated to assist in the pursuit of specific strategic goals or whether business strategy should be formulated in light of the human resource practices of the organization.

EXERCISE 3.3 WHAT'S YOUR BEST PRACTICE?

Table 3.2 sets out thirteen best human resource practices. Reflect on an organization with which you are familiar, either from experience or from the business literature, and answer the following questions:

- Which of these practices are in place? Which are absent?
- Why are some practices absent?
- What barriers exist in the organization to implementing these absent practices?
- What arguments would you use to convince your top management team to implement the absent practices or to retain the ones that are present?
- How important are these thirteen practices to the achievement of your organization's strategy? Explain why?

TABLE 3.2 *Pfeffer's best practices*

Best practice	Rationale	Business example
Employment security	Signals commitment, evokes norms of reciprocity	New United Motor Manufacturing (NUUMI) (Toyota-GM)
Recruitment selectivity	Productive employees; rigorous procedures symbolize elite organization	Southwest Airlines, Lincoln Electric
High wages	Produces diligence, especially where staff paid above market rates	Wendy's
Incentive pay	Share in benefits of productive work	Lincoln Electric
Employee ownership	Create common interests between staff and shareholders; create long-term view	Plenum Publishing, Tyson Foods, Wal-Mart, Circuit City, Southwest Airlines
Information sharing	Staff need information to be productive	Advanced Micro Devices, Bank of America
Participation and empowerment	Increase autonomy and control over work processes	Nordstrom, Levi Strauss
Self-managed teams	Team monitoring and peer expectations	Monsanto
Training and skill development	Skill acquisition and utilization	Advanced Micro Devices
Cross-utilization and cross-training (multi-skilling)	Work variety and interest; employability	Mazda
Symbolic egalitarianism	Signal comparative equality throughout company	NUMMI, Solectron
Wage compression	Facilitate co-operation and efficiency	Various
Internal promotion	Encourages training, participation and personal contact; fairness and workplace justice	Lincoln Electric, Nordstrom

Source: Adapted from Pfeffer, 1995: 57–65

Broderick and Boudreau[47] point to how different HRM practices (in their case, those that relate to the use of information technology) can be used to support different business strategies. For example, under a cost leadership strategy HRM practices should be aimed at streamlining, standardizing and decreasing production and other costs. In the event of a quality–customer satisfaction strategy, HRM practices should delegate decisions and educate staff about the need for customer focused performance. An innovation strategy requires HRM practices that attract and reward creative staff and provide opportunities for exploration and visioning. Taking the alternative position, Cappelli and Crocker-Hefter argue that 'people management practices are the *drivers* – the genesis of efforts to create distinctive competencies and, in turn, business strategies'.[48] If organizations can differentiate their people management practices from other organizations, they can use them to drive specific business strategies and create competitive advantage. In support of their argument, they point to Federal Express (Fedex) and United Parcel Service (UPS). Fedex employs a variety of empowerment practices, authority is decentralized and employees are encouraged to exercise discretion in getting the job done. In contrast, people management practices at UPS are tightly monitored in Taylorist fashion. 'Drivers are told, for example, how to carry packages (under the left arm) and even how to fold money (face up).' [49] While UPS staff enjoy little job enrichment, they are highly paid and productivity is argued to be about three times higher than at Fedex. The authors suggest that it may be easier to find a business strategy to fit existing practices than to develop new practices to go with a new strategy.

There are, then, debates within and between proponents of a universalistic, best practice approach and those of a contingency–fit approach. Perhaps the last word should go to Becker and Gerhart,[50] who argue that the two perspectives may not be in conflict with each other. While companies such as Lincoln Electric and Hewlett-Packard may have different HRM practices, they have similar HRM 'architectures' – although the details of their pay and selection policies are different, both link pay to desired behaviours and performance outcomes and both select and retain people to fit their cultures. Hence, the authors suggest that future research on the best practice–fit debate should consider the level of analysis.

Get competent or get dead?

Lawler[51] argues that many HRM practices are grounded in an outdated 'job paradigm' and that organizations which wish to gain a competitive advantage need to move to a new, competency-based approach to organizing. This requires a change in mentality to appreciate that individuals do not have jobs as much as they possess *value*. Interest in the competency-based approach 'has created a cottage industry among consultants eager to promote their expertise in identifying, measuring, and developing personal capabilities to lead in the new corporate environment'.[52] Managers are provided with advice on how to increase the competencies of their organizations, by buying in staff, training staff from within, borrowing staff from consultants and other external groups, removing non-performing staff and binding high-performance staff to the organization by making it an attractive place to work.[53]

One problem confronting managers seeking the right competencies for their organization is the disagreement concerning the level at which the appropriate competencies should be determined. The *single-job* model encourages managers to map specific competencies to specific jobs.[54] It has, however, been criticized for not creating flexibility in the organization in terms of the ability to move staff from job to job. The *one-size-fits-all* model identifies the broad competencies needed across specific types of jobs, such as managerial jobs,[55] but critics question whether a generic set of capabilities or competencies can be established across a wide range of positions. For this reason, Bartlett and Ghoshal[56] argue against the 'Russian doll model of management' which is based upon the premise that managers perform similar tasks, albeit at different levels in the organizational hierarchy. They maintain that while many companies, such as AT&T, British Airways, BP and Siemens, have sought to identify key competencies for their managers, they have encountered a variety of problems. First, there is little logic linking the required behaviours with the desired personality traits and beliefs. Second, competencies are almost always defined as a single ideal profile, which fails to meet the need for different competencies in different parts of the organization. For example, Kochanski and Ruse[57] identify three areas of competencies depending on whether the individual is working with customers, involved in inventing and discovering, or engaged in producing and delivering.

The *multiple-job* model identifies a broad set of 'building block competencies' generic to a wide number of jobs, but then customizes specific skills for specific jobs.[58] While acknowledging that, of the three models, the multiple-job model is the most complex, Mansfield[59] argues in favour of its ability to cross functional lines in an organization. Bartlett and Ghoshal[60] adopt a similar position, supporting the need to recognize different competencies applicable to different areas of managerial activity, such as specific personal characteristics, knowledge and experience and specialized abilities.

Interest in competencies is based on the assumption that competent organizations are composed of competent individuals and have organizational systems in place designed to maximize the exercise of individual capabilities.[61] Some writers maintain a distinction between individual and organizational competencies. Organizational competencies include systems, technologies, physical locations and infrastructure, and even HRM practices and policies. Managers need to pay special attention to these organizational systems because some are competence destroying, whereas others are competence enhancing. Moreover, as organizations change, so do the necessary competencies. This requires managers continually to monitor the appropriateness of an organization's competencies, the assumptions they make about what constitutes distinctive competencies,[62] and the extent to which HRM systems encourage or discourage the appropriate utilization of individual competencies (Exercise 3.4). It also involves paying special attention to ensuring that appraisal systems recognize that wider organizational systems may inhibit an individual's ability to exercise his/her competencies.[63]

EXERCISE 3.4 DECLARED COMPETENT?

Think about your current position, one that you have occupied recently, or one that you would like to occupy, and answer the following questions:

- What are the six most important competencies associated with your position?
- Of these six competencies, which are generic and apply to other positions in the organization? Which are specific to your particular job?
- What implications can you draw from this analysis regarding the 'one-size-fits-all' and the 'multiple-job' competency models?
- What is the relationship between your competencies and those that are important to your organization's success?
- What conclusions would you draw regarding the relationship between individual and organizational competencies?

Going external? Managing temporary employees

Employment security, listed by Pfeffer[64] as a 'best practice', is no longer a feature of many organizations. Medcof and Needham[65] note that in 1994 the largest private employer in the USA was Manpower, the nation's biggest temp agency. It had 600,000 people on its payroll – about 200,000 more than GM and 345,000 more than IBM. In the same year, the USA had around 1500 temporary employment agencies that handled over 1.5 million staff.[66] Since 1992 there has been a 360 per cent increase in the number of temporary employment agencies in the USA, with some 90 per cent of employers using the services of temporary employees.[67] These figures point to the changing nature of the employment relationship with the workforce being composed of three groups – core workers, contractors and the flexible workforce (temporary and part-time workers) – or what Handy[68] refers to as the three leaves of the shamrock.

The use of external workers, including temporary workers and contractors, is argued to complement the employment of a permanent, full-time workforce – internalization enhances organizational control and stability, while externalization increases organizational flexibility. Together, they provide a mechanism for developing stable yet adaptable work arrangements.[69] Other reasons for using an external workforce include cutting costs through lower wages, administration and training expenses; increasing organizational flexibility to deal with seasonal work flows; and the avoidance of legal or mandated restrictions associated with labour laws.[70] These advantages represent a far more complicated situation than the traditional use of temporary staff to replace permanent staff who are absent for short periods of time.[71]

One major impact of the move towards temporary employment and the massive organizational restructuring during the 1980s and 1990s[72] has been the shattering of 'good faith' employment relationships – the psychological contract. The concept of a social or psychological contract was a common way of describing the employee–employer relationship in the 1960s. It defined employee's beliefs about the reciprocal obligations between employee and organization based on perceived promises. Psychological contracts differ from legal contracts in that agents of the organization do not necessarily recognize them; they are based upon unspoken expectations and interdependence between parties; and they can be changed without a formal process.[73] Traditionally, the psychological contract was associated with a relational bond, involving mutual investment, between employers and employees, which was open ended, long term and based upon both social and economic exchange. In return for the organization living up to its obligations, employees were willing to work in and be trained for areas of work that were not necessarily envisaged at the commencement of the employment relationship.[74]

Over time, however, the nature of the psychological contract changed and became increasingly vulnerable. Employers' perceived obligations to their employees declined over time while the obligations they wanted from their employees increased.[75] If organizations are perceived to have violated the psychological contract, a number of problems may occur. They include a lack of trust, job dissatisfaction, a lessening of voluntary contributions to the organization, decisions to exit and, in some cases, revenge against the organization in the form of lawsuits, sabotage or other aggressive acts.[76] These problems have been exacerbated by the end of life-time employment brought about by downsizing and restructuring, even in those organizations traditionally associated with employment security – rules are being rewritten with little input from employees. In addition, middle managers may contribute to subordinates' dissatisfaction because they often downplay the extent of people problems when communicating with senior management in order to protect their own positions and perceived performance.[77]

These changes have led some to argue that the concept of a job is a 'social artefact that has outlived its usefulness',[78] especially since good work performance no longer guarantees job security. Managers are, therefore, being urged to establish a new set of understandings with their employees – a new psychological contract.[79] Burack and Singh[80] argue that it is time for managers to 'clear the smoke' so that employees know what is expected of them and can form their own expectations accordingly (Exercise 3.5). Managers are encouraged to be realistic in outlining jobs to potential employees; continually communicate expected behaviours and obligations; provide feedback; and ensure that the promises made to employees are accurate and fulfilled.[81]

On the other hand, Hall and Moss argue that the old contract was a myth. The long-term, relationship-based employment was never the norm in most

EXERCISE 3.5 PSYCHOLOGICALLY BOUND?

During the 1980s, AT&T's psychological contract 'crumbled' through organizational restructuring and downsizing. AT&T attempted to deal with this problem by establishing its own internal labour or flexible workforce called Resource Link. Employees who work in Resource Link are called associates and are high-performing employees who are cycled through a variety of short-term jobs throughout AT&T as the need arises. The programme aims to increase employee commitment by providing greater opportunity for redeployment within the organization, particularly for individuals in sections of the organization which are experiencing downsizing. It is also seen as a way of improving both individual and organizational learning by increasing the network of relationships among people within the organization, and diversifying individual experiences. By providing more stable employment, Resource Link is argued to contribute to the creation of a new psychological contract.

Questions

- Do you think Resource Link helps to create a new psychological contract? Explain your answer.
- How do you think you would feel about Resource Link if you were an AT&T employee?
- Do you think other actions are necessary to forge a new psychological contract? If so what are they?
- How applicable are initiatives like Resource Link to organizations where size, geographic dispersion, and other characteristics are different?

Source: Adapted from Sugalski et al. 1995: 390–8

US business organizations. It was operative only in a small subset of organizations, which had strong internal labour markets and whose human resource policies favoured long-term employment security. These authors estimate that, in 1975, less than 5 per cent of US workers had long-term employment security. However, because of the prominence and visibility of these large firms, they 'seemed to symbolize U.S. business, thus giving the appearance that their mode of managing people was the norm'.[82] Even if psychological contracts are based upon the mythological status of an earlier, golden employment age, it may be of little comfort to managers who are confronted with the need to manage the expectations of employees, unions and the public, who continue to believe in the myth (Exercise 3.6).

The use of temporary staff coupled with permanent staff also poses

---

EXERCISE 3.6 WHAT DID YOU EXPECT?

If you were working for an organization ten years ago, reflect on the psychological contract that existed then. If not, consult the business literature from ten years ago and explore how it described the employer–employee relationship. Answer the following questions:

- What were your expectations of the organization in which you worked? What did you see as your obligations to the organization?
- How have these expectations and obligations changed? Why? What has been the impact on you of these changes?
- Is your recollection typical of business organizations generally; what about government organizations and the public and voluntary sectors?
- In ten years time how do you envisage your expectations and perceived obligations to have changed?

---

problems because managers have to manage both temporary and permanent workforces. A range of problems confronts the management of temporary workers. They include dehumanized and impersonal treatment, insecurity and pessimism about the future, lack of access to benefits such as insurance, lack of honesty by employers about job requirements, feelings of underemployment and generalized bitterness towards the corporate community and its values.[83] These problems tend to occur when temporary staff lack the appropriate skills and commitment and 'become a wandering underclass in the labour pool'.[84] Friction can also occur between permanent and temporary staff, especially where reward inequality exists between them.[85] When this friction turns into 'malicious envy', the result can be hostile behaviour as individuals 'undercut their rivals by disrupting the efforts of competitors, negatively distorting competitors' successes, or positively distorting their own accomplishments. Such predator tactics have long been associated with the so-called "professional ambush" and are particularly common in fluid settings.'[86] The heavy use of externalized labour may lead permanent staff to worry about their own future job security, leading them to reduce their commitment to the firm.[87]

There are, then, a number of tensions that arise as a result of such changes in workforce profiles (Exercise 3.7). HRM managers have to formulate policies to deal with very different groups, as well as manage any friction between them.[88]

Opening up the books?

Sharing knowledge has become a 'motherhood' statement – it is assumed to be automatically beneficial.[89] In the context of human resource management,

EXERCISE 3.7 ROLE PLAY – GOING TEMPORARY?

You are a member of the senior manager team of a medium size, multi-divisional manufacturing company. You are in the process of establishing a new, 'green field' manufacturing site. You are aware that this creates the opportunity for putting into place a range of people management practices and policies. You decide to seek advice from two different human resources management consulting companies on what practices you should introduce. You are interested in what they propose, including the arguments and evidence they present in favour of their recommendations. The two companies are trying to convince you that their advice is best. After all, they will win a major contract to help you install the different HRM systems and procedures they recommend.

You develop a list of probing questions to ask representatives of the two companies. Each HRM consulting company will present its arguments at a meeting with you, during which time you will be able to ask your questions. You will have a brief opportunity to ask some final questions before making a decision and formal company announcement on the direction you will pursue – and why.

The first HRM consulting company – Flexible Providers Inc – is well known for its support of the use of temporary workers in an organization. For them, it represents a paradigm shift in the traditional techniques for managing people and is the way of the future. They have a range of advice, evidence and recommendations that they will present to the top management team regarding why this approach should be used, and what will be needed in order to make it work effectively.

The second HRM consulting company – Commitment Inc – is well known for its support for company commitment to employees, through the appropriate provision of job security and other related policies and procedures. The company believes that this approach produces greater commitment by employees which, in turn, leads to greater productivity and involvement. They have a range of advice, evidence and recommendations that they will present to the top management team regarding why this approach should be used, and what will be needed to make it effective.

Running the role play

Preparation
The top management team prepares a list of questions to ask each consulting company. Each consulting company prepares its

recommendations and arguments to persuade the top management team to adopt its advice.

The briefing meeting

- Flexible Providers Inc presents its advice and answers questions.
- Commitment Inc presents its advice and answers questions.
- The top management team confers and identifies the final questions it wishes to put to each company.
- The final questions are put to Flexible Providers Inc.
- The final questions are put to Commitment Inc to second consulting company

The announcement

The top management team announces its decision and explains its reasons.

---

this is reflected in the increasing interest in 'open book management' (OBM) techniques,[90] which have been traced back to 1983 when Jack Stack acquired Springfield Re-Manufacturing, a company that was about to collapse. He decided to 'open the books' to employees about the financial status of the company, provide information about its business operations and engage in profit sharing. Included in the approach was a commitment to educate employees so that they could properly evaluate company information (Table 3.3).

Other companies have also used the practice, including Ricardo Semler's Brazilian company, Semco (Table 3.4). The rationale underlying OBM is that by gaining involvement in the company and its operations, employees will be more committed to its financial success. Collins[91] suggests that participative management techniques can also be used as part of an ethical foundation for managing people. Nonaka and Takeuchi[92] refer to a similar process when they discuss information redundancy – 'intentional overlapping of information about business activities, management responsibilities,

TABLE 3.3 *Open-book management principles*

- Turn the business into a game in which employees can win
- Open the books to staff and share financial information
- Show staff how to read financial statements
- Show staff the impact of their work on the financial results of the company
- Link non-financial objectives to financial results
- Empower employees to make decisions in specific areas
- Establish accountability and jointly assess results
- Celebrate success
- Provide bonuses linked to company outcomes
- Encourage employee share ownership

Source: Adapted from Davis, T.R.V., 1997: 10–13

TABLE 3.4 *Managing openly the 'Semco' way*

Ricardo Semler, owner of a Brazilian company called Semco, is one of the most noted examples of open-book management. Over the past decade, and faced with a Brazilian economy which was highly turbulent, Semler instituted a radical experiment in new employment practices. His management of people is based upon three principles: employee participation, profit sharing, and open information systems. He deliberately set out to break down hierarchy, which he regarded as unproductive and a constraint on organizational productivity. In its place are self-control and the discipline of the community market place of jobs and responsibilities. He adopted an open-book management style in which information is made available to everyone. All meetings are open. Designs and specifications are shared. Major decisions are taken by majority vote among the staff. The company's books are open for inspection by employees and for auditing by their unions. The aim is to eliminate the filtering and negotiating information that goes on in so many corporations. Semler claims to be unconcerned about strategic information falling into the hands of his competitors because they reside in different countries and have to manage different contexts and the fast pace of environmental change means that such information offers little strategic value since it reflects yesterday's situation. He also argues that most people simply do not give away information.

Source: Adapted from Semler, 1994

and the company as a whole'. Redundancy facilitates knowledge creation through the exchange of tacit knowledge. It helps individuals to understand where they stand in the organization which, in turn, directs individual thinking and action.

Davis[93] argues, however, that it is time 'to pierce the veil of unbridled optimism that surrounds OBM and to bring a degree of rigour to the discussion of this approach to management'. He suggests that it is easier to introduce OBM into smaller companies rather than older and larger organizations. Other difficulties occur because managers are fearful of loss of control, distrust employees and feel that information sharing will result in damaging leaks to competitors. The resulting bonus schemes may be unfair or lead to conflicts of interest and some employees may not wish to be involved. Training programmes to facilitate participation take time, cost money and require a company-wide commitment to the process. Nonaka and Takeuchi[94] also point out that information sharing can lead to overload, which can decrease operational efficiency. Continuing in this critical vein, Hilmer and Donaldson[95] are sceptical of the claims of proponents of OBM, criticizing Semler's view of an egalitarian, self-regulating company. The question of 'who controls the agenda' and presents the issues for voting remains and they suggest that his company is still a hierarchy, in which 'voting works as an "escape valve," letting Semler, the unquestioned owner, know when the hierarchy is losing the support of the work force'.[96] (See Exercise 3.8)

Packing your own parachute?

In the past decade, career management counselling has become a big business with over 3000 books on the topic. It encourages 'employees to be

---

EXERCISE 3.8 OPENING UP THE BOOKS?

Select an organization with which you are familiar, either from experience or from the business literature, and answer the following questions:

- Of the open book management (OBM) principles outlined in Table 3.3, which ones are present in this organization?
- Would you encourage the implementation of any of the absent principles? Why? What would you hope to achieve by doing so?
- Evaluate the criticisms of OBM mentioned in the text. Which of these apply to the organization in question? Can you resolve them?

---

self-reliant, to realize that organizations are not prepared to enter into life-long partnerships with them, and to take charge of their own careers'.[97] In the current 'career pandemonium',[98] it is now up to employees to 'pack their own parachutes'[99] rather than rely upon organizations to plan their careers for them. By the same token, Feldman[100] notes that 'packing a parachute' does not help much if 'there's no field to land in and you don't bring along any survival rations'.

An underlying assumption of this literature is that as organization structures change, so will the career patterns within them.[101] Table 3.5 shows the difference between the traditional bounded career paradigm and the new boundary-less one.[102] Hierarchical progression is replaced by a sequence of experiences gained over time.[103] Fewer organizations have fixed career paths and, as a result, individuals look no further than one or two years ahead in their own careers[104] as contractual employability[105] rather than security and stability becomes the norm. In line with this change, managers are told to engage in strategies to discourage career entrenchment in their organizations.[106]

Peiperl and Baruch[107] suggest that, historically, there have been four career patterns (Table 3.6). Common to both the vertical and horizontal career models associated with modern bureaucracies was the assumption that careers occurred within specific organizations. In many respects the post-corporate career resembles the earlier pre-corporate career which is highly individual, lacks identification with specific organizations and blurs the distinction between family and working lives. These authors suggest that, in the twenty-first century, careers will change further, responding to globalization in services and communication and individuals' need for belonging. Temporary employment agencies, professional organizations and local communities will become the source of identification for many individuals, particularly as networks and virtual organizations provide new ways of linking individuals.

TABLE 3.5 *Shifting career paradigms*

Old career paradigm	New career paradigm
• Based on a contract of mutual loyalty where employee compliance is given in return for employment security. Some immediate rewards are deferred for future career advancement – which may entail politics.	• Based on direct exchange between individual and organization where rewards are received for performance against specified tasks; each has flexibility to terminate the relationship as situations change.
• Inward, one-employer focus with emphasis on training for current job. Knowledge of how company operates more important than acquisition of skills for future jobs.	• Individual excellence is in a continual phase of development including training for future needs. Orientation towards industry rather than a specific firm.
• In the top-down firm loyalty rather than enterprise is encouraged with corporate headquarters being responsible for entrepreneurial activities.	• Empowerment practices emphasize decentralized decision making and the value-adding individual.
• Fortress mentality of firm where other regional companies are seen as competitors and 'job hopping' among them prohibited.	• Identification with regional firms with people moving into and out of different companies over time, and being rehired.
• Allegiance is to the work group than the project.	• Allegiance is towards the project and task completion – not towards continuation of the project team.

Source: Adapted from Arthur et al.1995: 13

TABLE 3.6 *Career patterns*

Pre-organizational career	Prior to the advent of industrial bureaucracy, careers were low in security, highly individual and entailed a close integration of home and working life. Identification was with the work – a craft or trade – rather than with a specific organization.
Hierarchical career	With the advent of modern organizations came trust in the organization that, through diligence and hard work, individuals would be elevated in organizational rank. Except for senior management positions, such elevation was traditionally confined to the functional or technical path
Horizontal career	During the mid-1970s, as organizational growth slowed, generalists, rather than functional specialists, were encouraged. These people had a wide business experience in a range of functional areas, which may have included job rotation through sales, marketing, operations etc.
Post-corporate career	In the world of flexible organizations which need to respond to fast changing environments, come people who are refugees of large organizations – victims of downsizing and outsourcing practices. They develop service relationships with their former organizations, and identify with the professional service they offer rather than with specific companies.

Source: Adapted from Peiperl and Baruch, 1997

Before managers abandon any involvement in staff career planning, they should take account of some of the critics. Brousseau et al.[108] maintain that changes associated with newer career patterns will create pandemonium. They suggest that the move to a flexible, multi-skilled career concept ignores a number of issues. First, it is not clear that all staff can tolerate ambiguity and uncertainty – those who cannot simply become the new losers. Second, while knowledge work is seen as a major asset, there will be little incentive in the new organization for individuals to invest in depth in different skill and knowledge development if it will not offer continued job protection. Third, if individual identity is not aligned with organizations but rather with individualistic careers, organizations will be deprived of committed individuals who will help to grow and drive them. Nicholson points out that both models are really ideal types that do not accurately portray reality. The traditional model ignores the dominance of the small company sector and the ad hoc career systems associated with these organizations. Similarly, even in large organizations the traditional model did not apply to everyone. For such reasons he argues that the rhetoric regarding the new paradigm is 'running well ahead of its practice'.[109]

These writers suggest that managers should embrace aspects of both paradigms. Nicholson argues that as we move into the twenty-first century organizations will face pressures to be innovative and traditional at the same time which, in turn, will lead to a diversity of organizational structures, roles and careers.[110] Similarly, Brousseau et al.[111] advise managers to design organizations with diverse structures to meet the diverse elements of the environments in which they are located. This entails adopting a view of careers that incorporates more static career concepts with newer, more dynamic careers to develop a pluralistic strategy that accommodates both career and organization (Exercise 3.9).

Want loyalty and commitment? Get a dog!

Dunford[112] suggests that if senior managers want loyalty, they should get a dog. Stroh and Reilly[113] confirm a decrease in loyalty in an era of downsizing and restructuring, although managers who have taken responsibility for their careers and changed organizations display an increased loyalty to their new organization compared to the one they left. However, this loyalty, and the enhanced performance that goes along with it, may simply be part of a honeymoon period that erodes over time.

Other writers suggest that commitment can be fostered by reducing demands on employees, increasing resources to assist them and turning employee demands and problems into organizational resources by using exit interviews, giving consideration to family demands and involving employees in major decisions. Others have pointed to the need to provide stimulating workplaces if organizations are to motivate creative employees.[114] Rewards can also be used to foster commitment. Wallace[115] maintains that the perceived legitimacy of the distribution of rewards and promotional

---

EXERCISE 3.9 WHERE ARE THE BOUNDARIES?

Reflect on your career and think ahead to the next five to ten years. Answer the following questions:

- How likely is it that your career will be within the one organization – or will it be across a number of organizations?
- What are the key competencies that you have which currently make you employable?
- What key competencies will you need to develop in the next five years to remain employable?
- Why will you need to develop them?
- What options are available to you to develop these competencies?

---

opportunities are important factors in creating organizational loyalty. This suggests that lack of a career track and a perceived imbalance in rewards between permanent and temporary staff are likely to affect staff commitment adversely. However, Brett et al.[116] found that, compared to individuals with higher financial requirements, individuals with lower financial requirements exhibited greater performance and organizational commitment. Rather than strengthen an employee's identification with an organization, financial pressures may create a lack of choice that weakens the identification.

When linking rewards to commitment, managers need to clarify the extent to which reward systems are aligned with desired behaviours. Over two decades ago Kerr[117] wrote a classic article about the folly of rewarding A, while hoping for B (Table 3.7). Organizations apparently still suffer from this problem.[118] Creating commitment and improving performance is difficult if managers are unable to change their thinking about reward practices, if organizations do not have holistic performance-related systems in place and the emphasis remains on short-term responsiveness to shareholders (Exercise 3.10).

But how important is loyalty and commitment? While the commonsense view suggests that employees who are more committed to an organization will be more productive, research evidence has suggested that this view is

TABLE 3.7   *The continuing folly of rewarding A while hoping for B*

We hope for . . .	But we reward . . .
• Teamwork and collaboration	• Individual team members
• Innovation and risk	• Traditional methods and no mistakes
• Development of people skills	• Technical achievements and accomplishments
• Employee empowerment	• Tight control over employee work
• High achievement	• Another year's effort

Source: Adapted from Editors, 1995: 15

EXERCISE 3.10 HOPES AND REWARDS?

Select an organization with which you are familiar, either from experience or from the business literature. Use the matrix below to answer the following questions:

- List up to five behaviours expected of people in the organization.
- What rewards exist in the organization to encourage each of these behaviours?
- What reward systems go against the achievement of these desired behaviours?
- What changes would you make to more closely align expected behaviours and rewards?

Expected behaviours	Rewards that encourage this behaviour	Rewards which discourage this behaviour	Ways of eliminating discouraging rewards and implementing encouraging rewards
1			
2			
3			
4			
5			

inaccurate and that there is little relationship between commitment and performance. More recently, critics argue that this research conclusion may be the result of a narrow view of organizational commitment. Rather than viewing commitment and identification as being related to the organization, employee commitment should be seen as a multi-dimensional variable. For example, Becker et al.[119] distinguish between employee commitment to supervisors and employee commitment to the organization and show that commitment to *supervisors* is positively and significantly associated with performance. Ulrich argues that commitment must be accompanied by competence. Firms with 'high competence but low commitment have talented employees who can't get things done. Firms with high commitment but low competence have less talented employees who get things done quickly. Both are dangerous.'[120]

HORSES FOR COURSES: MANAGING PEOPLE IN NEW CONTEXTS

In this section we examine the management of people in new contexts – in networked organizations, in organizations that have outsourced their human resource functions and in international arenas.

Networking the people or peopling the network?

Some authors argue that the network organization poses significant challenges to managing people. It raises questions about how individuals identify with an organization, a job, a boss and a career in these new organizational forms. Managers need to change practices in order to accommodate the particular nature of 'organizational' culture, goals and careers in networks and to realign reward systems across networked arrangements.[121] Motorola provides an example of how to modify HRM practices by involving personnel from its alliance partners in the training programmes it provides for its own employees. In this situation, employees of one organization are processed through the HRM system of another.[122]

Quinn et al. argue that few organizations have been successful in arriving at systematic structures for developing the intellectual capabilities which networks are supposed to generate. The problem lies in knowing exactly where intellect resides in a network, the points at which it is converted into novel, creative solutions (customization), the direction in which this knowledge flows (intellectual flow) and the way intellect is harnessed (leverage).[123] These authors suggest that knowledge lies at the centre in infinitely flat organizations; in the nodes of the inverted and spider web forms; and in both the centre and nodes of starburst forms. They conclude that:

> Not only must a company design its recruiting, organizing, outsourcing and software support systems to focus and leverage its intellectual capabilities, it must also develop its measurement and reward infrastructures to reinforce its strategic intentions in four critical dimensions. These are professional skill

development, customer value creation, internal productivity, and intellectual asset appraisal.[124]

Blackler, however, provides a word of warning to managers who focus only on the intellect or 'expert knowledge worker'. He argues that the mystique which surrounds the use of terms such as 'knowledge worker' detracts attention from understanding that '*all* individuals and *all* organizations, not just so-called "knowledge workers" or "knowledge organizations", are knowledgeable'.[125] (See Exercise 3.11.)

Even people management systems get outsourced!

At a time when employees are cited as a valuable organizational asset, many companies are outsourcing not only their line employees but also the human resource systems that service them to save money, lower business risks and build core competencies.[126] In a survey of 69 US firms, Lever[127] found that 75 per cent outsourced benefits, 62 per cent outsourced payroll, 65 per cent

---

EXERCISE 3.11 LEVERAGING KNOWLEDGE THROUGH NETWORKING?

Select an organization with which you are familiar, either from experience or from the business literature. Identify an area in which it is engaged in external networking with clients, distributors, suppliers, marketing companies, lobbyists, etc. and answer the following questions:

- How easy is it to identify where the boundaries of your organization stop and start?
- Is there staff interchange between the organizations?
- Is there a sharing of organizational policies and systems (e.g. HRM policies, etc.)?
- How important is this network to the core business of your organization?
- In what ways does this network leverage the intellectual/knowledge capabilities of individuals or systems across each organization?
- How well does this network leverage the intellectual/knowledge capabilities (of individuals or systems) across each organization?
- What recommendations would you make to increase this leverage?
- What conclusions would you draw about key factors that should be considered when contemplating entering into a networked arrangement as a way of leveraging knowledge and capabilities?

outsourced training, 50 per cent outsourced recruiting, 30 per cent outsourced human resource information systems, and 17 per cent outsourced compensation. Companies like DDB Needham, a New York advertising firm, have outsourced their entire HRM staff, creating a new, external organization that contracts its services back to the original organization as well as to others.[128] Another outsourcing technique has been used by NCR, which leases individuals from a HR organization to perform services such as payroll or compensation, while continuing to manage other HR functions such as safety and regulatory compliance in house. Such diverse arrangements and the unprecedented degree of outsourcing are argued to have created a 'supra-organizational HRM system'[129] which exists outside individual organizations.

Barney and Wright[130] point out that HR outsourcing leads to problems if managers fail to assess the extent to which the HR function contributes to the sustained competitive advantage of the organization and to identify firm-specific skills. As we mentioned in Chapter 2 on organizational structure, outsourcing decisions made on the basis of cost alone can be dangerous because they ignore how those functions provide critical sources of value for the entire system.[131] Other problems found with outsourcing include higher costs, problems in co-ordinating a range of subcontractors, the time-consuming nature of this process, a loss of quality, a loss of competitive edge where outsiders take over responsibility for critical functions and a loss of control over process technologies.[132]

The use of external HR services still requires managers inside the client organization to carry out a number of managerial tasks. They must create systems to track the provision of HR services; co-ordinate internal and external providers and manage the associated uncertainties; ensure information technology compatibility and co-ordination between different systems; assess the risks associated with disclosing confidential information about staff; and plan strategically for the use of outsourced services.[133] Managers contemplating the outsourcing of HR functions still need to consider carefully the impact on their organization and the extent to which the benefits will outweigh the costs (Exercise 3.12).

Too close to home?

Adler and Bartholomew[134] argue that while organizations are going global in their strategies and operations, their HRM practices are staying closer to home, failing to reflect both local and global requirements. The perils of not understanding the importance of cultural differences when managing people are clear. For example, de Forest[135] points to the importance of harmony in the Mexican workplace and the public maintenance of honour. She cites a situation where a US manager attempted to avoid labour problems by introducing a three-stage grievance system in a Mexican organization. In the first instance, a complaint would go to an immediate supervisor and then further up the chain of command if it was not resolved. The manager, who thought

---

EXERCISE 3.12 OUTSOURCING HR?

Complete exercise 3.1, reflect on your answers and answer the following questions.

- Which HRM policies and practices carried out by the organization are best suited to outsourcing? Explain your answer.
- Which HRM policies and practices would you keep inside the organization? Explain your answer.
- What managerial responsibilities would need to be set up within the organization if you outsourced the specified HRM policies and practices? Explain your answer.

---

the system was working well, was astounded when the entire workforce walked off the site one day. The manager failed to recognize that Mexican workers typically avoid directly confronting their superiors with complaints because such behaviour is considered inappropriate in the context of this society. Other writers have identified similar problems in Mexico,[136] as well as in other countries, such as Asia, where the importance of establishing good relationships and good people connections is crucial to the successful conduct of business.[137] Critics argue that such problems also reflect the way in which HRM research is too 'culture-bound',[138] with the study of international HRM still being in its infancy.[139]

Others disagree, however, and argue that international HRM research is developing in a number of important areas. These include matching strategic HRM policies to the different stages of internationalization of the multinational corporation; and identifying the ways in which structure, culture, international experience and industry affect the strategic international HRM policies of an organization.[140] Two recent debates have emerged in relation to the developing areas of international HRM.

One debate centres on the nature of the strategic approach that should underpin HRM policies in multinational companies. For some writers, this debate is cast in terms of whether multinational companies should localize their HRM policies or whether they should import them from the parent country.[141] Others have pointed out that there are at least four different approaches which multinational companies can take.[142] For example, in an ethnocentric approach to managerial staffing policies, senior managers originate from the parent country. This approach can limit promotional opportunities for local staff and can create equity issues in regard to remuneration. In a polycentric approach, local managers are recruited to run the operation. This approach can create a gap (language, loyalty and culture) between local managers and the managers to whom they report in the parent country headquarters. It is often difficult for local managers in this situation to gain experience outside their own country. In a geocentric approach, appointment to positions is made on merit without regard to nationality. Problems can occur where the local country demands that its own citizens are employed in the multinational operation, or where others in the local company resist outside appointments on the grounds that it entails a loss of local autonomy. In a regiocentric approach, a mixed policy is adopted in which senior managers are selected from a number of countries, often related to the organization of the firm's business strategy. For example, if the business is 'oriented towards a particular area or region then the company will draw management from those countries and locate them in the host country company. In this case, there would be relatively few managers in the host country company who originated from the parent-country headquarters'.[143] Again, similar problems can occur in this approach to those found in the geocentric approach.

Kamoche[144] argues that international human resource management has tended to focus too narrowly on the staffing and socialization of senior management or high performers, which explains why a geocentric staffing approach has only been applied to small groups of senior managers:

> There is very little evidence in the literature about efforts to address the HR concerns of non-high-fliers and non-expatriate personnel. This issue is usually given cursory attention under the general sub-title of 'sensitivity to local circumstances' or 'local-level autonomy' in the implementation of corporate strategies or guidelines, for example in selection and training.

He takes an organization learning perspective and suggests that if organizations are to benefit from knowledge creation and renewal processes then international HR systems need to ensure that they are oriented towards the whole organization.[145] Another contribution to this debate suggests that the international HRM literature has focused too much on whether parent country policies should be applied to host country companies and not enough on actual HRM practices. It also ignores the way in which host country companies may reject, modify, or re-interpret HRM policies from the parent country as they are incorporated into local HRM practices.[146]

A second area of debate relates to arguments about the high failure rates of expatriates, placed at anywhere up to 40 per cent of international assignments.[147] These debates focus on issues such as their overseas performance, how to ensure cultural sensitivity and how to manage family adjustment and culture incompatibility problems.[148] Other writers dispute the high failure rates of expatriates. Harzing[149] argues that if failure rates are measured in terms of the premature re-entry of expatriates back to their home country, then there is little empirical evidence to support the assumption of high failure rates. Forster's study of expatriate managers in 36 UK-based companies found that less than 9 per cent returned home early – significantly less than the often-quoted figures of up to 40 per cent.[150] On these grounds, he argues that it is a myth to assume that most overseas postings are unsuccessful.[151] At the same time, he suggests that a wider definition of expatriate failure should be employed, including underperformance of expatriate managers, loss of expatriate managers to other companies and the post-expatriate experience, including what happens to family, careers and attitudes to future postings.[152] (See Exercise 3.13.)

MANAGING AT THE BOUNDARIES

In this section we explore two boundaries that impact upon the management of people in contemporary organizations. The first boundary cuts across individuals' lives, separating their work and family lives. The second boundary divides groups of diverse individuals in the workforce.

Do you feel at home at work?

While employees feel that their personal lives are important, managers often feel that the future growth of the organization depends on getting more out of these people, which often means impinging, in a variety of ways, on their family life.[153] For example, critics of continuous quality improvement programmes argue that they create health and safety problems and cause conflict between work and family by ignoring the 'whole' person and by the

---

EXERCISE 3.13 GOING INTERNATIONAL?

Select a multinational organization with which you are familiar, either from experience or from the business literature, and answer the following questions:

- Which of the following best describes the strategy taken in relation to its HR policies:
  - ethnocentric
  - polycentric
  - geocentric
  - regiocentric.
- Are these policies aimed at all staff, or mainly oriented towards senior management?
- If the latter, to what extent could these policies be applied throughout the organization – to all staff and in different countries? What barriers would need to be overcome?
- Is there a difference between HR policies in organizational units located in the parent country and the way in which those policies have been adopted and adapted in units in other countries? What implications do you draw from this about the relationship between units in the parent country and those in the host country?
- If you were asked to relocate to another country, what key issues would you face? What strategies might you use to address them? Which issues would be the hardest to address? Why?

emphasis on 'management by stress'.[154] The quality perspective simply sees employees as 'internal customers within their functional roles' and ignores the fact that they are people who need to balance pressures from both work and family.[155]

Many companies appear to adopt a 'separation' policy, akin to the separation of church and state, by ignoring altogether practices such as the provision of child care that are directly related to the family.[156] Many managers still see family-oriented programmes as costs rather than benefits. HR executives in a study of 400 US companies typically 'saw work/family programs as benefits for employees rather than as means of increasing the flexibility and productivity of their organizations'.[157] So, some work/family programmes may exist, particularly when institutional pressures such as professional norms, regulation and political influences, encourage or demand them. However, such programmes are often minimalist and, as Goodstein[158] points out, if organizations feel that institutional pressures conflict with organizational goals or that the programmes are too costly, they are unlikely to adopt them.

Some organizations adopt an 'integration' philosophy by weaving work and family issues together into the organization's culture,[159] for example, by organizing child care, flexible work hours and even elder care, which is becoming an increasingly important responsibility for many employees with elderly parents.[160] Osterman[161] found that high commitment organizations were associated with a greater awareness of, and sensitivity, to work/family boundaries. These organizations believe the key to productivity lies in the willingness of employees actively to engage themselves with the organization by offering readily their ideas and knowledge. By its nature, such engagement is not enforceable and always involves a substantial element of voluntarism on the part of the workforce. The task of the firm is, according to Osterman,[162] 'to find ways to induce or encourage this commitment'. His survey of 875 US organizations found that one common way to do this was to adopt work/family programmes. These initiatives are not, according to the author, a passing fad, since they have been adopted by large powerful organizations and are increasingly demanded as a result of the greater participation of women in the workforce.

Views of the ethics of such programmes vary widely, however. Some see them as examples of continuing personal empowerment and greater concern for personal welfare. A more critical view suggests that these benefits simply replace cuts in other areas, are unevenly provided and are in place only because they help employers, rather than employees. Osterman suggests that this debate parallels the broader debate about high commitment work systems. Are they 'genuine improvements, or are they clever devices to speed up work and use commitment as a form of self-supervision and regulation'?[163]

Hochschild argues that although work can complement family life, 'in recent decades it has largely competed with the family, and won'. In fact, parents now often act as Taylorist controllers at home, 'becoming supervisors with stopwatches, monitoring meals and bedtimes and putting real effort into eliminating "wasted" time'.[164] This spillover effect between work and family spheres has been found in other research. Williams and Alliger found that perceptions of task, personal control and progress towards work goals related to concurrent moods, both at home and at work. Ironically, unpleasant moods originating in one domain affected the other, while pleasant moods did not seem to spill over.[165] Emotions generated in one arena affect individual activities in the other but, apparently, only in negative ways. Chapter 10 on postmodern approaches discusses other aspects of the blurring of the boundaries between work and family life (Exercise 3.14).

Diverse peoples?

Researchers differentiate diversity into two broad categories.[166] Observable diversity includes distinct, identifiable differences such as gender, race and ethnic backgrounds. Non-observable diversity may include education, technical abilities, functional background, tenure in the organization and socio-economic background, personality, or values. These two categories are not mutually exclusive and, for example, gender differences may also be related to status and educational differences. Managing people involves managing these different boundaries, visible and invisible, that divide people.

EXERCISE 3.14 HOW FAMILY FRIENDLY ARE WE?

Select an organization with which you are familiar, either from experience or from the business literature. Mark on the continuum below, the position that this organization occupies in terms of its orientation to work–family policies.

Separation	Mixed	Integration

Answer the following questions:

- How appropriate is this orientation to work–family policies. Explain your answer.
- If you were to change this orientation, what would you change? What arguments would you use to support your recommendation, and how would you implement it? If you think that the orientation should not change, defend your case.
- What are the advantages and disadvantages of your recommendations from the point of view of the organization and from the point of view of the employees?
- How would these changes (or lack of change) contribute to the competitive advantage of the organization?

McDaniel and Walls[167] argue that diversity has been treated traditionally by both managers and scholars as a 'problem' that organizations have
to manage. These authors argue that diversity should be encouraged to proliferate, based on a model informed by quantum and chaos theories.
Viewed from these theoretical perspectives, greater diversity provides
organizational success, for two reasons. First, organizations are 'a rich and
complex world of relationships'.[168] The more diverse the workforce, the
more enriched are these relationships. Second, the future of an organization
is unknowable[169] and the environment is turbulent and complicated. Effective organizations will be those with sufficient diversity and variety to
respond to any situation that might arise. Diversity is, then, a way to
develop self-organizing systems through the generation of 'different ideas
and using them to make sense and guide decisions'.[170] Lack of diversity, on
the other hand, makes it difficult for organizations to deal with chaos and
make the creative frame-breaking changes needed to respond to environmental turbulence. Having a diverse workforce, according to this view,
does not reflect 'political correctness' but reflects the fact that 'fluctuations
generated by multiculturalism help to ensure the levels of instability that
may generate organizational renewal'.[171] Other reasons for encouraging
diversity in the workforce are given in Table 3.8.

Krefting et al.[172] take issue with McDaniel and Walls. They argue that
'identity-conscious' HRM practices of encouraging workforce diversity are
problematic for a number of reasons. First, organizations need requisite, not
finite, variety and they need it in their inventory of available *capabilities*
rather than in their inventory of demographic characteristics. Second, the
existence of a diverse workforce does not automatically stimulate diverse

TABLE 3.8   *Reasons for valuing diversity*

Cost savings	• Attention to diversity results in less turnover and absenteeism • Fewer discrimination and harassment lawsuits • Integrated workforces are more efficient
Resource acquisition	• Easier to attract and retain talented staff • Better staff are attracted to organizations with reputations for treating employees equitably
Marketing	• Can match profiles of customer and front-line staff • Internal diversity helps development of sensitivity to diverse customer base
Creativity and problem solving	• Greater range of perspectives enhances creativity • Staff heterogeneity produces better decisions
System flexibility	• Greater fluidity and flexibility among diverse employees
Public relations	• Avoidance of discrimination and harassment lawsuits that attract hostile media coverage • Best practices secure favourable coverage • Favourable treatment of diverse employees appreciated by diverse client base

Sources: Adapted from Cox and Blake, 1991; Robinson and Dechant, 1997

ideas because socialization and other processes lead to assimilation. Third, too much diversity can put loyalty in question, lead to ghettoization, dual standards, and 'silent' presence. Respectful interaction breaks down in the face of foreignness and 'otherness'. Fourth, 'identity-conscious' HRM practices are often responses to legal requirements and quota-driven practices where the aim is simply to get 'the numbers right'.[173] These authors argue that HRM policies and practices should be 'identity-blind'. They should encourage 'respectful interaction' and focus on how emotions, organizational dominance, affiliation and reciprocity affect the treatment of diverse workforces, inhibit the capacity for reframing and constrain the generation of diverse ideas in organizations.

The arguments in favour of diversity seek, in different ways, to move beyond the question of whether diversity management is a luxury or a necessity for organizations.[174] They exhort managers to recognize and capitalize 'on diversity rather than try to minimize and suppress it'.[175] Managers should assess the extent to which their organizations are intolerant, tolerant or appreciative of organizational diversity.[176] Intolerant organizations at best comply with legal requirements; tolerant organizations may actively seek a diverse workforce but fail to utilize their skills; appreciative organizations include the skills and talents of diverse members in the way the organization operates (Table 3.9; Exercise 3.15).

TABLE 3.9 *Mapping organizational approaches to diversity*

Issue	Intolerance	Tolerance	Appreciative
Power relationships between diverse groups	Latent struggles	Explicit struggles	Alliance building
Diversity of opinion between diverse groups	Disrespect when expressed	Expressed but not acted on	Expressed and used for competitive advantage
Views of other diverse groups	Stereotyping and hostility	Tolerance	Empathy, interest and respect
Representation and participation of diverse groups	Restricted	Tokenism: minority voices on committees	Expertise and qualifications are included and valued
Organizational action on diversity	None except where conflict emerges	Some individual responsiveness but weighed down by rest of system	Active monitoring and support

Source: Adapted from Joplin and Daus, 1997: 34

CONCLUSION: WHO HAS BEEN LEFT OUT?

This chapter set out to identify the debates associated with the management of people. We explored some of the debates associated with the nature of

---

EXERCISE 3.15 HOW TOLERANT ARE YOU?

Select an organization with which you are familiar, either from experience or from the business literature. Refer to the text and to Table 3.9 and answer the following questions:

- Is this organization intolerant, tolerant or appreciative of diversity? Explain your answer.
- What are the advantages and disadvantages of this position for the organization?
- What are the advantages and disadvantages of this position for the individuals who work in it?
- Would you make changes and, if so, what changes would you make? Explain your answer.
- Do you see this organization changing its position in the future? If so, how and why?
- How typical is this organization in your experience?

HRM and the role of the HRM department, as well as the relationship between HRM practices and organizational performance. We then examined specific HRM practices – identifying competencies, managing temporary employees, open-book management, coping with the problem of careers and issues concerning loyalty and commitment. We investigated some of the new contexts in which contemporary people management is taking place – networks, outsourced HRM practices and the international arena. Finally, we discussed the importance of recognizing the social boundaries between work and family and between different groups of employees.

There are, however, groups of people who have been left out of this analysis. Some of them are discussed in the next chapter on power, where we examine issues of social responsibility and accountability to different stakeholders. In this chapter, we remind readers of two other groups – the 'working poor' and the aged – who are often neglected in the context of people management. Kossek et al.[177] argue that, in a situation where the poverty rate is 13 per cent in the USA, around 7 per cent in Canada and Australia and 5 per cent in France and the UK, there are both economic and social reasons why employers should assist the working poor. For example, understanding the value of attracting and retaining minimum wage workers, a Burger King franchise with fourteen restaurants gave working parents $1.50 vouchers toward child care for every hour worked. Similarly, Marriott Hotels employs professional social workers to assist those in lower paid hospitality jobs with child care, housing and other domestic needs. Domino's Pizza and New York Telephone engage in literacy training and, in Atlanta, Days Inn employs homeless people when faced with a high turnover and contracting labour market. Such actions require organizations to change their mental frameworks to recognize the importance of partnerships with the community. Critics, however, might argue that if such organizations paid decent wages in the first place and governments changed punitive social welfare systems there would be fewer working poor in the first place and the need for such 'tokens' would be reduced.

Some organizations have also looked to the aged community as a pool of human resources. As our societies age, our preoccupation with youthfulness undermines the importance and wealth of experience offered by seniors.[178] A variety of myths are associated with the older worker, including the idea that they lack performance and learning capacity and are likely to be absent through injuries and sickness. Views that they should retire at the age of 65 and make way for younger staff are changing as some jurisdictions end mandatory retirement so that organizations can capitalize on the experience and wealth of knowledge they offer. However, while youth employment remains high, downsizing continues to occur and people, particularly in the 50+ age bracket, face difficulties in finding new jobs, so that privileging the older worker will remain a controversial issue.

NOTES

(See Bibliography at the end of the book for full references)

1 Lewis, 1994: 29; Lundberg, 1991; Davis, E., 1997
2 Lewis, 1994
3 Becker and Gerhart, 1996; Kiedel, 1994
4 Barney and Wright, 1998
5 Davis, E., 1997
6 Townley, 1993, 1994; Reed, 1996
7 Burack and Singh, 1995: 13
8 Coff, 1997: 375
9 Cooksey and Gates, 1995: 1
10 Kane, 1996: 116–23 provides an outline of this debate.
11 Sisson, 1990
12 Welbourne and Andrews, 1996; Wright and McMahan, 1992; Wood 1995
13 Legge, 1995
14 Truss et al. 1997: 53
15 Truss et al. 1997: 69
16 Cooksey and Gates, 1995: 2
17 Delery and Doty, 1996: 828
18 Guest, 1997: 263
19 Kane, 1996: 162
20 Bacon et al. 1996
21 Bacon et al. 1996: 96
22 Eisenstat, 1996
23 Eisenstat, 1996
24 Eisenstat, 1996: 14
25 Atchison, 1991
26 Medcof and Needham, 1998
27 Eisenstat, 1996: 9
28 Cited in Limerick and Cunnington, 1993: 43
29 Guest, 1997: 263
30 Lewis, 1994: 29–30
31 Becker and Gerhart, 1996
32 Huselid et al. 1997: 186; Wright et al. 1995: 272
33 Becker and Gerhart, 1996
34 Guest, 1997: 263
35 Guest, 1997
36 Becker and Gerhart, 1996
37 Pfeffer, 1998
38 Wright et al. 1995
39 Hannon and Milkovich, 1996
40 Barney and Wright, 1998
41 Blackburn and Rosen, 1993
42 Pfeffer, 1995
43 Pfeffer, 1998
44 Pfeffer, 1995: 56
45 Becker and Gerhart, 1996
46 Coff, 1997
47 Broderick and Boudreau, 1992
48 Cappelli and Crocker-Hefter, 1996: 7
49 Cappelli and Crocker-Hefter, 1996: 16
50 Becker and Gerhart, 1996
51 Lawler, 1994
52 Bartlett and Ghoshal, 1997: 104
53 Ulrich, 1998
54 Mansfield, 1996
55 Mansfield, 1996
56 Bartlett and Ghoshal, 1997
57 Kochanski and Ruse, 1996
58 Mansfield, 1996
59 Mansfield, 1996
60 Bartlett and Ghoshal, 1997
61 Lawler, 1994

62 Lado and Wilson, 1994
63 Caggiano, 1995; Ghorpade and Chen, 1995; Antonioni, 1996
64 Pfeffer, 1995
65 Medcof and Needham, 1998
66 Feldman et al. 1994
67 Cited in von Hippel et al. 1997: 93
68 Handy, 1990; Atchison, 1991
69 Davis-Blake and Uzzi, 1993
70 von Hippel et al. 1997
71 von Hippel et al. 1997
72 Rousseau, 1996
73 Morrison, 1994; Morrison and Robinson, 1997; Hall and Moss, 1998
74 Tsui et al. 1997
75 Robinson et al. 1994
76 Morrison and Robinson, 1997
77 Hallier and James, 1997
78 Bridges, 1994, cited in Burack and Singh, 1995: 13
79 Burack and Singh, 1995
80 Burack and Singh, 1995: 18
81 Morrison and Robinson, 1997
82 Hall and Moss, 1998: 23
83 Feldman et al. 1994
84 von Hippel et al. 1997: 93
85 Davis-Blake and Uzzi, 1993
86 Bedeian, 1995: 54
87 Davis-Blake and Uzzi, 1993
88 von Hippel et al. 1997
89 Stewart, 1998
90 Davis, T.R.V., 1997
91 Collins, 1997
92 Nonaka and Takeuchi, 1995: 80
93 Davis, T.R.V., 1997: 8
94 Nonaka and Takeuchi, 1995
95 Hilmer and Donaldson, 1996
96 Hilmer and Donaldson, 1996: 48
97 Carson and Carson, 1997: 62
98 Brousseau et al. 1996: 52
99 Hirsch, 1988, cited in Robinson et al. 1994: 137
100 Feldman, 1996: 159
101 Allred et al. 1996
102 Jones and De Fillippi, 1996
103 Arthur and Rousseau, 1996
104 Peiperl and Baruch, 1997
105 Arthur and Rousseau, 1996
106 Carson and Carson, 1997
107 Peiperl and Baruch, 1997
108 Brousseau et al. 1996
109 Nicholson, 1996: 42
110 Nicholson, 1996
111 Brousseau et al. 1996
112 Dunford, 1995
113 Stroh and Reilly, 1997
114 Cummings and Oldham, 1997; Amabile, 1997; De Vries, 1998
115 Wallace, 1995
116 Brett et al. 1995
117 Kerr, 1975
118 Editors, 1995
119 Becker et al. 1996
120 Ulrich, 1998: 16
121 Coyle and Schnarr, 1995
122 Medcof and Needham, 1998
123 Quinn et al. 1996
124 Quinn et al. 1996: 25
125 Blackler, 1995: 1026
126 Lever, 1997
127 Lever, 1997
128 Medcof and Needham, 1998
129 Medcof and Needham, 1998: 43
130 Barney and Wright, 1998
131 Becker and Gerhart, 1996
132 Medcof and Needham, 1998
133 Medcof and Needham, 1998
134 Adler and Bartholomew, 1992
135 de-Forest, 1994
136 Stevens and Greer, 1998
137 Yeung and Tung, 1998
138 Cooksey and Gates, 1995: 2
139 Welch, 1994
140 Taylor et al. 1996; Welch, 1994
141 Jain et al. 1998; Lu and Bjorkman, 1997
142 McGraw, 1997: 551–3
143 McGraw, 1997: 553
144 Kamoche, 1997: 215
145 Kamoche, 1997
146 Tayeb, 1998
147 Kamoche, 1997: 217
148 Kamoche, 1997
149 Harzing, 1995
150 Forster, 1997: 416
151 Forster, 1997: 429
152 Forster, 1997: 414
153 Bailyn et al. 1997
154 Cutcher-Gershenfeld et al. 1997: 24
155 Cutcher-Gershenfeld et al. 1997: 25
156 Cutcher-Gershenfeld et al. 1997
157 Mirvis, 1997: 50
158 Goodstein, 1994
159 Cutcher-Gershenfeld et al. 1997
160 Osterman, 1995
161 Osterman, 1995
162 Osterman, 1995: 686
163 Osterman, 1995: 697
164 Hochschild, 1997: 94
165 Williams and Alliger, 1994
166 Milliken and Martins, 1996
167 McDaniel and Walls, 1997
168 McDaniel and Walls, 1997: 366
169 McDaniel and Walls, 1997: 367
170 McDaniel and Walls, 1997: 368
171 McDaniel and Walls, 1997: 368
172 Krefting et al. 1997
173 Krefting et al. 1997; Konrad and Linnehan, 1995
174 Sanchez and Brock, 1996
175 Bartlett and Ghoshal, 1997: 115
176 Joplin and Daus, 1997
177 Kossek et al. 1997
178 Paul and Townsend, 1993

4   MANAGING POWER

Everything or Nothing?

As soon as we start to examine people in organizations and the relations
between them, issues of power inevitably arise. In this chapter, we continue
our exploration of people in – and around – organizations, using power as
an analytical framework (see Supplementary Reading box). Discussing
power is difficult because at the heart of the work on power is a debate on
what power is. For some researchers, power is so neatly defined and tightly
circumscribed that their critics argue that it amounts to nothing, scratching
only the surface dynamics. For others, power is a multi-faceted, all-embrac-
ing concept, the adoption of which, argue those who disagree with such
breadth, amounts to saying that power is everything.

In this chapter, we first re-examine this traditional debate by comparing
three approaches – managerial, critical and postmodern – to show how
different definitions of power have emerged. We then explore four specific
arenas – empowerment, feminist theory, corporate governance and ethics –
to demonstrate how a political analysis, which focuses on power dynamics,
can provide useful insights into management practice as well as raising some
important debates in these bodies of literature.

POWER . . . DID YOU SAY?

The traditional debate concerning power revolves around deciding exactly
what it is. There are countless ways of defining power and separate streams
of research have evolved based on differences in the conceptualization and
definition of power. In this section we discuss three broad approaches, which
we call *managerial*, *critical* and *postmodern*[1] and highlight their contributions to the debate about power.

Managerial approaches to power

The managerially oriented literature tends to see power in relatively negative terms. Since it adopts a functionalist approach, which seeks to make
organizations more efficient and effective, power is often cast as a 'dis-
organizing' tool usually employed by those opposing management, resisting
change, or pursuing vested self-interests. Consequently, decisions that

POWER: SUPPLEMENTARY READING

- Alvesson, M. and Deetz, S. (1996) 'Critical theory and postmodernism approaches to organizational studies', in S. Clegg, C. Hardy and W. Nord (eds), *Handbook of Organization Studies*. London: Sage.

- Bird, F. and Gandz, J. (1991) *Good Management*. Englewood Cliffs, NJ: Prentice-Hall.

- Bradshaw-Camball, P. and Murray, V. (1991) 'Illusions and other games: a theoretical view of organizational politics', *Organization Science*, 2 (4): 379–98.

- Calás, M. B. and Smircich, L. (1996) 'From the "woman's" point of view: feminist approaches to organization studies', in S. Clegg, C. Hardy and W. Nord (eds), *Handbook of Organization Studies*. London: Sage.

- Clegg, S. R. (1989) *Frameworks of Power*. London: Sage.

- Frost, P. J. (1987) 'Power, politics and influence', in F. M. Jablin, L.L. Putnam, K.H. Roberts and L.W. Porter (eds), *Handbook of Organizational Communications: An Interdisciplinary Perspective*. London: Sage.

- Hardy, C. and Clegg, S. (1996) 'Some dare call it power', in S. Clegg, C. Hardy and W. Nord (eds), *Handbook of Organization Studies*. London: Sage.

- Pettigrew, A.M. (1973) *The Politics of Organizational Decision Making*. London: Tavistock.

- Pettigrew, A. M. (1979) 'On studying organizational cultures', *Administrative Science Quarterly*, 24: 570–81.

- Pfeffer, J. (1992a) 'Understanding power in organizations', *California Management Review*, 34 (2): 29–50.

- Pfeffer, J. (1992b) *Managing with Power*. Boston, MA: Harvard Business School Press.

- Ranson, S., Hinings, R. and Greenwood, R. (1980) 'The structuring of organizational structure', *Administrative Science Quarterly*, 25 (1): 1–14.

'ought' to be rational become political as interest groups use power to influence decision outcomes in their favour. According to this view, power is sometimes used by managers but usually only in self-defence – to repel attacks, to bring about organizational change or to pursue organizational goals. As a result, this body of work sees power as a malleable, useful resource, which is 'good' when used by managers but 'bad' when used against them. See Table 4.1 for an example of various political games used by and against managers.

TABLE 4.1 *Political games*

Political game	Main players	Reason played
Insurgency	Lower level employees	To resist authority
Counterinsurgency	Senior managers	To counter resistance to authority
Sponsorship	Any subordinate	To build power base with superiors
Alliance building	Line managers	To build power base with peers
Empire building	Line managers	To build a power base with subordinates
Budgeting	Line managers	To accumulate resources
Expertise	Lower level employees and staff	To accumulate real or perceived skills
Lording	Unskilled operators	To build power through bureaucratic rules
Line vs. staff	Line managers and staff analysts	To defeat rivals
Rival camps	Any alliance or empire	To defeat rivals
Strategic candidates	Line managers, CEO, staff and operators	To bring about change
Whistle blowing	Usually lower level employees	To bring about change
Young Turks	Usually higher level managers	To bring about change

Source: Adapted from Mintzberg, 1983: 215–16

This body of work has identified different sources of power (Table 4.2) that can be used to influence decision-making. Most managerial writers relate power to the control of scarce, valued resources, which makes some individuals in an organization more powerful than others.[2] Some writers have also drawn attention to the symbolic aspects of power, pointing out that the ability to use symbols and language to secure legitimacy for their actions enables individuals to achieve them.[3] In addition, many writers argue that power sources have to be exercised or mobilized if they are to have any impact. The exercise of power is often referred to as politics,[4] although some writers reserve the term for the informal, illegitimate or unsanctioned use of power.[5] The conclusion that can be drawn from this body of literature is that those individuals who have the greatest access to these power sources and who are most adept at putting them to use are most likely to prevail in decision-making (Table 4.3; Exercises 4.1, 4.2, 4.3).

In summary, managerial approaches to power focus primarily on actions that fall *outside* legitimated organizational structures, processes and goals. Existing organizational arrangements are seen not as the embodiment of power but as *authority*. Power represents, for the most part, dysfunctional interruptions in the far more desirable flow of rational decisions. As a result, power has come to mean less and less. The extensive use of quantitative measures of power by researchers subscribing to this view of power emphasizes precision rather than breadth. Work on politics has restricted the reach of power, by defining its use as unsanctioned, self-serving, informal, illegal, illegitimate, conflict-ridden, duplicitous and anti-organizational behaviour.

TABLE 4.2 **Power sources**

• Charisma	The perception by others of being a leader whom they are willing to follow unquestioningly
• Credibility	Being perceived as someone with valued characteristics and/or a track record of achievements
• Expertise	Based on the possession of a valued skill or ability to do something that others cannot
• Group support	Having the support of many people
• Information	Access to and control over the dissemination of information that others do not possess
• Political access	Connections to powerful people
• Position, authority	The perceived right to control others by virtue of a formal position in the hierarchy
• Processes	The ability to control agendas, decision-making participants, and decision criteria
• Referent power	The ability to establish a personal rapport with others
• Resources	The ability to control and dispense critical scarce resources e.g. budgets, equipment, personnel
• Rewards	The ability to control and dispense valued rewards, both tangible and intangible
• Sanctions	Coercive power based on control of various punishments
• Strategic contingencies	The ability to control uncertainty
• Symbols	Access to symbols that confer particular meanings on particular actions and decisions

Note: For more information on power sources and mobilization strategies see, for example, French and Raven, 1968; Hickson et al. 1971; Pettigrew, 1973, 1979; Pfeffer, 1981; Astley and Sachdeva, 1984; Frost, 1987; Forester, 1989; Hardy, 1994

TABLE 4.3 **Mobilization strategies**

• Appealing	Appealing to senior levels for support
• Coalition building	Networking with strategically placed groups
• Directing	Issuing directives to act or not act in certain ways
• Empowering	Increasing the autonomy of others to produce particular actions
• Enrolment	Encouraging participation, obtaining consent of other parties
• Envisioning	Showing how co-operation in a particular initiative will produce mutual benefits
• Managing meaning	Making desired actions appear as legitimate, beneficial, or inevitable
• Negotiating	Making deals to secure support
• Personalizing	Establishing a personal relationship with individuals
• Persuading	Using information, analysis, expertise for or against particular actions or decisions
• Problematization	Becoming indispensable by defining – and therefore solving – the 'problems' of others
• Rallying	Rallying large blocs of support
• Sanctioning	Rewarding and/or punishing behaviour
• Score-carding	Using past or anticipated achievements for or against particular actions or decisions
• Socialization	Shaping the identification of new members of an organization

EXERCISE 4.1 WHO'S GOT THE POWER?

The pension investments division of a large firm consists of some twenty people. It is headed by a general manager and leads an isolated existence from the rest of the company. The work involves considerable contact with outside investment firms but relatively little with other employees in the company. Most of the employees have worked together for twenty years.

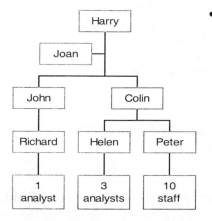

- **Harry** is the general manager. He was recently promoted to this position as a result of his predecessor having been 'relocated' following a $32 million write-off of the pension fund. There was some opposition to his appointment from John, although Harry is unaware of this and believes John to be one of his supporters. He was the most senior manager in the department and so his appointment was not a surprise, although both Colin and John could claim to have achieved superior performance in recent years.
- **Joan** is Harry's secretary. She worked for his predecessor for many years and is the longest serving employee in this group.
- **Colin** is a director whose recent promotion has been attributed to his connections with the CEO of the company, to whom he is related by marriage. When he was appointed director, Harry rearranged reporting relationships so that Helen now reports directly to him, instead of the general manager as before.
- **John** is a director who has moved up the hierarchy primarily because of his external contacts in the investment community and is considered to be the heir to Harry's position. He is independently wealthy and widely regarded as an expert in giving investment advice. He is, however, very selective in choosing to whom to give advice. He has advised Harry's secretary, Joan, on her investments over the years and she has become quite wealthy as a result. John was once highly supportive of Harry but, more recently, has started to speak derisively of him to the other members of the department. He is believed to be lobbying behind the scenes for Harry's job, although not all his colleagues are convinced of his ability to secure it.

- **Helen** is a manager whose expertise and competence is widely acknowledged. She is also famous for her temper. Her colleagues believe that this may be the cause of the reorganization of reporting relationships, requiring her to report to Colin, and the fact she has not yet been made a director.
- **Richard** is a newcomer. He is the only manager with a university degree. He has impeccable qualifications and his initial performance appears stunning. He is known to be a good friend of Harry, although his allegiances are not yet fully clear.
- **Peter** is the manager responsible for administration (rather than investments). His department is the largest. It includes the accounting and computer functions and is generally responsible for the smooth functioning of the office. He formally reports to John but since John is renowned for having no interest in these matters Peter has a considerable amount of autonomy.

Questions

- What sources of power do each of the players have?
- Who is the most powerful? Why?

Other writers reserve the exercise of power only for situations marked by conflict, [6] excluding both the idea that power might be embedded in culture, formal structures, procedures, routines and cultures (which they assume to be apolitical and functional) and the idea that acquiescence might be the result of power.

Critical approaches to power

Research in the critical tradition argues something quite different. It maintains that formal organizational structures and processes are not neutral, rational or logical but, rather, that power is embedded in them in ways that specifically serve managerial interests. Hierarchy is not authority, but *domination*; and actions taken to challenge it constitute *resistance* to domination, not the illegitimate or dysfunctional use of power. This tradition thus equates power with the ways in which dominant interests are protected.

Writers have often found relatively little evidence of resistance to domination in the workplace. Consequently, they have looked for ways in which managers use power to *prevent* resistance from occurring. As a result, in the critical literature power has become attached to a wide variety of organizational issues and processes. Studies have examined how power is embedded in structures, ideologies and narratives. These studies argue that much of what seems apolitical in organization is, in fact, both a product and medium of power.[7] Other critical writers on power examine more deeply how individuals manage meaning[8] in their attempts to prevent conflict from arising.[9]

EXERCISE 4.2 EARTH CALLING XAXOS?

The inhabitants of the planet Xaxos recently sent a space probe to undertake a detailed study of the inhabitants of earth. Hovering over a large urban area, the Xaxonians commenced their work. They sent this report back to their headquarters:

> Earthlings spend most of their time in one of three structures. The first are large, square immobile objects into which the majority of earthlings usually disappear at night. The second are larger, squarer and equally immobile objects in which they spend most of the daylight hours. Between these two objects, earthlings enter into small, square, mobile objects that subsequently move in conjunction with other such objects according to what appears to be a complex social ritual. The exact form and nature of this ritual is as yet unclear but one distinguishing feature has been noted. It appears that the earthlings' disappearance into the mobile object and their participation in a larger social group is part of some religious ceremony. In this ceremony, large totems wield a considerable amount of power by flashing different colours. By flashing red, the totem has the ability to render 98 per cent of its audience motionless; by flashing green, a similar percentage is induced to move forward. We intend to explore this power further.

Questions

- Do the totems have power?
- Explain your answer

Source: Adapted from Clegg, 1989: 78

In summary, critical theorists focus on the repressive side of power and how it is used in hidden ways by dominant groups to maintain the status quo, leaving other groups at a constant disadvantage since these invisible aspects are difficult to resist. Critical theorists believe that by revealing the hidden aspects of power it is possible for these groups to liberate themselves and achieve a situation that is free of the effects of power.

Postmodern approaches to power[10]

Postmodern writers, in particular Foucault,[11] have a very different view of power:

> Power must be analysed as something which circulates, or rather something which only functions in the form of a chain. It is never localized here or there, never in anybody's hands, never appropriated as a commodity or piece of wealth. Power is employed and exercised through a net-like organization ... [Individuals] are always in the position of simultaneously undergoing and exercising this power.[12]

EXERCISE 4.3 MOBILIZING SOME MUSCLE?

Take each power source (Table 4.1) and identify which mobilization strategies (in Table 4.2) represent an effective way to exercise it. Provide a *concrete* example of when you have used power in this way, or seen or read about someone else using it.

Power source	Mobilization strategy	Example
Charisma		
Credibility		
Expertise		
Group support		
Information		
Political access		
Position, authority		
Processes		
Referent power		
Resources		
Rewards		
Sanctions		
Strategic contingencies		
Symbols		

Foucault's work promotes a view of power that encompasses every facet of our lives. First, he challenged the idea that an individual could stand outside power and use it to achieve specific outcomes, arguing instead that power is embodied in a network of relations which captures everyone in its web, both those advantaged and those disadvantaged by it. So, individuals may have intentions concerning outcomes and they may act with the idea of achieving them, but whether pulling the necessary 'strings' of power actually brings them about is doubtful.[13] Second, Foucault drew attention to how these networks of power produce our subjectivity or identity. In other words, we recognize ourselves and others not in any objective way but because of systems of classification and categorization that teach us to see and experience particular things. In producing identity, power transforms 'individuals into subjects who secure their sense of what it is to be worthy and competent human beings.'[14] According to this view, individuals derive a positive experience from power relations, instead of just the negative effects discussed by critical theorists.

Third, Foucault illuminated the limitations of resisting power. The positive side of power – which gives meaning to the subject – leads to the continuation rather than the dismantling of power relations. Any resistance exerts a high price since the individual has to reject a part of him or herself in challenging existing power relations. In addition, the pervasiveness of power relations makes them difficult to resist, much less overturn. They are experienced as reality, which makes alternatives difficult to conceive of and, as a result, resistance often serves only to reinforce existing power relations.[15] Finally, Foucault argued that knowledge can never escape from the effects of power and therefore never constitutes the 'truth'. Instead, what we take to be true are those mechanisms which 'enable one to distinguish true and false statements . . . the techniques and procedures accorded value in the acquisition of truth; [and] the status of those who are charged with saying what counts as true'.[16] So, attempts by critical theorists to reveal the hidden side of power are themselves biased by the effects of power. Moreover, even if resistance were successful, the resulting situation could never be free of power – it would simply represent a *different* power regime.

In summary, Foucault's view of disciplinary power is hard to escape. Power is everywhere and we are totally enmeshed in it. It encompasses, surrounds and infiltrates us in ways that we may never realize. It is productive yet constraining; it makes us what we are, yet prevents us from becoming anything else.

We can see, then, that there is a fundamental debate concerning power – it means different things to different people. For some, power is something that goes on outside, and in ways detrimental to, formal organizational functioning. It can be seen and measured. For others, power is part of formal organizational functioning. It is largely invisible and difficult to measure and it affects, usually adversely, those at the bottom of the organizational hiearchy. For still others, power is everywhere – in what we know of ourself, in how we think of truth, in all the taken for granted aspects of

TABLE 4.4   *Summary of managerial, critical and postmodern views of power*

	Managerial	Critical	Postmodern
Focus on	Power as the mobilization of resources	Power as the management of meaning and/or as embedded in structure	Power as embedded in networks of relations
Concept of power	Deliberate, causal, visible, has a direct and measurable effect on decision outcomes	Deliberate, causal, invisible, has a direct effect on producing acquiescence	Arbitrary, invisible, pervasive, cannot be managed or manipulated
Ethics of power	Neutral or functional when used by management; dysfunctional when used against management	Repressive but revealing the way in which power works helps to engender resistance to its dominating effects	Productive and constraining; any assessment of the ethics of power is inevitably a position affected by power

our lives – and it shapes all our experiences, both positive and negative (Table 4.4).

This debate can never be resolved – it is bound up with deeply held assumptions about the way societies and organizations operate. So, we do not attempt to resolve it. Instead, we use it to broaden our understanding of the different ways in which power works. Other writers have combined these different views to show that power operates in a multitude of different ways. Sometimes it involves the management of dependencies in situations of overt conflict, sometimes the management of legitimacy to prevent conflict, and sometimes it is embedded in the fabric of organizational and societal life (Table 4.5).[17] Consequently, in the following sections, we explore four particular arenas – empowerment, women in organizations, the board and ethics – to examine other, more recent debates concerning power and management practice.

UPSIDE DOWN: THE POLITICS OF EMPOWERMENT

Some writers have hailed the 1990s as the 'empowerment era'. As noted in the structure chapter, empowerment practices are often associated with overturning traditional organizational structures and the introduction of new organizational forms. Empowerment is argued to benefit 'shareholders through improvements in the bottom line, customers through value and service, suppliers through more effective partnership agreements and employees through a higher quality of work life'.[18] At the same time, there is growing evidence that empowerment programmes often fail to improve performance;[19] while other critics question whether employees are empowered at all, but simply subjected to different kinds of managerial controls.[20] There may also be more talk than action: a survey of Fortune 1000

TABLE 4.5   ***Different faces of power***

Lukes: three dimensions of power	• First dimension (decision-making): the ability of A to make B do what s/he otherwise would not do. • Second dimension (non-decision-making): the ability to mobilize the bias of decision-making processes to exclude issues and participants from the decision-making area and confine the agenda to 'safe' questions. • Third dimension: the ability to shape people's perceptions and preferences in such a way that they accept the existing order, either because they cannot see any alternatives, view it as natural or because they value it as beneficial.
Clegg: circuits of power	• Episodic: causal power used by an actor to secure outcomes. • Dispositional: fixing relations of meaning or membership for the purposes of domination. • Facilitative: conditions of empowerment and disempowerment in terms of power's productive capabilities; transformation of an existing configuration of episodic power networks.
Bradshaw-Camball and Murray: tri-focal view	• Functional: overt political fame playing by adversaries. • Interpretive: management of meaning through language, symbols, myths. • Radical: power effects of social structure to maintain status quo.
Fincham: perspectives on power	• Processual: power at the level of social interaction e.g. coalition formation, manipulation of information. • Institutional: mandated authority and social structure, e.g. class, markets, occupations. • Organizational: hierarchical mechanisms, e.g. selection, career, dominant coalition.
Hardy: four dimensions of power	• First dimension (power of resources): the control of scarce, critical resources and management of dependencies. • Second dimension (power of processes): the ability to control decision-making processes, agenda, participants and arenas. • Third dimension (power of meaning): the ability to use symbols to create legitimacy for desired actions or 'delegitimize' undesired actions. • Fourth dimension (power of the system): power embedded in the system – in the unconscious acceptance of values, traditions, structures, etc. – which cannot be consciously mobilized.

Sources: Adapted from Lukes, 1974; Clegg, 1989; Bradshaw-Camball and Murray, 1991; Fincham, 1992; Hardy, 1994

firms indicated relatively low rates of employee participation, leading others to argue that empowerment is 'just another vacuous corporate buzzword, denuded of all meaning by loose and excessive usage'.[21]

Empowerment works in different ways (Table 4.6).[22] The motivational approach is believed to leave employees optimistic, involved, committed, able to cope with adversity and willing to perform independently and responsibly. In short, it is supposed to enhance the individual's belief that she or he can do the job by countering feelings of powerlessness, regardless of whether or not the practices involve any significant delegation of power and authority.[23] So, while the relational approach advocates increasing the

TABLE 4.6   *Motivational and relational approaches to empowerment*

Motivational[*]	Relational[†]
• Aim is to help employees feel that they have power over their work and to develop a sense of pride and ownership.	• Aims at reducing the dependencies that make it difficult to get a job done.
• Open communication and inspirational goal setting increases commitment and involvement.	• Delegates power by: involving employees in decision-making; establishing self-managing teams; by allowing workers to set performance standards, monitor performance, schedule work, select their own equipment, participate in recruitment decisions, and deal with co-worker discipline.
• Attainable objectives are set to help motivate employees.	
• Exemplary co-worker and supervisory role models provide learning opportunities.	
• Encouragement and feedback bolsters self-confidence.	• Employees are typically permitted to take decisions only within specified policies and procedures set by management, e.g. organizational goals and compensation are predetermined; a shared vision is communicated, reinforcing organizational goals; training and education heighten employees' awareness of organizational goals
• Emotional support offsets stress.	
• Jobs may be redesigned but the primary aim is to provide feelings of ownership, responsibility, and capability.	
• Typically relies on less delegation of power.	

Sources: * Adapted from Conger and Kanungo, 1988; Thomas and Velthouse, 1990; Sheridan, 1991a, b; Eccles, 1993
            † Adapted from Belasco, 1989; Topaz, 1989/90; Doyle, 1990; McKenna, 1990; Velthouse, 1990; Brymer, 1991; Carr, 1991; Eisman, 1991; Eubanks, 1991; Fleming, 1991; Gonring, 1991; Penzer, 1991; Schaeffer, 1991; Welter, 1991a, b; Lawler, 1992; Eccles, 1993

power of lower level employees by reducing their dependency, the motivational approach recommends reducing feelings of powerlessness without necessarily making any structural changes. Both approaches hinge on the belief that employees thrive on stress and are keen to perform above and beyond the call of duty,[24] even though Ashkenas et al.[25] argue that the idea that all staff wish to be empowered is a myth. People have different motivations for working: some 'enjoy being told what to do, or they feel most secure in a structured, well-ordered environment, or they get satisfaction out of doing one thing well, over and over'.

In this section, we draw on managerial, critical and post-modern insights to explore three debates about empowerment. We examine whether empowerment really does involve handing over power to employees; why it is not achieving more success for the organizations employing it; and whether managers are adversely affected by empowerment.

Empowerment: power to the people – more or less?

Does empowerment involve handing over power to employees or not? Do empowerment practices benefit the employee or not? The answers to these questions differ, depending on the way in which power, and hence empower-ment, is conceptualized – according to managerial, critical or postmodern views.

Most of the work in the business literature on empowerment adopts a managerial view of power. It focuses on the sources of power specified in Table 4.2, and especially those associated with the control of critical resources. Consequently, writers, particularly those with the relational approach, argue that business empowerment practices do, indeed, transfer some resources to employees by allowing them to take decisions and control tasks that were previously the purview of senior management. These researchers argue that the enhancement of decision-making latitude and self-worth of subordinates enables them to work in ways that are aligned with the preferences of their supervisors while, at the same time, increasing their perceptions of control over their organizational situations.[26] Superiors who do not trust subordinates and are reluctant to share power with them are less likely to receive satisfying performance from them.

Critical approaches challenge these conclusions by pointing out that empowerment programmes are usually implemented for instrumental reasons: to improve productivity, lower costs, or raise customer satisfac-tion; rather than to enhance morale or democratize the organization per se. 'The purpose of shifting decision making to the employees is not to remove managers totally from making decisions, or to turn the operation into a democracy.'[27] Consequently, empowerment is often part of a broader initiative, such as continuous improvement, total quality or downsizing, that is intended to improve organizational effectiveness and enhance com-petitive advantage.[28] They also argue that senior management continues to control important resources and uses the management of meaning – sym-bolized by the term empowerment – to maintain its dominance. They note that senior managers retain the right to hire, fire, promote, hand out rewards and control budgets. Similarly, while empowered employees may secure access to decision-making processes from which they were previ-ously excluded, ultimate control continues to rest elsewhere. Senior man-agers establish the parameters within which subordinates are forced to operate by setting the agenda – usually improved performance and profitability – and determining the strategic direction of the company. In other words, the empowered organization is 'not participative but rather dictatorial'.[29]

Critical theorists also suggest that empowerment practices rely on the increased use of 'hidden' forms of power by managers, such as selection, socialization, socializing, training and communication to legitimate organizational goals. The power of language reduces conflict by emphasiz-ing consensus and co-operation, through such terms as 'associates', 'team members', 'players' and 'coaches'.[30] Peer pressure controls behaviour more effectively than managerial threats – employees 'are less likely to call in sick if they have to face team members the next morning'.[31] Individuals who oppose empowerment are 'delegitimized' by being labelled 'Neanderthals' or 'dinosaurs'. Dissenters, if they are not fired, are marginalized as unco-operative, or in need of education or training.[32] Hierarchical controls are replaced by 'concertive' controls in the form of team pressures to identify strongly with team values, goals, norms and rules. Resistance may involve risking 'human dignity' and 'being made to feel unworthy' as a teammate.[33]

According to this view, empowerment is an exercise in the management of meaning to enhance the legitimacy of organizational goals and to create the perception that organizational and employee interests converge. Empowerment programmes reduce the necessity of having to use more visible or coercive forms of power to ensure that organizational goals are met and to quell resistance. The power of senior managers, who usually dictate the form and timing of the overall empowerment initiative, remains untouched[34] and, confident that employees will not use their newly found power in an adversarial way, managers agree to cede some power and authority:

> It is tempting to conclude that many companies are attracted to a fantasy version of empowerment and simultaneously repelled by the reality. How lovely to have energetic, dedicated workers who always seize the initiative (but only when 'appropriate'), who enjoy taking risks (but never risky ones), who volun-teer their ideas (only brilliant ones), who solve problems on their own (but make no mistakes), who aren't afraid to speak their minds (but never ruffle any feathers), who always give their very best to the company (but ask no unpleas-ant questions about what the company is giving back). How nice it would be, in short, to empower workers without actually giving them any power.[35]

Postmodern approaches challenge these pessimistic views by acknow-ledging that the practices that constitute business empowerment do result in positive experiences for some individuals. If power relations stimulate 'a positive sense of self-discipline by transforming individuals into subjects who secure their sense of identity, meaning, and reality through partici-pating in [certain] practices',[36] should not *em*powerment relations produce a similar effect? In other words, empowerment practices that grant auton-omy, provide variety and challenge, relax formal controls, enhance the opportunity for personal initiative and generate an emotional attachment to collective goals help to produce subjects who believe themselves to be more highly valued. As a result, they may feel more excitement and passion in their work and derive a more rewarding work experience. In other words, individuals may *enjoy* being empowered.

So, rather than dismiss empowerment out of hand, as critical theorists do, the postmodernist approach draws our attention to the complexity and ambiguity of empowerment as it is experienced by those being empowered. While aware that empowerment contains a risk of exploitation, this view acknowledges that it also encompasses changes in the organizational environment that may improve the experience of working life for some, even if not all, employees.

Empowering the organization . . . more or less?

Critical approaches illuminate the contradictions of business empowerment, namely that while the language of empowerment *promises* the acquisition of power in exchange for an increase in effort and responsibility, practices often *limit* the devolution of power to subordinates. These critics argue that managerial approaches to empowerment adopt a line of reasoning which suggests that, as long as employees can be made to *believe* they are empowered, it does not matter whether they actually are or not. Managers can 'claim to be empowering their workforce when in fact they are merely deceiving them'.[37] This might not matter to managers except that some research indicates that participation or collaborative decision-making will not improve satisfaction and performance unless it is accompanied by a broader decentralization of power, such as the delegation of authority, the opportunity to reject assigned goals and voluntary participation.[38]

There is also risk of a backlash if employees find out they have been deceived. Researchers have noted that 'promise-making language'[39] like empowerment creates beliefs about fairness and, in so doing, forges a psychological contract between employer and employee. This contract encompasses the latter's beliefs concerning the commitments and obligations of the employment relationship. If the employer meets these perceived commitments, organizational loyalty is fostered and co-operation and consensus are engendered. But if employees consider the organization to have breached the contract, trust and commitment can decline and employees may withdraw from their obligations, all of which can have a negative effect on performance (also see Chapter 3 on people).[40]

In summary, the tendency of managerial work to skirt the issue of power and circumscribe its definition restricts the redistribution of power in empowerment initiatives. This may be contributing to the failure of empowerment programmes. Rather than avoid power, it would appear that it is, perhaps, time for managers to address it more directly.

Empowerment . . . for managers?

The effect of empowerment on managers is often neglected. Managerial writers assume that they will jump at the chance of empowerment because of its assumed impact on the bottom line. Critical writers are too busy taking up the cause of lower level employees and dismiss managers[41] as members of a homogeneous dominant elite whose exclusive interest lies in exploiting workers. Postmodern insights remind us, however, that the manager is also affected by empowerment.

Managers often experience distress and alienation as a result of empowerment. As Keller and Dansereau[42] point out, the need for control is necessary to individual well-being and integral to self-esteem. With empowerment comes a loosening of control, no matter how superficial, which undoubtedly affects some managers adversely because their sense of identity, grounded in 'traditional' management authority and practice, is threatened. Moreover, the scope for management resistance is limited because the rhetoric of empowerment has become intertwined with ideas of 'good' and 'enlightened' management practice. Those who have previously been successful in hierarchical organizations and define themselves in the context of more authoritarian styles of management may find empowerment particularly repressive and difficult to manage.

In summary, by examining the power of empowerment we are in a position to learn more about these business practices. It is clear that it is debatable whether empowerment benefits employees, whether it improves organizational performance and whether managers are better off or worse off in an empowered organization (Exercise 4.4).

INSIDE OUT: THE POLITICS OF WOMEN IN (AND AROUND) ORGANIZATIONS

In this section we examine some of the debates associated with women in organizations. To do so we draw on feminist theory. It is important to note that there is no single feminist theory, but rather a richness of diverse voices which are often 'difficult to incorporate alongside each other and within the realms of management'.[43] Consequently, this body of literature encompasses

---

EXERCISE 4.4 POWER TO THE PEOPLE?

Select an organization with which you are familiar, either from experience or from the business literature, that has introduced an empowerment programme and answer the following questions:

- Explain why this initiative succeeded or failed or predict whether it will succeed or fail?
- If the programme ran into problems (or if you anticipate problems), explain how you would manage it differently to avoid them.
- What are the critical success factors for successful empowerment from the organization's perspective? Define what you mean by success.
- What are the critical success factors for successful empowerment from the individual's perspective? Define what you mean by success.
- How do you think managers experience empowerment? Why do they experience it this way?
- What can be done to help managers who have negative experiences as a result of empowerment?

a wide range of approaches (Table 4.7). Regardless of the approach, however, feminist theories are about power, even though theories of power are often blind to women's experiences.[44] Feminist theorizing challenges existing distributions of power in society, questions the nature of organizations and their purposes and critiques social practices based on public and private gender differentiation.[45] 'Power is both the source of oppression in its abuse and the source of emancipation in its use.'[46]

Early feminist writers differentiated between sex, considered to be biological, and gender, which comprised the socially constituted categories of 'female' and 'male'. More recently, writers have challenged this separation of body and mind. They argue that human experience revolves around the occupation by a physical, material body of a moment in time, which is socially and historically constituted. Consequently, attention has turned to gender relations – the relations whereby 'men' and 'women' are created as their bodies are connected to the ideas, norms, images and practices of a particular culture at a particular time.[47] Writers argue that gender and gender relations are neglected in organization and management theory, even though most of us 'spend most of our days in work organizations that are almost always dominated by men'.[48] By ignoring gender relations, organization theory has helped to promote the view that organizations are gender neutral while, at the same time, suggesting that men are the norm and women are the 'other'.[49] By studying gender, feminist writers help women to emerge from the shadows and take their place in the foreground.[50] By trying to 'out' gender (as well as sexuality and race), they show how these relations are produced on the inside as well as the outside and underside of organizational life.

In examining power in the context of gender, we first document some of the ways in which power relations in society, organizations and organization theory oppress women. We then look at some of the different ways in which feminist researchers treat power.[51]

TABLE 4.7   ***Themes in gender research in management****

Women in management	• Counting, describing, explaining them
	• Barriers faced by women in management and how to overcome them
	• Whether men and women are really different[†]
Power and gender	• Male-dominated cultures and their consequences for women
	• Processes by which gender differentiation is created, sustained and resisted
	• Linking organizational power effects to those in wider society
	• Challenging supposedly gender neutral concepts
Rewriting gender in organization studies	• Reclaiming 'lost' gender-associated issues
	• Alternative organizational forms
	• Critical studies of men and masculinities

Sources: * Adapted from Marshall, 1995a: S57; Calás and Smircich, 1996
        † Adapted from Bacchi, 1990; Rosener, 1990

Powering down: sources of oppression inside and outside organizations

Women's 'liberation' has come a long way in the last thirty years but, as Calás and Smircich[52] point out, there is still a long way to go both inside and outside paid work. Sex segregation still occurs in occupations and organizations; pay inequity prevails; poverty touches mostly women; globalization adversely affects many women;[53] and attempts to assert the rights of women have met with a backlash in countries like the USA.[54]

Outside paid work
Popular culture still reinforces stereotypical behaviour, objectifying women sexually and either restricting them to subordinate roles or showing negative consequences to non-stereotypical behaviour.[55] Unattached women are better able to organize and develop political power than married women – the latter tend to have relatively poor mental health compared to their male partners, particularly those in the role of traditional housewife.[56] As a result of their participation in household labour, studies show that even women who work full time outside the home have only 24.6 hours per week of leisure time, compared with 33.5 hours for men.[57] Women also continue to be the victims of sexual, emotional and other violent actions and attacks.[58]

Inside paid work
Improvements for women in the area of paid work have been undeniable over the last thirty years as women's participation in the workforce and relative income, although still not equal, have climbed.[59] Despite these improvements, however, women are still concentrated in ghettos of low-pay occupations and denied access to senior positions. Women continue to lack power through their low representation in state institutions such as legislatures, political parties, the judiciary and civil service. For example, Canadian women represent only 4.6 per cent of the House of Commons and 9 per cent of senior civil service levels.[60] Women predominate in low-paying occupations. Occupational crowding, a high incidence of part-time work and a lack of union support depress wages and benefits. [61]

Women also face difficulties in permeating the barriers that keep them out of the higher echelons of management.[62] A *Fortune* magazine article on women in senior management in the USA noted that of the 4012 names listed in the proxy statements of the 800 largest companies, only 19 were female.[63] Men even dominate the management ranks in companies and industries that rely on female labour and female patronage.[64] This form of discrimination often results from the pro-male bias of job performance evaluation. A study found that professional articles written for academic journals were given higher evaluations when attributed to men rather than women; while another found that actions of an individual during an emergency situation were evaluated as more logical when attributed to 'Larry' than to 'Linda'.[65] Another form of discrimination occurs when women are systematically assigned less challenging, lower status work than their male counterparts with equal or even lesser abilities, which undermines equal pay for equal work[66] and inhibits promotion.[67]

In summary, then, the evidence suggests that women remain at a disadvantage in many different arenas. However, organization and management theory has been relatively oblivious to these inequities, as we discuss in the following section.

Deaf and blind: the gendering of organization and management theory

Many writers have pointed out that organization and management theory is 'blind and deaf' to issues of gender. Until recently, few women have been acknowledged as leading exponents in the field.[68] Consequently, their authorial presence in the literature has been diminished. In addition, organizations have been studied from male-oriented perspectives that either treat women as peripheral to organizational life or assume they are the same as men,[69] helping to preserve the privileges of white, usually Anglo-Saxon, males[70] simply by denying gender exists. Rosabeth Moss Kanter's work was among the first to take gender seriously in terms of the power and opportunities available to men and women in the corporation. Until then, women had been, at best, relegated to the role of 'company wives' and, at worst, completely ignored. Studies talk of an 'abstract, bodiless worker, who occupies the abstract, gender-neutral job, has no sexuality, no emotions, and does not procreate'.[71] For example, Bass and Avolio argue that the leadership literature has largely ignored the role of gender in organizational change. They conclude 'that women managers, on average, tend to be more transformational and more proactive in addressing problems. As a consequence, they are likely to be seen as more effective and satisfying as leaders by both male and female followers.'[72] Most of the literature, however, tends to ignore women leaders, while glass ceilings ensure that not many women get the chance to be leaders.

More recently, scholars have become aware of the gender blindness of organization studies[73] and interest in the contribution of early female researchers, such as Mary Follett,[74] has burgeoned. Key texts have also been reassessed to explore how their contribution is often premised on unspoken assumptions about gender and methodologies that completely remove women from the frame (Table 4.8).[75] In the remainder of this section, we examine the potential contribution of the managerial, critical and postmodern conceptualizations of power in redressing gender blindness and deafness.

Women in management: harnessing managerial power

The women in management literature uses predominantly quantitative studies either to document the inequities and barriers facing women or to dispute the basis for discrimination. First, the work on gender-based

TABLE 4.8 *Forgotten women*

- The Hawthorne studies examined the differential increases in output of an experimental group and a control group of workers following changes in working conditions. The authors did not use gender as a category of analysis even though the experimental group comprised females, while the control consisted of men.
- F.W. Taylor's exclusive focus on male manual workers in steel and metal manufacturing industries is rarely mentioned.
- Maslow's theory of motivation treats gender as inconsequential. Self-actualization reflects stereotypical male traits and defines concepts such as risk taking in ways that reflect male experiences.
- Crozier in studying supposedly low-power maintenance workers, whose job was to fix machine breakdowns referred to them by production workers in a French state-owned tobacco monopoly, found that their control of uncertainty accorded maintenance workers considerable power over the production workers. He drew no conclusions from the fact the maintenance workers were all men while the production workers were all women.
- Even though women had the least skilled and most repetitive jobs, Blauner argued that the women in his study were not dissatisfied with their work, although he provided no evidence to support his case.
- Simon's concept of bounded rationality is grounded in male-centred assumptions that exclude alternative modes of organizing, e.g. that preclude the role which emotionality plays in decision-making.
- Burawoy's study of how employees consent to the labour process even as they engage in games designed to resist it did not include women.
- Braverman's analysis paid no attention to the gendered dimensions of the relationship between the struggle for control of the labour process and the effects of deskilling in twentieth-century capitalism.

Sources: Adapted from Mumby and Putnam, 1992; Mumby, 1996; Wilson, 1996

inequities[76] documents the persistence of segregation through measurable constructs. Psychological-based research focuses on the individual and examines sex–gender differences in such areas as leadership, stress, commitment and recruiting. More macro-level work looks at the organizational level – the existence of a glass ceiling, organizational demography, careers and social networks. Finally, work on equal opportunities, affirmative action, sexual harassment and work–family issues examines the broader social system. Recommendations for change in this literature, which Calás and Smircich argue are thin on the ground, confine themselves to incremental changes within existing power distributions.[77]

The second stream in this literature, which challenges discrimination, has spent thirty years trying to demonstrate that 'women are people too'.[78] This approach attempts to prove that women are similar to or, in certain circumstances, even better than men and are therefore credible managers. In other words, there is no logical basis for the discrimination that exists. Management is 'feminized' as stereotypical values and character traits of women are linked to effective management skills and alternatives to traditional bureaucracies.[79] Scholars argue that women managers use a 'different voice' than their male counterparts and develop 'a communicative style that encourages participation, shares information and power, and enhances the self-worth of others'.[80] Employers are exhorted to take women seriously – that labour shortages, new organizational forms, collaborative strategies and global competitiveness require the subtle insights and inter-personal skills that only women can provide. In other words, women add value.[81]

The solutions that follow from these two analytic perspectives revolve around traditional power sources. The work on the inequities suffered by women, implicitly or explicitly, suggests that were they to acquire these power sources – status, expertise, credibility, money, access to political net-works – women could take their rightful place alongside men at the top of the business pyramid. The idea that women add value effectively suggests that women already have the necessary power bases for the global infor-mation age but that, perhaps, men are a bit slow in recognizing that fact. Once they do, women will be the obvious choice for senior positions.

Critical theory: revealing structures of oppression

Critical work argues that gender is not separate from organization but, rather, is deeply embedded within it. Organizations and the society that sur-rounds them are, themselves, 'gendered'.[82] Men and women do not have inherently different traits but, rather, the meanings of maleness and female-ness are socially constructed which, in turn, creates different 'realities' or experiences for men and women. In other words, gender is not a peripheral aspect of organizational life, but a defining and constitutive feature of it. It does not overlay neutral organizing processes but is an integral part of those processes.[83] Organization members 'do' gender every day through a variety of communicative practices. Moreover, argue Calás and Smircich,[84] the 'private sphere cannot be separated from the public one, since organizations, families and societies are mutually constituted through gender relations'. The public–private divide is itself associated with gender since mainly men dominate the public world of politics and business, while women are pri-marily responsible for the private sphere in which children are procreated and nurtured.[85] Persistent structuring along the lines of gender, and also class and race, are thus further reinforced by practices external to the organization (Exercise 4.5).

Rather than contribute to the existing patriarchal system by being better at it, as suggested by the women in management literature, some feminists have attempted to create new types of organization. These organizational heterarchies[86] emphasize participatory decision-making, rotating leader-ship, flexible and interactive job design, an equitable income distribution and political accountability. Their aim is not only to enact practices and values that provide a counterpoint to male domination inside the organiz-ation, but also to act as a mode of social and political transformation within the larger society.[87] There is, however, considerable debate around the sustainability of these alternative forms of organizing. If women are

---

EXERCISE 4.5 ORGANIZATIONS DOING GENDER?

Select an organization with which you are familiar, either through your working experience or from the business literature. Examine the following:

- Organizational structure
- Key policies and procedures (e.g. job evaluations, selection decisions, promotions, work assignments, mentoring, formal meetings and informal interactions, decision-making)
- Organizational publications (e.g. newsletters, annual reports, etc.)
- Images and symbols of successful managers
- Self-presentation by women and men (e.g. what they wear, when they speak, how they speak)
- Organizational attitudes to maternity leave, paternity leave, working mothers, working from home, crèche facilities, etc.

Questions

- Discuss and document how these reinforce gender stereotypes and differences.
- Who benefits from these stereotypes? In what ways?
- Who is disadvantaged by these stereotypes? In what ways?
- How would you change things and why?

---

disadvantaged because power is embedded in societal structures and meanings, these wider pressures will permeate organizational boundaries and undermine the organization.[88] While feminist organizations have survived, few have managed to sustain the radical democratic form and are continually confronted by the bureaucratic, ideological and economic exigencies of the larger society.[89] Sometimes the reality has been embarrassing as women have failed to co-operate, conflict has emerged and power has been used to exploit other women.[90]

Postmodernism and feminist theories
In the context of the feminist literature, postmodern perspectives emphasize the complexity of power relations and their role in constituting 'gender'. The mechanism of power referred to here is the construction of the female subject. Flax[91] argues that postmodern approaches cast doubt on the existence of a stable, coherent self (also see Chapter 10 on postmodern approaches). Postmodern writers challenge the duality of male and female making gender more tenuous, fragile and less stable than even critical theorists would have us believe.[92] In other words, 'gender' cannot be treated as

a natural fact. Unless 'we see gender as a social relation, rather than as an opposition of inherently different beings, we will not be able to identify the varieties and limitations of different women's (or men's) powers and oppressions with particular societies'.[93]

These lines of thinking have led to a number of developments within the literature. First, postmodern insights remind us that there are many different kinds of women and 'none of us can speak for the "woman" because no such person exists except within a specific set of (already gendered) relations'.[94] There are, then, many different kinds of women. Second, postmodern approaches point out that both men and women are 'prisoners of gender', albeit in different ways.[95] Consequently, men's voices are being heard as men write about men and men's experiences.[96] Postmodern perspectives draw attention to the contradictions that stem from this: 'And what about men, who have caused us so much trouble, our brothers, lovers, fathers, work-mates, comrades, oppressors. There are no simple answers to this one, for sure. We shall need to fight with them and against them at the same time, often at the same moment.'[97] Third, postmodernism has made space for other, traditionally marginalized voices, such as those of lesbians and homosexuals,[98] the disabled[99] and various racial and ethnic groups.[100] Postmodern research on race and ethnicity,[101] in particular, has had an increasing impact, with work on 'racing' organizations challenging the more conventional 'managing diversity' literature (Table 4.9).[102]

A third development is the increasing interest in sexuality and the body.[103] Burrell[104] points out that organization and management theory tends to ignore sexuality, even though few would deny the existence of sexual relationships in organizational settings. He provides examples to show that, as many Western societies have become more 'civilized', so have feelings of shame increased in association with human sexual relations. The time for sexual relations is out of working hours as the world is divided up into private (home – love and comfort) and public (organization – efficiency, performance) spheres.

TABLE 4.9 *Managing diversity vs. 'racing' organizations*

Managing diversity	'Racing' organizations
• How can organizations manage diversity?	• How are societal race relations reproduced in the workplace?
• Does discrimination exist in recruitment and selection?	• To what extent is race built into the definition of a manager?
• Is there racial bias in performance evaluations?	• How do organizational processes contribute to racial domination?
• Can members of ethnic minorities become CEOs?	• How does racial identity affect organizational experiences?
• How can minorities be assimilated into organizations?	• What are the implications of racial identity for organization theory?

Source: Adapted from Nkomo, 1992: 506

In summary, then, postmodern insights open up feminist theory so that it is not only about gender. Unitary notions of gender identity are replaced with 'plural and complexly constructed conceptions of social identity, treating gender as one relevant strand among others, attending also to class, race, ethnicity, age'.[105] In addition, the complex interconnections between the physical and the ideational; between the body and the mind; and between the body and power are highlighted in this work (Exercise 4.6).

Despite its contributions, postmodernist theorizing is not free from debate because it undermines the notion of feminist theory itself. Feminist theories cannot claim that the mind, the self and one's identity are socially constituted and then maintain that feminist theory will uncover the truth regarding women's oppression or find a solution to its problems.[106] By contrast, some feminist writers argue that postmodern theories represent the voices of the powerful that are attempting to co-opt those who challenge Western male rationality.[107]

EXERCISE 4.6 BODILY CONTROL?

We have a young woman who is extraordinarily important to the launching of a major new [product]. We will be talking about it next Tuesday in its first worldwide introduction. She has arranged to have her Caesarean yesterday in order to be prepared for this event. . . **We have insisted that** she stay at home and this is going to be televised in a closed circuit television, **so we're having this done** by TV **for her**, and she is staying home for three months and **we are finding ways of filling in to create this void for us** because **we think it's an important thing for her to do**. (Statement by a CEO of a large multinational corporation at a conference sponsored by a major US university)*

Questions

- What does this statement say about the public/private sphere?
- What does this statement say about the control of the body?
- What do the specific phrases marked in bold convey?
- What impression does the overall statement convey?

We have a young man who is extraordinarily important to the launching of a major new [product]. We will be talking about it next Tuesday in its first worldwide introduction. He has arranged to have his coronary bypass operation yesterday in order to be prepared for this event . . . We have insisted that he stay at home and this is going to be televised in a closed circuit television, so we're having this done by TV for him, and he is staying home for three months and we are finding ways of filling in to create this void for us because we think it's an important thing for him to do.†

Questions

- Compare this statement with the one above.
- What are your impressions?
- How do they differ from your reactions to the first statement?
- What conclusions do you draw?

We have a young woman who is extraordinarily important to the birth of her new child. We will be talking about her baby next Tuesday in its first worldwide introduction. She arranged to have her product launched early in order to be prepared for this birth.‡

Questions

- What does this statement say about the public/private sphere?
- What does this statement say about the control of the body?
- What impression does the overall statement convey?
- How does it compare with the first statement?

Sources: * Quoted in Martin, 1990: 339
          † Quoted in Martin, 1990: 346
          ‡ Paraphrased from Martin, 1990: 351

In summarizing this section on feminist theories, we can see that the matter of resistance is problematic for all the approaches discussed here. Women in management writers continually show that men and women are not that different and, in the areas which they are, women promise important contributions to organizational effectiveness. So, why do women continue to be discriminated against? Critical theorists find an answer in the deeply embedded nature of power in processes and structures. But why cannot other forms of organizing supplant these structures? Postmodern perspectives, by illuminating the social constructed nature of gender itself, show the attendant problems of transforming the power relations that gave rise to it. But with this insight, resistance fades ever more into the distance. 'If power is not to be viewed as an entity, as so many analyses of a post-Foucauldian nature proclaim, then how do we obtain it? And if it is so diffuse as to be inscribed on our very lives, our bodies, at every turn, then how do we know we have it?'[108]

OUTSIDE IN: THE POLITICS OF CORPORATE GOVERNANCE[109]

Corporate governance refers to 'the processes, structures, and relationships through which the shareholders, as represented by the board of directors, oversee the activities of the business enterprise'.[110] Simply stated, 'corporate governance refers to the overseeing and directing of a corporation, as distinguished from the day-to-day managing of one'.[111] It brings the board face to face with senior management, shareholders and other stakeholders. We examine these relationships in terms of the power relations between different stakeholders and show that many of the debates in this literature stem from assumptions concerning what motivates managers. On one hand, agency theory argues that managers are opportunistic and self-interested, making decisions that benefit themselves rather than the overall organization or its shareholders. According to this view, a strong board is needed to monitor managers and hold them accountable for their decisions. In contrast, proponents of stewardship theory[112] challenge this view, arguing that managers are good stewards of the corporation and work diligently to secure high levels of profit and shareholder returns. Allowing 'amateur' outsiders access to the board compromises sound managerial decisions and hampers strong leadership.

Legally, the board is responsible for the overall management and direction of a corporation. It supervises and oversees the business of the company while managers deal with the day-to-day management. Consequently, directors are responsible for such activities as declaring dividends; issuing and redeeming shares; approving disclosure documents and financial statements; ensuring compliance with regulatory standards; approving financial transactions; establishing compensation for themselves and senior executives; and selecting and evaluating the CEO. In addition, boards have a strategic role, particularly when they balance risk and potential return in decision-making; ensure that effective communication and control systems are in place and appoint, monitor, evaluate and, when necessary, replace the CEO and other senior executives.[113]

In carrying out their responsibilities, directors are expected to act in the best interests of the corporation. As such, they have two fundamental duties. First, the duty of loyalty means that directors must adhere to a strict fiduciary standard of behaviour whereby they always act in the best interests of the corporation. Second, the duty of care 'also requires reasonable inquiry and monitoring of corporate affairs'.[114] 'Directors cannot simply react to issues and information submitted by management, but must implement procedures and make sufficient inquiry to assure that management is properly discharging its duties and presenting the appropriate issues to the board.'[115]

These duties embody a complex network of relationships, which we examine with reference to recent critical studies of the way in which boards function.[116] First, the board's responsibilities mean it must work in partnership with management to achieve organizational goals by contributing expertise and experience to the strategy making process, as well as by providing objectivity and independence in monitoring progress towards it. Second, the board's ultimate objective is to maximize the value of the corporation over the long term. In acting in the best interests of the corporation, directors are considered to act in the best interests of shareholders as a whole, rather than any single shareholder or shareholder group, including majority shareholders. Third, many writers argue that the board must also consider other stakeholders, such as employees, unions, creditors, suppliers, customers, government, special interest groups and community members and incorporate a political analysis to complement efficiency-oriented approaches to corporate governance.[117]

Too close for comfort: the board and senior management

It has been argued that boards have become close to the managers they are supposed to be monitoring, especially the CEO to whom they are often beholden for their position. The bonds become stronger when a large proportion of board members are insiders – executive directors – who are closer to management than to shareholders. Another aspect of closeness concerns the offices of chair of the board and CEO. If held by one person, power is centralized in the hands of the senior executive; if separate, an independent outside, non-executive director serves as chair, providing more distance between board and management.

Boards that are too close to management, argue critics, serve largely ceremonial roles (Table 4.10).[118] Such directors have a rubber-stamp mentality and try to 'confirm and conform' rather than take action consistent with effective corporate governance. These directors and boards are associated with ineffective monitoring, a reluctance to replace an incompetent CEO, the provision of inadequate strategic direction, the failure to protect shareholder interests and the awarding of excessive compensation for directors and CEOs.[119] Consequently, the seeds of the well-publicized problems of companies such as Royal Trustco in Canada, General Motors and IBM in the USA, and Coles Myer Ltd in Australia, have been associated with inadequate corporate governance.[120]

The result has been calls for greater independence on the part of the board in relation to management. Critics argue that directors lack independent information and analysis regarding a company's performance since virtually all information comes to the board from management. CEOs can use this

TABLE 4.10   *Directors who display ceremonial behaviour*

- Display total loyalty to the chairman
- Support management at all times
- Be compatible, always try to get along and never let differences surface
- Be legally correct
- Participate correctly and constructively, but within limits so as not to upset the chairman or your colleagues
- Do not take the job too seriously
- Go through the right channels
- Be discreet by watching what you say and to whom you say it
- Take your perks and keep quiet
- Do not rock the boat

Source: Sexty, 1995: 89

information to ensure that the bad news is sugar coated or never even emerges. Similarly, those 'arguing for separation identify the inherent conflict of interest in having one person act as chair and CEO. How can a board chaired by the most senior member of management function independently of management and monitor and assess management performance?'[121] Separating these positions, advocates argue, avoids CEO entrenchment, provides effective board monitoring and offers an extra source of insight in the form of a chairperson who can advise a CEO. To create further board independence, these writers also call for an increase in the number of outside directors[122] who can dismiss poorly performing executives.[123]

Other writers, however, continue to argue in favour of the need for a dominant CEO. They point to the lack of clear empirical evidence to support any link between outsider dominated boards and improved performance.[124] They argue that if the board is too strong it may result in executives who are less willing to undertake risky strategies or build long-term, trusting relationships with stakeholders.[125] Hilmer and Donaldson[126] maintain that the independence of non-executives does not compensate for the insight, expertise and intuition of executive directors. They also argue that there is little evidence to suggest that having more insiders stifles innovation, promotes unwise diversification, or results in excessive compensation (although see Table 4.11 for examples to the contrary).[127] They cite the example of successful Japanese firms which, typically, have large numbers of inside directors on their boards. Moreover, they point out that while some US organizations have experimented with separation of chair and CEO, notably GM, 80 per cent of US companies continue to combine the two positions and many that have separated them later recombined them, GM among them.[128]

These writers argue that combining the two positions also helps to provide strong leadership, unity of command, eliminate conflict and avoid the confusion of having two spokespersons. Combining the positions of chairman and CEO provides a single focal point for company leadership and avoids questions about who is boss or who is responsible. Daily and Schwenk[129] suggest that such CEO dominance is particularly important in periods of organizational change, although they concede that board dominance may be more appropriate when firms need resources from other organizations and institutions that can be acquired through outside directors. These writers argue that a balanced board produces the worst case scenario by invoking a power struggle between the players and reducing performance.

In summary, there are divergent opinions about the power relationship between the board and its senior management in terms of whether they are too close or not close enough (Exercise 4.7).

Fighting back: the board and shareholders

Some writers argue that relations between the board and its shareholders have changed radically with the increasing activism of institutional investors and organization of independent investors. Public and private pension funds, mutual funds and insurance companies have increased their power, as share ownership has become more concentrated. Whereas institutional holdings in the USA were less than 15 per cent of direct equities outstanding in 1960, they had reached 53 per cent by 1995.[130] The proportion is

TABLE 4.11 *Examples of executive compensation*

- In 1997 the average pay rise in the USA was 2.6 per cent for blue-collar workers and 3.8 per cent for white-collar staff; for CEOs it was 35 per cent, although this was lower than 52 per cent in 1996.
- The president of FirstService Corp received a bonus of nearly half a million dollars in 1995 even though the company lost nearly twenty million dollars.
- Warner executives were guaranteed a minimum bonus of 125 per cent of their salary.
- In 1991, the compensation of ITT's CEO more than doubled while ITT's stock price dropped significantly.
- Ivaco president was paid a $435,000 bonus in addition to a $1 million salary to recognize his contribution since 1991 while the price of its class A shares fell from $27 in 1986 to $9 in 1994 and sales almost halved.
- The CEO of US Surgical received so many options over four years that even a $1 increase in the stock price would net him nearly $6 million.
- Between 1990 and 1994, the chairman and CEO of the Toronto Dominion Bank received more compensation than any other CEO of the major Canadian banks, even though $100 invested in TD stock during that period increased 56 per cent compared to 65–300 per cent at the other banks.
- Between 1993 and 1995, the president of Molson Ltd, a diversified brewer, received twice as much in compensation as the president of John Labatt, a similar firm. Even though Molson lost $28 million in its US operations in 1995 and shareholders saw their investments decline 35 per cent between 1992 and 1995.
- Laura Ashley directors changed the remuneration scheme partway through the financial year when it became clear that the set of targets was not going to be met.
- A proposed new incentive scheme at British Telecom could mean an extra £5 million for the CEO even if BT's performance does not improve.
- In 1995, top UK executives gave themselves pay rises of nearly 19 per cent – roughly five times both inflation and the average increase in earnings and despite an inquiry by Sir Richard Greenbury, chairman of Marks & Spencer's, that established guidelines on boardroom salaries and perks.

Sources: Adapted from Monks and Minow, 1995; Mathias, 1995: 11; *The Guardian Weekly*, 9 June 1996: 19; 27 July 1997: 11; 19 April 1998: 19; also the Greenbury Report, 1995

EXERCISE 4.7 TOO CLOSE FOR COMFORT?

Take a well-publicized example of an organization that has encountered severe financial problems and answer the following questions:

- Examine the role that the board played in these problems. Could it have done more to prevent them?
- Examine the relationship between management and the board. Were they too close for comfort?

also increasing in other countries.[131] Moreover, institutional investors are typically holding larger long-term stakes in corporations. In effect, a new class of 'permanent' investors is emerging,[132] who are virtually locked into their investments. Unable to sell their shares quickly when dissatisfied with a firm's performance because they trigger a fall in the share price, these institutional investors believe that their best option is to use their power to pressure an under-performing company's board and management to make radical changes.[133]

For example, the California Public Employees' Retirement System (CalPERS) is the largest public pension fund in the USA with assets in excess of $80 billion. It targets poorly performing companies and attempts to improve them by meeting with management, issuing shareholder resolutions, or voting against their boards, publicizing the names of companies that do not adequately address their problems. A 1994 study of 42 CalPERS campaigns revealed that companies that had underperformed the S&P 500 Index by 60 per cent prior to CalPERS' involvement subsequently outperformed the index by 40 per cent.[134] See Table 4.12 for other examples of activism by institutional investors and other shareholders.

In summary, the power balance between board and shareholder appears to have changed. The debate here concerns whether these changes are having a beneficial effect in terms of serving shareholder interests (Exercise 4.8).

Tied to the stake: boards and stakeholders

Most boards are notable for their homogeneity – they are 'predominantly male, middle-aged or older, WASP businessmen and professionals' who are typically 'higher income, and by and large, well educated and experienced gentlemen'.[135] While such a situation may increase harmony, the lack of diversity tends to reinforce the status quo and promote resistance to change as important stakeholders, inside and outside the organization, are frozen out (Table 4.13; Exercise 4.9). Some writers are arguing that globalization and

TABLE 4.12 *Examples of how institutional investors have used their power*

- Forcing out CEOs
- Voting against management in conjunction with other institutional investors
- Threatening to exercise dissent rights
- Suing to enjoin a transaction
- Enlisting the support of securities regulators to stop a transaction
- Publicly expressing dissatisfaction with management or its actions
- Engaging in a proxy battle to unseat management
- Supporting other lobby groups, such as the Pension Investment Association of Canada or the Australian Shareholders Association and voting en bloc against motions
- Meeting with management to discuss matters of concern
- Influence nominations for board seats

Sources: Adapted from Stewart, 1993; MacIntosh and Schwartz, 1995; Conner, 1995; Kirby, 1996

consumer confidence, in the light of such demographic changes as increasing numbers of working women and ethnic minorities, demand more diversity[136] to combine 'competence and varying backgrounds and viewpoints'.[137] A group of older, white male executives of the same nationality 'represents a dangerously narrow profile of exposure for a board' in a rapidly changing world that demands 'aggressively creative approaches to business, and it is through diversity that much of that creativity can be found'.[138]

TABLE 4.13 *Board diversity**

Women	Minorities	Foreign nationals
• Although 84 per cent of Fortune 500 companies in the USA had at least one woman on their boards, women held only 10 per cent of all directorships on public corporations in 1995 and only 181 companies had more than two women directors. • In Canada, less than 5 per cent of the members of the boards of directors of private sector organizations are women. • In 1997, the percentage of women directors increased from 4 per cent to 6 per cent of directorships.	• Ethnic representation has increased and ethnic minorities sit on 55 per cent of all major US boards. African-Americans are represented on 37 per cent of all boards, but only 3 per cent of directors of major US companies are African-American.	• Only 14 per cent of the boards of major US corporations have a single foreign representative.[†]

Sources: * Adapted from Bryan, 1995: 7; Burke, 1997; Caudron, 1998; http://www.advancingwomen.com/womnews.html; Australian Business Online http://www.abol.buswomen.htm

Note: [†] There are often restrictions on the percentage of foreign citizens serving on boards and significantly higher costs are involved.

EXERCISE 4.8 ACTIVE INVESTORS?

You are an investor in an organization that is a poorly performing company which, nonetheless, has considerable potential. Consequently, you are reluctant to withdraw your capital. A friend of yours is a senior manager in a large pension fund that has a considerable investment in this company. Answer the following questions:

• What power can you use to influence the company?
• What strategies will you use?
• What changes will you try to bring about?

EXERCISE 4.9 CHANGING YOUR STAKE?

In 1975, Sara Lee's board consisted of fifteen directors – twelve insiders, two bankers and a prominent lawyer. The board lacked the necessary diversity, independence and expertise to make it an effective strategic contributor to its long-term plans to expand globally. Consequently, the board reorganized. Seven insiders were replaced by prominent outsiders, leaving the company with an eighteen-person board made up of four insiders and fourteen outsiders, including two women, two minority groups and three foreign nationals. During this time, Sara Lee transformed itself from a domestic company into a global marketer of branded consumer products. From a base of virtually no international presence, Sara Lee now derives over one-third of its earnings from products sold in 120 countries around the world; sales have grown to (US)$17 billion in 1995; earnings per share have increased at an annual rate of 13 per cent over the last ten years and total return to investors has averaged 20.6 per cent per year.

Questions

- Why do you think Sara Lee reorganized its board?
- What would outsiders, as opposed to insiders, contribute to Sara Lee's strategy?
- What would the representation of women, members of minority groups and foreign nationals contribute to Sara Lee's strategy?
- What are the disadvantages of a reorganization like this one?

Sources: Bryan, 1995; *Fortune*, 1996

Stakeholder thinking has expanded conceptions of corporate responsibility with the notion that it is accountable to groups other than simply shareholders,[139] including customers, suppliers, local communities, governments, public health and safety institutions and environmental organizations.[140] By taking into account all groups who have a stake in the firm, it argues that the organization is more likely to engage in ethical behaviour and increase both social and economic performance.[141] One way to achieve this is to have representatives of stakeholder groups on the board. So, for example, many businesses have appointed non-executive directors with environmental credentials (Table 4.14). A variety of other ways[142] have, however, also been offered as means to control the corporation (Table 4.15).

Stakeholder theory appears to be descriptively accurate in that organizations engage in some form of stakeholder management. Moreover, in the

TABLE 4.14 *Companies adding environmental directors to their boards*

Company	Affiliation of director
Ashland Oil Inc.	President, Conservation Fund
Atlantic Richfield Co.	Conservation Fellow, World Wildlife Fund/Conservation Fund
Baxter International	Director, Chesapeake Bay Institute
Chevron Corp.	Senior Counsellor, World Resources Institute
Du Pont Co.	Former Administrator, US Environmental Protection Agency
Exxon Corp.	Senior Scientist, Woods Hole Oceanographic Institution
Metclad Corp.	Founding Director, National Association for Environmental Management
Monsanto Co.	Former Administrator, EPA
Niagara Mohawk Power	President and CEO, Earth Conservation Corps
Union Carbide Corp.	Chairman, World Wildlife Fund; Former Administrator, EPA
Waste Management Inc	President, World Wildlife Fund and Conservation Foundation
Weyerhaeuser Co.	Former Administrator, EPA

Source: Adapted from Lawrence and Engleman, 1993: 25

TABLE 4.15 *Controlling the corporation: juggling economic and social goals*

• Nationalize it	• Ensure the corporation pursues social goals by guaranteeing government dominance over the organization and among external stakeholders
• Democratize it	• Ensure the corporation pursues social goals by changing the formal power base by broadening representation on the board of directors
• Regulate it	• Ensure the corporation pursues social goals by increasing government power through the imposition of formal, legal constraints
• Pressure it	• Mobilize special interest groups and pressure campaigns to make the corporation pursue social goals
• Trust it	• Trust managers to be socially responsible and allow them to retain control of the corporation
• Ignore it	• Society can afford to ignore the corporation because it 'pays' to be socially responsible and pursue social goals
• Induce it	• The conflict between economic and social goals can be overcome by rewarding corporations if they act in a socially responsible manner
• Restore it	• The shareholders are the 'rightful' owners of the organization which should pursue only economic goals

Source: Adapted from Mintzberg, 1983: 528–9

USA legal changes in many states are forcing even more consideration of stakeholders by increasing the range of permissible concerns by boards to a variety of non-shareholder constituencies.[143] Against this view, however, is a lack of empirical evidence to support the view that corporations whose boards include representatives of the society in which it operates are any better in meeting social responsibility obligations,[144] let alone conventional financial and market objectives.[145] Whether this is because existing board members and/or management are already responsive to social responsibilities, or whether the current power of stakeholders is too small to combat tokenism or co-optation, is unclear (Exercise 4.10).

EXERCISE 4.10 CONTROLLING THE CORPORATION

Select a company with which you are familiar, either though the business literature or from experience. Take each of the positions in Table 4.15 and apply them to the company in question. Draw conclusions about the appropriateness of each for controlling the corporation.

In summary, then, within the corporate governance literature there is debate about where power should lie – with the management through a compliant board or with independent directors, well-represented shareholders and involved stakeholders (Table 4.16). The constitutional board centralizes power while the collegial board shares it. Many conceptual and theoretical models suggest that the collegial board is the route to organizations that are both effective and ethical; the empirical findings are, however, more equivocal.

RIGHTSIDE UP: THE POLITICS OF BUSINESS ETHICS

For many people, ethics and politics are mutually exclusive. Ethical behaviour is seen as a matter of individual conscience and personal integrity. However, we argue that, power and ethics are inextricably linked. First, what constitutes ethical behaviour is the result of power relations. Second, managers will only realize ethical objectives if they use power.[146] Even with the most sincere of intentions, conclusions about appropriate behaviour are often hard to draw and people may differ in their assessment of a situation. Moreover, ethical issues arise in arenas where actions are influenced by other organizations with power – boards, regulatory agencies, creditors, trade

TABLE 4.16   *Governance configurations*

Constitutional	Collegial
• Joint CEO/Chair	• Separate CEO/Chair
• Insider dominated board	• Outsider dominated board
• Executive directors	• Non-executive directors
• Homogeneous top management team	• Heterogeneous top management team
• Centralized decision-making	• Working committee structure
• Nomination processes controlled by the CEO	• Nomination processes controlled by committee
• Passive board members	• Active decision-makers
• Infrequent meetings	• Regular meetings
• Little diversity represented	• Diverse stakeholder groups represented

Sources: Adapted from Vance, 1983; Bazerman and Schoorman, 1983; Molz, 1995; Daily and Schwenk, 1996: 185

unions, managers, operating committees and interest groups. Consequently, reformers who seek to bring about responsible business practices need more than good intentions and articulate arguments: they need to discover ways of mobilizing power to support their proposals.

Ethical debates

There are a variety of frameworks for evaluating ethical behaviour. Three broad ethical frameworks categories are typically used in business based on utilitarian considerations, social justice and individual rights (Table 4.17).[147] The problem, however, is that these frameworks tend to produce different, often contradictory, assessments. For example, a reluctance to reschedule Third World debt without the imposition of austerity measures by the International Monetary Fund may be justified as ethical on the grounds that the short-term costs will be outweighed by the long-term advantage of placing the economy on a stable footing. Such action may be seen as unethical, however, when other arguments are employed. On the basis of individual rights, one can argue that the poorer sections of an already poor society will be violated. Social justice might dictate restitution in the form of more flexible treatment by pointing out that the Westernized countries were irresponsible in lending the money in the first place. Similarly, affirmative action legitimated on the grounds of social justice may be countered by arguing that positive discrimination transgresses individual rights. Even a single utilitarian argument can produce contradictory answers. Is a plant closure unethical because it will cause unemployment in an isolated community; ethical because it will save the jobs of workers in other towns; unethical because the work will go to non-unionized labour in

TABLE 4.17 *Ethical frameworks*

Framework	Ethical behaviour	Example
Utilitarianism	Ethical behaviour benefits the greatest number in the most efficient way	A plant closure may be justified as ethical on the basis that it will protect the viability of the larger organization
Individual rights	Ethical behaviour respects individual rights, such as rights of privacy, free consent, freedom of conscience, free speech and due process	A plan to test employees for drug use on the grounds that it impedes productivity may be rejected as unethical because individual rights to privacy are violated
Social justice	Ethical behaviour involves fair treatment for all, a fair application of rules, and fair compensation and restitution	Affirmative action and equal pay programmes may be justified on the grounds that all minorities and both genders deserve fair treatment and compensation

Sources: Based on Cavanagh et al. 1981; Velasquez et al. 1983; Bird and Gandz, 1991

another country; or ethical because the resulting fall in prices will benefit consumers and protect profitability? Postmodern conceptualizations of power reinforce this ambiguity further by locating 'values', 'justice', 'rights' and 'ethics' in a historical and social context. In other words, what is considered to be 'right' and 'good' is the result of power (Exercise 4.11).

Putting power into ethics

Ethical concerns arise in a broad social context with organizational or interorganizational ramifications. Ethical issues that emerge at the organizational level often do so when organizations establish ethical expectations

---

EXERCISE 4.11 IT ALL DEPENDS?

Select one of the following scenarios and answer the following questions.

- You are a general manager of a pulp and paper plant in northern Canada. It provides a large number of jobs for members of local native groups, among whom unemployment rates are usually high. However, the plant also causes considerable pollution. The plant is only just making a profit – changes to upgrade the pollution controls will be too expensive and corporate management will be tempted to close the plant.
- You are a new hire in an Australian government department that is a large lender of funds to developing countries. The government of one such country has requested a major rescheduling of payments in which a large proportion of the debt is written off and you have been asked to prepare a position paper. Your research tells you that this country is one of the most poor and least democratic in the world. You also find out that one consequence of previous investment has been a major effort by the country's dictatorial government to improve the education of women. However, this programme is threatened if the country is forced to make its original debt payments.
- You are a human resource manager in a division of a US conglomerate, with a non-unionized workforce of 3000, facing a bid for unionization. You know that this division has previously made a profit only because the unskilled, non-unionized employees have had no choice but to accept low wages and questionable safety practices. Corporate headquarters is unhappy about the prospects of unionization and has indicated that it will close the division if the union organizers are successful and relocate production south of the border.

Questions

- Use the utilitarian, social justice and individual rights framework to evaluate the situation. Provide an analysis using each of the three frameworks.
- How would this analysis change if it had been conducted twenty years ago?
- How would this analysis change if it had been conducted by a woman compared to a man, a Western European compared to an Eastern European, a member of a First Nations or Aboriginal group compared to someone from the UK or the USA?
- What is your ethical position, i.e. what action would you wish to take to conform to your ethical standards?
- What actions will you take to achieve it?

for their members – formally, informally or, sometimes, simply by default. Members may fail to live up to these normative expectations in the ways described in Table 4.18. Ethical concerns arise in an interorganizational arena when stakeholders make claims upon an organization which, correspondingly, makes counter-claims on them. As with the individual, organizations may respond to these claims in a variety of ways.

Power can be used to bring about ethical behaviour in the organizational arena. Sanctions may be used to discourage non-role acts and role distortion, through the punishment of offenders and/or the reward of adherents, and by internal audits and performance appraisals to create a system of surveillance whereby the inappropriate behaviour is identified. The debate is, however, whether the use of such coercive power simply provokes strategies designed to conceal non-compliance.[148] Similarly, tying rewards to acceptable behaviour may simply produce the lowest common denominator and, since ethical issues change over time, there will often be situations when the rewards, punishment and surveillance systems lag behind actual practice. Consequently, more sophisticated political strategies may be necessary to produce ethical behaviour of a more enduring nature. Managers might, then, use power to create legitimacy for a particular ethical issue – to try to redefine what is ethical and unethical behaviour – in addition to using power sources to reward and punish appropriate and inappropriate behaviour.

Similarly, stakeholders wishing to ensure ethical behaviour on the part of an organization may also mobilize power. Resistance can be countered by sanctions, although observers debate whether rewards or coercion are most appropriate: rewards elevate the cost of good behaviour; while penalties increase the inclination to find loopholes. Avoidance is more passive and might be confronted with new procedures and sanctions that prevent the organization taking the easy way out. For example, Dow Corning did nothing throughout the 1980s in response to safety concerns regarding

TABLE 4.18 *Forms of non-ethical behaviour**

Organizational arena	Interorganizational arena
• **Non-role acts** are inconsistent with organizational definitions of the individual's role, not approved by the organization, and are often illegal. Examples include cheating on expense accounts, embezzling funds, stealing supplies, insider trading and conflict of interest activities. • **Role distortion** occurs when individuals distort their role mandates in ways incompatible with broader moral standards to benefit the organization. Examples include bribery to secure contracts, pirating computer software, contravening work safety regulations and falsifying safety and environmental test results. Such acts are often 'encouraged' by management turning a blind eye. • **Role failure** occurs when employees fail to act in accordance with 'ideal' role expectations. For example, managers fail to carry out accurate performance appraisals; fire incompetent individuals; take on unreasonable union demands to avoid conflict, extra work, or unpleasant consequences. The organization may suffer as a result of an individual's desire for an 'easy life' but, on the other hand, it may have contributed to the problem by failing to provide the support necessary to facilitate a problem-solving, proactive response.	• **Resistance** occurs when organizations actively resist the claims of stakeholders. For example, the US tobacco firms have defended themselves against health concerns by manipulating information to downplay and challenge the evidence linking cancer to smoking. They also directly confronted the regulatory body and stopped its attempt to ban cigarette advertising. As a result, health concerns initially raised in the 1950s did not translate into an advertising ban until 1970 when fragmented opposition groups had sufficiently mobilized to counter the power of the tobacco firms.[†] • **Avoidance** occurs when organizations ignore demands from stakeholders for changes in their behaviour. • **Absorption** involves co-opting dissident stakeholders in the hope of heading off confrontation, perhaps by allowing representatives of workers or community groups to sit on the board. The aim is, that, once co-opted, organizational interests can be promoted. • **Tokenism** occurs when organizations make minor concessions to pressure groups in an attempt to avoid larger ones.

Sources: * Adaped from Bird and Gandz, 1991
[†] Miles and Cameron, 1982

silicone breast implants. Once these medical devices were brought under the responsibility of the Food and Drug Administration, however, they were required to supply safety data. Unable to do so, the company voluntarily ceased production of the implants.[149] Crusades for ethical change in the interorganizational arena are far more problematic. Often they occur only as new stakeholders are admitted, forcing a redefinition of values and norms.[150] For example, environmentally responsible behaviour has been brought about only gradually, as the environment has been redefined as a relevant, societal concern in recent years; as new processes and procedures (round tables, 'green' board members) have been put into place; and as legal sanctions and informal penalties – such as bad press – have increased.

In summary, debates about what is or what is not ethical, coupled with the existence of competing interest groups, mean that the successful implementation of ethical action in an organizational or interorganizational arena is a political challenge. Yet combining politics and ethics is, in the eyes of many people, a debatable practice. It certainly raises the question of does the ethical end justify any political means? There is, perhaps, a need to strike a balance between being pragmatic and principled. Too much emphasis on political idealism can lead to futile, rhetorical goals that are admirable but unattainable; but political action without regard to ethics is a frightening prospect indeed (Exercise 4.12).

CONCLUSIONS: ROUND AND ROUND?

In this chapter, we have shown that power is a slippery concept – so much so that to study this subject seems to take us around in circles. Certainly, different assumptions underlie the concept of power that are not always made apparent. The first part of this chapter exposed these assumptions and identified the different views that exist. We then used the different approaches to power to explore issues such as empowerment and gender. We found that these multiple lenses – or perspectives – were useful in making sense of the debates that exist in these literatures, although they did not help us to find a definitive conceptualization of power.

Raising the issue of ethics in the context of power brings us full circle. While power is integral to bringing about ethical behaviour and, some writers would argue, to the very definition of what such behaviour constitutes, ethics is also at the heart of the study and definition of power. Managerial views of

---

EXERCISE 4.12 ACTING ETHICALLY?

Consider an example of one of the forms of non-ethical behaviour (listed in Table 4.18), either from your experience or from the business literature, and answer the following questions:

- Why is this an ethical issue? Explain your answer.
- What ethical action should be taken? Explain your answer.
- What are the political dynamics of the relevant – organizational or interorganizational – arena?
- Which political strategy should be used to act effectively in that arena?
- How can power be secured and used to carry out the strategy? Who should be using it? What counter-strategies are likely to emerge?

power tend to avoid explicit discussions of ethics – writers usually implicitly assume that managers will automatically use power responsibly to achieve organizational objectives, while everyone else uses it irresponsibly to resist those objectives. As a result, potential abuses of power by dominant groups are downplayed, while those who challenge managerial prerogatives are automatically discredited, often by the label 'political'. In this way, the managerial approach is often ill-equipped to deal with the ethical issues associated with the abuse and exploitation of power.[151] Critical theorists have railed against such neglect. For them, power is exploitation; to study it is an ethical project designed to expose its dominating effects and, if possible, to resist and overturn it. Postmodern writers dismiss such moralizing hand-wringing. For them, power is everywhere, while ethics are nowhere and certainly not in the hands of researchers. So, the story continues.

NOTES

(See Bibliography at the end of the book for full references)

1 See Hardy, 1995; Hardy and Clegg, 1996; Hardy and Leiba, 1998 for extended discussions of the different approaches to power.

2 French and Raven, 1968; Pfeffer and Salancik, 1974, 1978

3 Pfeffer, 1981; Pettigrew, 1979; although see Hardy, 1985a, 1994; Hardy and Clegg, 1996 for a more detailed discussion of this point.

4 Pettigrew, 1973; Hickson et al. 1986

5 Mayes and Allen, 1977; Gandz and Murray, 1980

6 Pettigrew, 1973, 1985; MacMillan, 1978; Pfeffer, 1981, 1992a, b; Narayanan and Fahey, 1982; Gray and Ariss, 1985; Schwenk, 1989

7 Ranson et al. 1980

8 Pettigrew, 1979

9 Clegg, 1975; Gaventa, 1980; Hardy, 1985b

10 See chapter on postmodern approaches

11 Foucault, 1979, 1980, 1982, 1984; Dreyfus and Rabinow, 1982; Smart, 1985; Turner, 1990

12 Foucault, 1980: 98

13 Hoy, 1986; Parry and Morris, 1975; Deetz, 1992a, b

14 Knights and Morgan, 1991: 269

15 Clegg, 1989; Knights and Willmott, 1989; Knights and Morgan, 1991; Alvesson and Willmott, 1992a

16 Foucault, 1980: 131

17 Frost, 1987; Clegg, 1989; Hardy, 1994

18 Gandz, 1990: 74; also Burke, 1986; Conger and Kanungo, 1988; Thomas and Velthouse, 1990; Bowen and Lawler, 1992; Ford and Fottler, 1995

19 Bernstein, 1992; Brown, 1992; Matthes, 1992; Eccles, 1993; Eccles and Nohria, 1993

20 Barker, 1993; Parker, 1993; Cullen and Townley, 1994

21 Lawler et al. 1992, cited in McCaffrey et al. 1995: 608

22 See Leiba and Hardy, 1994; Hardy and Leiba, 1998 for more details

23 Kizilos, 1990; Conger, 1989; Feldman, 1991; Schlossberg, 1991; Conger and Kanungo, 1988; Thomas and Velthouse, 1990; Velthouse, 1990; Shelton, 1991; Block, 1990

24 Conger and Kanungo, 1988; also Burke, 1986; Bell and Zemke, 1988; Sherwood, 1988; Stewart, 1989; Topaz, 1989/90; Block, 1990; Kizilos, 1990; Manz, 1990; Velthouse, 1990; Beatty and Ulrich, 1991; McKenna, 1991a, b; Schaeffer, 1991; Sheridan, 1991a, b; Bowen and Lawler, 1992; Lawler, 1992

25 Ashkenas et al. 1995: 55

26 Keller and Dansereau, 1995

27 Odiorne, 1991: 66; also Bell and Zemke, 1988; Von der Embse, 1989; Early, 1991; Goski and Belfry, 1991; Eisman, 1991; Schlossberg, 1991; Shelton, 1991; Eccles, 1993

28 Beatty and Ulrich, 1991; Lawler, 1992; O'Connor, 1995; Dean and Bowen, 1994; Feldman and Leana, 1994; Freeman, 1984; Spencer, 1994; Waldman, 1994

29 McKenna, 1990: 18; also O'Connor, 1995

30 Parker and Slaughter, 1988; Deetz, 1992b; Barker, 1993; Parker, 1993

31 Manz, 1990: 21
32 O'Connor, 1995
33 Barker, 1993
34 Barker, 1993; Parker, 1993; O'Connor, 1995
35 Kizilos, 1990: 56
36 Knights and Morgan, 1991: 194
37 Skaggs and Labianca, 1993: 7
38 Leana, 1987; Latham et al. 1988; Vroom and Jago, 1988; Leana et al. 1992; Ledford and Lawler, 1994
39 Rousseau and Parks, 1993: 20
40 Rousseau and Aquino, 1992; Rousseau and Parks, 1993
41 Nord and Jermier, 1992
42 Keller and Dansereau, 1995
43 Marshall, 1995a: S55; also see Alvesson and Billig, 1992; Calás and Smircich, 1996
44 Radtke and Stam, 1994
45 Czarniawska-Joerges, 1994; Marshall, 1995a; Calás and Smircich, 1996
46 Radtke and Stam, 1994: 1
47 Calás and Smircich, 1992
48 Acker, 1990: 139
49 Acker, 1990; Calás and Smircich, 1992, 1996; Wilson, 1996
50 Marshall, 1995b
51 Radtke and Stam, 1994; Marshall, 1995a; Calás and Smircich, 1996
52 Calás and Smircich, 1996
53 Parker, 1996: 497
54 Faludi, 1991
55 Walby, 1990
56 Faludi, 1991
57 Walby, 1990
58 Walby, 1990; Kitzinger, 1994; MacLeod, 1989
59 Peitchinis, 1989; Vianello and Siemienska, 1990
60 Vianello and Siemienska, 1990: 255
61 Nieva and Gutek, 1985
62 Peitchinis, 1989
63 Fierman, 1990
64 Peitchinis, 1989
65 Nieva and Gutek, 1985
66 Peitchinis, 1989: 26
67 Ohlott et al. 1994
68 Wilson, 1996: 825; also Acker, 1990; Calás and Smircich, 1992, 1996; Marshall, 1995a
69 Hearn and Parkin, 1987
70 Calás and Smircich, 1992
71 Acker, 1990: 151
72 Bass and Avolio, 1994: 557–8
73 Mills and Tancred, 1992
74 Follett, 1924
75 Acker and Van Houton, 1974; Calás and Smircich, 1991, 1992
76 See Calás and Smircich, 1996: 222–7 for detailed references.
77 Calás and Smircich, 1996; Marshall, 1995a
78 Calás and Smircich, 1996: 222; also Marshall, 1995a
79 Ferguson, 1984; Rosener, 1990; Mann, 1995
80 Mumby, 1996: 271
81 Marshall, 1995a: S58–9
82 Acker, 1990: 145–50
83 Mumby, 1996
84 Calás and Smircich, 1996: 233
85 Martin, 1990: 343
86 Mumby, 1996
87 Calás and Smircich, 1996: 228; Iannello, 1993; Martin, 1990; Morgen, 1994; Mumby, 1996
88 Ferree and Martin, 1995; Arnold, 1995; Calás and Smircich, 1996: 228
89 Mumby, 1996: 281
90 Acker, 1990
91 Flax, 1987
92 Calás and Smircich, 1996: 235–43; Liff and Wajcman, 1996
93 Flax, 1987: 641
94 Flax, 1987: 642
95 Flax, 1987: 637
96 Collinson, 1988; Collinson and Collinson, 1989; Collinson and Hearn, 1994; Connell, 1994
97 Coote and Campbell, quoted in Burrell, 1984: 101
98 Hall, 1989
99 Stone and Colella, 1996
100 Nkomo and Cox, 1996
101 Nkomo, 1992; Nkomo and Cox, 1996
102 Mumby, 1996: 288; see the people chapter.
103 Burrell and Hearn, 1989; Mills, 1989; Gutek, 1989
104 Burrell, 1984; Kitzinger, 1994
105 Fraser and Nicholson, 1988: 393
106 Rosenau, 1992
107 Mumby, 1996: 261; also see Rosenau, 1992
108 Radtke and Stam, 1994: 1
109 The authors wish to acknowledge the contribution of Vittorio Mario Grascia whose report *Corporate Governance In North America*, prepared under the supervision of Professor Cynthia Hardy, proved invaluable in writing this section.
110 Sexty, 1995: 216
111 Priest et al. 1995: 3
112 Donaldson and Davis, 1994; Davis et al. 1997
113 This approach to the strategic role of boards is closely based on the Final Report of the Toronto Stock Exchange, TSE Committee on Corporate Governance in Canada, December 1994: 17–19.

114 Bailey, 1988: 6
115 Bailey, 1993: 3–4
116 For example, the Cadbury Report in the UK, the TSE Committee on Corporate Governance in Canada.
117 TSE Committee on Corporate Governance in Canada, 1994: 21; see also Mintzberg, 1983
118 Thain et al. 1994
119 Hills, 1994; Mathias, 1995; Monks and Minow, 1995; Sexty, 1995
120 Also see TSE Committee on Corporate Governance in Canada, 1994 and the Cadbury Report, 1992.
121 TSE Committee on Corporate Governance in Canada, 1994: 41
122 The Cadbury Report, 1992; TSE Committee on Corporate Governance in Canada, 1994; Lorsch, 1995
123 Cannella, 1995
124 Daily and Schwenk, 1996; Hilmer and Donaldson, 1996; Daily and Dalton, 1997
125 Cannella, 1995
126 Hilmer and Donaldson, 1996
127 Donaldson and Davis, 1994
128 Daily and Dalton, 1997
129 Daily and Schwenk, 1996
130 Stewart, 1993
131 Daniels and Morck, 1995
132 Montgomery and Leighton, 1993: 41
133 Montgomery and Leighton, 1993; Delorme, 1993; Conner, 1995
134 Foerster, 1995
135 Leighton and Thain, 1993: 19
136 Bryan, 1995: 7
137 Leighton and Thain, 1993: 21
138 Bryan, 1995: 7; see people chapter for arguments which parallel these.
139 Hill and Jones, 1992; Huse and Eide, 1996
140 Freeman, 1994
141 Preston and Sapienza, 1990; Kotter and Heskett, 1992; Clarkson, 1995
142 Mintzberg, 1983
143 Donaldson and Preston, 1995
144 Kesner et al. 1986; Molz, 1995
145 Donaldson and Preston, 1995
146 See Bird and Hardy, 1994 for more details.
147 Cavanagh et al. 1981; Stead et al. 1990
148 Waters, 1978; Jackall, 1988
149 *Montreal Gazette*, 1992, 20 March: A1
150 Hardy and Phillips, 1998
151 Hardy and Clegg, 1996

5 MANAGING CULTURE

Guiding Light or Black Hole?

We continue with our task of understanding people in organizations by examining culture. One debate here is whether culture has had its fifteen minutes of fame. Some view culture's heyday as the 1980s, when cultural perspectives were applied to a wide range of organizational and management issues, especially as an alternative to organizational structure, in controlling people and their behaviours[1] (see Supplementary Reading box). But, despite having become, by the mid-1980s, 'a staple in the business press's vocabulary',[2] interest in culture may now be on the wane.[3] Indeed, some have even proclaimed the death of culture,[4] asserting that managers, burned by experiences of failed cultural interventions in their organizations,[5] are turning 'elsewhere to find another "quick fix" for corporate ills'.[6] Other writers argue, however, that organizational culture is nowhere near ready to be consigned to the graveyard of organizational history.[7] Preston[8] maintains that the management of culture remains an important part of top management activities. Moreover, the concept has much left in it to be explored; especially how organizational cultures are produced, reproduced and changed.[9]

CULTURE: SUPPLEMENTARY READING

- Cartwright, S. and Cooper, C.L. (1993) 'The role of culture compatibility in successful organizational marriage', *Academy of Management Executive*, 7 (2): 57–70.

- Cook, S.D.N. and Yanow, D. (1993) 'Culture and organizational learning', *Journal of Management Inquiry*, 2 (4): 373–90.

- Denison, D.R. and Mishra, A.K. (1995) 'Toward a theory of organizational culture and effectiveness', *Organization Science*, 6 (2): 204–23.

- Fedor, K.J. and Werther, W.B. (1995) 'Making sense of cultural factors in international alliances', *Organizational Dynamics*, 23 (4): 33–48.

- Harrison, M.T. and Beyer, J.M. (1993) *The Cultures of Work Organizations*. Englewood Cliffs, NJ: Prentice-Hall.

- Hatch, M.J. (1993) 'The dynamics of organizational culture', *Academy of Management Review*, 18 (4): 657–93.

- Hofstede, G. (1993) 'Cultural constraints in management theories', *Academy of Management Executive*, 7 (1): 81–94.

- Kolb, D.G. and Shepherd, D.M. (1997) 'Concept mapping organizational cultures', *Journal of Management Inquiry*, 6 (4): 282–95.

- Kotter, J.P. and Heskett, J.L. (1992) *Corporate Culture and Performance*. New York: Free Press.

- Kunda, G. (1995) 'Engineering culture: control and commitment in a high-tech corporation', *Organization Science*, 6 (2): 228–30.

- Lundberg, C.C. (1990) 'Surfacing organisational culture', *Journal of Managerial Psychology*, 5 (4): 19–26.

- Martin, J. (1992) *Cultures in Organisations: Three Perspectives*. New York: Oxford University Press.

- Martin, J. and Frost, P. (1996) 'The organizational culture war games: a struggle for intellectual dominance', in S. Clegg, C. Hardy, and W. Nord (eds), *Handbook of Organization Studies*. London: Sage: 599–621.

- Ricks, D.A. (1993) *Blunders in International Business*. Cambridge, MA: Blackwell.

- Schein, E.H. (1985) *Organizational Culture and Leadership*. San Francisco: Jossey-Bass.

- Schneider, B., Brief, A.P. and Guzzo, R.A. (1996) 'Creating a climate and culture for sustainable organizational change', *Organizational Dynamics*, 24 (4): 7–19.

This paradoxical situation can be explained by the way in which the term has been used. Alvesson[10] maintains that the term culture has been applied to such an array of phenomena that it has become 'a word for the lazy'. 'Culture is rather like a black hole: the closer you get to it the less light is thrown upon the topic and the less chance you have of surviving the experience.'[11] Debates over the meaning of culture have been likened to academic 'war games', which have little relevance for managers who are more concerned about 'the considerable expense and unwanted consequences of ill-thought-out cultural change interventions'.[12]

This chapter explores these debates and assesses their relevance to management practice. We examine the continuing struggle to define the term culture; disputes over the appropriate method to uncover culture; conflicting perspectives or ways of thinking about culture; different ideas about its impact on organizational performance and productivity; and the controversy about changing culture.

TAMING THE BEAST: DEFINING CULTURE

Culture had a long history in anthropology and sociology before it migrated to the field of organization studies in the early 1970s, taking hold in the 1980s[13] with the appearance of studies such as Deal and Kennedy,[14] Ouchi,[15] and Peters and Waterman.[16] Since then it has been used to explain such management issues as commitment, socialization, turnover, problems of productivity, competition and the practices of Japanese management.[17]

Culture has always been an elusive term. A study in the field of anthropology in the 1950s identified 164 different definitions of culture.[18] In the early 1970s, Spradley and McCurdy[19] concluded that 'the concept of culture has come to mean so many different things that it is not possible to discuss them all'. In borrowing this term, many management academics and practitioners have displayed little knowledge of its background and complexity. Yet this complexity has bedevilled its application to the study of organizations and researchers continue to devote themselves to taming what is clearly an ambiguous and contested beast.

Endless definitions

A range of management definitions of culture can be found (Table 5.1). Some of these definitions mention beliefs and values; others emphasize 'knowledge'; some highlight shared meanings; others point to an organization's 'ethos'; some mention myths, symbols and rituals. Some writers maintain that agreement exists around the fact that culture is holistic, historically determined, anthropological, socially constructed, soft and difficult to change.[20] Others, however, question even this degree of consensus arguing that culture has become a buzzword meaning 'many different and sometimes contradictory things'.[21]

Even definitions that are widely used, such as that of Schein (Table 5.1), have been the source of dispute. It has been argued that his definition does not so much define culture as describe its creation and transmission. It is essentially 'unitarist' in orientation (that is, an organization is treated as having one culture); and fails to pay enough attention to the role of symbols, symbolic behaviour and organizational processes or the extent to which culture is the outcome of the continual production and reproduction of these features.[22] Sathe[23] argues that it is pointless to argue about which definition of culture is correct because it does not have a 'true and sacred meaning that is to be discovered'. However, as can be seen in Table 5.1, he nevertheless goes on to gives his own definition.

What's the weather like: climate or culture?

Another definitional debate concerns the link between climate and culture. Studies on organizational climate preceded the current interest in organizational culture. As the interest in organizational culture caught hold, there

TABLE 5.1 *Definitions of culture*

Definition	Authors
The 'knowledge people use to generate and interpret social behaviour. This knowledge is learned, and, to a degree, shared'	Spradley and McCurdy (1972: 8)
The 'set of important understandings (often unstated) that members of a community share in common'	Sathe (1983: 6)
The 'taken-for-granted and shared meaning that people assign to their social surroundings'	Wilkins (1983: 25)
A 'pattern of basic assumptions that a given group has invented, discovered, or developed in learning to cope with its problems of external adaptation and internal integration, and that have worked well enough to be considered valid, and, therefore, to be taught to new members as the correct way to perceive, think, and feel in relation to these problems'	Schein (1985: 9)
A 'social process associated with a unit in which members share a common set of elements – assumptions and worldviews, values, behavioural norms, patterns of activities, and material artefacts'	Rousseau (1990: 160)
'At the deeper and less visible level, culture refers to values that are shared by the people in a group and that tend to persist over time even when group membership changes. At the more visible level, culture represents the behaviour patterns or style of an organization that new employees are automatically encouraged to follow by their fellow employees.'	Kotter and Heskett (1992: 4)
A 'set of values, beliefs, and feelings, together with the artefacts of their expression and transmission (such as myths, symbols, metaphors, rituals), that are created, inherited, shared, and transmitted within one group of people and that, in part, distinguish that group from others'	Cook and Yanow (1993: 379)
The 'collective programming of the mind which distinguishes one group or category of people from another'	Hofstede (1993: 89)
The '"way we do things around here", the "unwritten rules" of what constitutes intelligent behaviour in an organization, the shared values which people have'	Peters (1993: 34)
The 'firmly implanted beliefs and values of organizational members'	Schneider, Brief and Guzzo (1996: 11)

was a corresponding decline in interest in organizational climate,[24] although the link between the two has become a source of debate. In arguing in favour of retaining a distinction between climate and culture, Rousseau[25] says:

> climate reflects individual perceptions of the organization and thus focuses on a class of cognitions or *descriptive beliefs* individuals hold regarding organizational properties (managerial trust, supportiveness, participativeness in decision making, and so on) . . . Climate as a product of individual psychological processes (and the individual's potentially idiosyncratic experience of the organization) and culture as a unit-level phenomenon that is derived from social interaction are distinct constructs.

Conversely, Schneider et al.[26] argue that the practices that senior managers introduce and the values they communicate determine both climate and culture. So, according to the first view, climate is derived from individual psychological processes, while culture is found at the unit level and derives from social interaction. In the second view, climate resides in a variety of organizational processes, while culture is found in people's beliefs and values. Despite such confusion, and the acknowledgement by some that 'the concepts do slide greyly into one another', a valiant fight is still fought by those who wish to retain the distinction between the two.[27]

Attempts to retain the climate–culture distinction are not very helpful to managers. As Denison[28] points out, the convergence between studies of both culture and climate means that they are not particularly different. These 'two research traditions should be viewed as differences in *interpretation* rather than differences in the *phenomenon*' being studied. Researchers need to adopt the language of the context in which the organization operates (whether climate, culture or some other term) if they are to contribute to the management of social contexts.

It all depends on where you sit

The confusion regarding the definition of culture translates into fundamental differences concerning conflicting levels of analysis. While organizational culture remains a primary focus, the role of the individual in an organization's culture is also a source of research; and, within organizations, many writers have studied the emergence of subcultures. In addition, the interest in organizational culture is being supplemented with an emphasis on culture at the levels of the industry and country. These different levels of analysis have given rise to a number of debates, which we consider here.

The individual and culture

Views vary regarding the role that the individual plays in producing and being produced by the organizational culture. A number of interrelated lines of enquiry can be identified. One focus is on how individuals experience organizational culture. One schema suggests that individuals entering a new organization can be an adapter, a good soldier, a maverick or a rebel.[29] An alternative framework denotes team players, warriors, isolates or outsiders.[30] This work allows for individuals to be absorbed into a culture (team player or good soldier) and to play a role in changing culture (rebel, warrior). Writers also draw conclusions regarding the benefits of each in the context of cultural change programmes.[31] Variations of this approach include the interest of human resource management in whether individuals are able to deal with 'culture shock' when sent on foreign assignments;[32] and in whether individual commitment to an organization can be enhanced through different types of organizational cultures[33] or organizational values.[34]

A second body of literature is more interested in how individual values can be aligned with those of the organization, i.e. how individuals can be absorbed into the organizational culture. Some writers have explored the malleability of particular types of persons. Work on dissonance between personality and behaviour argues that behaviour results from both personal characteristics and organizational context or culture. Consequently, an individual's behaviour may differ, in different times and places, from their personality. In a simulation of organizational cultures, Chatman and Barsade found that individuals with a high personal disposition to co-operate displayed low levels of co-operation when they work in an individualistic culture.[35] Consequently, they argued that co-operative people are more malleable than individualists. Another interpretation is that it may be possible to change behaviours without changing underlying individual values, and that at least some people can tolerate a discontinuity between their underlying values and the behaviours expected of them. In other words, it may not be necessary to change individuals' underlying values in order to achieve behavioural and cultural change.

Fitzgerald[36] points out, however, that 'we have no comprehensive theory to account for the process by which values are relinquished and replaced, either through the inner work of the person, or by outside agency (inducements, coercion, threats, modelling, persuasion, whatever)'. It is, therefore, difficult to draw many conclusions. He also argues that we lack a theory of 'resistance' – comprehensive knowledge of the psychological processes through which individuals protect themselves from attempts to change them. This argument suggests that individuals may be more resistant to attempts to bind them to a particular organizational culture than is often portrayed in the business literature.

Subcultures

Much like culture, the use of the word 'subculture' is commonplace. Yet what constitutes a subculture is much more complex than is often portrayed in many writings in the literature.[37] Rose[38] points out that subcultures or 'multiple cultures' have different meanings. They can refer to a loose constellation of unique cultures, in terms of meanings and values, which are 'not connected to an overarching core culture'; or they can refer to 'an array of distinct subcultures that exist in relationship to a core umbrella culture'. In the latter case, subcultures consist of enclaves of individuals within a broader culture of shared values, meanings and structures. Whereas Rose opts for the latter meaning, other writers adopt the former position, or a combination of the two.

Schein[39] suggests that there are three different cultures operating in many organizations – an operator culture (those who do the work); an engineers' culture (those who design and monitor the technology); and an executive culture (those who manage the process). Engineering and executive cultures represent occupational communities that go beyond the organization, reminding us of the porous nature of organizational boundaries.

Consequently, we cannot understand *organizational* cultures, even though they appear to be internal to an organization, without reference to wider social influences, pressures and processes.

Sackmann[40] presents an interesting argument for understanding subcultures, maintaining that there are four different kinds of cultural *knowledge* (Table 5.2) which can be identified in organizations. People may participate simultaneously in different subcultures depending upon the type of knowledge and meanings being analysed. Sackmann found seven different cultural sub-groupings associated with dictionary knowledge. One subgrouping, relating to directory knowledge, spanned three divisions. The top management group was associated with axiomatic knowledge; while no particular groupings or subcultures formed around recipe knowledge.

This framework directs managers' attention to the way in which particular subcultures may form around particular types of knowledges; to how some types of knowledges are more widely shared across the whole organization; and to how some knowledges cross organizational boundaries. Subcultures, then, are not so much fixed as they are fluid groupings that exist in and around different themes and understandings. They permeate through and beyond organizational boundaries and people may belong to more than one simultaneously (Exercise 5.1).

Industry cultures

In the 1990s there has been a shift in focus away from the organization as the unit for studying culture to the industry.[41] Phillips[42] claims that industry

TABLE 5.2   *Cultural knowledges*

Knowledge type	Underlying theme	Main identifiers	Innovation/change example
Dictionary knowledge	'What'	Descriptive words and labels of organizational situations	'An incentive plan to produce organizational innovation/change is one which is easily measurable by employees'
Directory knowledge	'How'	Common knowledge about cause and effect relationships; descriptive, not evaluative	'This particular innovation/change was introduced by manager X at Y manufacturing facility'
Recipe knowledge	'Should'	Judgements for repairing and improving organizational situations	'Organizations should initiate innovations in one location and then into subsequent locations, adapting and improving the idea throughout the process'
Axiomatic knowledge	'Why'	A priori explanations for why things occur	'In order to be innovative we employ a particular type of person who is self-motivated, an initiator, profit-oriented, takes responsibility and is a good communicator'

Source: Adapted from Sackmann, 1992

EXERCISE 5.1 WHAT DO YOU KNOW?

Select an organization with which you are familiar, either through experience or from the business literature, and answer the following questions:

• Identify the way in which the four knowledges described in Table 5.2 manifest themselves in this organization. How widespread is each of these? How does each impact on the organization?
• To what extent do different social groupings exist around each of these knowledges within this organization?
• Are there social groupings in this organization that cut across organizational boundaries? What effect does this have on the organization?
• Identify an issue or innovation that you would like to implement in your organization.
• Which of the subgroups you have identified require special attention? Why? How would you deal with them?

---

cultures exist – mindsets that 'transcend suborganizational, transorganizational, and organizational boundaries to be held in common by members of discrete industries'. Abrahamson and Fombrun[43] maintain that 'in an ocean of micro-cultural heterogeneity, islands of greater macro-cultural homogeneity tend to emerge and persist along vertical, horizontal, and diagonal dimensions of value-added networks'. There is some empirical evidence to support such statements. Chatman and Jehn[44] found, in studies of fifteen firms across four service sector industries, that there was less cultural variation within the industries than across them. Phillips's[45] study of the wine industry and museum industry in California also supported this finding.

Others debate the value of industrial cultures. Chatman and Jehn[46] suggest that firms should 'consider the benefits of imitating the cultures of successful players in their industries', although they acknowledge that the conditions under which organizations should endeavour to do so remain to be researched. Similarly, Abrahamson and Fombrun[47] maintain that 'macro-cultures' of industries – composed of shared beliefs of managers across industry organizations – may facilitate interorganizational negotiation and trust among top managers; lead to agreement on the strategic issues facing their industry; and enable managers to develop common interests. However, these macro-cultures are also said to lead to inertia, inhibit inventiveness and prevent innovation, causing the 'collective failure of industries'.[48]

Going global: national cultures
Adler and Jelinek maintain that most studies of organization cultures treat members as separate from the rest of society. They also point out that much

of the work has adopted a US perspective, leading to a cultural 'blind spot'[49] because US assumptions are treated as universal. Other writers[50] have pointed out how a lack of attention to differences in language and meaning in different cultural contexts can have potentially disastrous effects on developing new product markets. To solve such problems Adler and Jelinek[51] recommend 'careful attention to societal culture' so that managers can create an organizational culture that is in harmony with societal culture or work toward a 'transcendent' organizational culture that draws on multiple cultures. It is not clear, however, how managers can create such 'harmony' or even which aspects of societal culture they should be attempting to harmonize. Nor is it clear how such alignment benefits organizational performance.

Even identifying a country's culture is problematic. Hofstede has argued that a country's culture can be assessed on five dimensions:

- *power distance* – the extent of inequality;
- *individualism* – the extent to which individual rather than groups dominate action;
- *masculinity/femininity* – the extent to which 'male' or 'female' values predominate;
- *uncertainty avoidance* – the extent to which rules govern behaviour compared to a more flexible, less structured society;
- *long/short term orientation* – the extent to which values are oriented towards the future or the past/present.

However, even Hofstede also points out that only 49 per cent of variance in his sample is explained by the first four (most cited) factors, while others dispute his model altogether. In other words, national cultures are not easily reduced to similarities across a small number of dimensions and differences may be more important than similarities.[52]

Magic metaphors

Lundberg[53] suggests that the multiplicity of definitions of culture is partly due to our 'excessive familiarity' with the concept. It may, therefore, be instructive for managers to reflect upon the nature of their own 'familiarity' with the term, and how taken for granted assumptions both illuminate and shield different features of culture. Such reflection requires a more imaginative way of 'defining' culture. Morgan[54] suggests using metaphors to help us see culture in different ways. Viewing culture as an iceberg may conjure up a view of culture as large, cold and difficult to move or change; or it may convey the idea that the tip – surface behaviour – can only be understood by exploring the deeper structures below it – values, beliefs, etc. Viewing culture as an umbrella might involve views of broad organizational values providing the overarching fabric to house an array of subcultures; or the 'shelter' that culture provides in helping organizational members to cope with a stormy, external environment. The point of this work is not, then, to identify which metaphor is the most 'accurate', but to use metaphors to recognize the multiple meanings that people attach to culture and to trace how these images and meanings affect the actions they take (Exercise 5.2).

In summary, there are many diverse opinions concerning what and where culture is. This has led to myriad definitional struggles that open up a series of debates, many of which appear to be largely unrelated to managerial concerns. We conclude that efforts to tame the beast of culture in the search for the 'best' definition are unlikely to be fruitful. Instead, it might be more effective to consider that when people refer to culture, it is akin to the blind person touching an elephant – each may be experiencing different parts of the beast, 'seeing' it from different vantage points which hide other perspectives.

EXERCISE 5.2 MIXING YOUR METAPHORS?

For each metaphor below, one possible meaning of the nature of an organization's culture is given. Think of at least one other meaning for each and explain what it says about organizational culture.

Metaphor	Possible meaning
Social glue[*]	'It serves to bind individuals, and creates organizational cohesiveness'.
Exchange regulator[†]	'A control mechanism that can handle complex exchange relations'.
Compass[‡]	'The direction-pointing capacity of the shared value system'.
Sacred cow[§]	'Stresses the limits of instrumental reason and focuses on deeper value commitments and the stability of the cultural core'.
World closure[**]	'Social reality is in principle open and negotiable: culture makes it appear given, natural, and, when it comes to basic premises, impossible (or at least very difficult) to question'.
Personality[††]	'Culture is the real "personality" of an organization; the way it actually works'.

Sources:	[*]	Cartwright and Cooper, 1993: 60
	[†]	Alvesson, 1993: 18
	[‡]	Alvesson, 1993: 18
	[§]	Alvesson, 1993: 20
	[**]	Alvesson, 1993: 23
	[††]	Tucker et al. 1990: 10

IN SEARCH OF CULTURE: METHODS GALORE!

As Hofstede[55] reminds us, culture is a *construct* that is 'not directly accessible to observation but inferable from verbal statements and other behaviours and useful in predicting still other observable and measurable verbal and non-verbal behaviour'. Given the disagreements about how to define this construct, it should not be surprising to learn that a variety of aspects of organizational behaviour are studied as manifestations of culture and that a range of different techniques have been used to reveal culture. In many respects, these differences stem from whether researchers view culture as one of a number of variables within an organization or whether they see the organization as a culture.

A menagerie of different organizational features has been targeted in attempts to identify manifestations of culture. They include rites and ceremonies;[56] symbols, heroes and values;[57] corporate architecture;[58] organizational stories,[59] including their formative aspects in regulating the expression of emotions;[60] and the norms attached to the use of time in organizations.[61] For many researchers, culture is to be found in the symbolic aspect of organizations although, as Alvesson[62] notes, almost everything can have a symbolic component. Even the most rational or objective aspects of organizations can be 'conceptualized as involving important symbolic dimensions, anchored in the shared meanings of the organizational collective'.

Both quantitative and qualitative methodologies have been used. The former is typically associated with the view of culture as an organizational variable. Quantitative surveys of organizational members assume that culture is measurable and is composed of a series of other constructs, such as access to decision-making, commitment, extent of rules, commitment to quality, degree of innovativeness, extent of risk taking and the like. Such surveys are often referred to as cultural audits or cultural databases.[63] For example, the audit used by Fletcher and Jones[64] is seventeen pages long, and is designed to reveal culture along a series of different dimensions.[65] More qualitative techniques used to uncover cultural assumptions include projective drawings, metaphors, scenarios and other visualization techniques. They attempt to identify 'what the people in the organization worship'[66] and often utilize group processes such as workshops and retreats.[67] Ethnographic techniques (where the researcher acts like an anthropological participant-observer) and discourse analysis (entailing deconstruction of organizational 'texts') have also been employed in the search for culture.[68]

Proponents of the various approaches have mounted vigorous defences of their techniques. Advocates of quantitative approaches[69] point to the limitations of the qualitative study of many of the 'manifestations' of culture referred to above, especially the use of individual case studies that make generalizations difficult.[70] These critics also argue that study of stories, symbols and myths by themselves 'provide little leverage for explaining central theoretical issues, for example why and how consent in a particular set of shared meanings forms, sustains, changes or has specific impacts'.[71] Conversely, Schein maintains that one of the problems with understanding organizational culture is the obsession with measurement. 'When I see my colleagues inventing questionnaires to "measure" culture, I feel that they are simply not seeing what is there, and this is particularly dangerous when one is dealing with a social force that is invisible yet powerful.'[72]

As we have indicated, these differences reflect deeper divisions[73] concerning whether culture is seen as a variable, something which the organization *has*, much like a structure or a strategy; or whether it is seen as a perspective where the culture *is* the organization and the organization *is* the culture. The former view assumes that culture can be identified, measured, analysed and managed. It has an objective, existence, independent of the people who wish to study or change it. Users of quantitative methods are most likely to share this attitude. The latter view argues that culture cannot be reduced to an independent or dependent variable. Moreover, it maintains that what is seen as culture is a product of how the person is 'doing' the seeing. In other words, the frameworks or perspectives used to identify culture shape what is perceived to be the culture. This treatment of culture denies any 'objective' existence and instead focuses attention on the interwoven nature of language, meanings, symbols and rituals.[74] Users of qualitative methods are most likely to share this view. Studying culture in this way has been associated with a challenge to the dominant, positivist view of organization studies, with culture becoming 'the code word for the subjective side of organizational life'.[75] As a result, academic trench warfare exists as to which methods are the most appropriate (Exercise 5.3).

IT'S A MATTER OF PERSPECTIVE

These differences in the study and conceptualization of culture have led to the identification of different perspectives adopted by those who study culture. Meyerson and Martin[76] identify three such perspectives. The *integration* perspective sees culture as unified and monolithic, something that binds individuals into a coherent organization. There is a strong emphasis

---

EXERCISE 5.3 A MATTER OF PERSPECTIVE?

Answer the following questions:

- What is your view of culture: is it something an organization *has* or is it something an organization *is*?
- What are the implications of this for identifying culture?
- What are the implications of this for managing culture?

on the 'sharedness' of organizational culture, which leads people to look for those elements of culture that reaffirm consistency and cohesion. Ambiguity is denied as a picture of harmony emerges. In addition, people who adopt this perspective tend to have an optimistic view of the ability to manage culture and enhance organizational effectiveness.[77]

The *differentiation* perspective emphasizes inconsistency, a lack of consensus and contradictory values and beliefs. Organizations are thought of as fragmented subcultures – 'islands of clarity' in a 'sea of ambiguity'.[78] Subcultures may be oppositional, orthogonal or complementary to any dominant organizational culture that surrounds them. People who adopt this perspective are more likely to point to the complexities that confront those seeking to manage culture.

The *ambiguity* perspective is the least developed of the three perspectives. It views organizations as composed of differing interpretations, inherent paradoxes and irresolvable differences. Ambiguity is a permanent state of affairs. Attempts to hide the contradictions and complexities of organizational life are simply attempts to mask differences. This perspective views individuals as being temporarily connected with other individuals for particular issues and, as these issues change, so too do the connections. Unlike the differentiation perspective, which sees subcultures as relatively enduring, the ambiguity perspective treats all alignments as transient. Individuals 'share some viewpoints, disagree about some, and are ignorant of or indifferent to others. Consensus, dissensus, and confusion coexist, making it difficult to draw cultural and subcultural boundaries.'[79] This perspective parallels one image of new organizational forms, which views them as consisting of a series of continual reorganizations that occur as interorganizational alliances are formed and broken, and network arrangements are shaped and reshaped.[80]

Meyerson and Martin[81] suggest that all three perspectives should be adopted to 'avoid the usual blind spots associated with any single perspective' because 'any culture at any point in time will have some aspects congruent with all three perspectives'.[82] However, this position implies that concrete cultural patterns – or variables – exist in the organization under study, and therefore multiple perspectives are needed in order to reveal this multi-faceted 'reality'. This view is at odds with the idea that cultural patterns are *constructed* – as opposed to being revealed – by the perspectives brought to bear on them, and that they do not have any independent existence outside the disposition of the analyst. It would appear that, in relation to the debate above about whether culture is a variable or a perspective, Meyerson and Martin have a foot in both camps (despite protestations to the contrary).[83] Another question has been raised by critics who ask why there are only these three perspectives. Are other perspectives being ignored? Other critics question whether ambiguity really is a perspective and whether, while ambiguity may exist in organizations, there may well be shared understandings for how to deal with it, making it explicable with reference to one of the other perspectives.[84]

While these arguments might seem esoteric, they do have practical implications. In any cultural analysis managers need to consider whether the results will tell them more about the analyst (e.g. consultants, change managers, etc.) and how they view organizations, than about any supposed 'facts' about the culture or cultures of the organization under review (Exercise 5.4).

THE BOTTOM LINE: DOES CULTURE AFFECT PERFORMANCE?

Managerial interest in organizational culture lies not so much with these academic debates (although, as we discuss, they do have implications for practice), but with the relationship between culture and organizational performance. We discuss three different arguments about this relationship: the role of a 'strong' culture; cultural 'fit'; and adaptability and learning arguments.

Stronger is better

Peters and Waterman's 1982 study *In Search of Excellence* promoted the idea that strong cultures and strong performance go hand in hand:

> Without exception, the dominance and coherence of culture proved to be an essential quality . . . the stronger the culture and the more it was directed toward the marketplace, the less need was there for policy manuals, organization charts, or detailed procedures and rules. In these companies, people way down the line

---

EXERCISE 5.4 THROUGH A LENS?

Find either a consultant's report on an organization's culture or statements about an organization's culture that appear in a company newsletter, annual report or other documentation. Alternatively, ask some organizational members how they view their organization's culture. Answer the following questions:

- Is there a dominant perspective(s) – integration, differentiation, fragmentation – that underpins these reports of culture?
- What assumptions are made about what constitutes the culture and to what extent is ambiguity acknowledged?
- How do these assumptions affect the conclusions of the report (what's good/bad/in need of change)?
- Select another perspective on culture: what would the conclusions look like now? Are these any less valid? What new directions might they suggest?

know what they are supposed to do in most situations because the handful of guiding values is crystal clear.[85]

The message to managers was clear: to enhance performance, they needed to ensure that their organization contained a strong, value-driven culture.

This view of culture still has popular appeal. Collin and Porras[86] in their 1994 book on visionary companies take a 'strong culture' view in their recommendation that managers *'build an organization* that fervently preserves its core ideology in specific, concrete ways. The visionary companies translate their ideologies into *tangible* mechanisms aligned to send a consistent set of reinforcing signals. They indoctrinate people, impose tightness of fit, and create a sense of belonging'.

Critics have pointed out that the 'strong' culture argument assumes a causal direction in which good performance results from a strong culture; an alternative argument is that a strong culture only emerges in companies which are experiencing good performance.[87] Strong cultures may undermine performance in that with success comes arrogance, politics and bureaucracy which prevent management from identifying new strategic directions, and also inhibit change, as with Goodyear's 'bureaucratic' culture, Proctor and Gamble's 'risk-averse' culture and Citycorp's 'arrogant' culture. Strong cultures may initially be high performers, but barriers to the emergence of new and innovative ideas may replace 'co-operativeness'.[88]

Other writers, however, have challenged the notion of strong cultures. They point out that the term 'strong' has been used in myriad inconsistent ways (Table 5.3).[89] Researchers challenge claims to have found support for strong cultures,[90] because of 'the impossibility of operationalizing cultural strength'.[91] Other observers point out that cultures may be strong in some areas and influence certain types of behaviours, but weak in others.[92] Finally, even if agreement may be reached on what is a strong culture, others argue that this is no substitute for an effective organizational structure. Organizations such as Apple and General Electric, often cited as examples of strong corporate cultures, continue to use hierarchy and structure to drive the organization.[93]

TABLE 5.3   *Definitions of strong cultures*

- The more one organization has of a particular ritual or artefact compared to another organization, the stronger is assumed to be its culture.
- The more diversity of artefacts – jargon, stories, myths, ceremonies, etc. – an organization has, the stronger is its culture.
- It is not the quantity or diversity of artefacts which is important in assessing strength, but rather the consistency in meaning across them.
- The extent to which control is exerted over organizational members, i.e. a strong culture is one which demands adherence to a particular organizational 'self', even where this is potentially inconsistent with other identities which individuals may wish to express.

Source: Yanow, 1993: 211–12

Fitter is better?

Contingency or 'fit' arguments assume that a specific culture is needed – one which is aligned strategically to internal processes and external conditions.[94] There is no point in having a strong culture if it is the wrong one. 'Unless strategic plans, culture and internal policy are all in line, the organization won't work properly.'[95] Since the costs of a sub-optimal culture may be high, changes to realign it may be well worth considering because 'even marginal changes can be very cost-effective'.[96] Tailor-made examples of cultures designed to suit every occasion include the following:[97] humanistic-helpful cultures, affirmative cultures, approval cultures, conventional cultures, dependent cultures, avoidance cultures, oppositional cultures, competitive cultures, competence/perfectionist cultures, achievement cultures, and self-actualization cultures (also see Table 5.4).[98]

This approach has some shortcomings. It suggests that there is a culture for every occasion. Other writers have argued that a particular culture 'can only be a source of *sustained* competitive advantage if it has positive economic consequences, if it is rare, and if it is imperfectly imitable'.[99] If every organization in a similar situation has the same culture, that culture will no longer offer any strategic advantages by being unique. Other critics point to the static nature of the 'fit' approach, questioning how these relationships will cope with future strategic or environmental changes. Northwest is cited as an example of such a failure – its cost-cutting culture did not fit in the 1980s with the newly deregulated airlines industry, where customer service was demanded.[100] The question this raises is whether managers have to make continual cultural adjustments as circumstances change and, if so, how (Exercise 5.5)?

EXERCISE 5.5 TYPOLOGICALLY SPEAKING . . .

Consider the cultures listed in Table 5.4 and answer the following questions:

- Identify the circumstances (industry, stage of product life cycle, environment, etc.) to which each is most suited.
- What are the potential drawbacks of trying to institute these cultures in these circumstances?
- Which of the cultures have you personally experienced?
- To what extent did it 'fit' the organization's strategy and environment?
- How adaptable was this culture to new circumstances?

TABLE 5.4 *Examples of cultural typologies*

Type	Author	Meaning
Appreciative culture	Barrett, 1995: 39–40	'Accentuate the successes of the past, evoke images of possible futures, and create a spirit of restless, ongoing inquiry that empower members to new levels of activity'.
Legitimate culture	Ebers, 1995: 151	'Built around established environmental norms and values which it incorporates as a result of immediate adoption and environmental sanctioning . . . Members . . . pay particular attention to acquiring external support, resources, and legitimacy. They are bound by a common ideology and mission'.
Efficient culture	Ebers, 1995: 151	'Comprises patterns of effective conduct that originate from the various demands of its constituencies. Members . . . are mainly bound by common task goals and codes of conduct. Co-ordination . . . is achieved through a shared technology'.
Traditional culture	Ebers, 1995: 151	'Based on the coincident values, beliefs and traditions of its bearers that have developed over time as a result of initial accord, self-selection of group members, mutual adaptation, and consensual validation'.
Utilitarian culture	Ebers, 1995: 152	'Based on its bearers' compatible, interlocking explicit and tacit (self-) interests. Its members are mainly tied together by functional interdependencies'.
Innovation culture	Peters, 1993: 34	'Holds its entrepreneurs, research and development stars and technologists as its role models. Its people will feel more inclined . . . to take risks'.
Action culture	Peters, 1993: 35	'A belief that the strong survive, and the weak fall by the wayside. Its stars will be its CEO, and its sales and marketing people . . . Initiative is welcomed, but mistakes may well be punished'.
Control culture	Peters, 1993: 35	'Its people may feel secure but stifled. Taking risks will not be perceived as intelligent behaviour. People will be proud of the organization's history and success . . . a clear hierarchy'.
Harmony culture	Peters, 1993: 36	'Often a fiercely loyal one. Its vision statement will state its belief that "people are paramount". Most tasks will be undertaken by teams or committees'.
Constructive culture	Lahiry, 1994: 51	'Members are encouraged to interact with others and approach tasks in ways that will help them meet their higher-order satisfaction needs'.
Passive/ defensive culture	Lahiry, 1994: 51	'Members believe they must interact with people in ways that will not threaten their own security'.
Aggressive/ defensive culture	Lahiry, 1994: 51	'Members are expected to approach tasks in forceful ways to protect their status and security'.

Cultural typologies are also associated with specific management practices such as re-engineering and mergers and acquisitions. For example, in re-engineering an organization, Champy[101] argues for the need to develop a culture of 'willingness' to be subservient to the customer, whatever shape that takes. This cultural type is '*strongly* supportive of trust, respect, and teamwork'. Champy draws upon popular root metaphors such as 'horticulture' in

TABLE 5.5 *Different types of culture*

• Power culture	'Depends on a central power source, with rays of power and influence spreading out from that central figure. They are connected by functional or specialist strings but the power rings are the centres of activity and influence'.
• Role culture	'The role, or job description, is often more important than the individual who fills it. Individuals are selected for satisfactory performance of a role, and the role is usually so described that a range of individuals could fill it'.
• Task culture	'The whole emphasis . . . is on getting the job done. To this end the culture seeks to bring together the appropriate resources, the right people at the right level of the organization, and to let them get on with it'.
• Person culture	'The individual is the central point. If there is a structure or an organization it exists only to serve and assist the individuals within it'.

Source: Adapted from Handy, 1993: 183–91

imploring managers to '*cultivate your culture*. Only a very strong, constantly cultivated culture can prevent the weeds of mistrust, disrespect, and unco-operativeness from taking over the garden'.[102] Paradoxically, this type of culture may be difficult to achieve in the context of re-engineering processes that involve the loss of jobs, eradication of status and changes in power relationships. In addition, Hofstede et al.[103] argue that while customer-oriented cultures are relevant for particular industries (e.g. service; custom-made manufacturing, etc.), they may be dysfunctional for other industries (e.g. where adherence standards or government regulations dictate manufacturing standards, etc.), regardless of whether they are being re-engineered or not.

Fedor and Werther[104] argue that cultural fit is also important in international alliances – a dimension often ignored by managers in favour of matters concerning strategy, finance and law. In order for an alliance to be successful, cultures do not have to be totally similar, but they should be complementary. Alliance 'designers' should choose partners with cultures that will maximize the success of the alliance. Using the four cultural types of power, role, task and person (Table 5.5), Cartwright and Cooper[105] argue that mergers are unlikely to be successful when the dominant partner has a power culture. This is because centralization will impede the assimilation of the other organization. Similarly, mergers where the dominant partner has a role culture and the other organization has either a task or a person culture will run into problems since managers in the junior organization will resist the bureaucracy, either because it prevents getting the job done or because it neglects human issues. The authors maintain that successful mergers are most likely where the dominant organization has a role culture and the junior organization has either a power or a role culture. In the former case, members of the junior organization will value the 'fairness' of the role culture; in the latter, assimilation will occur through the rewriting of a new rulebook.

The fit approach to culture adopts an integrationist view of organizational culture, allowing little room for internal inconsistency within an organization, or for the influences of wider industry and societal cultures. Also, little theoretical rationale exists for the assumptions about why certain cultural types are more compatible with others, the duration of the alignment, or how realignment might occur.

Adaptability is everything

A third view of the relationship between culture and performance maintains that only cultures which help organizations to 'anticipate and adapt to environmental change will be associated with superior performance over long periods of time'.[106] These cultures are compared to non-adaptive cultures, which are reactive and do not encourage risk taking, innovation or creativity. There are strong parallels here with the organizational learning literature (see Chapter 8 on learning).[107] Barrett[108] discusses the need to develop appreciative or 'generative learning' cultures which encourage continual experimentation and generate organizational innovation. However, it is not clear that every organization needs to be adaptive or to engage in learning, particularly where they operate in stable or relatively unchanging environments.[109]

In summary, managers in search of a definitive answer to the question of whether culture improves performance are likely to be disappointed. In a review of empirical studies, Siehl and Martin[110] found little in the way of support for linking culture and performance. A fundamental problem lies in the methodological difficulties concerning how both culture and performance are operationalized, making it unlikely that definitive evidence, either supporting or refuting the link between culture and performance, will ever be found.

CHANGING CULTURE: MANAGEMENT OR MANIPULATION?

An assumption underlying much of the literature on culture is that it can be changed.[111] The cultural engineering[112] position assumes that top management is able to 'create, maintain, and change'[113] organizational culture. In other words, the influence of managers on employees is greater than the influences from other sources. Culture is thus a technical 'push-button control'[114] tool. Managers use cultural symbols such as myths and stories to represent and create change processes[115] and consultants who work with this view provide prescriptive steps for creating new cultures.[116] People are assumed to be malleable and open to change, if not in their values, then at least in their behaviour. It is also assumed that managers know the appropriate values and behaviour that will enhance organizational success.

A more reserved position emphasizes the limits and difficulties in changing culture. 'Managers can influence the evolution of culture by being aware of the symbolic consequences of their actions and by attempting to foster desired values, but they can never control culture in the sense that many management writers advocate.'[117] In her study of management development programmes, Preston[118] found managers' attempts to instil particular symbols and images were not received uniformly by participants. They conflicted with other work-based images derived from their experiences. Also unplanned cultural symbols emerged and affected socialization processes. According to this view, individuals are not passive recipients of managerial cultural interventions. 'Individual men and women may be shaped by circumstance and history, but as active agents they also make their circumstances and themselves.'[119] Cultural change is thus 'participative, communal, or interactive'.[120]

Other writers question whether culture can be managed separately and distinctly from the rest of the organization.[121] While managers might attempt to provide guidance as to cultural beliefs and values, such 'meaning cannot be engineered'.[122] Salaman and Easterby-Smith[123] argue that if managers wish to achieve cultural change they will have to modify their own values. They maintain, on the basis of their study of cultural change at British Nuclear Fuels, British Airways, Jaguar Cars and British Airports Authority that 'changing culture is a complex, long-term undertaking'.

A very different view draws attention to the 'dark side' of cultural change. It points out that in attempting to change culture managers may be encouraging people to 'suppress or suspend independent thought and action',[124] while reinforcing their own power over others in the organization.[125] Because of its role in constructing an individual's 'self', cultural change opens up 'experience itself' as a 'target for corporate control'.[126] Yanow[127] maintains that ethical questions are raised where managers deliberately set out to change the meanings associated with organizational artefacts in ways that have consequences for organizational members' meanings and identities. Individuals risk being treated as objects to be manipulated through the commodification of artefacts, which divorces them from the meanings they represent for individuals.

Some writers have attempted to separate ethical and non-ethical manipulation of symbols and values. Sathe[128] argues that 'it is in the nature of the manager's job to influence organizational behaviour in a responsible and professional manner, so it is his or her job to conscientiously shape organizational beliefs and values in the appropriate direction'. In taking this stand, he distinguishes between shaping organizational values and beliefs from shaping personal and political ones – the implication being that attempts to shape the latter are unethical. Similarly, Mason[129] suggests that it is possible to distinguish between manipulative uses of symbols and 'inspiring' uses of symbols. The former involves a lack of correspondence between symbol and substance; in the latter case there is an integration of the two, with implications of empowerment and welfare. In practice, however, it may be difficult to distinguish between the ethical and non-ethical manipulations of symbols (see also Chapter 4 on power, especially critical approaches to power).

In summary, there are different opinions regarding the ability of management to change culture and its right to do so. As far as the former issue is concerned, writers vary considerably over the degree of cultural control that managers have. Regarding the latter, opinions vary as to whether such change is ethical or not (Exercise 5.6).

CONCLUSIONS: DEAD, DOMINANT, DECONSTRUCTED OR DOUBLE-EDGED SWORD?

The literature on culture is fraught with debate – regarding definitions, methodologies, perspectives and applications. 'Different people think of different slices of reality when they talk about culture.'[130] Consequently, when people talk about culture, they may be talking about quite different things.[131] When researchers focus on one particular aspect of culture, they define what is left out as less important. [132] Not surprisingly, then, news of the death of culture has also come from very different sources.

One view attributes the death of culture to its limited practical relevance – so many attempts to change it and improve organizational performance have failed. Some pallbearers argue that the positive effect of culture on the bottom line has yet to be proven and may even be a distraction since widespread cultural change in an organization is the exception rather than the rule. Most 'organizations are *not* engaged in drastic culture change all the time'.[133] Other observers blame practitioners who 'oversimplify the meaning of organizational culture as they borrow, adapt, or are fed the latest theory'. This produces a high probability of failure, especially in attempts

---

EXERCISE 5.6 MANAGING TO MANAGE CULTURE?

Think of a cultural change programme in which you were engaged either as a change initiator, change recipient or as an observer or select a cultural change programme documented in the business literature. Answer the following questions:

- How was the cultural change programme carried out and with what success?
- To what extent did it involve manipulation of cultural symbols, artefacts and meanings?
- Relate this change programme back to arguments about the ability to change culture and the ethics of changing culture. Which of these arguments sheds new light or interpretations on what happened?
- What new implications emerge in thinking about managing culture in organizations?

to improve productivity and performance. 'This, in turn, leads to disillusionment and dismissal of the cultural approach as a fad.'[134]

A second view suggests that culture is 'dominant, but dead'.[135] According to these academics, culture was originally an antidote to predominantly functionalist, normative and, particularly, quantitative research on organizations. Culture offered a way to explore the 'soft' side of organizations and offered a means to challenge unthinking managerialism. Over time, however, research on culture has become absorbed into the mainstream of organizational analysis. Agendas driven by practical matters have infiltrated and contaminated research on culture.[136] Accordingly, some writers call for a revitalization of culture's 'dissident' status by adopting a postmodern approach.[137] This work rejects a managerial viewpoint and tries to 'deconstruct' the organizational 'texts' that support culture, challenging their supposed intentions. For example, Goodall[138] deconstructs the Nordstrom Employee Handbook in order to identify the ways in which it claims to empower employees. Others, such as Linstead and Grafton-Small use postmodernist ideas to provide a commentary on those who are writing about culture and to draw attention to the creativity of *consumers*, and not just managers, in the production of culture. 'Both authors and readers, creators and consumers, are inseparably bound together in and are constituted by the continual process of the emergence of meaning.'[139]

These two positions seem irreconcilable. The first suggests that the only way to breathe life into culture is to make it more managerially relevant. The second offers techniques for revitalization that must seem esoteric to most managers. Perhaps it is in this ambiguity that the future of culture lies. 'Culture not only serves "positive" functions such as fulfilling people's needs for meaning, guidance and expressiveness but also leads to closure of mind, restriction of consciousness, and reduction of autonomy. Culture provides direction but also prevents us from "seeing".'[140] Culture is, then, a double-edged sword.

We cannot view culture simply as a managerial tool and accept 'utility' as a benchmark for its definition, conceptualization and theorizing – if only because its utility is fiercely contested. The use of 'superficial methodologies which merely skim the surface of organizational events and which characterize much of the 'culture magician' literature can only fail to capture the multiple meanings attributed to organizational events by different interests'.[141] On the other hand, managers cannot afford to wash their hands of it, simply handing it over for postmodern deconstruction. The concept continues to offer insight into one of the key paradoxes of organizational life – conflicting tensions of organization and disorganization.[142] Understanding culture may not offer any trite answers but it does provide a way to understand integration and harmony; at the same time as developing 'sensitivity for differentiation, inconsistency, confusion, conflict, and contradiction'.[143]

NOTES

(See Bibliography at the end of the book for full references)

1 Harrison and Carroll, 1991: 552
2 Barley et al. 1988: 32
3 Bate, 1990
4 Smircich, 1995: 233
5 Yanow, 1993: 209
6 Martin and Frost, 1996: 608
7 De Lisi, 1990: 84; see also Wilkinson et al. 1996
8 Preston, 1993: 18
9 Ebers, 1995: 129
10 Alvesson, 1993: 3
11 Grint, 1995: 162
12 Martin and Frost, 1996: 602
13 Hatch, 1993: 657
14 Deal and Kennedy, 1982
15 Ouchi, 1981
16 Peters and Waterman, 1982
17 Harrison and Carroll, 1991: 552
18 Kroeber and Kluckholn, 1952, cited in Green, 1988: 122
19 Spradley and McCurdy, 1972: 7
20 Hofstede et al. 1990: 286
21 Wilkins, 1983: 24
22 Green, 1988: 122; Hatch, 1993: 658–87
23 Sathe, 1983: 6
24 Ashforth, 1985: 841
25 Rousseau, 1990: 159–60
26 Schneider et al. 1996: 18–19
27 Ashforth, 1985: 841; Rousseau, 1990
28 Denison, 1996: 654
29 Sathe, 1983: 15-16
30 Van Maanen, 1976: 112–13
31 Westley, 1990
32 McEnery and DesHarnais, 1990
33 Lahiry, 1994
34 O'Reilly et al. 1991: 487
35 Chatman and Barsade, 1995: 439
36 Fitzgerald, 1988: 10–11, 13
37 Sackmann, 1992: 140
38 Rose, 1988: 142–3
39 Schein, 1996: 236–9
40 Sackmann, 1992
41 Gordon, 1991
42 Phillips, 1994: 398
43 Abrahamson and Fombrun, 1994: 737
44 Chatman and Jehn, 1994: 522
45 Phillips, 1994
46 Chatman and Jehn, 1994: 548
47 Abrahamson and Fombrun, 1994: 728, 750
48 Abrahamson and Fombrun 1994: 728
49 Adler and Jelinek, 1986: 81
50 Ricks, 1993
51 Adler and Jelinek, 1986: 87
52 For a summary of his work see Hofstede, 1993.
53 Lundberg, 1990: 19
54 Morgan, 1989
55 Hofstede, 1993: 89
56 Trice and Beyer, 1984: 657
57 Hofstede et al. 1990: 291
58 O'Connor, 1988
59 Boje, 1991, 1995; Boyce, 1996; Feldman, 1990
60 Van Buskirk and McGrath, 1992: 9
61 Schriber and Gutek, 1987
62 Alvesson, 1993: 214–15
63 Harrison and Stokes, 1992
64 Fletcher and Jones, 1992: 31
65 See Harrison and Stokes, 1992 for an example of another culture audit instrument.
66 Schneider et al. 1996: 9
67 Lundberg, 1990; Morgan, 1993
68 Hatch, 1993: 678; Sackmann, 1992: 141
69 Tucker et al. 1990
70 Ebers, 1995: 131
71 Ebers, 1995: 155
72 Schein, 1996: 239
73 Sackmann, 1992: 140; Rousseau, 1990: 166
74 Smircich, 1983; Meyerson and Martin, 1987: 623–4
75 Meyerson, 1991: 256 cited in Denison, 1996: 619
76 Meyerson and Martin, 1987 refer to these as 'paradigms' although this changes in Martin, 1992; Martin and Frost, 1996 where they refer to them as 'perspectives'.
77 Meyerson and Martin, 1987: 627 appear, at times, to conflate the view of 'organization as variable' with a view of culture as an organization, i.e. culture as perspective, although they also contrast these views.
78 Meyerson and Martin, 1987: 633
79 Meyerson and Martin, 1987: 637; also see chapter on organizational structure.
80 Alvesson, 1993: 4; see structure chapter.
81 Meyerson and Martin, 1987: 643
82 Martin and Frost, 1996: 610
83 Meyerson and Martin, 1987: 623
84 Alvesson, 1993: 110–18; Ebers, 1995
85 Peters and Waterman, 1982: 75–6
86 Collins and Porras, 1994: 135–6
87 Kotter and Heskett, 1992: 24
88 Hilmer and Donaldson, 1996: 124–31
89 Yanow, 1993: 211–12
90 Hofstede et al. 1990: 302
91 Alvesson, 1993: 32
92 Sackmann, 1992: 156; Ebers, 1995: 157
93 Hilmer and Donaldson, 1996
94 Kotter and Heskett, 1992: 28

95 Peters, 1993: 34
96 Fletcher and Jones 1992: 30
97 Cooke and Rousseau, 1988, cited in Klein et al. 1995
98 Fletcher and Jones, 1992: 30
99 Grint, 1995: 176
100 Kotter and Heskett, 1992
101 Champy, 1995
102 Champy, 1995: 84
103 Hofstede et al. 1990: 314
104 Fedor and Werther, 1996
105 Cartwright and Cooper, 1993
106 Kotter and Heskett, 1992: 44
107 See chapter on organizational learning.
108 Barrett, 1995
109 Kotter and Heskett, 1992: 50–1
110 Siehl and Martin, 1990: 268
111 Ashforth, 1985: 843; Schneider et al. 1996: 18–19
112 Green, 1988: 121
113 Adler and Jelinek, 1986: 82
114 Green, 1988: 121
115 Feldman, 1990; Preston, 1993: 20–1
116 Price Waterhouse, 1996
117 Morgan, 1986: 139
118 Preston, 1993: 20–8
119 Fitzgerald, 1988: 10
120 Bate, 1990: 101–2
121 Salama and Easterby-Smith, 1994: 32
122 Lundberg, 1990: 25
123 Salama and Easterby-Smith, 1994: 31
124 Hilmer and Donaldson, 1996: 139
125 Preston, 1993: 20
126 Kunda, 1995: 229
127 Yanow, 1993: 212
128 Sathe, 1983: 17
129 Mason, 1994: 27
130 Sathe, 1983: 6
131 Ebers, 1995: 134
132 Rousseau, 1990: 160
133 Trice and Beyer, 1995: 227
134 Martin and Frost, 1996: 614
135 Smircich, 1995: 233
136 Barley et al. 1988
137 See chapter on postmodern approaches.
138 Goodall, 1992: 25
139 Linstead and Grafton-Small, 1992: 344
140 Alvesson, 1993: 120
141 Young, 1989: 202
142 Dougherty, 1996; Weick and Westley, 1996
143 Alvesson, 1993: 120

6 MANAGING STRATEGY
Walking the Talk or Talking the Walk?

Strategy is another means of providing an organization with direction. It is also one of the 'hot' topics in contemporary business education. In 1990 Marjorie Lyles[1] identified strategy as one of the most important areas for future research. Three years later, Richard Whittington[2] noted the existence of at least thirty-seven books in print called *Strategic Management*. Strategy started to emerge as a management discipline in the 1960s, with the work of Chandler[3] on strategy and structure and Ansoff[4] on corporate planning. In the 1970s and 1980s 'business policy' was a key component of many business school curricula and has since given way to courses on strategy and strategic management.[5] Accordingly, Whipp,[6] reflecting on the field, argues that the term is now firmly embedded in managerial discourse; while Knights and Morgan[7] argue that 'strategic' now has connotations of importance and helps to elevate the status of functions like human resource management.

While talk of strategy is commonplace today (see Supplementary Reading box), this talk covers some very different matters. In this chapter, we introduce the reader to five different ways of talking about strategy. We examine the implications of each for some of the traditional debates that revolve around strategy. We then present some of the newer talk on strategy, drawing out the implications for business practice. Finally, we explore a relatively recent stream of work on strategy, which sees strategy as an artificial, linguistic construct where meaning is imposed on actions and decisions – where the walk is turned back into talk.

STRATEGY: SUPPLEMENTARY READING

- Andrews, K.R. (1980) *The Concept of Corporate Strategy*. Homewood, IL: Dow-Jones Irwin.

- Ansoff, H.I. (1965) *Corporate Strategy*. New York: McGraw-Hill.

- Chandler, A.D. (1962) *Strategy and Structure: Chapters in the History of the Industrial Enterprises*. Cambridge: MIT Press.

- Hamel, G. and Prahalad, C.K. (1994) *Competing for the Future*. Boston: Harvard Business School Press.

- Inkpen, A. and Choudhury, N. (1995) 'The seeking of strategy where it is not: towards a theory of strategy absence', *Strategic Management Journal*, 16: 313–23.

- Knights, D. and Morgan, G. (1991) 'Strategic discourse and subjectivity: towards a critical analysis of corporate strategy in organisations', *Organisation Studies*, 12 (3): 251–73.

- Mintzberg, H. and Waters, J.A. (1985) 'Of strategies, deliberate and emergent', *Strategic Management Journal*, 6: 257–72.

- Mintzberg, H. (1987) 'Crafting strategy', *Harvard Business Review*, 65 (4): 66–75.

- Mintzberg, H. (1990a) 'Strategy formation schools of thought', in J.W. Fredrickson (ed.), *Perspectives on Strategic Management*, Vol. 5. Greenwich, CT: JAI Press. pp. 1–67.

- Porter, M. (1980) *Competitive Strategy*. New York: Free Press.

- Whipp, R. (1996) 'Creative deconstruction: strategy and organizations', in S.R. Clegg, C. Hardy and W.R. Nord (eds), *Handbook of Organization Studies*. London: Sage. pp. 261–75.

- Whittington, R. (1993) *What is Strategy and Does it Matter?* London: Routledge.

INTRODUCTION TO THE KEYNOTE SPEAKERS

There are a number of approaches to strategy, which have been classified and categorized in a plethora of different ways (Table 6.1). There are, as a result, major differences in the way that strategy is conceptualized (Table 6.2). We review these differences by presenting five broad perspectives on strategy: rational, processual, contingency, evolutionary, and institutional approaches and draw attention to their implications for practice.

Rational approaches: planning properly

One stream of literature can be classified as a classical, or rational, view. The firm is reduced to a single decision-maker, a rational economic man (*sic*) who pursues clear, financial goals through rational and analytic means.[8] Here, perhaps, lie the traditional roots of the field with the work of Chandler and Ansoff, who both drew from the writings of Alfred Sloan on General Motors and, particularly, his interest in 'policy' – which revolved around positioning the firm so as to maximize profit – as distinct from operations. Central to this work is an emphasis on a top-down,

TABLE 6.1   ***Categorizing the strategy literature***

Author	Categorization
Chaffee*	*Three mental models* • Linear: focuses on sequential planning. • Adaptive: focuses on adapting to internal and external situations, especially the environment. • Interpretive: focuses on processual aspects of strategy and extent to which it affords legitimacy.
Mintzberg[†]	*Ten schools of thought* • Design: strategy is a controlled, conscious process of thought, normally carried out by the CEO, in which formulation is separate to implementation. There is a unique strategy to confer competitive advantage. • Planning: strategy is a formal analytic process which is broken up into distinct steps, supported by techniques, and carried out by staff planners. Strategy is implemented through programmes, budgets and schedules. • Positioning: strategy is a formalized, deliberate thought process in which positions are staked out in the light of industry characteristics through 'generic' strategies. • Entrepreneurial: strategy follows from the intuitive, instinctive vision of the entrepreneur, which may or may not be articulated. • Cognitive: strategy is a mental process of decision-making/information-processing. • Learning: strategy formation is an emergent process of collective learning; strategies emanate from different parts of the organization; formulation and implementation are intertwined; strategy making is a process of trial and error. • Political: strategy is either the result or medium of power plays. It either results from internal (organizational) political processes or is the means by which the organization exerts political influence on its environment. • Cultural: strategy formation is a collective process that is rooted in shared beliefs, norms, values, etc. • Environmental: environmental forces dictate strategy and strategy formation is thus a process of adaptation whereby strategies find viable niches or respond to contingencies. • Configurational: strategy involves a fit between organization, environment and strategy, strategic change involves episodic movement between these configurations.
Whittington**	*Four perspectives* • Classic: formal strategy, profit maximization goal, analytical process, economics and military influences. • Processual: crafted strategy, political process. • Evolutionary: strategy is efficient; the rationale is survival; the emphasis is on markets that engage in Darwinian processes. • Systemic: strategy is embedded in the local context; emphasis is on social processes.
Zan[‡]	*Four types* • Evaluative/policy making: strategy as winning choices, as a project for dominance. • Descriptive/policy making: strategy as a unique choice or intention. • Evaluative/interpretive: strategy as winning (dominant) behaviour. • Descriptive/interpretive: strategy as the logic of the firm's behaviour.
Rouleau and Séguin[§]	*Four forms of discourse* • Classical: managers as rational actors; other participants as non-rational; the organization as a unitary system. • Contingency: structural determinism; organization results from structural variables. • Socio-political: recognition of a capacity for action; organizations as coalitions. • Socio-cognitive: the individual is constituted from his/her experiences and interactions; the organization as a subjective reality.

Sources: * Adapted from Chaffee, 1985
[†] Adapted from Mintzberg, 1990a
** Adapted from Whittington, 1993
[‡] Adapted from Zan, 1990
[§] Adapted from Rouleau and Séguin, 1995

TABLE 6.2 *Conceptualizations of strategy*

- Strategy as artful design and master plan
- Strategy as competitive positioning
- Strategy as a pattern in a series of decisions or actions
- Strategy as the rational development of core competencies
- Strategy as opportunism
- Strategy as the release of human potential
- Strategy as commitment
- Strategy as employee participation
- Strategy as adaptation to the environment
- Strategy as co-operating with customers
- Strategy as the achievement of total quality and ever escalating benchmarks
- Strategy as uniqueness

planned, rational approach to strategy making and an assumption that strategies which position organizations effectively in particular industries can be deduced logically and rationally from an analysis of the industries and firms in question.[9]

Two focal points preoccupy work in this area: the planning process and the formulation of particular strategies to guarantee competitive success. First, work on the planning process revolves around the use of a variety of techniques to help formulate strategy.[10] They range from a fairly straightforward process of SWOT (strengths, weaknesses, opportunities, threats) analysis, objective setting and the development of action plans, to highly technical procedures such as nominal group technique, dialectic inquiry, and metagame analysis.[11] Second, writers concerned with the formulation of specific strategies take a greater interest in the content of strategy – finding ways to exploit a firm's uniqueness by devising strategies either to capitalize on external market conditions or to exploit the internal resource-base within the firm. Organizational economics[12] focuses on external market conditions by arguing that success is related to the attributes of industry structure, especially industry concentration, level of product differentiation and barriers to entry.[13] Strategies thus revolve around selecting the most attractive industry if managers want to earn above normal returns and positioning the firm within it so as to exploit it effectively. As we have already noted in Chapters 3 and 5 on people and culture, the resource-based view of the firm[14] is concerned with the internal resources and capabilities controlled by a firm that are valuable, rare, costly to imitate and difficult to substitute. The strategic goal is to discover markets where those resources can be exploited.

What do the various bodies of work described as rational offer the practitioner? Taken together, they offer the manager an idealized view of how an effective strategy might be forged, based on sophisticated planning techniques, assessments of market characteristics and a thorough understanding of the organization's resources.

Processual approaches: from cognition to intuition

The emphasis in this broad and diverse body of literature is on the imperfect and intuitive processes whereby strategy is made rather than the clear, distinct techniques associated with the rational view; and on the difficulties of managing strategic change rather than the problem-free rational approaches to strategy formulation. Within this literature, a number of different emphases can be found. *Cognitive* approaches[15] have examined how individuals take strategic decisions and the limits and biases inherent in this process. Quinn[16] coined the term *logical incrementalism* in his portrayal of strategy making as a series of discrete steps which, when aggregated over time, produced strategic change. Pettigrew[17] took a more explicit *political* stance and argued that successful strategy making depended on the effective mobilization of power. Mintzberg[18] developed the notion that strategy is not necessarily planned or intended but often *emerges* from a series of decisions and actions that converge in a pattern and which, if effective, might then be made deliberate. More recently, his work has focused on the learning component in strategy making, i.e. the ability to recognize effective patterns and capitalize on them. Interpretive and social constructionist work has examined how environments, organizations and strategies are socially constructed – or enacted – by individuals selecting and making sense of particular information.[19] By conceptualizing strategy as a process of *sense making*[20], links are also established with organizational learning, where collective sense is made, often of discontinuous or contradictory information.[21] Finally, there is a large body of work on the role of *visionary* leaders and how they introduce new and, typically, transformational strategies to revitalize their organizations through intuition and instinct.[22]

Processual approaches to strategy challenge many of the assumptions of the rational approach. Writers point out that there are cognitive limits to rational action; that multiple, conflicting goals often exist; that intuition and vision are an important part of strategy making; that people often resist change; and that existing behaviour becomes entrenched in routines and procedures, making strategic change difficult. Strategy thus emerges from bounded rationality; from a series of incremental steps; from political deals and compromises; from accident and luck; or from the insights of a visionary leader. Whereas rational approaches separate formulation and implementation, in processual approaches they become intertwined. Consequently, managers do not plan strategy, they craft it; envision it; muddle or politick through it; make sense of it; or even look back and find, perhaps to their surprise, a strategy hiding amid what appeared to be disconnected actions.

The contribution to practice from this body of literature revolves around a more 'realistic' appreciation of strategy making. It takes into account cognitive, practical and political limitations that impede strategy making. It also offers insights into the way in which power, sense-making, collective learning, intuition and vision might be harnessed to facilitate strategy making.

Configurational approaches: forcing a fit

Configurational approaches to strategy making argue that structural and strategic characteristics typically combine in a limited number of ways that produce distinct organizational types or configurations.[23] One of the earliest examples is the work of Burns and Stalker,[24] which differentiated between organic and mechanistic forms of organization. Miles and Snow's[25] typology includes three viable configurations. The defender focuses on the efficient production and distribution of goods and services, which are facilitated by a functional organization, formal planning and extensive controls. The prospector engages in a continuous search for new market and product possibilities and requires environmental monitoring, innovation and flexibility to allow the quick exploitation of opportunities. The analyser tries to combine differentiation and low cost strategies and must be both responsive and efficient, often through a matrix structure that emphasizes product development and technical specialization. In general, this work[26] highlights a finite number of organizational configurations, the transitions between them[27] and the relevance of particular configurations to particular contexts.[28] Strategy making thus revolves around aligning a variety of organizational characteristics to support the strategy.[29]

Cultural perspectives are a variant on the work on configurations. This work tends to adopt a more normative perspective than the work above, which has been more descriptive. For example, the 7-S framework[30] recommends a fit between strategy, structure, superordinate goals, systems, staff, skills and style. Miller[31] discusses a similar theme when he talks about an architecture of simplicity in which there is a clear consensus about goals and means; decision-makers share clear priorities and world views; and strategy, structure, process, systems, routines and culture are all shaped by a central focus.[32] This cultural perspective argues that competitive advantage is achieved through alignment and integration, rather than by any single, individual aspect of strategy:

> Much to their benefit, some organizations possess a powerful unifying theme that gives them a sense of mission and direction. As a result, strategies are clear, efforts are focused, goals inspire, co-ordination is easy and complementarities among strategy, structure, and systems are great. So distinctive competencies emerge and strategic implementation is facilitated.[33]

This body of work suggests how practitioners might balance and align organizational parameters in a mutually reinforcing way, thereby increasing the chances of successfully carrying out a particular strategy. It also suggests how strategic advantage might be derived from particular constellations and offers some suggestions as to how organizations might move between them as they engage in strategic change. At the same time, we have already visited this 'fit' perspective in the culture chapter – where we noted a number of problems associated with the integrationist assumptions that underpin it.

Determinist approaches: strategic sterility

Economic thinking clearly underlies rational approaches to strategy; it also influences determinist views, but in a very different way. Whereas rational approaches have an optimistic view, i.e. that economic ideas and rational thinking can help managers to form effective strategies; determinist views use economic thinking to undercut the notion of strategy altogether. They argue that the constraining nature of the environment removes any scope for strategic decisions to help the organization to *adapt*. Instead, organizations are *adopted* by that environment, regardless of any strategic choices that are made.[34]

Evolutionary perspectives[35] consider economic competition to be the survival of the fittest, arguing that regardless of what managers do, markets will choose the best performers. Managers find it difficult to anticipate and respond to shifts in the environment – success in finding the clue to environmental fit is more likely to be a matter of luck and will quickly be imitated by competitors.[36] Proponents argue that, unless a firm has a commanding market position as in a monopoly or at least an oligopoly, a strategy simply reduces flexibility and locks the company into a position that will either be quickly copied or will be selected out by the environment. In any event, the public is best served not by clever strategies but by the ruthless weeding out of failures and the replenishment of the 'gene pool' with newcomers.

Other deterministic approaches include contingency theory,[37] which argues that strategy must fit the prevailing environment to enhance performance. In other words, a particular set of circumstances will dictate the type of strategy that will succeed. Transaction Cost Theory[38] explains vertical integration, the multi-divisional form and multinational enterprises in terms of the inevitable results of the costs of co-ordination and the bounded rationality of managers.

In many respects, determinist approaches represent an anti-strategy view of strategy. They portray management's role in strategy making as largely superfluous and subservient to environmental factors. While, not surprisingly, this body of work has had relatively little practical impact, it does provide insight into the limitations of strategy and strategic choice by identifying constraints on action. It also serves as a salutary reminder of what cannot be done through strategy.

Institutional approaches: incomplete inertia

Institutional theory examines how pressures of isomorphism[39] and legitimacy[40] force organizations to adopt practices 'demanded' by their institutional environment. It draws attention to the way in which the surrounding context limits and orients strategic actions. Institutional pressures relate to social and economic institutions – capital markets, accounting systems, and government intervention, etc. – which make certain actions feasible and others infeasible. So, much of what goes on inside Japanese companies has been attributed to differences in the structure of Japanese industry, its capital markets and the role played by government.[41] A second form of institutional pressure relates to the quest for legitimacy, which differs according to the broader social context. Managers will, therefore, adopt different behaviours to demonstrate their legitimacy depending on the country, industry, time period, etc. in which they are making strategic decisions.

The constraining nature of these pressures has led some to categorize institutional approaches as determinist.[42] More recently, however, some institutional theorists have argued for greater attention to be given to the scope of agency and the role of institutional entrepreneurship.[43] Insofar as strategy making is concerned,[44] there appears to be sufficient room for managerial discretion. For example, institutional economists[45] reject deterministic and static models and, instead, see market relations and competition as the product of human experience. In this way, 'competition' and 'markets' are simply reoccurring patterns of behaviour that are informed by the social institutions which surround them.

According to this view, strategies will be influenced by the social and economic systems of which they are a part, in particular, the local interplay of state, family and market structures.[46] Whittington[47] argues that decision-makers are not detached, calculating individuals engaged in purely economic transactions but are entwined in complex social systems that encompass their family, profession, country, education, etc. Whipp,[48] in documenting studies of UK industry, notes that they have shown how social institutions in Britain – such as family controlled business, the lack of involvement of banks in industry and the nature of the educational system – restrained the growth of mass production techniques found in other countries. However, while the prevailing context may set limits on feasible or legitimate strategic action, within those limits the manager has the latitude to find the particular actions that will 'work' in a particular situation.[49]

In summary, institutional approaches remind managers of the context in which strategy making occurs and which demands the customization of strategies. It also offers scope to managers to search for more creative and effective ways of customizing and tailoring their strategies within these parameters.

OLD-SPEAK: THE TRADITIONAL DEBATES

The different approaches discussed above tell different stories regarding the practice of strategy making. As a result, they contribute to a number of debates that emerge at their intersection (Table 6.3). These traditional debates are, then, associated with struggles between some of the more established speakers. In this section, we briefly present the debates concerning the link between strategy and structure; the question of whether planning improves performance; the issue of strategic leadership; different views concerning the velocity and dynamics of strategic change; and the role of strategy research (Exercise 6.1).

TABLE 6.3 *The traditional debates: five approaches*

	Rational	Processual	Configurational	Deterministic	Institutional
Contributions to strategy practice	The Ideal Story: how to make strategy using planning techniques and an informed understanding of market/external environment and the resources/capabilities of the organization	The Real Story: how to make strategy in the real world, taking into account both the limiting and enabling effects of cognitive, practical, political sense-making, and intuitive factors	The Balanced Story: how to align aspects of the organization in a mutually reinforcing way; how to derive strategic advantage from a configuration; how to move between them	The Other Story: the identification of the limits to action and a salutary reminder of what cannot be done	The Tailor-made Story: the need to tailor strategy to institutional demands for legitimacy and effectiveness, within which there is scope to find more effective or more creative responses
Strategy/structure debate	Structure should follow strategy	Causality is unclear; lags occur; structure may lead strategy	Structure will be realigned to fit strategy	Structure has no choice but to follow strategy	Structure will vary according to context but with some managerial discretion
Planning debate	Planning will produce the best strategy	Planning can impede strategy, but may serve other purposes	Planning is less important than the actions taken to implement the strategy	Planning is largely irrelevant since the environment selects in or out	Planning is (or is not) institutionalized in the particular context
Strategic change debate	(Senior) strategists should instigate strategic change	Strategists instigate strategic change through a variety of means, usually in an evolutionary way; strategy making can be bottom up	Senior strategists usually instigate strategic realignment (although others may be involved) strategic change occurs in quantum leaps	Actions of strategy makers are largely irrelevant since the environment selects in or out	The role of strategists is more or less relevant depending on the context
Role of research debate	Mainly prescriptive	Descriptive cases on basis of which prescriptions may be drawn	Mainly prescriptive based on some descriptive cases or concepts	Mainly descriptive	Mainly descriptive although some prescriptions may be inferred

---

EXERCISE 6.1 SO WHAT *IS* STRATEGY?

Which of the five approaches presented in the chapter best describes the way in which strategy making is carried out in your organization (or consider the way strategy making is taught in your university)? What does it say about the following?

- the nature of formal strategy making sessions
- the way the market/environment is analysed
- the way in which strategy is implemented in the organization
- the people involved in strategy making
- the expectations people have regarding the impact of strategy on organizational performance
- the role that strategy making plays in the organization
- the barriers to effective strategy making
- the outputs of the strategy making process
- the language used to describe and talk about strategy

Select one or more of the other approaches. How would strategy making change if the other approaches were adopted?

Strategy/structure: fit, lag, or geographic accident?

Whittington[50] points out that the relationship of strategy to structure is a matter of great theoretical debate. Chandler[51] fired the opening shots when he argued that structure should follow strategy. Using the example of large US organizations like Du Pont and General Motors, he argues that their early attempts at diversification were unsuccessful because the existing centralized, functional structures precluded the type of co-ordination needed in the case of multiple businesses. The complexity of diversified lines of business overwhelmed the capacity of central managers. Eventually the divisional form emerged, where divisional managers take responsibility for co-ordinating particular businesses, while headquarters management deals with the overall strategic direction of the company. Organizational economists[52] argue that this form works because it minimizes the transactions costs associated with multiple businesses. Similarly, contingency theory matches particular structures to particular strategic contingencies, albeit with a time lag between the adoption of a strategy of diversification and the change to a multi-divisional structure.[53] Thinking such as this has led to relatively deterministic discussions of how structure moves from simple to functional to divisional (or strategic business groups) as the organization develops strategies that allow it to grow in scale, market and product. Configurational approaches, while less deterministic, also see a fairly strong fit between strategy and structure as organizational realignment proceeded as part of strategy implementation.[54]

Some writers have, however, criticized the structure follows strategy line of thought. Hall and Saias[55] argue that strategy follows structure. In other words, a multi-divisional structure predisposes senior managers to adopt strategies that involve the acquisition or divestment of whole businesses, which can easily be added to or subtracted from the overall divisional arrangements, rather than pursuing new strategies regarding particular businesses with which they are relatively unfamiliar. Mintzberg[56] argues that one cannot easily separate out the causality between structure and strategy since they are inextricably intertwined and change in tandem with each other.

Institutional perspectives suggest that the relationship is less between strategy and structure, but between context and organizational form. So, for example, the prevalence of a diversified form – *keiretsu* – in Japanese companies is due to the history and culture of Japanese industrialization rather than the particular nature of these firms' strategies. While large Japanese firms may appear to resemble their US counterparts, the reasons for and nature of this divisionalization are quite different.[57] This work questions whether a universal model of efficient and strategic organization can exist, regardless of the prescriptions of many writers adopting the rational and deterministic perspectives. Instead, it posits a view of structure that is largely a product of the institutional pressures deriving from history and culture which produce such diverse forms as US conglomerates, Japanese *keiretsu*, Korean *chaebol*, and traditional family businesses in Taiwan.[58]

Planning a performance

The role of planning and design in strategy making is another traditional arena of contention. Rational writers base their whole approach on the careful planning and design of strategy.[59] Their basic premise is that an analysis of competitive forces and internal strengths and weaknesses – in other words the use of rational decision-making techniques – is the route to more effective strategies which will, in turn, produce a stronger financial performance. In this regard, writers have introduced increasing degrees of complexity and sophistication in the form of such variants as flexible planning, stakeholder analysis and cultural audits.

The notion of planning strategy focuses attention on intended strategy, i.e. the realization of deliberate strategies.[60] In contrast, Mintzberg[61] has long been associated with the concept of emergent strategy. He takes issue[62] with virtually all aspects of strategic planning: from the definition of planning, which has become too broad to be useful, to the literature's promotion of planning techniques that merely formalize existing strategies rather than actually create strategy. He argues that planning is, in fact, strategic programming, i.e. the articulation of strategies that have already been created. Mintzberg argues that we need to understand strategy making fully before we can programme it through planning. We have not yet reached the necessary level of awareness and knowledge concerning strategy, especially since successful strategy making relies on collective intuition and we have yet to learn how intuition works on an individual basis, let alone collectively. Nor can we forecast the future because it does not yet exist and we cannot, therefore, attain the level of predictability necessary to make planning effective. Scenario or contingency planning does not work either, because hedging one's bets disrupts commitment or particular scenarios become self-fulfilling. Mintzberg goes on to question the separation of formulation and implementation, arguing that better strategies are made when managers immerse themselves in the details of their business. Finally, he challenges the emphasis on analysis, saying that managers need to see the big picture, but analysis, by its very nature, tends to break it down, giving only fragmentary clues.

A number of writers have questioned whether formal strategic planning actually improves organizational performance. Some even attribute economic decline in the USA to behaviours associated with planned approaches to strategy.[63] Research findings are equivocal. Some studies do suggest a positive correlation between planning and performance,[64] but their sampling and methods have been criticized.[65] Planning may, however, be important for quite different reasons than performance. Langley[66] argues that planning is useful because it provides control, serves public relations function and creates an opportunity for 'group therapy' in the organization. Other writers attribute formal strategic planning to institutional pressures present in particular countries such as the UK and the USA, as opposed to Japan;[67] or particular political pressures, such as Thatcherism and the New Right.[68]

Despite their concerns, few critics of planning suggest that it should be abandoned altogether because of its symbolic and political benefits. Even Mintzberg[69] suggests that it is appropriate in the case of stable, mature, capital intense, large organizations that have elaborate structures and tightly coupled and simple operations. He concedes that there is room for both emergent and intended strategy since without the former we would never learn and without the latter we could never control.

Strategic change: orchestration or adaptation, continuity or quantum leaps?

The various approaches to strategy raise a number of issues concerning strategic change. The first concerns whether there is a role for strategists in orchestrating strategic change. Deterministic views reduce the role of strategic choice and argue that the actions of organizational members, whether senior managers or not, are largely irrelevant since it is the environment that does the selecting. Other approaches place more emphasis on the role of strategic 'leadership'. The rational model of strategy focuses on the role of the CEO, who orchestrates strategic change as a result of careful planning and analysis. Some processual writers emphasize the 'heroic' leader who, instead of planning and analysis, uses charisma and vision to bring about the right strategy; others emphasize the political skills of leaders.[70]

Configurational approaches suggest that effective implementation depends on managers whose style, personality and/or functional background match the requirements of the particular strategy.[71] Other research, however, suggests that managers may be able to adapt to the type of strategy they are implementing and are, therefore, relatively flexible; or that strategic teams compensate and complement the styles and personalities of individuals.[72] In other words, the 'fit' of senior managers may be less important than configurationalists might have us believe.

Brodwin and Bourgeois[73] have identified different types of strategic 'leadership' (Table 6.4), of which it seems safe to say that we know least about the crescive form of strategic management. Westley[74] points out that researchers, who often assume strategy to be the responsibility of top management alone, rarely consider middle managers.[75] As a result, 'strategic planning systems continue to be designed as top-down planning systems with bottom-up information flows'.[76] Accordingly, middle managers are typically given only a supporting role in most approaches to strategy, despite the fact that involving middle management can contribute greatly to strategy making, by reducing resistance, generating energy, creating commitment and providing different viewpoints.[77] Moreover, despite Mintzberg's[78] attempts to draw attention to the role of 'strategists' throughout the organization, the bottom-up crafting of strategy has, so far, received relatively little academic analysis.

Finally, Whittington[79] points out that 'leadership' has different connotations in different countries. There is no direct translation of this word in French; while in German the word has a negative connotation. Similarly, leadership is bound up with a masculine orientation in which 'traditional' female leadership styles receive short shrift. In other words, the role played by leadership in strategy making may have a lot to do with social and historical assumptions.[80]

A second debate concerning the nature of strategic change revolves around whether it occurs gradually, as a series of incremental steps, or whether transitions occur in the form of quantum change. Mintzberg and Waters[81] suggest that strategic change is both slow and rare. Their studies have shown that over time the most striking element is continuity, not change. They conclude that managers should resist constant strategic change and not interfere with strategic direction unless something is radically wrong. Writers like Quinn and Pettigrew[82] suggest that an accumulation of incremental and political steps eventually may produce radical change. John Harvey Jones at ICI orchestrated, behind the scenes, a series of small, political moves over a period of nine years that put him in a position to bring about more fundamental changes only when he was finally elected as CEO. Conversely, Miller[83] argues that all change should be held back until pressures build sufficiently to ensure revolutionary change, from one configuration to another. As such, he advocates episodic revolution rather than gradual, incremental steps. Other configurational writers adopt a mid-point, arguing that organizational change is marked by periods of evolution (with incremental changes) followed by a major revolution.[84]

TABLE 6.4 *Strategic leadership styles*

	Commander	Change	Collaborative	Cultural	Crescive
How are goals set?	Dictated from the top	Dictated from the top	Negotiated among top team	Embodied in culture	Stated loosely from top, refined from bottom
What is the CEO's role?	Rational actor: how do I formulate the optimum strategy?	Architect: how do I implement my strategy?	Co-ordinator: how do I involve top management and secure commitment?	Coach: how do I involve the whole organization in implementation?	Premise-setter: how do I encourage managers to promote sound strategies?
What signifies success?	A good plan, judged by economic criteria	Organization and structure to fit the strategy	An acceptable plan with top management support	An army of busy implementers	Sound strategies promoted by effective champions
What factors are considered?	Economic	Economic, political	Economic, social, political	Economic, social	Economic, social, political, behavioural
What are the dynamics?	CEO formulates plan, based on analysis and logic; others are then instructed to implement it	Once the strategy has been developed, the CEO puts into affect by realigning the organization	CEO involves senior team in strategy formulation to guarantee their support	Middle and lower levels are involved and strategy is implemented through culture management	CEO addresses formulation and planning together by encouraging managers to come forward with own strategies

Source: Adapted from Brodwin and Bourgeois, 1984

The role of research: describing the obvious or prescribing the ridiculous?

The strategy literature can be divided according to whether it is descriptive or prescriptive.[85] Rational approaches tend to be the most prescriptive; the deterministic literature tends to be most descriptive; while the remaining perspectives are a mixture of both. Processual approaches often use case studies to describe how strategy making evolves in a particular situation, from which prescriptions are then explicitly or implicitly drawn. Configurational approaches tend to be relatively prescriptive in their emphasis on the need for strategic alignment, but these ideas are based on conceptual or empirical descriptions of organizations. Institutional approaches are also mainly descriptive of the different institutional pressures that exist in a given setting, but prescriptions about how best to demonstrate legitimacy in that setting often follow.

Mintzberg[86] suggests we should focus on description since we still do not really know how strategy is made. He argues that academics can best help managers by showing how strategies are made and helping them to reflect on these processes. Only managers have the in-depth knowledge necessary to make strategy; academics are too distanced and their knowledge is too abstracted to be of much practical help. Much of the interest in strategy as a discipline, however, revolves around its potential to tell managers exactly *how* they might successfully establish or implement a competitive advantage. For this reason, pressure will undoubtedly continue to move at least part of the field towards prescriptive work.

In summary, a number of traditional debates are associated with the strategy field. We present these debates not in order to resolve them, but to explore them and to link them to different views of strategy. We have framed these debates to highlight the contribution that academic work makes to the practice of strategy.

WALKING THE (NEW) TALK

Strategy, as both a discipline and a practice, does not stand still. As we move through the 1990s, we can see elements of a new strategic language emerging. Table 6.5 summarizes some of the traditional language in strategy making and Table 6.6 contrasts the 'old' and the 'new' approaches to strategy. In this section, we present an overview of what some have called a new strategic paradigm,[87] and discuss some of its implications for practice.

The concept of *strategic stretch* encompasses a cluster of ideas promoted, in particular, by the work of Hamel and Prahalad.[88] It proposes using strategy to reinvent industries by rewriting the rules of the game, rather than to compete more effectively within the confines of existing industry/market rules. Consequently, strategy is devoted more to the exploiting of opportunities to create new environments. Strategic analysis and intuition pushes – or stretches – the status quo to find new competitive spaces. Instead of

TABLE 6.5 *The traditional lexicon*

- Five competitive forces – suppliers, buyers, substitutes, new entrants, and competitors – that determine level of competition in an industry.
- Experience/learning curve – the percentage decline (20%–30%) in unit production costs as the total accumulated volume of production (or experience) doubles.
- Business/competitive strategy – means of competing in a particular business.
- Corporate strategy – company's overall direction based on a balanced portfolio of businesses.
- Generic strategies – cost leadership is a low-cost strategy that allows the company to compete on price; differentiation adds value by differentiating on the basis of service, design, quality, image, etc., allowing it to charge a premium price; focus involves the location of a profitable niche.
- Vertical integration – taking over a supplier (backwards) or customer (forward) to grow and/or control costs.
- Portfolio matrix/BCG growth-share matrix – portfolio of investments plotted against growth rate of industry and relative market share. Stars are leaders in high growth markets; cash cows are milked as market leaders in mature businesses; dogs have low shares in unattractive industries; question marks require investment to develop market share in growing industries.
- Organizational life cycle – birth, growth, maturity, decline and death.
- PIMS (profile impact of marketing strategy) – models of a large database that purport to predict performance on the basis of market growth, market concentration, market share, etc., thereby identifying the most effective corporate strategy and portfolio mix.
- Product life cycle – sales over the life of a product from its introduction, growth, maturity and decline.
- Strategic business unit – organizational groups consisting of separate, independent product market segments which have responsibility for managing their own business.
- Strategic group – a group of firms that pursue similar strategies within an industry.
- SWOT analysis – assessment of the internal strengths and weaknesses of a company and of the environmental opportunities and threats.
- Value chain – chain of activities whereby 'value' is added to the product or service by the activities that transform it from input to output, either through low cost transformation of inputs or the differentiation of outputs. By identifying exactly where in the chain value is added, a firm's distinctive competence can be ascertained.

focusing on the served market, managers are urged to consider the customers who are not being served. Instead of concentrating on the existing position in the value chain, managers should explore whether profits could be extracted at a different point in the chain. Instead of fine-tuning the existing skill sets and resource configurations, managers must examine alternative configurations. Instead of settling for flexibility, managers are exhorted to identify the extent to which they are vulnerable to new 'rules of the game'.

The idea of strategic stretch revolves around the concept of *organizational learning*[89] through *strategic thinking*, a term which has been attracting increasing attention.[90] Strategic thinking is differentiated from strategic planning, as being a state of mind rather than a process or technique.

> Strategic thinking is a term intended to communicate the presence of some prior evaluation and is the prelude to designing an organization's future. The outcome of strategic thinking is an integrated perspective of the enterprise, and loosely

TABLE 6.6   *'Traditional' and 'New' approaches to strategy*

Strategic Dimensions	Traditional	New
Relationship between strategy and environment	Strategy as fit: transform the firm to fit the environment	Strategy as stretch: reinvent industry to fit the firm
Nature of competitive analysis	Competing within an existing industry structure: generic strategies to lock in markets	Competing to shape future industry structure: create new markets
Goal of competitive advantage	Competing for market share and product leadership: aim is incremental improvements in existing market share or position	Competing for opportunity share and core competence leadership: aim is to rewrite industry rules and create competitive space
Strategic intent captured in	Strategic plan	Strategic architecture
Resource priorities	Capital budgeting and allocation of resources between competing projects	Leveraging resources through competence acquisition and forcing competitors on to more expensive migration paths
Problem-solving logic	Formal planning: • rational analysis • formulaic and ritualistic • existing industry/market structure is base line • industry structure analysis (segmentation, value chain, cost structure) • individual businesses as the unit of analysis	Strategic thinking: • intuition and sense-making • exploratory and open-ended • potential future discontinuities are base line • a search for new ways of doing things internally and externally • corporation as the unit of analysis
Nature of strategic change	Linear, incremental	Breakthrough, quantum
Role of alliances	Competing as a single entity	Competing as an alliance
Role of competitors	Cost reduction	Learning
Role of customers	Marketing tools	Learning
Role of suppliers	Contractual	Learning
Role of employees	Distant from strategic thinking/actions	Integral to strategic thinking/actions

articulated vision of direction. It identifies the organization's driving force and highlights the different ways for organizations to obtain their chosen objectives . . . the strategic thinker is therefore more like an artist or inventor.[91]

Strategic thinking thus involves synthesis, intuition and creativity; it emphasizes vision, curiosity and wisdom; it is concerned with the future; and is qualitative, holistic and conceptual, rather than quantitative, linear and routinized.

Through strategic thinking, managers gain industry foresight by probing into what drives an industry and changing customer interfaces in more productive ways. By delivering on this, the company achieves a sustainable *competitive advantage*. The route to competitive advantage encompasses what

Hamel and Prahalad call *strategic intent,* which 'envisions a desired leader-ship position and establishes the criterion the organization will use to chart its progress'. It focuses attention on winning; motivates and communicates the value of the target; leaves room for individual and team contributions; sustains enthusiasm by providing new operational definitions as circum-stances change; and provides consistency to guide resource allocation.[92] This intent is not articulated through any strategic plan, but by what Hamel and Prahalad refer to as *strategic architecture,* which identifies what must be done now to 'intercept' the future: what competencies must be built, what customers must be explored and what priorities must be pursued. It is an 'opportunity approach' plan.[93]

Integral to the creation of competitive advantage is the concept of *core competencies* (Table 6.7), around which the organization and its strategy *converge.* Hamel and Prahalad's use of this term has been associated with a bundle of skills and technologies that is embedded, organizationally, in a collectivity, rather than in an individual or small group. It offers real bene-fits to customers, is difficult to imitate and provides access to a variety of markets. The term emphasizes a more fluid conceptualization of organiz-ational resources, strengths and abilities, which cuts across departments, divisions and strategic business units. Other work has used the term to com-prise tangible and intangible resources, specific knowledge, specialized assets and tacit knowledge.[94] Competencies are generally considered to be technological or knowledge-based expertise that add value at specific points along the value chain, while the term *distinctive capabilities* has been used to refer to strengths that are rooted more in process and business routines[95] and which encompass the entire value change.[96] Capabilities are, then, defined as the ability to make use of resources[97] – organizational know-how

TABLE 6.7   *Comparison of the concept of SBU and core competence*

SBUs	Core competencies
• Compete on basis of today's products	• Organization competes in order to build competencies
• The organization is organized into separate businesses on the basis of distinct products and markets	• Organization is organized to embrace a portfolio of competencies, core products and businesses
• Boundaries between business units are designed to be relatively self-contained and permanent	• Boundaries between business units are designed to be fluid and permeable
• Reorganization and reconfiguration of SBUs occurs only periodically	• Reorganization and reconfiguration of competencies occurs regularly
• The SBU is highly autonomous and possesses its own resources	• The business unit is a potential reservoir of core competencies
• Capital is allocated to individual businesses	• Capital is allocated across businesses and competencies
• Corporate managers optimize returns by trading off capital allocations between businesses	• Corporate managers optimize returns by building competencies to secure the future

Source: Adapted from Prahalad and Hamel, 1990: 86

embedded in the shared decision rules that constitute an organization's identity, which produces particular actions.

Acting on strategic intent involves the management of *migration paths* – the way forward – by investing in core competencies; creating and managing alliances with other organizations; learning and experimenting in the market; building global brands and distribution; and setting standards and influencing regulation.[98] By pre-emptively building core competencies; reconfiguring the customer interface; and assembling alliances, competitors are forced onto longer and more expensive migration paths in order to keep up, thereby ensuring competitive advantage for the firm. Part of this process involves *leveraging resources*: specifying precise goals; building consensus on these strategic goals; emphasizing high-value activities; using all employees; accessing the resources of partners; securing complementary assets; recombining and recycling skills in new ways; shielding resources from competitors; and minimizing the time to payback.[99]

Part of the new strategic paradigm is a strong emphasis on *collaboration* – both internal and external. The latter emphasizes a role for 'collective' strategy[100] – co-operative arrangements, or *relationship strategies*, between organizations, in such forms as *strategic alliances*; *network organizations*; *modular corporations*; *virtual organizations*, and *outsourcing*.[101] One way to reinvent industries is to transform the competitive profile by collaborating with suppliers, competitors, buyers, government and other organizations in order to enhance learning, spread risk, leverage resources and acquire competencies.

The notion of *strategic identity* is another relatively recent addition to the literature on strategy. Eccles and Nohria[102] use the example of Biogen to show how organizational identity changed as its strategy changed. They argue that identity is a social process that shapes decisions and actions but their analysis very much emphasizes identity resulting from strategic decisions; another approach is that of Dutton[103] who discusses how organizational identity affects strategy making in two ways. First, through the motivation of individuals to act on issues: particular issues are seen as legitimate, important and feasible depending on the extent to which they fit in with notions of organizational identity. Moreover, since organizational identity also helps constitute individual identity, issues that reinforce attractive components (or revise unattractive components) of the organizational identity are likely to secure individual attention and commitment.

Second, an organization's identity becomes embedded in routines and programmes that shape the strategy-making process. Links between belief systems and routines, programmes and structures of an organization converge in 'paradigms' or 'archetypes'.[104] In a study of a firm whose identity was nurturing and paternalistic, Johnson[105] found human relations practices (promoting from within), socialization behaviour and marketing routines reproduced organizational identity. In other words, organizational identity leads to routines and practices concerning the type of strategic information that is collected; patterns of participation that include particular individuals in strategic decisions (and exclude others); and forms of strategic communication and customer involvement which, in turn, produce particular types of strategy.

In summary, we can see that the theory and practice of strategy involves some new ideas and practices, three of which we consider here: the notion of strategic stretch, collaborative strategy and global strategy. In each case, we present some of the new debates associated with them (Exercise 6.2).

Stretched out of shape

The idea of using core competencies to stretch organizational capabilities has captured the imagination of the contemporary strategy literature. It is a seductive idea, but not without its problems. One question concerns the recognition of exactly what constitutes an organization's core competencies. Getting it wrong can lead to large amounts of wasted investment. Even if core competencies can be recognized, senior managers (at least) have to agree on them. Given that they are tacit, complex bundles of skills and know-how that might be combined in many different ways to produce diverse products and services, there is considerable scope for disagreement.[106] Consequently, identifying core competencies and then building them into a strategy may be more problematic than the literature suggests.

Another problem arises with the flip side of core competencies – core rigidities. The tacit knowledge associated with core competencies is inevitably institutionalized and standardized into routines and procedures. Research has found that core competencies become reified, recreating an organizational reality that is increasingly out of touch with both the organization's capabilities and the market's needs and making it difficult for innovators to break out of routines. While these routines are problematic, it may

---

EXERCISE 6.2 REINVENTING THE WHEEL?

According to Hamel and Prahalad (*Competing for the Future*, Boston: Harvard Business School Press, 1994: Table 1–2), CNN, Wal-Mart, Bell Atlantic, Compaq, AT&T, British Airways and Hewlett-Packard are all companies which have reinvented their industry and/or regenerated their strategy instead of simply restructuring their organizations or re-engineering business processes. Select one of these companies and, by consulting the business press, ascertain the following:

- What were the strategies of these companies?
- How did they reinvent the industry?
- Why do you think Hamel and Prahalad believe that the strategies of these companies correspond to the 'new' paradigm?

not be sensible to eradicate them, even if it were possible, since they serve an important role by providing a short cut to decision making and action, and preventing people from continually having to reinvent the wheel and create new rules.[107]

However, this process can lead to a dysfunctional trajectory as core competencies are rigidified; tacit knowledge and intuition become displaced by conventional wisdom and unchallenged assumptions (Table 6.8). For example, organizations that became successful through their commitment to precision quality start to focus myopically on tinkering, producing over-engineered, over-priced products. Growth-driven entrepreneurial companies get carried away with continual expansion, acquisition and diversification to end up as over-extended imperialists. Pioneers, once renowned for their innovative differentiation, revert to idealistic escapism as they invent countless new products with little regard to the end-user (Exercise 6.3). Organizations whose success derived from exemplary marketing drift into an emphasis on marketing minutiae rather than offering new products and services.[108]

Collaborating with the enemy

The value of collaboration, as opposed to competition, has started to become part of the new conventional wisdom in the strategy field. Collaboration has, as a result, acquired a very positive connotation despite the suspicion with which economists and policy-makers have traditionally viewed it. Accordingly, new forms of organization[109] are advocated to bring together organizations in arrangements that hinge on effective inter-organizational collaboration. Table 6.9 categorizes these forms under three main headings, and describes their strategic advantages.

TABLE 6.8 *Examples of core competencies and incompetencies*

Core competencies	Core incompetencies
• Developing useful applications from core material; figuring out and solving users' needs quickly and completely; helping users see the value of the innovation	• Ideas always come from the field; minimal market analysis is necessary because company is competitive; little investment made in technology and manufacturing
• Deep knowledge of speciality process is applied creatively to specific needs; emphasis on low cost but high quality and elegant solutions	• Concentrate on the technical properties of quality, low cost and convenience in the abstract; elegant technology always wins; technologists dominate innovation
• Appreciation of how data processing can enhance productivity of office work flows; ability to solve information flow problems; orchestration of complex development processes	• Contact with users through a large salesforce; paternalistic attitude to users; emphasis on plans rather than needs for product planning; only produce expensive, high quality equipment

Source: Adapted from Dougherty, 1995: 119

EXERCISE 6.3 PACKAGING COMPETENCIES?

Select an organization with which you are familiar, either from experience or from the business literature, and answer the following questions:

- Identify the 'packages' of skills, expertise, knowledge and know-how that allow this organization to add value to its product or service.
- How much do these packages rely on tacit, informal, fluid, flexible relationships?
- How much do they rely on conventional wisdom, past ways of doing things, rules and procedures?
- How easy is it to reorganize and reconfigure the components of this package?
- Does this organization have effective core competencies or is it in danger of developing core incompetencies?

First, the most familiar category is, perhaps, mergers and acquisitions (M&As) in which two existing entities become one. Here, the problem of collaboration is brought 'in-house', albeit a new house. Even so, the management challenges of ensuring the newly formed entity works the way that it is supposed to are considerable. The literature is full of failed mergers and acquisitions where the strategic advantage was lost due to the inability to overcome the management difficulties. The merger mania of the 1980s has since been criticized for a considerable amount of activity that failed to produce the anticipated benefits. Interestingly, the 1990s have been associated, after a brief hiatus, with a steady increase in such activity. While proponents argue that this round of M&As is more strategic, other writers are more critical. They argue that diversification still fails to create synergies between unrelated businesses[110] and that the Boston Consulting Group (BCG) portfolio concept does not create value because 'dogs' and 'cows' become self-fulfilling prophesies; while managers overpay to acquire 'stars'.

Second, joint ventures involve the creation of a new entity through a partnership between two or more existing entities. This form has proved to be particularly important in the context of international and global strategies, although this is by no means the only arena in which joint ventures are found. The key here is effective collaboration between the two partners in setting up and managing their progeny. Partners must be chosen carefully, ownership and management details have to be agreed and the ongoing relationship between the players must be worked out. Problems might also occur when a conflict of interest arises – to be expected when partners may be involved in multiple forms of collaboration and if they are unbalanced in terms of dependency and power.

TABLE 6.9 *Advantages and challenges of interorganizational collaboration*

Form of interorganizational relationship	Strategic advantages	Implementation challenges
Mergers and acquisitions: absorption of an existing entity	• Synergy/complementarity • Diversification of risk • Rapid growth • Acquisition of skills • Absorbing the competition • Control of key resources	• Unknown business • Organizational fit • Culture clash • Colonization and destruction of unique characteristics
Joint ventures: creation of a new entity	• Access to new skills • Access to new markets • Reduction of risk • Co-opting the competition	• Managing the new entity • Discontinuities in culture, policies, etc. • Unbalanced dependencies • Switching-out costs
Alliances: multiple co-operative relations between existing entities	• Farm out non-core activities • Benefit from skills, economies of scale, specialization without having to acquire or develop them • Reduce capital requirements, training needs, etc.	• Hollowing out of organization • Creation of trust • Loss of proprietary knowledge

Third, the most recent impetus in collaboration can be generally described as strategic alliances, which cover a host of different forms including networks, outsourcing and modular firms. Here, the original entities remain separate but new arrangements link them as tasks and responsibilities are transferred. Given that one organization may be involved in a number of such different relationships, the multiple interfaces can become difficult to manage. Consequently, considerable care must be taken with developing effective communication and either trust or contracts must be well articulated between partners. Other managerial issues are also important, such as how to manage the displacement of individuals who are transferred to partner organizations; safeguarding against the release of proprietary knowledge; and ensuring the organization is not 'hollowed out' to the extent that it becomes too focused (Exercise 6.4).

Going global

The globalization of business has also been taken for granted in the rhetoric of the new strategic language. As such, it has posed new challenges for strategy makers. In recent years, many organizations have developed an increasingly global or worldwide perspective. In response to this, research has also developed a broader strategic interest in global issues compared to the narrower disciplinary orientation of international business.[111] Definitions of exactly what constitutes a global firm or a global strategy are, however,

---

EXERCISE 6.4 FRIENDS OR ENEMIES?

Select an interorganizational collaboration with which you are familiar, either from experience or from the business literature, and answer
the following questions:

- Identify the strategic advantages that might be expected from this
  collaboration.
- Were those strategic advantages achieved?
- Explain why/not.
- What implementation problems did the collaboration run into?
- Why do you think that was?
- How might those problems have been overcome?

---

unclear. A global enterprise is supposedly different from multinational enterprises that are headquartered in a particular country and whose culture and
practices are dominated by the traditions of that country. Research has
found empirical support for three types of organizations with an international presence. The international organization is a co-ordinated federation in which the parent company transfers knowledge and expertise to
foreign markets. The multinational is a decentralized federation in which
foreign operations respond to local differences. The global organization is
a centralized hub which has a worldwide presence but in which most assets
and decisions are centralized. It offers a standardized product, manufacturing at whichever sites afford most efficiency.[112] However, each of these has
been found to run into difficulties when competing in a worldwide arena,
leading to the proposal of an ideal type – the transnational organization.

The transnational organization is supposed to address the contradictory
demands of standardization and flexibility (Table 6.10) – achieving competitive advantage through worldwide standardization to reduce costs, at
the same time being responsive to local market demands. It is, however,
unclear how these conflicting demands might be reconciled in the form of
specific reporting relationships, communication systems, human resource
policies, etc. Nor is there much in the way of empirical support for the existence of these organizations. A way around this has been to relate different
strategies to different industries. So firms in industries like cola beverages
might benefit from strategies to attain cost reduction through standardization; while consumer electronics and automobiles lend themselves to strategies that exploit more of a customized, market-by-market orientation to
find and serve market segments across the world.[113] In this regard, we can
see the thinking behind Porter's generic strategies being applied to a global
context: the successful firm is the one that recognizes and responds to the
demands of its particular environment (Exercise 6.5).

TABLE 6.10   *Global strategy assumptions*

Assumption	Standardization	Flexibility
Country market/product characteristics	• Similar, not segmented • Stable, few changes or new products	• Different and segmented • Dynamic, new products
Customer	• The global customer is willing to buy standardized products if the price is right ·	• Customers in different countries have different preferences
Cost position	• Manufacturing costs are important • Economies of scale can be derived in many areas • Experience-curve result from long runs of few products • Choice of production location is critical	• Marketing costs are significant • Flexibility in manufacturing makes up for scale • Economies of scope as well as scale in manufacturing, marketing and distribution • Markets stimulate new product development
Trade and investment barriers	• None	• Regulation • Tariff barriers • Protectionism, nationalism, regionalism

Source: Adapted from Wortzel, 1991

EXERCISE 6.5 GOING, GOING, GONE GLOBAL?

Select an organization with which you are familiar, either from experience or from the business literature, and answer the following questions:

• To what extent has this organization 'gone global'?
• What strategic advantages does it hope to derive from this move?
• What has been the impact on the organization?
• What additional changes do you expect to arise in the future both in the way the organization functions and in your particular job as a result of globalization?

In summary, the 'new' strategic language focuses our attention on new strategic practices, including those to do with core competencies and strategic stretch; collaborative strategy; and globalization. Despite the claims of some writers, we question whether these themes constitute a new *paradigm*.[114] First, they have roots in more traditional approaches. The idea of core competencies can be traced back to configurational approaches. Strategic thinking has its roots in sense making and enactment. Collaboration has concerned economists for many years, albeit from a somewhat different perspective. One of the main themes in globalization revolves around an application of generic strategies to a worldwide context and has evolved out of a relatively longstanding lineage of international business. In fact, much of the 'new-speak' can be directly related to the concern of processual writers with intuition and insight, coupled with the concern of configurational writers with synthesis, and applied to the driving force of the rational concern with content.

Second, many of the problems that plague traditional approaches remain, such as the details of how to *manage* strategy and make strategic choices. For example, the identification of core competencies is as problematic as deciding 'what business are we in?' Trying to prevent tacit, flexible competencies from becoming mechanistic recipes is reminiscent of the search for flexible planning. Collaborative strategy is still ill-served by concrete ideas on how to manage cultural differences and how to merge structures and policies, in much the same way that the entire field has generally neglected implementation in order to concentrate on formulation. Globalization continues to suffer from definitional problems and tensions between prescription and description that mirror those in the broader strategy literature.

CONCLUSIONS: TALKING THE WALK

This chapter has reviewed five broad approaches to the field of strategy. It has examined traditional debates that evolve from differences in the assumptions of some of the more established approaches. We then examined some of the new strategic language, concepts and practices that evolved in strategy research and practice. We argue that this new language does not represent a new paradigm in the strategy field. Instead, its roots are to be found in the more traditional literature. However, the emphasis on strategic *language* does shed light on a newly evolving approach to the study of strategy – that of strategy as discourse. It emphasizes strategy as a social and, in particular, a linguistic construction. Within this approach, we can identify a pragmatic perspective that revolves around a link between talk and action; as well as an academic orientation that seeks to problematize the very concept of strategy.

The pragmatic aspects of discursive approaches focus on the power of words. Eccles and Nohria[115] consider strategy to be a particular kind of rhetoric that provides a 'common language used by people at all levels of an organization in order to determine, justify, and give meaning to the constant stream of actions that the organization comprises'. They argue that strategy does not merely reflect an organizational reality but actually creates it. Thus strategy has become an important new rhetoric which makes sense of, legitimates and *produces* certain activities. Eccles and Nohria[116] suggest that the effective use of strategic language can galvanize organizations into action and, thereby, guarantee financial success by defining powerful core concepts and providing a means for communication.

One criticism that might be made of this work is that the link between talk and action is not well understood. Consequently, we have only an unclear idea of how linguistic constructions relate to actions by specific individuals in specific organizations[117] and so the practical lessons for managers are somewhat vague. There are major questions concerning how thinking up or

---

EXERCISE 6.6 FITNESS OR STRETCHING EXERCISES?

Below are two different ways of talking about strategy. Select an organization with which you are familiar, either from experience or from the business literature, and answer the following questionnaire. Indicate how strategy is talked about in this organization. If both terms are talked about equally, circle number 3; if one term is used exclusively, circle numbers 1 or 5; if one term is predominant but the other is occasionally used, circle 2 or 4.

strategy as fit	1 2 3 4 5	strategy as stretch
strategic plan	1 2 3 4 5	strategic architecture
position in the industry	1 2 3 4 5	reinvent the industry
SBU	1 2 3 4 5	core competence
strategy formulation	1 2 3 4 5	strategic thinking
analysis	1 2 3 4 5	intuition
controlling resources	1 2 3 4 5	leveraging resources
competition	1 2 3 4 5	collaboration
SWOT analysis	1 2 3 4 5	rewriting industry rules
certainty	1 2 3 4 5	ambiguity
the organization has a good/bad strategy	1 2 3 4 5	we don't talk about strategy in this organization

Reflect on the pattern in strategic discourse and answer the following questions:

- How is strategy talked about in this organization?
- What does it say about the organization?
- Which organizational members and activities are privileged by this discourse?
- What organizational members and activities are marginalized by this discourse?
- What is the relationship between discourse and practice? Are they consistent or are there gaps between what the organization 'says' and what it 'does'?
- Can you conceive of a way of talking about what this organization does and its successes and failures without using the term strategy?

to be more precise – talking up – a new strategy translates into organizational actions or reinvents new industries. In some regards, this is not a new question: Mintzberg[118] asks how can an organization transform itself simply through thinking up a new strategy.

The second, more theoretical, body of work[119] sees strategic discourse as a space where language and action constitute each other. Strategic plans, mission statements, academic papers, articles in *Fortune* or *The Economist*, strategy taskforces, as well as specific actions or practices, such as acquisitions, restructuring and selling in overseas markets, make strategy what it is. Similarly, the way in which research questions are posed, methodologies are selected and publishing conventions are imposed help to constitute strategy as a field of inquiry which, since there are interactions between academia and practice, also has implications for management practice. Consequently 'strategy' is a construction that serves to make sense of the world, and which is reproduced by a variety of texts and practices. We only know about strategy because we talk and write about it and because some activities get talked about as strategy whereas others do not.

The way we talk about strategy and categorize particular actions as strategic has political implications. The top-down conceptualization of strategy embodied in much of the literature helps to reproduce hierarchical relations and most views of strategic management, it has been argued, help to constitute a conservative political ideology centred on profit, managerial power and the reinforcement of existing capitalist relations.[120] Strategy's widespread acceptance and association with organizational performance also advantages those groups associated with it; while others, such as accountants and human resource managers, strive to make themselves more 'strategic'.[121] Within strategic discourse, some subjects – senior managers, academics, business journalists – have a clear mandate to speak and act, while other actors are invisible.[122]

In summary, the aggregation of actions by researchers and managers in their search for strategy, by attributing a meaning to particular events, has produced a phenomenon from which it has become difficult to escape. Strategy has become so well ingrained in business language that it is commonly accepted as a determinant of success and failure: whether by having a good strategy, a bad strategy, or no strategy at all. The term strategy is ever present – in hospitals, universities, governments as well as businesses.[123] Inkpen and Choudhury[124] argue that strategy is simply an artefact of research conventions. It says more about how academics theorize than how firms secure competitive advantage since strategies are simply assumed to exist. The walk – actions and practices – has been turned into strategic talk!

NOTES

(See Bibliography at the end of the book for full references)

1 Lyles, 1990
2 Whittington, 1993: 1
3 Chandler, 1962
4 Ansoff, 1965
5 Johnson, 1992
6 Whipp, 1996
7 Knights and Morgan, 1991
8 Whittington, 1993
9 See Foss, 1996 on the convergence between industrial organization and resource-based views of strategy; also Ghemawat, 1991.
10 Examples include Andrews, 1980; Christensen et al. 1982; Ansoff, 1984, 1988; see also Mintzberg, 1990b on the design school and 1994 on the planning school.
11 Webster et al. 1989
12 Barney, 1996
13 Porter, 1980, 1985, 1990
14 Rumelt, 1984; Rumelt et al. 1991; Barney, 1991; Grant, 1991
15 Schwenk, 1984; Huff, 1990; Reger and Huff, 1993
16 Quinn, 1978
17 Pettigrew, 1977
18 Mintzberg and Waters, 1985
19 Daft and Weick, 1984; Smircich and Stubbart, 1985.
20 Gioia and Chittipeddi, 1991; Weick, 1995
21 Orr, 1990; Weick and Westley, 1996.
22 Bennis and Nanus, 1985; Westley and Mintzberg, 1988, 1989
23 Meyer et al. 1993; Miller, 1996
24 Burns and Stalker, 1961
25 Miles and Snow, 1978
26 Other examples of configurational typologies include those of Mintzberg, 1983; Greenwood and Hinings, 1988.
27 Miller and Friesen, 1977, 1980, 1984
28 Bowman and Johnson, 1992
29 Spender, 1989; Johnson, 1992; Hardy, 1994
30 Waterman et al. 1980
31 Miller, 1993
32 Other writers who emphasize, explicitly or implicitly, the cultural alignment of strategic goals as a means of implementing strategy include Ouchi, 1981; Peters and Waterman, 1982; Barney, 1986; Lorsch, 1986; Johnson, 1992.
33 Miller, 1996: 510
34 Bourgeois, 1984; Whittington, 1993
35 Aldrich and Pfeffer, 1976; Hannan and Freeman, 1977
36 Whittington, 1993
37 Hofer, 1975; Bourgeois, 1984; Child, 1997
38 Williamson, 1975, 1985
39 DiMaggio and Powell, 1983
40 Meyer and Rowan, 1977
41 Abegglen and Stalk, 1985; Aoki, 1990; Clegg, 1990; see also Whittington, 1993: 32–5
42 For example, Child, 1997
43 See Roberts and Greenwood, 1997 on pre-conscious and post-conscious institutionalization; Tolbert and Zucker, 1996
44 For example, Whittington, 1993
45 Schotter, 1981; Langlois, 1986; Hodgson, 1988
46 Whitley, 1991
47 Whittington, 1993: 28–35
48 Whipp, 1996
49 Whittington, 1993
50 Whittington, 1993: 112–22
51 Chandler, 1962
52 Williamson, 1975
53 Donaldson, 1996
54 Also see the chapter on organizational structure.
55 Hall and Saias, 1980
56 Mintzberg, 1979
57 Hamilton and Biggard, 1988; see also Whitley, 1990; Whittington, 1993
58 Clegg, 1990
59 For example, Grant, 1991; see Whittington, 1993: chapter 4
60 Mintzberg, 1994
61 Mintzberg and Waters, 1982, 1985
62 Mintzberg, 1994
63 Hayes and Abernathy, 1980
64 For example, Pekar and Abraham, 1995
65 See Mintzberg, 1994: chapter 3; Whittington, 1993: chapter 4
66 Langley, 1988, 1991
67 Horowitz, 1980
68 Whipp, 1996
69 Mintzberg, 1994
70 For example, Taylor, 1995; Graetz, 1996; Gratton, 1996
71 Hambrick and Mason, 1984
72 Waldersee and Sheather, 1996
73 Brodwin and Bourgeois, 1984
74 Westley, 1990
75 Daft and Weick, 1984
76 Shrivastava, 1986: 369
77 Floyd and Wooldridge, 1992; Westley 1990
78 Mintzberg, 1987
79 Whittington, 1993
80 See the leadership chapter.

81 Mintzberg and Waters, 1985
82 Quinn, 1980; Pettigrew, 1985
83 Miller, 1982
84 Greiner, 1972
85 Zan, 1990
86 Mintzberg, 1994
87 Prahalad and Hamel, 1994; see also Eccles and Nohria, 1993
88 Hamel and Prahalad, 1989, 1993, 1994
89 See chapter on organizational learning.
90 Zabriskie and Huellmantel, 1991; Bates and Dillard, 1993; Hendry et al. 1994; Lavers, 1996
91 Lavers, 1996: 1
92 Hamel and Prahalad, 1989: 64
93 Hamel and Prahalad, 1994: 111
94 Wernerfelt, 1984; Barney, 1991; Collis, 1991; Leonard-Barton, 1992; Dougherty, 1995
95 Marino, 1996
96 Stalk et al. 1992
97 Henderson and Cockburn, 1994
98 Hamel and Prahalad, 1993
99 Hamel and Prahalad, 1993
100 Bresser and Harl, 1986
101 See chapter on organizational structure.
102 Eccles and Nohria, 1993
103 Dutton and Dukerich, 1991; Dutton and Penner, 1993
104 Johnson, 1987; Hinings and Greenwood, 1988
105 Johnson, 1987
106 Marino, 1996
107 Dougherty, 1995
108 Miller, 1990
109 See chapter on organizational structure.
110 Lubatkin and Lane, 1996
111 Parker, 1996
112 Bartlett and Ghoshal, 1989
113 Wortzel, 1991
114 Prahalad and Hamel, 1994
115 Eccles and Nohria, 1993: 88
116 Eccles and Nohria, 1993: chapter 5
117 Hardy et al. 1998
118 Mintzberg, 1994: 281
119 Knights and Morgan, 1991; Whipp, 1996; Barry and Elmes, 1997
120 Shrivastava, 1986
121 Knights and Morgan, 1991
122 See people chapter.
123 Whittington, 1993; Whipp, 1996
124 Inkpen and Choudhury, 1995

7 MANAGING CHANGE

Is the Soft Stuff Really the Hard Stuff?

Organizational change is said to be as inevitable as birth, death and taxes.[1] It is a fundamental part of organizational life and represents a mainstream field within management studies (see Supplementary Reading box). Most of the other topics covered in this book assume the need for organizational change in one form or another. For example, to gain competitive advantage managers are encouraged to engage in 'strategic change'.[2] To respond to the hypercompetitive business environment, managers are told to change their organizational structures. To enhance organizational performance, managers have been told to change organizational cultures. This emphasis on change has led some commentators to suggest that organizations today 'are immersed in a virtual cyclone of change'.[3] In fact, one US study claimed that 84 per cent of US firms were conducting a major change programme.[4]

CHANGE: SUPPLEMENTARY READING

- Amburgey, T.L., Kelly, D. and Barnett, W. (1993) 'Resetting the clock: the dynamics of organizational change and failure', *Administrative Science Quarterly*, 38: 51–73.

- Argyris, C. (1993) *Knowledge for Action: A Guide to Overcoming Barriers to Organizational Change*. San Francisco: Jossey-Bass.

- Bunker, B.B. and Alban, B.T. (1996) *Large Group Interventions: Engaging the Whole System for Rapid Change*. San Francisco: Jossey-Bass.

- Burke, W.W. (1995) 'Organization change: what we know, what we need to know', *Journal of Management Inquiry*, 4 (2): 158–71.

- Colby, W.D. (1996) 'The five great management myths', *Business Quarterly*, 61 (2): 93–5.

- Cummings, T.G. and Worley, C.G. (1993) *Organization Development and Change*, 5th edn. Minneapolis/St. Paul: West.

- Ford, J.D. and Ford, L.W. (1995) 'The role of conversations in producing intentional change in organizations', *Academy of Management Review*, 20 (3): 541–70.

- French, W.L. and Bell, C.H. (1995) *Organization Development: Behavioral Science Interventions for Organization Improvement*. Englewood Cliffs, NJ: Prentice-Hall.

- Greenwood, R. and Hinings, C.R. (1993) 'Understanding strategic change: the contribution of archetypes', *Academy of Management Journal*, 36 (5): 1052–81.

- Jick, T.D. (1995) 'Accelerating change for competitive advantage', *Organizational Dynamics*, 24 (1): 77–82.

- Kotter, J.P. (1996) *Leading Change*. Boston, MA: Harvard Business School Press.

- Marshak, R.J. (1993) 'Managing the metaphors of change', *Organizational Dynamics*, 22 (1): 44–56.

- Van de Ven, A.H. and Poole, M.S. (1995) 'Explaining development and change in organizations', *Academy of Management Review*, 20 (3): 510–40.

- Vince, R. and Broussine, M. (1996) 'Paradox, defense and attachment: accessing and working with emotions and relations underlying organizational change', *Organization Studies*, 17 (1): 1–21.

The aim of this chapter is not to provide a comprehensive review of change models. Rather, we wish to identify contemporary debates that traverse the change literature. While not all of these debates are new, they continue to influence research and practice concerning the management of organizational change. We first outline a sample of contemporary change models that exist in the literature and discuss some of the key debates associated with them. Second, we examine the impact of reframing on change processes. Third, we explore theoretical explanations of organizational change – why change occurs in organizations. Fourth, we examine the issue of resistance to change and some of the solutions that have been proposed to overcome it. Finally, we examine some of the reasons why, despite such a prodigious literature, many organizational change programmes fail, pointing out that it's the soft stuff – the people side of change – that is often the hardest to get right.

GET WITH THE PROGRAMME: CONTEMPORARY CHANGE MODELS

Organizational change has attracted considerable attention by both academics and practitioners. The result is a bewildering array of change models to confront the manager. They can select from a 29-step model,[5] a 15-point 'manifesto',[6] a 13-point plan,[7] and a number of 6-step approaches.[8] In this section, we first explore the traditional model of change developed by Kurt

Lewin and some of the debates that have arisen around it. We then investigate some of the debates associated with the nature and the scale of organizational change. Finally, we examine the 'improvisational' model of change.

Is it chilly out there?

Despite the apparent variety, many change models continue to adhere to the logic developed by Kurt Lewin[9] in his 1947 classic three-phase change model. This entails *unfreezing* the way the organization currently operates, *changing* the organization in a specific direction, and then *refreezing* these changes and the associated behaviours into the operations of the organization. While other writers expanded the number of phases and embellished it in other ways,[10] this logic remains embedded in many change models.[11]

This model is particularly influential in what is known as the organization development (OD) approach to change. While there are a variety of definitions of the OD approach,[12] Cummings and Worley[13] define it as 'a system-wide application of behavioural science knowledge to the planned development and reinforcement of organizational strategies, structures, and processes for improving an organization's effectiveness'. It incorporates both traditional and contemporary views in seeing change as consisting of a number of planned stages or phases. As Burke, a prominent OD writer recently suggested, this phased approach to change 'fit my experience and probably yours as well'.[14]

But not all change writers are so enamoured of Lewin's simple unfreezing-changing-refreezing model. Kanter et al. argue that this 'quaintly linear and static conception – the organization as ice cube – is so wildly inappropriate that it is difficult to see why it has not only survived but prospered, except for one thing. It offers managers a very straightforward way of planning their actions, by simplifying an extraordinarily complex process into a child's formula'.[15] The view of these authors is that organizations are never static but, rather, are 'fluid entities with many "personalities"'. Change stages 'overlap and interpenetrate one another in important ways', while change is 'ubiquitous and multidirectional'. Organizations are 'bundles of activity'[16] which are in a constant state of motion and consist of multiple stakeholders and interest groups. For these writers, change is often in the eye of the beholder. Announcements of change often merely formalize activities that have already been in train for some time, rather than indicate fundamentally new actions.

Consequently, a variety of alternatives to the Lewinian approach have been proffered. The models in Table 7.1 each present a planned approach to producing organizational change. The work of these writers is distinguished from that of Lewin, either by differing over the number and nature of individual phases, by presenting them as less linear and more iterative, by recognizing the need to adapt them to particular situations, or by changing and omitting particular phases.[17] These models also address, to varying degrees, issues associated with organizational politics[18] or 'turf barriers',

TABLE 7.1 *Contemporary change models*

Kanter et al. 1992: The Ten Commandments	Kotter, 1996: The eight-stage process of creating major change	Cummings and Worley, 1993: Effective change management	Ghoshal and Bartlett, 1996: Blueprint for corporate renewal	Morris and Raben, 1992: Large-scale change
• Analyse the organisation and its need for change	• Establishing a sense of urgency	• Motivating change	• Simplification	• Surface dissatisfaction with the present state
• Create a shared vision and common direction	• Creating the guiding coalition	• Creating a vision	• Building front-line initiative	• Promote participation in change
• Separate from the past	• Developing a vision and strategy	• Developing political support	• Building discipline	• Give rewards for supporting change
• Create a sense of urgency	• Communicating the change vision	• Managing the transition	• Embedding support	• Provide time and opportunity to disengage from the present state
• Support a strong leader role	• Empowering broad-based action	• Sustaining momentum	• Integration	• Develop and communicate a clear image of the future
• Line up political sponsorship	• Generating short-term wins		• Realigning cross-unit relationships	• Use multiple/consistent leverage points
• Craft an implementation plan	• Consolidating gains and producing more change		• Creating stretch	• Develop organizational arrangements for the transition
• Develop enabling structures	• Anchoring new approaches in the culture		• Developing trust	• Build in feedback mechanisms
• Communicate, involve people and be honest			• Regeneration	• Assure the support of key power groups
• Reinforce and institutionalize change			• Ensuring continuous learning	• Use leader behaviour to generate energy in support of change
			• Integrating the contextual frame	• Use symbols and language
			• Maintaining a dynamic imbalance	• Build in stability
			• Leading the renewal process	

Sources: Adapted from Kanter et al. 1992: 383; Kotter, 1996: 21; Cummings and Worley, 1993; Ghoshal and Bartlett, 1996; Morris and Raben, 1995: 64

which the traditional OD approach has tended to avoid.[19] This can be seen in Morris and Raben's last four steps,[20] in Step 5 of Kotter's model, Step 6 in Kanter et al. and Step 3 in Cummings and Worley. (See Exercise 7.1.)

Some of these models try to redress the mechanical nature of the Lewinian model. For example, Kanter et al. point out that the meaning associated with each step may vary, depending on who is interpreting it: change strategists, who identify the need for change; change implementers, who make the change happen; or change recipients, on whom the change impacts. While strategists may be easily convinced of the need for change, change implementers may be disheartened by the fact that they have not yet finished implementing the last change programme, and change recipients view it as yet another confusing direction from the top.[21] Hence, Kanter et al. are explicit in pointing out how different interest groups in organizations will lead to multiple interpretations of change steps which will affect how each change step is received within the organization.

Despite these embellishments, it is clear that the underlying logic of the Lewinian model is retained: change is viewed as consisting of different phases and most of the models contain steps that look very much like unfreezing and refreezing. In addition, most of these writers advocate the utilization of all the steps in their models, Kotter maintains that successful change 'of any magnitude goes through all eight stages, usually in the sequence shown'.[22] Similarly, Ghoshal and Bartlett[23] argue in favour of change occurring through 'carefully phased or sequenced processes'. Even Kanter et al. with the use of the ten 'commandments' of change, indicate that it is an unwise manager who chooses to ignore one of the steps.

EXERCISE 7.1 SO, HOW DID IT GO?

Reflect on an organizational change with which you are familiar, either from experience or from the business literature, and answer the following questions:

- Which of the steps described in the various models in Table 7.1 were implemented?
- Describe how the steps were implemented – what actions and decisions were taken and by whom?
- Does one particular model describe the change or was it a combination of steps from different models?
- Which steps were most important for successful change?
- Which steps were associated with problems or failure?
- What steps would you put together to create your own 'planned change model'?
- What, if anything is missing from these models?

An interesting criticism of the Lewinian model comes from Marshak who points out that Lewin's model is very much rooted in North American assumptions of change, which are quite different from other cultures. He compares the assumptions of the Lewinian OD model with the assumptions behind a Confucian/East Asian model. In the Lewinian model, change is linear, progressive, destination oriented, based on disequilibrium, planned and managed by people intent on achieving goals, and separate from what is 'normal'. In the Confucian model, change is cyclical, processional, journey oriented, associated with equilibrium, managed in a way which is designed to create universal harmony, and seen as normal as the universe is treated as dynamic and in a constant state of flux.[24] So, even if the Lewinian model is appropriate to North American organizations, which others now dispute, it may not be appropriate to organizational change in other countries and cultures.

In summary, traditional OD approaches to change, despite acknowledging that planned organization change is 'messy and never as clear as we have written in our books and articles',[25] remain wedded to the Lewinian model. Critics of that model have introduced new ideas concerning power, fluidity, circularity and multiplicity but remain committed to a logic of phased change, albeit different phases from Lewin's. Other observers point out the cultural assumptions embedded in Lewin's model that may limit its use in other geographic and cultural locations.

How much do you want and when do you want it?

The scale of change is another issue relevant to understanding differences in change models. Many OD change models tend to focus on incremental change, rather than on sudden transformational or revolutionary organizational changes. Some writers explicitly argue against the continual implementation of transformational change. Kilcourse[26] views the continuing attempts of managers to implement transformational change as a 'trap' enslaving them to the current management fashion, an issue which we will examine in more detail below. He maintains that managers should keep change programmes small, a position shared by other writers. Thus Weick[27] maintains that a 'small wins' approach is best as it can uncover new opportunities and create momentum for other wins. In this way, 'the real power of small wins as a strategy for social change comes in the capacity to gather and label retrospectively a series of relatively innocuous small wins into a bigger "package" that would have been too threatening to be prospectively adopted'.[28]

Other writers not only focus on the need for transformational change, but also advocate speeding it up. Jick[29] points out that the standard textbook time for transformational change often involves a five- to seven-year time frame but, typically, executives want to achieve change in around a year. To speed up the process he suggests a change model composed of three 'change accelerators'. The first accelerates people's understanding of the need for change and endeavours to engage, early on, their commitment to a change process through targeted education and training processes. The second accelerates change through modelling and leading change behaviour. The third accelerates change by keeping the momentum of change going through 'spotlight' slogans and constant customer involvement. Similarly, Bunker and Alban[30] outline a range of accelerating techniques including the search conference, future search, real time strategic change, ICA strategic planning process, conference model, real time work design, fast cycle full participation work systems design, participative work design, simu-real, work-out and open space technology. Such techniques typically entail meeting for three or more days and, unlike more micro-OD techniques,[31] can include up to 2000 participants, depending on the technique.

According to authors such as Dunphy and Stace,[32] the scale of organizational change may vary and, in so doing, require differences in the style of change management. They identify four types of change (Table 7.2). Participative evolution and charismatic transformation both warrant a collaborative and consultative style of change management akin to the approach advocated by many OD models. Forced evolution and dictatorial transformation require a directive and coercive change management style. So, whereas the models presented in Table 7.1 tended, to varying degrees, to be based on the logic of the 'one-best way' of conducting change, the Dunphy and Stace model entails a contingency approach which assumes that the best change technique will depend upon the type of change being undertaken.

Nadler and Tushman also present a contingency approach when they argue that successful change management strategies and techniques will depend upon the type of change that is being implemented. They identify two types of organizational change. *Incremental* changes occur during periods of relative stability and 'are aimed at continuing to improve the fit among the components of the organization'. *Discontinuous* changes occur where the 'demands of a radically changing environment require equally radical changes in the organization'.[33] The authors argue that these changes are affected by time – whether they are implemented in anticipation of the need for change, or whether they are reactive, i.e. managers are forced into responding to pressures for change. On this basis, they identify four change

TABLE 7.2   *Dunphy and Stace's model of change*

Type 1	Participative evolution: involves fine tuning or incremental adjustment of the organization
Type 2	Charismatic transformational change: involves major change in a situation where people recognize the need for change and 'buy into' the charismatic vision of the CEO
Type 3	Forced evolution: even incremental change is resisted within the organization
Type 4	Dictatorial transformation: top-down transformational change, usually in situations where the luxury of time for employee involvement in decision-making is deemed to be unavailable

Source: Dunphy and Stace, 1990

types. *Tuning* occurs when an organization makes incremental changes in anticipation of future change events. *Adaptation* occurs when an organization makes incremental changes in reaction to changes in the external environment. *Reorientation* occurs when an organization makes radical or discontinuous changes in anticipation of future environmental changes. *Re-creation* occurs when an organization makes radical changes in its core values in reacting to environmental changes. They argue that each of these types of change requires different types of change management techniques.[34]

Underlying both these models is the assumption that the scale and nature of change has an important effect on the type of change management techniques that should be employed. Huy[35] provides a more sophisticated contingency approach in what he calls 'navigation' styles (Table 7.3), when he combines the scale of change (from general to specific) and the nature of change (whether it is viewed as an objective or instrumental activity or as social, subjective affair) with two other factors. They include views of knowledge (objective and abstract or interpretive, embedded and tacit) and the distribution of power in the organization (from unitary to pluralist). From this, he suggests that a *designing* style is best suited to formal, structural change in organizations where change agents have both power and knowledge and the pressure to change is high. A *converting* style suits when the aim is to change values and norms, change agents are knowledgeable and the change process is gradual. *Programming* also addresses work processes in a gradual process and suits change agents who lack the necessary tacit knowledge but have moderate power. An *animating* style works best with specific changes in work processes, where change agents have the necessary tacit knowledge, power is divided and the change process is gradual. The problem, however, is that as the sophistication of the model increases to accommodate more contingencies, the number of possible permutations increases, leaving the manager more and more confused (Exercise 7.2).

EXERCISE 7.2 NICE CHANGE, SHAME ABOUT THE STYLE!

Reflect on an organizational change with which you are familiar, either from experience or from the business literature. Consult Tables 7.2 and 7.3 and answer the following questions:

- What was the nature of change, e.g. scale, scope, speed of change, reactive, proactive, structural, cultural, work processes?
- What was the style used by management to bring it about?
- What are your observations? Did the management style suit the type of change being pursued? Should management have used a different style? Should the type or focus of change have been different?

TABLE 7.3 *Change navigation styles*

	Designing style	Converting style	Programming style	Animating style
View of change	Wide-scale, structural change based on objective, codified, explicit knowledge	Wide-scale, cultural change based on interpretive, tacit practical knowledge	Specific structural change based on objective, codified, explicit knowledge	Specific cultural change based on interpretive, tacit practical knowledge
Target	Structure	Beliefs and values	Tasks	Relationships
Power distribution	Unitary power distribution	Pluralist power distribution	Unitary power distribution	Pluralist power distribution
Diagnostic model	Strategic analysis of environmental factors	Analysis and surfacing of individuals erroneous assumptions	Analysis of work processes and redesign	Socio-technical systems analysis and employee involvement in redesign
Intervention theory	Competitive analysis, strategic planning to restructure	Exposing shared tacit assumptions, theories in use to build culture	Work process redesign, re-engineering to change specific tasks	Participative action research, socio-technical redesign to build teams
Goals	An efficient, effective organization	A community of responsible, mindful individuals	Well-designed and efficient work systems	A democratic community of semi-autonomous workgroups
Change agent	Strategy implementor who acts as a commander	Process consultant who acts as psychologist to enhance cognitive skills	Systems, process analyst who acts as teacher and expert	Technical expert in work design who acts as co-ordinator, facilitator and role model
Change tactics	Power, coercive	Normative, re-educative	Empirical, rational	Empirical, normative

Source: Adapted from Huy, 1998

Can we improvise?

All models above embrace the idea of *planning* for change to a greater or lesser extent. A relatively new entrant to the change literature, on the other hand, takes a more spontaneous approach. Orlikowski and Hofman outline an improvisational model for managing the introduction of technological change into organizations. They assume that change is not an event but rather an ongoing process and that it is not possible to anticipate all the consequences of the change process. They use the metaphor of a jazz band:

> While members of a jazz band, unlike members of a symphony orchestra, do not decide in advance exactly what notes each is going to play, they do decide ahead of time what musical composition will form the basis of their performance. Once

the performance begins, each player is free to explore and innovate, departing from the original composition. Yet the performance works because all members are playing within the same rhythmic structure and have a shared understanding of the rules of this musical genre.[36]

This model assumes that technological change occurs through the evolution of an iterative series of steps which produce outcomes that management could not have predicted at the start. In this model, managers become nurturers and facilitators of the change process. The authors acknowledge,[37] however, some limitations to their model. First, it is most appropriate to 'open-ended, customizable technologies or for complex, unprecedented change'. Second, 'some people are incapable of playing jazz'. In other words, some people will not have the skills or the inclinations to participate in such an unplanned, open-ended approach to change. Third, this model remains relatively untested and, like the early OD approaches, it could be argued that it downplays the impact of differing interests and politics associated with change. People may be capable of 'playing jazz', but not willing to do so because it is not in their interests to engage in a particular change programme. Nevertheless, this approach does serve as an alternative to planned approaches to change which, as Vince and Broussine[38] argue, 'over-emphasize the rational and consequently do not take into account the complexity, ambiguity and paradox acknowledged to be an integral part of organization'.

REFRAMING THE PICTURE

The use of reframing to understand change goes back over twenty years to psychiatric writings. Watzlawick et al. argued that reframing changes 'the conceptual and/or emotional setting or viewpoints in relation to which a situation is experienced' and places it in another frame. It is based on three assumptions. First, it assumes that our perception of the world is based upon mental constructs. Second, it assumes that these constructs define our reality. Third, it assumes that reframing is an effective change tool since once an alternative frame is realized, it is difficult to 'go back to the trap and the anguish of a former view of "reality" '.[39] Recent organizational change writings have picked up these ideas and used them to develop a diagnostic tool for effective change management and to explore the change process. This work has also engendered a debate concerning whether deframing, rather than simply reframing, is the key to strategic change.

Frame breaking change requires organizational members to change their schema or current mode of thinking. It takes individuals beyond first order change – a series of incremental adjustments that do not alter fundamental understandings about how the organization should operate – into second order change, which entails the establishment of a new schema or a new way of operating. (Third order change occurs, not when one schema is swapped for another, but when organizational members transcend schemata by becoming aware of how they enable and restrict organizational choices and influence understandings and behaviours.[40] It is probably fair to say that most changes are either first or second order changes.) Consequently, many writers are interested, not so much in 'frame bending' changes that occur within the dominant organizational 'frame' but in discontinuous or transformational change, which involves 'frame breaking'.[41] Frame breaking change is similar to what Old refers to as the need, when engaged in transformational change, to address 'deep structure-underlying patterns', that is the 'deep reflexive patterns of thinking and action',[42] if the change is to be successful.

The potential for reframing is influenced by the degree of commitment to existing frames. Greenwood and Hinings[43] suggest that knowledge of organizational members' commitment to current schemata or frames is 'a key potential dynamic of change' and necessary for understanding the receptivity of organizational members to engage in frame breaking changes. They argue that there are different 'archetypes' of change, that is, different patterns of achieving change which depend upon the commitment of organizational members to prevailing frames or schemata. They identify four patterns of commitment. First, a status quo commitment involves a widespread commitment to an existing interpretive schema. Second, a reformative commitment indicates a widespread commitment to an alternative interpretive schema. Third, a competitive commitment revolves around a substantial commitment to two or more interpretive schemata. Fourth, an indifferent commitment represents low commitment to prevailing and alternative interpretive schemata. The greater the reformative commitment of organizational members, the easier it should be to introduce frame breaking changes.

A four by four?

Bolman and Deal argue that frames are 'both windows on the world and lenses that bring the world into focus. Frames filter out some things while allowing others to pass through easily. Frames help us order experience and decide what to do. Every manager, consultant, or policymaker relies on a personal frame or image to gather information, make judgements, and determine how best to get things done'.[44] They suggest that four frames dominate understandings of organizations: a structural frame, a human resource or people frame, a power or political frame and a cultural or symbolic frame. Managers who see the organizational world in structural terms focus on concepts such as rules, roles, goals and policies. Those with a human resource approach focus on needs, skills and relationships. Organizational members with a political approach tend to identify power, conflict and competition. Finally, those with a symbolic approach focus on meanings, rituals, culture and stories.

These authors argue that managers who engage in single frame thinking will identify only a limited number of solutions to organizational problems because they lack the ability to 'reframe' the situation. In other words, they are unable to see it in a new light and identify alternative actions and approaches. Effective change managers are multi-frame thinkers who are able to reframe organizational situations and identify change actions and options. As indicated in Table 7.4, each frame alerts change managers to different facets of organizational change, and the use of all frames is argued to create more effective change outcomes. However, it might be asked why these particular frames form the basis of effective change. Bolman and Deal recognize that there may be other frames available to participants, which are not recognized or employed but which may be equally useful to organizational change. For this reason they challenge change agents to identify whether a 'fifth' frame may also dominate particular organizational settings (Exercise 7.3).

TABLE 7.4   *Reframing organizational change*

Frame	Change barriers	Strategic options
Human resource	Fear, uncertainty, incompetence	Counselling, skill development, involvement in change decisions
Structural	Loss of goals, direction and clarity	Communicating new goals and directions; renegotiating roles and responsibilities
Political	Conflict, confrontation, lack of empowerment	Renegotiating alliances, establishing new coalitions
Symbolic	Past traditions and meanings	Establish transition processes to let go of the past; embracing the future

Source: Adapted from Bolman and Deal, 1997: 321

EXERCISE 7.3 FRAMES AWAY!

Reflect on an organizational change with which you are familiar, either from experience or from the business literature, and apply each of the four frames to the change:

- Compile a list of organizational characteristics you would focus on for each frame.
- Identify the change barriers associated with each frame and see whether they played a part in the change.
- Explain how you would overcome these barriers for each of the four frames by identifying explicit actions you would take.
- Integrate your analysis by providing an action plan for each frame.
- Explain how the use of the four frames together contributes to managing change.
- Are there any other frames that could be used?

Frame by frame?

Reger et al.[45] argue that managers use cognitive schemata or frames to make sense of their organizational world and convey to subordinates their interpretations through sensemaking and sensegiving processes. They suggest that transformational change programmes such as total quality management (TQM), which require a major paradigm shift, can fail because of the disjuncture between the current cognitive frames and those required for the full implementation of TQM. Instead, they propose that managers reframe in stages in order to narrow the gap between current perceptions and desired future states. Managers should establish 'tectonic' changes – ones that shake up the organization into perceiving the need for change, but do not overwhelm it into thinking that the change needed is unobtainable.

There are, however, a number of criticisms of this approach. First, it neglects the arguments of Greenwood and Hinings, noted above, that there may be varying degrees of commitment in the organization to the current frame which will affect the ability of change managers to introduce new frames. Second, it adopts a unitarist and instrumental view of change that others have criticized.[46] Third, it is doubtful that reframing can be applied in such a mechanical and controlled fashion.

Taking the frame away?

Dunbar et al. argue that we need to 'deframe' in order to approach change. This 'does not imply that we must obliterate all previous ways of thinking. That is not possible. What it does imply is the need for an ability to step back from a reliance on the particular frames we currently rely on'.[47] For example, we often attribute success to ourselves and attribute failures to the actions of others. This stops us from seeing how external forces may have contributed to 'success and, conversely, how our own actions contributed to failure'. 'Discrediting' processes, which get us to reverse such assumptions, are 'likely to open up new possibilities for change'.[48] They suggest that Sun Microsystems is an example of an organization that 'deframed' to recognize change possibilities in the computing industry. By employing an open systems approach they made their computing technology freely available to other competitors in the industry. They 'deframed' by moving away from a view that revenues should be generated by getting customers to commit to exclusive computing hardware systems, to a view that revenues could be generated from customers who saw a benefit in being able to access multiple computing systems.

Porac and Rosa take issue with this view, noting that deframing and opening up managers to multiple frames does not necessarily enhance business outcomes. They argue that narrow 'well-learned frames are inherently *enabling* because they channel behaviour in directions that are consistent with a firm's knowledge and abilities . . . it is interpretive narrow-mindedness that provides the clarity of purpose that cuts through market ambiguities and builds a solid epistemic foundation for action'.[49]

They suggest that a firm's success is associated with their ability to impose such frames onto their environment. In response, Dunbar et al.[50] agree that firms should attempt to shape their environments, but that in times of rapid change, narrow-framed thinking rooted in past practices acts as a constraint on future possibilities.

Reframing has become a popular approach to envisage new possibilities for organizational change. Not unlike Morgan's metaphors,[51] it promises new ways of seeing. A fundamental debate plagues this approach, however, concerning the distinction between deframing and the more prosaic matter of re-examining assumptions. If deframing – and reframing – are different in that they represent mental constructs that fundamentally shape the way in which we view and experience the world, how can they be swapped and abandoned at will, and what are the implications of an individual being left frameless? If, on the other hand, frames are like any other reflective technique[52] which help us to see different aspects of a problem and its solution, are they not simply a matter of old wine in new bottles – or maybe old pictures in new frames?

BUT *WHY* DO ORGANIZATIONS CHANGE?

In this section we discuss some of the different ways that writers use to explain why change occurs. Two explanations of organizational change – life cycle and population ecology – use biological analogies. Life cycle theory is the most common perspective used to explain organization change. It presents it as an inevitable passage from birth, through growth, to death. Population ecology and evolutionary approaches have a similar deterministic orientation but focus on populations of organizations and how they change over time, rather than individual organizations.[53] They draw on notions of competitive survival in which 'change proceeds through a continuous cycle of variation, selection, and retention'.[54] Dialectical theory is based on the notion of opposition and conflict leading to change. In other words, opposing forces clash, changing the status quo, when one side gains sufficient ascendancy or power.

All three perspectives view organizational change as a form of 'punctuated equilibrium', a dominant model in change and strategy literatures.[55] Organizations go through periods of stability, punctuated by organizational upheavals as new stages are reached or new environmental pressures are experienced.[56] Brown and Eisenhardt argue, however, that punctuated equilibrium does not describe the experiences of companies such as Sears, Wal-Mart, 3M, Hewlett-Packard and Gillette which experienced continuous change. Successful managers in such companies should, therefore, link 'products together over time through rhythmic transition processes from present projects to future ones, creating a relentless pace of change'.[57] Van de Ven and Poole[58] argue that punctuated equilibrium and continuous change may serve as complementary explanations, depending on whether single or multiple organizations are the focus, and the extent to which the change is prescribed.[59]

More recently, new explanations have been introduced that modify and challenge these perspectives. We examine three of them: trilectics, chaos theory and neo-institutional theory.

From dialectics to trialectics

Nielsen suggests that there are five different versions of dialectic change. In *iteration* ideas, not people, are in conflict. *Transformation* means that ideas, actors and external worlds are changed simultaneously. *Upbuilding* involves a clash of local traditions and external 'macro' worlds. *Action-science* revolves around experimentation to improve and modify advocated actions. In *strategic dialectical inquiry*, different groups hold different plans which, through critique, are synthesized into new plans.[60] Regardless of such fine distinctions, Mason points out that dialectic change is based on a premise that contradiction leads to a mediated resolution. 'There are at least two parties involved (let's call them a protagonist and an antagonist) and there is some difference between them that communication, exchange, or some other activity will help resolve.'[61]

Ford and Ford move beyond a dialectical view of change to 'trialectics'. Whereas dialectic change occurs through the 'opposition' of differing perspectives or events, trialectic change emerges through 'attraction'. Instead of being pushed, pressured or opposed, change occurs through individuals being 'pulled, drawn toward, or attracted to different possibilities'. Trialectical change involves establishing the desired result, active and attractive forces, and processes that can 'engage both the active and attractive forces to produce the desired result'.[62] However, Carini et al.[63] suggest that Ford and Ford present an overly simplistic view of dialectics, in which the idea of conflict in change processes is presented as unequivocally 'bad'. Moreover, there is no clear-cut distinction between dialectics and trialectics, nor is there any convincing argument that trialectics is viable. Little in the way of evidence has been brought to bear on either side of this debate and it would appear that both theoretical and practical benefits of trialectical change have yet to be realized.

Chaos theory

Building upon a critique of the life cycle theory,[64] chaos theory has emerged as a new contender for explaining organizational change. Dubinskas suggests that there are a number of flaws with the life cycle view of transformational change. First, 'sudden infant death syndrome is far more common than smooth growth to maturity in businesses, and sudden cardiac arrest strikes firms in their prime as well as in old age'. Second, it relies on a simplistic biological view of evolution that differs from biological data. 'In nature, species rise and decline sporadically, often with radical and sudden population changes. Some species explode in variety, then contract to extinction. Still others survive virtually unchanged for eons.' Third, it assumes that external forces produce change as opposed to change being self-generated. Fourth, it assumes that change occurs along a simple linear trajectory, rather than through multiple paths or paths in which different stages are skipped.[65]

Proponents of chaos theory argue that it is best suited to explaining transformational change. It sees organizations as being 'in constant flux, with periods of temporary stability. Considering stability as the unusual case should force an examination of those influences at the edge of stability which are likely to precipitate movement into chaos'.[66] It explores the chaotic patterns in organizational systems that are heavily context dependent. The context of behaviour is all-important. 'Tiny differences in alignment of conditions occasion large differences in outcomes. Every context thus becomes very important for understanding the dynamics of what will happen. Yet the bounds of the system's outcomes are knowable.'[67] Consequently, contingency theories of organizational change are inadequate because in abstracting static relations among structure, technology and environments, they fail to consider context-specific dimensions.

The chaotic system has thus become a new metaphor for understanding transformational change and self-organizing.[68] However, it is important to note that, like any metaphor, chaos theory both illuminates and hides different features of change. What is left unexplained in chaos is why a focus on 'instability' should be any more revealing than a focus on 'stability' in explaining change. A second problem concerns the organizational application of complex models from other disciplines. Evolutionary theory has been criticized for failing to keep up with developments in the biological sciences. Given that chaos theory derives from theoretical mathematics, then simplistic management applications, without a corresponding awareness of the mathematical nuances and complexities, appear highly likely.

Neo-institutional theory and management fashion

Recent writings acknowledge that 'institutional theory is not usually regarded as a theory of organizational change, but as usually an explanation of the similarity ("isomorphism") and stability of organizational arrangements in a given population or field of organizations'.[69] Greenwood and Hinings accept that 'neo-institutional theory is weak in analysing the *internal* dynamics of organizational change. As a consequence, the theory is silent on why some organizations adopt radical changes whereas others do not, despite experiencing the same institutional pressures'. Consequently, these authors provide a framework for understanding strategic change by studying the interaction between external influences and internal organizational dynamics. They suggest that radical change will vary depending on how tightly coupled are organizations in their sectors, and how insulated they are from changes occurring elsewhere. At the same time, radical change also depends upon the internal dynamics of organizations, specifically, the 'interests, values, power dependencies, and capacity for action'[70] that exist in an organization.

Abrahamson draws on institutional theory when he argues that one way of understanding change is through a conception of managerial fashion and fads. Whereas aesthetic fashions take hold when they are deemed beautiful and modern, fashionable management techniques are those that appear rational, i.e. they are efficient means to achieve important ends, and progressive, i.e. they are seen as new and improved relative to older management techniques.[71] When this occurs, managers face pressures to adopt such techniques as ways of dealing with technical and environmental pressures for change. Similarly 'root' metaphors emerge in popular management writings, helping to establish the legitimacy of such management practices and place pressure on managers to adopt them.[72] As a result, change techniques proliferate, as organizational change becomes fashionable. One study identified fifty-five new management techniques in use in 1996; while another study of twenty-five management fads between 1990 and 1994 found that, on average, companies experimented with twelve of them.[73]

In summary, theoretical explanations of *why* organizations change are much like change models and techniques which suggest *how* organizations should change – subject to the whims of fashion. Over the last forty years, organization theory has swung like a pendulum on these issues.[74] In the 1950s and 1960s, writers such as Selznick[75] and March and Simon[76] saw the organization as an organism, in which senior managers were responsible for adapting it to a variety of political, economic and social pressures. Thompson[77] and Lawrence and Lorsch[78] used an open systems approach to develop this further by advocating change to adapt organization structures to the external environment. In both cases, the room for manoeuvre was limited since change was dictated largely by external pressures. Weick's[79] view of organizations 'enacting' their environments increased the role of senior management in the change process since their task was to mould particular environments through the use of effective strategic choices.[80] In the 1980s and 1990s, organization theory returned to a more deterministic view of how organization change occurs. Population ecology and evolutionary theory, with an emphasis on environmental selection, accorded managers little control over the direction and speed of change. Similarly, new institutionalism theories emphasize normative and coercive pressures emanating from the external environment. Failure to heed such pressures spells the death of the organization. According to this logic, managers are largely puppets of external pressures. However, recent change literature is much enamoured of transformational change orchestrated by visionary leaders. And so the pendulum swings again (Exercise 7.4).

PIÈCE DE RÉSISTANCE

A common topic in the change literature is dealing with resistance to change. Ironically, the current fascination with change and the availability of change techniques may well be part of the problem. As one manager

---

EXERCISE 7.4 YOUR BEST SHOT!

Select one of the following theories as it has been applied to organizational change:

- Life cycle
- Population ecology
- Dialectics
- Trialectics
- Chaos theory
- Neo-institutional theory
- Managerial fad and fashion

Carry out the following exercises:

- Defend the theory on the grounds that it presents a good explanation for explaining why organizational change occurs.
- Now critique it – what are its shortcomings?
- Select another theory and carry out the last two steps.
- Reflect back upon the two theories you examined. What general lessons can be drawn in terms of why managers are confronted with the need to change organizations?

---

complained, 'I've been transformed, reengineered and tinkered with so many times I don't know what we are doing any more.'[81] Resistance to change appears to plague change efforts. One study found that nearly 75 per cent of US firms claimed to have faced resistance during change processes.[82] Morris and Raben[83] argue that resistance to change is natural and occurs because individuals experience a loss of self-control, autonomy, status and benefits, or because they perceive the change to be detrimental to the organization or to undermine core organizational principles. However, most change analysts suggest that the way in which change is handled causes the resistance, rather than the change itself.[84] In this section, we examine the role played by CEOs, emotions and communication in addressing – or causing – resistance.

It's the boss's fault

Greiner suggests that researchers might consider dusting off the resistance to change literature, especially with regard to the role of the CEO. While the business press is replete with stories of CEOs like Jack Welch and Irwin Federman, who engineered dramatic company turnarounds, these are only one side of the transformational change story. In contrast, many research studies indicate that financial performance is often not enhanced by CEO turnaround action. Nor do CEOs stay long in their position – the average CEO tenure is six years, with an annual turnover rate of around 35 per cent.[85] In such situations CEOs are unable to see through long-term trans-formational change and their turnover acts as an inhibitor to successful change. Moreover, while middle managers are usually blamed for being the source of resistance, six 'fatal errors' made by CEOs may account for many failed change attempts (Table 7.5). These 'fatalities' occur when CEOs view middle managers simply as transmission belts for implementing announced changes. Middle managers who experience change in this manner are likely to exhibit apathy or resistance to implementing such changes. This high-lights an interesting change lesson, that 'resistance among middle managers may only be a symptom of a deeper problem rooted in the intervention models being used by CEOs, senior managers, and consultants'.[86]

TABLE 7.5 *Fatal change errors of CEOs*

Fatal errors	Consequences	Alternative actions
Too preoccupied with external events; experience great pressure from stockholders to perform	Ignore internal strengths and dynamics of the organization	Micro-dynamics can generate macro-changes; include middle managers in planning processes
Too general a view of changes; assume everything must change at once	Ignores micro-politics of change, and management of resistance and emotion	Recognize cultural strengths of company; pay more attention to strengths than weaknesses
Too much focus on rational change and design strategies	Assumption that middle managers are like Pavlovian dogs and will fall in line with top managers' rational plans	Mould change process with desire of employees and involve them – and their fears – in planning and visioning
Assume that charismatic leadership will produce change	Simplistic assumptions of influence – and recipients usually only have sporadic contact with the 'charismatic' leader	Make leadership a collective process involving all of top management acting as role models
Assume that 'Do as I say' will produce change	Other top managers may only pay lip service to new pronouncements for change; reliance on training and incentives programmes is not enough	Top management should work alongside middle managers, sponsor their efforts and facilitate action on proposals
Place burden of change on 'decentralized' middle managers	Perversion of meaning of decentralization whereby top managers simply judge the actions of middle managers on their change abilities	Share burden of change; allow external consultants to represent middle managers; and remind top managers of impact of their actions elsewhere in the organization

Source: Adapted from Greiner, 1992

Don't get emotional

French and Delahaye identify two broad responses to resistance: 'gap closure' and 'gap connection'. The former tries to close the gap between individuals' experiences of the old situation and their experiences of the new situation. It uses 'power and conflict to force movement through the process by overcoming resistance and encouraging the driving forces of change'.[87] In 'gap connection', a more time-consuming change management style is employed that entails 'easing the passage of the individual through change'. It is a 'bridge-building' approach, identifying what individuals will need to perform effectively in the new situation and helping them develop in these ways. The latter approach implicitly recognizes the need to manage people's emotional reactions to change, including their attachment to past practices.

Many change models neglect the emotional aspects of change for a variety of reasons. First, for the rational manager, emotions are irrational and therefore irrelevant. Second, some organizational cultures stifle the expression of feelings and emotions. Third, where managers have a task or high 'strategic' orientation, they find it difficult to articulate emotions and feelings. Fourth, organizations tend not to structure opportunities to focus on feelings and emotions.[88] Successful change managers need to recognize the importance of managing emotions by acknowledging individual defensive mechanisms associated with change, as well as the nature of attachments to past practices which have occurred and through which individuals have structured their identities.

Highlighting emotions serves to indicate how 'resistance to change' may be due, in part, to a lack of management attention to individual emotions.[89] The 'rational' manager who dutifully follows the steps of any change programme may run into trouble if he or she fails to give due regard to managing emotions, which may explain why many change programmes fail (Exercise 7.5).

Speak clearly

Another approach to resistance involves overcoming interpretive and communication barriers. Interpretive barriers occur when people have differing interpretations of strategic goals and the priorities associated with them. Communication barriers emerge when people do not share a common language or 'code' for understanding and communicating change issues and tasks.[90] Most change models refer to the importance of 'communicating change' as a means of avoiding resistance and may even include a 'communications strategy' for change.[91] Managers are exhorted to communicate openly, although it is not always clear exactly what this involves. Communication is not so much a mechanism by which change occurs but, rather, change is 'a process that is created, produced, and maintained by and within communication'.[92] Ford and Ford argue that rather than issuing glib statements to managers about the need for good communication, change agents

EXERCISE 7.5 HERE WE GO AGAIN!

Step 1: You are about to participate in the next round of organizational changes. Circle the words below which best describe how you feel about this.

1 adjust	11 different	21 opportunity
2 alter	12 disruption	22 rebirth
3 ambiguity	13 exciting	23 replace
4 anxiety	14 fear	24 revise
5 better	15 fun	25 stress
6 challenging	16 grow	26 transfer
7 chance	17 improve	27 transition
8 concern	18 learn	28 uncertainty
9 death	19 modify	29 upheaval
10 deteriorate	20 new	30 vary

Step 2: Scoring your 'Reaction to change' inventory, add up the value of your inventory in the following way:
- Record a score of 10 for each word you circled from 5, 6, 13, 15, 16, 17, 18, 20, 21, 22
- Record a score of 0 for each word you circled out of: 1, 2, 7, 11, 19, 23, 24, 26, 27, 30
- Record a score of –10 for each word you circled out of: 3, 4, 8, 9, 10, 12, 14, 25, 28, 29
- Total your score

Step 3: Interpret your scores:
- Scores of 40 + = strong support for change
- Scores of 20 to 30 = moderate support for change
- Scores of –10 to 10 indicate willingness to comply with change
- Scores of –20 to –30 indicate moderate resistance to change
- Scores of –40 + show strong resistance to the change

Step 4: Reflect
- Why do you react to change in the way you do?
- How representative are your reactions compared to those of others in your organization?
- Do you consider your reaction to be positive or negative?
- If you consider your reaction to be negative, what would it take to turn it around?
- How would you manage others with a similar negative reaction?

Source: Adapted from DeMeuse and McDaris, 1994: 55

need to ensure that managers are trained in four types of change conversations (Table 7.6).

Five breakdowns in conversations can occur. First, initiative conversations may take place with the wrong people, i.e. individuals who are not in a position to take action relating to change. Second, when shared understandings about the proposed change have not emerged, there is a lack of clarity in communicating what the change is, where it is headed, and what expectations are associated with it. A third breakdown occurs when there is agreement about the need for change, but a lack of understanding about what needs to be done and who has responsibility for specific actions. When requests for action do not lead to expected results, a fourth form of breakdown will occur, often because expectations or deadlines have not been adequately communicated to change actors. A fifth breakdown occurs when people feel that their past contributions are unacknowledged or unappreciated and they fail to participate fully. In this case, insufficient attention is given to closure mechanisms.

This framework alerts managers to the need to employ different modes of communication to different aspects of the change process. However, this approach assumes that conversations can be neatly ordered and sequenced in a clearly defined, self-contained change programme, whereas in many organizations different change programmes, at different stages, may be nested within other ones; and organizational members may be contemporaneously involved in multiple changes. Moreover, if organizations are in a state of constant change, how easy is it to identify 'closure' in organizational change situations?

Another initiative in the work on communicating change argues that different types of change require different types of talk.[93] *Developmental*

TABLE 7.6   *Change conversations*

Conversation	Implication	Example
Initiative conversations	Proposes to listeners what needs to be done	'I propose . . .' 'We should . . .' 'Why don't we start to . . .'
Conversations for generating understanding	Specifies the conditions for change; creates involvement, participation and support from those engaged in change; provides decision makers' interpretations and understandings	Making claims, providing evidence: 'We've got too many complaints . . .'
Conversations for performance or action	Mobilizes action through requests, promises; acknowledges liability; allocates responsibility	'I request that you . . .' 'I accept that I need to . . .' 'You've forgotten about the need to . . .' 'Will you do . . .'
Conversations for closure	Acknowledges the finality of change; provides disengagement	'I want to thank you . . .' 'Your willingness has made possible . . .'

Source: Adapted from Ford and Ford, 1995

change, which is incremental and aimed at building upon past performance, uses imagery of 'developing', 'building', 'growing' or 'nurturing'. *Transitional change*, which entails moving from one situation to a different one, such as from a hierarchical organization to an empowered organization, requires the use of words such as 'leaving the old behind', 'taking the best route' and 'avoiding obstacles and dead ends'. In *transformational change*, the fundamental state of the organization alters by moving into new markets and new modes of operating. The language associated with this mode can include 'recreating ourselves', 'reinventing', 'waking-up' and being visionary. Using the 'wrong' words to communicate a particular type of change can lead to problems. For example, a CEO encountering difficulty in achieving the change he desired was found to be trying to achieve a transitional change by using language that was more suited to developmental change, thus sending a mixed message and adding confusion to the change process.[94]

However, another analysis suggests that talk about change may relate more to the underlying value structure of the organization than to the nature of the change.[95] In portraying change, elite organizations talk about change in a top-down manner. Organizations with leadership values have a strong, top-down accountability theme, but combine it with the need to persuade employees to engage in change. Meritocratic organizations emphasize the constructive role of employees in changing organizations. Collegial organizations, unlike the other three, are more apt to talk about change by conveying positive images of change including employee involvement and benefits. This research reminds us that communication strategies for change which fail to appreciate its 'contextual' nature will run into problems when they do not achieve a degree of compatibility with underlying organizational values (Exercises 7.6 and 7.7).

CONCLUSIONS: CAN YOU SPARE SOME CHANGE?

The field of organizational change has been active for at least fifty years – Lewin's work dates back to the 1940s.[96] Some maintain that we are now at the stage where 'researchers' interest in organizational change has peaked'[97], especially where large-scale changes are concerned. At the same time, others claim that theory development on organizational change remains inadequate,[98] is dominated by 'atheoretical pragmatism'[99] and consists of 'stereotypes and prescriptions'[100] that are applied without regard to the change context. This reflects 'the different foundational points of view, perspectives, or frames that we in the field of management employ'.[101] It also reflects the fact that writings on change are a mixture of research-based, academic theory and recent reports from front-line, battle-weary change consultants and practitioners.

Miller et al.[102] argue that there is considerable divergence between the academic and the practical literatures for three reasons. First, the academic literature may be slow in recognizing how organizations experience major

---

EXERCISE 7.6 20/20 HINDSIGHT VISION

Analyse an organizational change with which you are familiar, either from experience or the business literature.

1 Was the change a success or failure? Briefly explain your answer.
2 Did it encounter resistance?
   • If so describe the cause, nature, location and consequences of this resistance (see Table 7.8).
   • If not, briefly explain the various groups who supported the change.
3 Analyse the reasons behind the existence/absence of resistance.
   • Did CEO make or avoid the fatal errors (Table 7.5)?
   • How was emotion dealt with?
   • Were the different conversations (Table 7.6) employed effectively or did they break down?
   • Was the type of language used appropriate to the type of change?
4 What conclusions do you draw for dealing with resistance to change?

---

economic and social pressures to change, since it is difficult to demonstrate empirically that such pressures are indeed greater now than in past times. Second, the two groups have very different interests. Normative, practitioner-oriented writers are more focused towards the goals of senior managers' interests and assume that what is good for top managers will be beneficial for the rest of the organization. Academic writers are more apt to see competing interests at work in change processes. Third, the academic literature tends to reflect upon what has happened in the past, whereas the normative literature wants to achieve change in the future. To narrow the gap between these two sets of writings, Miller et al. recommend that academics continually assess the practical relevance of their conceptual ideas. At the same time practitioner writers should avoid simplistic models of change, acknowledge the political aspects of change, assess the need for change against the benefits of stability and more clearly identify the problematic aspects of managing change. Until these steps are taken, however, there will remain two change management literatures, each of which embodies different assumptions (Table 7.7).

Perhaps this gap explains some of the problems that change programmes encounter. As many as 70 per cent of change initiatives fail.[103] Where the change is an acquisition, synergies are not often realized; where the change involves re-engineering, both time and costs can escalate; where the change entails downsizing, financial performance may be weaker; and where it

---

EXERCISE 7.7 TALK ABOUT CHANGE!

Reflect on an organizational change with which you are familiar, either from experience or from the business literature, and answer the following questions:

1 Evaluate the organization's values. Would you describe them as:
   • elite
   • meritocratic
   • leadership oriented
   • collegial
2 Evaluate the nature of the change. Would you describe it as:
   • developmental
   • transitional
   • transformational
3 Analyse the words used to talk about change:
   • Who used them?
   • Did everyone use similar language or did the language differ depending on who was talking about the change?
   • Did they reflect the organization's values?
   • Did they reflect the type of change?
   • To what extent can the success/failure of the change be related back to such 'talk'?
4 What conclusions do you draw for talking about change and successful change management?

---

involves quality programmes, the expected results are not always produced.[104] For 'every successful corporate transformation, there is at least one equally prominent failure. GE's dramatic performance improvement starkly contrasts with the string of disappointments and crises that have plagued Westinghouse. ABB's ascendancy to global leadership in power equipment only emphasized Hitachi's inability to reverse its declining fortunes in that business. And Philips's successful revitalization since 1990 only highlights its own agonizingly slow turnaround in the preceding ten years'.[105] A survey of electronics companies reported that, while almost three-quarters of the companies were engaged in TQM initiatives, only around 10 per cent reported the programme as successful, and nearly two-thirds failed significantly to improve the rate of product defects.[106]

A number of reasons have been given for such failures (Table 7.8) but the fact is that we still remain far from clear on how to go about orchestrating a successful organizational change, even if we have some idea about why change fails. There is considerable rhetoric about organizational change: embracing change is the hallmark of a progressive manager; resisting it

TABLE 7.7   *Two change literatures*

Practitioner	Academic
Normative and prescriptive	Empirical and theoretical
Optimistic view of the possibility of achieving desired change	Pessimistic view of the possibility of achieving desired change
Transformational organizational change is necessary and beneficial; organizations need constantly to reinvent themselves to survive	Transformational organizational change is likely to be risky, costly; it will destabilize the organization and probably fail
Top managers can control and manage change	Inertia and resistance hinder transformational change
Organizations are loosely coupled systems and, therefore, change programmes can occur in some units, independently of the rest of the organization	Organizational sub-units are tightly integrated, change in one part of the organization has implications for the rest of the organization
Managers are rational and have the information needed to systematically change their organization	Managers rarely process information rationally; organizational systems are unpredictable; managers favour previous practices even in the face of evidence to the contrary
Political aspects of change are unimportant	Political obstacles and vested interests affect organization change

Source: Adapted from Miller et al. 1997

TABLE 7.8   *Barriers to successful change*

- Difficulty in making changes 'stick'
- Actions that managers can take are limited because of the range of interests and groups in organizations
- Change programmes are swamped by the wider organizational system
- Those people who are good at leading one type of change may be not well suited to leading other types
- Change programmes are too ambitious
- Change may be unnecessary
- The urgency for the change is not established
- Insufficient support from powerful coalitions for the changes
- Insufficient vision or communication of this vision
- Obstacles are not identified and dealt with
- Short-term wins are not built into the change process
- The completion of the change process is declared too early
- The change is not institutionalized into the organizational culture

Sources: Adapted from Kanter et al. 1992: 5–9; Kilcourse, 1995: 40; Kotter, 1996

represents a lack of commitment to the organization, an unwillingness to leave behind past practices or an inability to cope with the new business environment. The paradox is that the practice of organizational change often fails to live up to these expectations, and academic research appears to be of limited help.

Organizational change is paradoxical in a number of other ways (Table 7.9), and one of the biggest paradoxes is that what has been referred to, in a derogatory fashion, as the 'soft people stuff' is really the 'hard stuff' when it comes to managing change in organizations.[107]

TABLE 7.9 *Paradoxes of change*

- Change is often needed at times when organizations can least afford to invest in change.
- The ability of organizations to change often coincides with an inclination to stay the same.
- Positive change requires significant stability.
- To build an enterprise, focus on the individual.
- Focus directly on culture, indirectly.
- True empowerment requires forceful leadership.
- In order to build you must tear down.
- Those organizations with the resources to change are often the most bureaucratic and, therefore, resistant to change.
- The longer the change effort drags on, the more effort has to be spent keeping the 'spotlight' on.
- Why do organizations bother attempting change if change may increase the risk of organizational failure?

Sources: Adapted from Haveman, 1992: 51; Hall, 1996: 190; Jick, 1995: 81; Price Waterhouse Change Integration Team, 1996: 19–21

NOTES

(See Bibliography at the end of the book for full references)

1 Burke, 1995: 159
2 Worley et al. 1996
3 Siegal, 1996: 54
4 Romano, 1995
5 Vrakking, 1995
6 Price Waterhouse Change Integration Team, 1996
7 Iskat and Liebowitz, 1996
8 Zimmerman, 1995; Schneider et al. 1996
9 Lewin, 1947
10 Lippitt, et al. 1958; Schein, 1987
11 Cummings and Worley, 1993
12 French and Bell, 1995: 26–8
13 Cummings and Worley, 1993: 2
14 Burke, 1995: 159
15 Kanter et al. 1992: 10
16 Kanter et al. 1992: 12
17 Kanter et al. 1992: 391–2; Morris and Raben, 1995: 65
18 Cummings and Worley, 1993: 153
19 Hutt et al. 1995: 23
20 Morris and Raben, 1995
21 Kanter et al. 1992
22 Kotter, 1996: 23
23 Ghoshal and Bartlett, 1996: 23
24 Marshak, 1993b
25 Burke, 1995: 159
26 Kilcourse, 1995
27 Weick, 1984; Meyerson and Scully, 1995
28 Meyerson and Scully, 1995: 595
29 Jick, 1995
30 Bunker and Alban, 1996
31 Mink et al. 1993; McWhinney et al. 1993
32 Dunphy and Stace, 1990
33 Nadler and Tushman, 1995: 22
34 Nadler and Tushman, 1995: 22–9
35 Huy, 1998
36 Orlikowski and Hofman, 1997: 13
37 Orlikowski and Hofman, 1997: 21
38 Vince and Broussine, 1996: 3
39 Watzlawick et al. 1974: 99
40 Bartunek and Moch, 1994
41 Nadler and Tushman, 1995: 29-30
42 Old, 1995: 12
43 Greenwood and Hinings, 1993: 1075
44 Bolman and Deal, 1997: 12
45 Reger et al. 1994
46 See chapter on culture.

47 Dunbar et al. 1996a: 26
48 Dunbar et al. 1996a: 30
49 Porac and Rosa, 1996: 36
50 Dunbar et al. 1996b
51 Morgan, 1986, 1993
52 See chapter on learning.
53 See strategy chapter.
54 Van de Ven and Poole, 1995: 518
55 Brown and Eisenhardt, 1997
56 Greenwood and Hinings, 1993
57 Brown and Eisenhardt, 1997: 3
58 Van de Ven and Poole, 1995
59 See strategy chapter.
60 Nielsen, 1996
61 Mason, 1996: 294
62 Ford and Ford, 1995: 776
63 Carini et al. 1995
64 Large, 1996
65 Dubinskas, 1994: 356–7
66 Dubinskas, 1994: 365
67 Dubinskas, 1994: 359
68 Dubinskas, 1994
69 Greenwood and Hinings, 1996: 1023
70 Greenwood and Hinings, 1996: 1032
71 Abrahamson, 1996
72 Dunford and Palmer, 1996
73 Ghoshal and Bartlett, 1996: 24
74 Hirsch and Lonsbury, 1997
75 Selznick, 1957
76 March and Simon, 1958
77 Thompson, 1967
78 Lawrence and Lorsch, 1967
79 Weick, 1979
80 Child, 1972
81 Doerr, 1996: 5
82 Romano, 1995
83 Morris and Raben, 1995: 48
84 Spiker and Lesser, 1995
85 Greiner, 1992
86 Greiner, 1992: 64
87 French and Delahaye, 1996: 22
88 Vince and Broussine, 1996
89 See chapter on postmodern approaches.
90 Hutt et al. 1995
91 Klein, 1996: 34
92 Ford and Ford, 1995: 542
93 Marshak, 1993a
94 Marshak, 1993a
95 Kabanoff et al. 1995
96 Lewin, 1947, 1951
97 Greenberg, 1995: 206
98 Robertson et al. 1993
99 Hendry, 1996: 621
100 Sinclair, 1994: 32
101 Ford and Ford, 1994: 756–7
102 Miller et al. 1997
103 Spencer, 1996
104 Kotter, 1996
105 Ghoshal and Bartlett, 1996: 23
106 Siegal, 1996
107 Spencer, 1996: 91

8 MANAGING ORGANIZATIONAL LEARNING

Has the Time Come or Gone?

'That organizations learn is an idea whose time has come,' argues Mirvis.[1] This comment emerges after nearly fifty years of foundation work in related disciplines, such as physics, biology, cybernetics and psychology and particularly since the publication of Peter Senge's 1990 book, *The Fifth Discipline*.[2] The result has been more than six times as many academic articles on organizational learning during the 1990s than in the 1980s[3] (see Supplementary Reading box). Interest in organizational learning stems from both practical and theoretical sources. Insofar as management practice is concerned, organizational learning is attracting interest because of its links to action – change and innovation[4] – as well as its association with new organizational forms such as strategic alliances and international joint ventures which offer new opportunities for organizational learning.[5] From a theoretical perspective, researchers argue that organizational learning offers an opportunity to redress the atheoretical tendencies of the organizational change literature, mentioned in the previous chapter.[6]

LEARNING: SUPPLEMENTARY READING

- Argyris, C. and Schon, D. (1978) *Organizational Learning: A Theory of Action Perspective*. Reading, MA: Addison-Wesley.

- Brown, J.S. and Duguid, P. (1991) 'Organizational learning and communities-of-practice: toward a unified view of working, learning and innovation', *Organization Science*, 2 (1): 40–57.

- Cook, S.D.N. and Yanow, D. (1993) 'Culture and organizational learning', *Journal of Management Inquiry*, 2: 373–90.

- Daft, R.L. and Huber, G.P. (1987) 'How organizations learn: a communication framework', *Research in the Sociology of Organizations*, 5: 1–36.

- Dodgson, M. (1993) 'Organizational learning: a review of some literatures', *Organization Studies*, 14 (3): 375–94.

- Easterby-Smith, M. (1997) 'Disciplines of organizational learning: contributions and critiques', *Human Relations*, 50 (9): 1085–113.

- Fiol, C. and Lyles, M. (1985) 'Organizational learning', *Academy of Management Review*, 10: 803–13.

- Garvin, D.A. (1993) 'Building a learning organization', *Harvard Business Review* (July–August): 78–91.

- Huber, G. (1991) 'Organizational learning: the contributing process and the literatures', *Organization Science*, 2: 88–115.

- Isaacs, W.N. (1993) 'Taking flight: dialogue, collective thinking and organizational learning', *Organizational Dynamics*, 22 (2): 24–39.

- March, J. (1991) 'Exploration and exploitation in organizational learning', *Organization Science*, 2 (1): 71–87.

- Miller, D. (1996) 'A preliminary typology of organizational learning: synthesizing the literature', *Journal of Management*, 22 (3): 485–505.

- Nicolini, D. and Meznar, M.B. (1995) 'The social construction of organizational learning: conceptual and practical issues in the field', *Human Relations*, 48 (7): 727–46.

- Nonaka, I. (1994) 'A dynamic theory of organizational knowledge creation', *Organization Science*, 5 (1): 15–37.

- Schein, E.H. (1993a) 'On dialogue, culture and organizational learning', *Organization Dynamics*, 22 (2): 40–51.

- Senge, P. (1990) *The Fifth Discipline*. New York: Doubleday.

- Shrivastava, P. (1983) 'A typology of organizational learning systems', *Journal of Management Studies*, 20 (1): 7–28.

- Weick, K.E. and Westley, F. (1996) 'Organizational learning: affirming an oxymoron', in S.R. Clegg, C. Hardy and W. Nord (eds), *Handbook of Organization Studies*. London: Sage. pp. 440–58.

Weick[7] admits to some unease with the notion that organization studies theorists are taking up the matter of learning just as psychologists are dropping it. Nevertheless, most researchers assume that organizational learning produces only positive benefits on performance[8] through such factors as competitive advantage, efficiency, productivity, environmental realignment and technological development. Indeed, some writers suggest that we have reached the point where discussions of learning organizations are often 'reverential and utopian, filled with near mystical terminology'.[9] For example, Senge[10] argues that learning organizations afford people the opportunity to 'continually expand their capacity to create the results they truly desire'. They are places 'where new and expansive patterns of thinking are nurtured, where collective aspiration is set free, and where people are continually learning how to learn together'.

Agreement concerning the beneficial returns to both organizations and individuals afforded by organizational learning has not yet translated into definitional consensus. There are countless definitions of organizational learning scattered throughout this literature.[11] Some writers have urged the field to ignore definitional debate, arguing that, while researchers are bickering about what organizational learning is, organizations are already doing it.[12] Instead, these writers suggest that the challenge for theorists lies in exploring learning practices and their outcomes, with a view to designing more organizations that are capable of more learning.

In this chapter we argue that differences concerning definitions of organizational learning have profound ramifications for management practice. We argue this initially by examining three debates that surround different conceptualizations of organizational learning and tracing their implications for management practice. The first debate relates to views about whether organizational learning is primarily an individual phenomenon, even though these individuals work in organizational settings. The second debate concerns the systems-structural approach to learning, including work on the learning organization. The third debate relates to the interpretive perspective, which looks at organizational learning as a process of meaning creation. Following an outline of these three debates, we then explore the paradox of organizational learning and discuss debates around convergence of meaning, tacit and explicit knowledge, and organizing for learning. Finally, we debate some of the reasons put forward to justify why organizations should bother to learn. To examine these debates, we will draw from the literature on organizational learning, the learning organization, as well as some of the work on innovation and technology that relates to organizational learning.[13]

WHAT IS ORGANIZATIONAL LEARNING?

Definitions and views of organizational learning abound (Table 8.1).[14] Fiol and Lyles[15] noted in 1985 that no theory or model of organizational learning had achieved widespread acceptance, an observation that remains true today.[16] Easterby-Smith[17] argues that one of the reasons behind the lack of consensus stems from the fact that organizational learning has been studied from a number of different disciplinary perspectives, each providing distinct contributions and conceptions of problems (Table 8.2). The result is a plethora of views on organizational learning. Some writers argue that learning consists primarily of the development of insights and knowledge; others suggest that learning must translate into actions and outcomes.[18] Some approaches focus on learning only as an outcome; others see learning mainly as a process.[19] For some researchers, organizational learning can be quantified, measured and separated from the context in which it occurs; for others, it is intangible, a product of social construction that cannot be disentangled from the people, processes and cultures that give it meaning.[20]

TABLE 8.1 *Views of organizational learning*

- Organizational learning as acquiring knowledge that is recognized as potentially useful to the organization.
- Organizational learning as knowledge acquisition, information processing and distribution, information interpretation and organizational memory.
- Organizational learning as knowledge acquisition (the development of skills, insights and relationships); knowledge sharing and dissemination: and knowledge utilization (the integration of learning to make it widely available and generalizable to new situations).
- Organizational learning as the assumption-sharing modification of cognitive maps.
- Organizational learning as the development of knowledge about action–outcome relationships, including the effectiveness of past and future actions and the impact of the environment on these relationships.
- Organizational learning as the enhanced ability to perform in accordance with a changing environment through the search for strategies to cope with those contingencies, and the development of appropriate implementation systems and structures.
- Organizational learning as systems that acquire, communicate and interpret organizationally relevant knowledge for use in decision-making and which transform individual knowledge into an organizational knowledge base.
- Organizational learning as a different response to the same stimulus.
- Organizational learning as adaptation and change.
- Organizational learning as the process of improving actions through better knowledge and understanding.
- Organizational learning as a process where known objects and phenomena acquire new meaning.
- Organizational learning as acquiring, sustaining and changing the meanings embedded in the organization's cultural artefacts through collective action.
- Organizational learning as the construction of meaning from a wide range of materials, including social and physical circumstances and the histories and social relations of the people concerned.
- Organizational learning as the development of organizational efficiency through the creation and organization of knowledge and routines around and within organizational activities and cultures.
- Organizational learning as institutionalized experience.

Sources: Adapted from Shrivastava, 1983; Fiol and Lyles, 1985; Duncan and Weiss, 1979; Brown and Duguid, 1991; Huber, 1991; Weick, 1991; Cook and Yanow, 1993; Nevis et al. 1995; Nicolini and Meznar, 1995; Thatchenkery, 1996; Boland and Tenkasi,1996

Some writers emphasize individual learning; others assume that organizations can, in one form or another, learn collectively.[21] Some views insist on behavioural change before learning can be said to occur; others believe that new ways of thinking are enough.[22] For some commentators, information processing is fundamental to organizational learning; for others it is shared meanings. Depending on the commentator, organizational learning is rare, common or even, in some cases, inevitable.[23]

The existence of such diverse approaches means that it is difficult to pin down exactly what organizational learning does constitute. 'It remains unclear just what learning is, how it takes place, and when, where, and why it occurs.'[24] Numerous types of organizational learning have been identified

(Table 8.3), but the nature of the relationships between learning[25] and individuals, organizations, change and innovation[26] remain far from clear. For our purposes, we consider organizational learning to encompass both the acquisition of new knowledge and its translation into organizational action. Hence, the role played by learning in innovation and technology development is important, especially since many managers are interested in organizational learning precisely because it promises innovation and transformation.[27] As Miller[28] points out, new knowledge that does not relate to organizational action is really only relevant to individual learning, not organizational learning. Similarly, action that does not contribute to organizational knowledge does not constitute organizational learning. Consequently, organizational learning is related to, but not the same as organizational change.[29]

Within this broad conceptualization of organizational learning, a key debate that is crucial to our understanding of organizational learning concerns whether learning is an individual or a collective matter. Cook and Yanow[30] argue that most work focuses on learning and the individual: either by exploring how individuals learn in organizations or by applying theories of individual learning to the organization. The first approach explores how individuals learn because 'individuals are the primary learning entity in firms'. It is individuals who create organizational forms to 'facilitate organizational transformation',[31] and organizational learning is manifested only through the experiences of individuals.[32] The second view acknowledges that organizational learning is more than, and different to, the sum of individual learning[33] and that there is the possibility of embedding human cognition and the capacity to learn and produce knowledge through expert systems.[34] But it does so by applying an information-processing framework, based on individual theories of learning, to organizational processes,[35] arguing that organizations have collective minds or memories and can, therefore, learn in a manner similar to individuals.[36]

There is, in fact, very little of the organization in either of these two literatures on organizational learning.[37] Consequently, Cook and Yanow[38] offer a third approach. They agree that learning is organizational – it is about group practice and collective action, rather than about what goes on inside individuals' heads. It 'is neither empirically or conceptually the same thing as either learning by individuals or individual learning in organizations'. It is inappropriate to superimpose cognitive processes on to an organizational 'mind' since organizations are not cognitive entities. Nor should the limitations of theories of individual cognition be allowed to hamper our understanding of organizational learning. These writers argue that the question to be explored is what is the nature of learning when it is done by organizations. Work in this vein has been described as interpretive – it focuses on the role that social construction and meaning creation play in learning.

We can, then, identify three broad arenas of study: learning by individuals who work in organizations; learning by organizations in a manner akin to individual learning; and organizational learning as a non-cognitive process

TABLE 8.2 *Approaches to the study of organizational learning*

Approach	Contributions	Perceived problems facing organizational learning
Psychology • hierarchy of learning • cognitive processes of learning • experiential learning • learning styles • difficulties of learning	• The existence of different hierarchical levels of individual learning • The recognition of the importance of context • The assumption that ideas concerning individual learning can be adjusted to relate to organizational learning • The recognition of importance of cognitive maps and frames of thinking • The recognition of the interrelationships between thinking and action	• How to move from learning by individuals to collective learning • How to overcome the defensive reactions of individuals and groups • How to improve poor communications between organizational members
Management science • information gathering and processing • systems thinking • organizational knowledge	• An understanding of the creation and dissemination of information • The development of the concept of organizational knowledge • The promotion of progressive levels of learning • An holistic view of organizational learning	• How to overcome the distorting effect of organizational politics • How to overcome other forms of non-rational behaviour • How to reconcile conflicts between short-term and long-term agendas • How to 'unlearn' • How to facilitate dissemination of information between hierarchical levels and through political barriers
Sociology and organization theory • functional views • contingency theory • learning as social construction • critical views	• Different types of learning according to contingent factors • The exploration of the processes of social construction that underpin organizational learning • The study of politics and conflict as inevitable organizational processes that affect learning • Questioning whose interests are served by organizational learning • A fundamental questioning of the nature of organizational learning	• How to reconstruct knowledge following perceived discontinuities in organizational functioning • Questioning who is to direct organizational learning; whose knowledge is to be privileged; whose interests are served • Questioning whether organizational learning should be a lever to be pulled at the behest of senior executives

Approach	Contributions	Perceived problems facing organizational learning
Strategy • competitive advantage • environmental alignment • population-level learning	• Organizational learning produces competitive advantage • Contribution to the debate concerning whether organizations can adapt to their environments • Further explication of levels of learning the importance of direct experience and tacit knowledge in organizational learning • Exchange of knowledge and technology transfer between organizations	• How to facilitate higher level learning in highly complex and ambiguous contexts • Whether organizational learning will have an impact on the environment or whether the environment selects out organizations • How to facilitate technology transfer between organizations • How to facilitate organizational learning when members are tied to strict deadlines • Whether ideas from countries such as Japan can be transferred to different cultures
Production management • learning curve • exogenous affects on organizational learning • technology and working arrangements	• The use of productivity to measure organizational learning • The concept of the learning curve • The debate about exogenous and endogenous factors on organizational learning • The role of organizational design in facilitating organizational learning	• How to compare learning across different organizational configurations • How to compare learning across national boundaries and cultural differences • How to assess organizational learning in the absence of longitudinal studies • How to overcome methodological weaknesses of comparative research
Culture • organizational learning in Japanese firms • organizational learning as shared meanings • organizational learning as embedded in a context	• Focus on values and beliefs • Investigation of how culture affects organizational learning • Whether some cultures have an advantage in facilitating organizational learning	• How to transfer ideas between national and organizational cultures • How to transfer tacit knowledge which cannot be articulated • How to change cultures that do not generate organizational learning
Learning organization • organization development • human development • action research	• Identification of success factors associated with organizational learning • How to implement organizational learning • Cyclical and evolutionary models of organizational learning	• Problems of implementation • How to address different levels or types of learning • How to overcome utopian recommendations in the literature

Source: Adapted from Easterby-Smith, 1997

TABLE 8.3 *Types of organizational learning*

- **Single loop learning**: the correction of error within a given set of governing variables, norms, policies, objectives, etc. Those activities that add to the knowledge base and specific competencies of the organization.
- **Double loop learning**: the correction of error in ways that change the governing variables themselves. Changes to the knowledge base and competencies.
- **Deutero-learning**: when organizations reflect on previous episodes of learning to discover what facilitated or inhibited it, develop new strategies for learning, and evaluate what these new strategies have produced. A consideration of why and how to change.

- **Lower level learning**: routine learning that occurs through repetition within a given set of organizational rules and structures to produce behavioural outcomes, including the institutionalization of formal rules, adjustments in management systems, the development of problem-solving skills.
- **Higher level learning**: takes place within an ambiguous context and involves changing rules and norms that govern behaviours and activities through the use of heuristics and insights to produce new missions, new agendas, problem-defining skills.

- **Generative learning**: addresses the underlying causes of behaviour at a level that enables patterns of behaviour to change through the redesign of underlying systems.
- **Adaptive learning**: focuses more on short-term and the surface issues, which may lead to some changes in behaviour but not system change.

- **Reliable learning**: produces shared understandings of experience and shared, public and stable interpretations of those experiences.
- **Valid learning**: enables organization to understand, predict and control its environment.

- **Exploitation**: refinement and extension of existing competencies, technologies and paradigms producing positive, short-term, predictable returns.
- **Exploration**: experimentation with new alternatives whose returns are uncertain, distant, and possibly negative.

- **Analytical learning**: methodical learning in an unconstrained environment that takes place mainly at upper echelons through rational analysis of environment and organization; uncertainty and conflict are relatively low; criteria and standards are clearly defined; relies on and produces largely explicit knowledge.
- **Synthetic learning**: emergent learning in an unconstrained environment that takes place mainly at upper echelons whereby individuals' creative capacities allow them to see patterns and opportunities in conditions of high uncertainty where others only see a jumble of elements; criteria and standards are aesthetic and subjective; relies on and produces primarily tacit knowledge; outcomes are likely to be radical.
- **Experimental learning**: methodical learning that takes place at middle levels of the organization where actions are constrained; small experiments circumvent some of the constraints that limit organization-wide action and help overcome high uncertainty about how best to achieve goals; effects of learning are applied locally.
- **Interactive learning**: emergent learning that takes place at middle levels of the organization where actions are constrained; negotiations between individuals circumvent political constraints on learning and high levels of conflict regarding both goals and the means to achieve them.
- **Structural learning**: highly constrained, in terms of both action and thought, methodical learning which is embodied in organizational routines that guide – and circumscribe – learning throughout the organization.
- **Institutional learning**: highly constrained, in terms of both action and thought, emergent learning that derives from institutionalized practices and ideologies that affect all organizational members.

Sources: Adapted from Shrivastava, 1983; Fiol and Lyles, 1985; Argyris, 1986; Senge, 1990; March, 1991; March et al. 1991; Dodgson, 1993; Miller, 1996

of social construction. In the following sections, we examine the management implications of these debates concerning the definition and conceptualization of organizational learning (Exercise 8.1).

'Organizational' learning: many little brains?

A considerable amount of work on organizational learning draws on research into how individuals acquire knowledge. This involves a focus on the investigation of memory, information acquisition and processing, and the organization of knowledge.[39] The aim is to enhance the ability of individuals – who happen to work in organizations – to learn more effectively.[40] Miller[41] (Table 8.3) categorizes this work as an analytic approach to learning.[42] It encompasses a predominantly rational analysis of scanning the environment, collecting information, analysing it to generate alternatives, and choosing effective actions. Improvements in individual cognitive processes should, theoretically, enhance learning by providing managers with a better understanding of critical environmental forces, identifying areas that need improvement, and helping managers to reflect critically on their assumptions.[43] Daudelin recommends four steps to aid reflection by articulating the problem, analysing it, formulating and testing a tentative theory to explain the problems, and acting.[44]

Synthetic learning[45] is also individual, but the result of a more intuitive, exploratory, open-ended path of discovery. Normally associated with creative, insightful individuals, recommendations for enhancing this type of learning are few and far between, although Senge's[46] techniques concerning systems thinking are argued to aid the ability of individuals to see patterns and connections. Despite writing about the learning organization, Senge's work emphasizes the individual. He argues that 'organizations learn only through individuals who learn. Individual learning does not guarantee organizational learning. But without it no organizational learning occurs'.[47]

EXERCISE 8.1 SO HOW DO *YOU* SEE LEARNING?

Examine the various views, approaches and types regarding organizational learning in Tables 8.1, 8.2 and 8.3. Answer the following questions:

- How would you define organizational learning?
- Explain your answer.
- What does your definition focus attention on (e.g. the individual, various different aspects of the organization)?
- What does it tell you about the likely barriers to effective learning?
- What does it tell you about improving organizational learning?

He advocates personal mastery, being aware of our mental models, shared vision, team learning and systems thinking as the five disciplines of learning.

Argyris's work also focuses on individual learning. 'Just as individuals are the agents of organizational action, so they are the agents for organizational learning.'[48] Organizational learning occurs when individuals detect errors, in the form of a mismatch between expectations and outcomes, and take steps to correct them. This involves discovering the sources of error, inventing new strategies based on new assumptions, and transforming those strategies into actions. Argyris adopts a social psychological perspective which aims at overcoming the defensive practices and routines exhibited by individuals that prevent learning. The aim is to free managers of the conceptual frameworks that imprison them (such as the self-reproducing nature of cognitive structures),[49] by helping them to differentiate between their espoused theories and their theories-in-use; to confront those differences; and to change theories-in-use rather than simply defend them.[50] Interventions like 'dialogue'[51] (Table 8.4) are intended to help managers to identify such disparities and enhance learning.

In summary, the work on individual learning provides an understanding of why individuals resist learning and offers ways to overcome this resistance. However, its focus is purely on the individual and it fails to recognize that barriers to individual learning do not reside only in the individual, but also in the very fabric of organizations.[52] While dialogue extends the level of analysis to the group, it offers few suggestions as to how such learning should be transmitted outside the dialogue group and transformed into collective action on the part of the organization (Exercise 8.2).

'Organizational learning': discovering the truth?

Some writers argue that although organizational learning occurs 'through individuals, it would be a mistake to conclude that organizational learning is nothing more than the cumulative results of their members' learning'.[53]

TABLE 8.4 *Dialogue*

- Dialogue helps groups reflect on ways of knowing, on language and on the embodied experience of meaning.
- Dialogue creates a 'container' – a setting that allows a free flow of meaning and a vigorous exploration of collective assumptions.
- Dialogue is not consensus. It seeks to enable individuals to surface fundamental assumptions and to open up inquiry, rather than to analyse and solve problems.
- Dialogue is based on the idea that shared tacit thought among group members comprises a field of meaning that is the underlying constituent of human experience.
- As fields of meaning are altered so, too, is behaviour.
- Unstable, incoherent fields of meaning involve defensive behaviour.
- Dialogue helps to build trust, confront assumptions, build common ground and build a new shared field of meaning that is more amenable to learning.

Source: Adapted from Isaacs, 1993

EXERCISE 8.2 LEARN YOUR LESSON

Select and read one of the following articles or books on organizational learning and answer the following questions.

- Argyris, C. and Schon, D. (1978) *Organizational Learning: A Theory of Action Perspective*. Reading, MA: Addison-Wesley.
- Senge, P. (1990) *The Fifth Discipline*. New York: Doubleday.
- Schein, E.H. (1993a) 'On dialogue, culture and organizational learning', *Organization Dynamics*, 22 (2): 40–51; Isaacs, W.N. (1993) 'Taking flight: dialogue, collective thinking and organizational learning', *Organizational Dynamics*, 22 (2): 24–39.

Questions

- Summarize their main recommendations for enhancing learning.
- What are the strengths of these recommendations?
- What are the weaknesses, especially with regard to *organizational* learning?

Organizational learning involves a different level of complexity. For example, defensive routines that militate against learning emanate from individual resistance and also from organizational factors such as conflict between interest groups with a stake in the outcomes of organizational learning. Individual-based approaches have little to say about how knowledge might become organizationally available, for example, through processes such as assimilation, absorption and utilization.[54] This view suggests that organizations develop learning systems whereby individual learning is transmitted to others through a variety of processes, structures, histories and norms, which are then translated into collective action. Thus research is devoted to understanding how organizations acquire, disseminate, interpret, apply and institutionalize knowledge.[55]

These tasks raise particular challenges in organizational settings where knowledge must be distributed and applied across different sub-units and hierarchical levels (Table 8.5). Even organizations that create and acquire new knowledge find it rather more difficult to disseminate it and apply it to their activities. Schein[56] argues that the increasing rate of environmental change and technological complexity demands organizational forms in which knowledge-based information is widely distributed. This outcome is difficult to achieve where fragmented sub-units exist with different sub-cultures and limited communication between them. Organizational learning, therefore, depends upon the evolution of structures, processes and shared mental models that cut across the subcultures of the organization and remove error and biases in organizational knowledge creation and dissemination process.

TABLE 8.5 *Phases of organizational learning and their challenges*

Phase	Challenges
Becoming aware of and identifying new knowledge	• How is the environment scanned? • How is new knowledge identified? • What sources and forms of knowledge are deemed legitimate and illegitimate? • What filters exist to screen out potential new knowledge?
Transferring/interpreting new knowledge	• How is new knowledge transferred across the different parts of the organization? • How is tacit knowledge transferred? • What happens to knowledge as it is transferred? • How likely are multiple interpretations to arise? • How are multiple interpretations addressed? • Whose interpretations will be deemed legitimate?
Using knowledge by adjusting behaviour to achieve intended outcomes	• How is knowledge transformed into action? • What is the absorptive capacity of the organization to adopt new ideas? • How is collective action orchestrated? • What forms of organizational resistance to changes in behaviour exist? • How can they be overcome?
Institutionalizing knowledge by reflecting on what is happening and by adjusting behaviour	• How can knowledge be institutionalized? • Is there an organizational equivalent of memory in which experiences can be deposited? • What are the inertial results of institutionalizing knowledge? • How can institutionalization be reconciled with future learning?

Source: Partially adapted from Levinson and Asahi, 1995

Much like the attempts to improve information-processing capabilities of individuals, researchers believe that organizational learning can be improved through more effective systems, structures and cultures (Table 8.6). So, while organizations may not have brains, they do have 'cognitive systems and memories. As individuals develop personalities, personal habits, and beliefs over time, organizations develop world views and ideologies'.[57] Consequently, as with individuals, organizational barriers to learning exist. Similarly, if individuals can be helped to learn through improving their cognitive processes so, too, can organizations through the more effective design of their 'cognitive' systems. In the same way that individuals can be encouraged to put their learning into practice, organizations can be helped to translate new knowledge into new behaviours. In other words, organizational learning mechanisms can be put in place to improve the organizational equivalent of the human nervous system[58] as theories developed from individual learning are applied to the organization.[59]

Recommendations include both structural and cultural mechanisms to

TABLE 8.6 *Barriers to and facilitators of organizational learning*

Barriers	Facilitators
• Lack of resources, incentives, training • Pressure to meet deadlines • Fragmented and hierarchical structures • Top-down leadership and conflicting strategic priorities • Lack of multi-functional teams or domination of multi-functional initiatives by particular functions • Communication bottlenecks and poor communication • Role constraints, role complexity, role ambiguity • Organizational politics • Fear of change • Low employee morale • Defensive routines where people say they learn but do not manifest it in their behaviour and resist admitting any inconsistency, making it difficult to challenge the status quo • Inability to deal with tacit knowledge • The activities associated with learning and change, e.g. risk taking, making mistakes are deemed illegitimate in the larger organization • Highly institutionalized cultures	• Hiring key individuals • Training and continuous education • Individual (e.g. compensation) and organizational incentives (e.g. patents) • Motivation, including high cost of errors, need for continuous improvement, performance gap • Curiosity about the environment • Concern for measurement of learning activities and outputs • Committed, involved leadership and multiple advocates • Involvement of middle managers • Decentralized structure and diffusion of information • Cross-cutting, open communication and co-ordination mechanisms • High levels of trust • A strong culture that values learning and high organizational commitment • High absorptive capacity – ability to pick up new ideas • Willingness to experiment; variety of methods to facilitate experimentation • Centrality of R&D function • TQM, reverse engineering, benchmarking and customer input • Systems perspective • Diversification, strategic and cross-national alliances, outsourcing

Sources: Adapted from Argyris, 1986; Dodgson, 1993; Garvin, 1993; Levinthal and March, 1993; Pennings et al. 1994; Inkpen and Crossan, 1995; Elmes and Kassouf, 1995; Levinson and Asahi, 1995; Nevis et al. 1995; Nicolini and Meznar, 1995; Beer and Eisenstat, 1996; Dougherty and Hardy, 1996; Lipshitz et al. 1996; Hardy and Dougherty, 1997; Easterby-Smith, 1997

enhance organizational learning.[60] For example, many writers advocate the careful design of organizational structure,[61] although disputes arise concerning exactly how.[62] Some writers advocate decentralization to help the assimilation of new knowledge and increase flexibility.[63] Others support a contingency approach where the most appropriate structure depends upon the perceived environment[64] or upon the amount and ambiguity of the information that the organization needs to process.[65] Writers also advocate the introduction of more formal information, planning and control systems, as well as systems of procedures and regulations. The aim is to incorporate learning gained from both experience and technology and to integrate it into formal systems to enable the flow of information.[66] In general, formal structural mechanisms revolve around the idea that rigorous data collection and analysis will aid learning through the reduction of uncertainty (see Miller's analytic mode of learning in Table 8.3).

Other recommendations emphasize cultural adaptation to improve learning. Much like an individual whose propensity to learn can be enhanced through reflection, dialogue and contrasting espoused theories and theories-in-use, organizations will learn more effectively if their cultural arrangements enhance 'mythological learning' and 'information-sharing'.[67] If formal structure provides the appropriate organizational 'hardware' for organizational learning, culture provides the 'software' through such means as socializing newcomers to transfer knowledge, developing informal organization-wide ways of sharing knowledge and creating cultures where innovation and knowledge acquisition are valued. Other suggestions include the promotion of climates that encourage individuals to learn; the extension of the learning culture to embrace customers, suppliers and other stakeholders; and ensuring that human resource management plays a key strategic role through investments in training.[68] Schein[69] suggests that organizational learning can be enhanced by ensuring that leaders learn something new, by creating a change management group, by making sure that groups also learn, by designing a learning process and a change programme, and by maintaining communication. In these ways, individual learning is transmitted throughout the organization.

Organizations that deliberately develop such strategies to enhance learning have been called 'learning organizations' (Table 8.7).[70] Wishart et al.[71] say that a learning organization is skilled at acquiring information, storing it and retrieving and applying it to guide action. Garvin[72] defines a learning organization as one able to create, acquire and transfer knowledge, and to change its behaviour to reflect new knowledge. New ideas, from flashes of insight, systematic reflection, or from the importation of outsiders and outside ideas, can only trigger improvements if they are translated in changes in the way in which work is carried out. Organizational learning involves systematic problem-solving, experimentation with new approaches, learning from experience and best practice, and transferring knowledge quickly and efficiently through the organization in ways that manifest themselves in measurable output.

Writers have pointed out that designing an organization-wide system that supports learning and produces innovation is difficult. While problems that relate to particular instances of individual learning or to specific innovation projects can often be resolved relatively easily, it is far more difficult to engender learning that translates into continuous innovation, particularly in the case of large, mature organizations.[73] Dougherty and Hardy[74] provide an organizational blueprint that incorporates both structural and cultural aspects. They argue that innovation can only be sustained if *resources* are made available for new product development; collaborative *processes* exist to connect innovations to the larger organization; and innovation is a valued component, which has positive *meaning* for the organization's strategy (Table 8.8). In this way, three dimensions of power are directed towards

TABLE 8.7 *Characteristics of the learning organization*

- A learning approach to strategy
- Leaders who model risk taking and experimentation
- Participative policy making
- Decentralized decision-making
- Skill inventories and audits
- Systems and enabling structures for sharing learning and internal exchange
- Flexible rewards and human resource practices that encourage employee initiatives
- Information technology and accounting systems that inform and empower individuals across the organization
- Consideration of long-term initiatives
- Cross-functional teams – collaboration and team learning
- Opportunities to learn from experience
- A culture of feedback and disclosure
- Continuous learning opportunities and self-development
- Promotion of inquiry and dialogue
- Continuous experimentation
- A learning culture and a commitment to learning
- Learning-based information systems
- Connections to the environment and boundary workers who act as environmental scanners
- Inter-company learning such as interorganizational networks and alliances
- Ideas are shared across vertical, horizontal, external, geographic and temporal boundaries

---

Sources: Adapted from Watkins and Marsick, 1993; McGill and Slocum, 1993; Ulrich et al. 1993

organization-wide innovation. Many large bureaucracies find it difficult to innovate because, instead of being aligned with innovation, the three dimensions reinforce each other to produce an *anti*-innovation configuration (Exercise 8.3).

EXERCISE 8.3 DOES YOUR ORGANIZATION LEARN?

Reflect on your organization or select one from the business literature. Refer to Tables 8.7 and 8.8 and answer the following questions:

- Is this organization a learning organization and/or a pro-innovation configuration? Explain your answer.
- If it is, explain the critical success factors that make this organization capable of innovation and/or learning.
- If it is not, what changes would you make to enhance learning and innovation? How would you implement them?
- Are learning and innovation the same process or different? Explain your answer.

TABLE 8.8 *Organizational configuration and innovation*

	Anti-innovation	Pro-innovation
Resources	Access to critical resources are systematically controlled by individual groups, departments and individuals rather than being readily and widely provided by the organization	Seed money, equipment, and expertise from all functions are available; budget control is decentralized; information about customers, operating costs, development expenses is dispersed; training and rewards are consistent with innovation
Processes	Decisions on new products are centralized, excluding people familiar with specific technologies or business opportunities; decision processes rely on vague, unclear criteria; allocation systems such as annual budgeting are fixed by date rather than opportunity; jobs; interdepartmental relations are rigidly defined.	Collaborative structures and problem-solving processes are extensive; agenda setting is open and participative; decision criteria are based on collective judgement and link new products to existing businesses; decision-making procedures move innovations through development steps in a visible manner; regular reviews clarify and renegotiate targets and assure follow-through
Meaning	Activities associated with innovation are penalized; individuals are reassigned without concern for innovation projects; short-term results are rewarded over long-term capability development; projects killed when sponsors are moved; connections between projects and strategy are not made.	The symbols of management show that innovation is clearly valued; constituent activities of innovation are understood as proper and legitimate for all organization members; open strategic conversations involve the participation of many people in enacting innovation and constructing its meaning
Impact on innovation and learning	Innovation and learning are repudiated in favour of the routine; change only occurs due to the efforts of individuals who are able to create innovative 'bubbles' that are protected from the wider organization.	Innovation and learning are deeply ingrained in the fabric of the organization, and not dependent on particular individuals or groups; it occurs on a continuing basis.

Source: Adapted from Hardy and Dougherty, 1997

In summary, this approach to learning, which has been termed systems-structural[75] or modernist,[76] seeks to address the limitations of individual-based accounts of learning that fail to address how individual learning is transferred into an organizational context. It is based on logical, positivist assumptions concerning the processing of information.[77] Organizational learning lies in discovering the 'truth' about how the environment works and developing appropriate responses to it. Knowledge is assumed to be finite and capable of being itemized; the world works according to definite principles; and people are – or at least should try to be – rational. Within the organizational context, the object is to grasp the organizational 'systems that portray the processes of the world and to apply this knowledge to rectify or to eliminate problems'.[78] Structural and cultural organizational mechanisms are designed and implemented to enhance learning by improving the collection and analysis of information, the acquisition of knowledge and the transfer of information and knowledge into collective action.

Organizational 'learning': making sense of madness?

A different approach to organizational learning places more emphasis on the interpretation of meaning within specific cultures. It challenges the anthropomorphism of organizational 'minds' and 'memories' and questions whether organizations can 'think'. Instead, this literature focuses more on the meaning of information and intangibles such as the tacit knowledge of experienced people.[79] But meaning and tacit knowledge are not objective phenomena – they are embedded in a particular time and place. Thus learning, whether by individual or organization, cannot be separated from its institutional and social context.[80] The interpretive approach[81] is based on different assumptions and generates different implications for management practice than the systems-structural approach discussed above (Table 8.9).[82] It holds that events and organizational problems are constituted through people's subjective understanding and focuses on how people shape their reality. So, while systems-structural organizational learning aims at reducing uncertainty, interpretive views do not remove doubt about the future, or even the past, because both are open to multiple interpretation. In this context, ambiguity is inevitable, rationality is impossible and understanding is associated with plausibility rather than veracity. In this situation, learning becomes a form of meaning creation and sense-giving/making rather than an objective set of techniques aimed at discovering the 'truth'.[83]

Through the lens of an interpretive perspective, the seemingly fixed and concrete yields to social construction. For example, technology is not a neutral tool used to accomplish human action, but is a creation of human action.[84] It may seem to be 'part of the objective, structural properties of the organization' because 'once developed and deployed, technology tends to become reified and institutionalized, losing its connection with the human agents that constructed and gave it meaning'.[85] However, this meaning, despite appearances, is always flexible. Consequently, technology

TABLE 8.9   *Systems-structural and interpretive views*

	Systems-structural view: discovering the truth	Interpretive view: making sense of madness
Modus operandi	To reduce uncertainty by detecting the correct answer in an analysable situation and sharing it throughout the organization	To acknowledge ambiguity and then create meaning from it in an unanalysable situation
Key assumptions	Organizations are information-processing systems that scan, interpret and diagnose environmental events	Organizations are networks of shared meanings that are sustained through a common language and everyday social interactions
Knowledge acquisition	Environmental scanning and formal search procedures to collect and measure information	Informal and haphazard information collection from diverse informal sources. Multiple meanings are created from ambiguous environment through actions taken throughout the organization
Information distribution	Information is distributed through formal processes that connect parts of the organization and/or by breaking down cultural barriers to sharing and understanding information	Experiential knowledge is distributed horizontally within and across communities-of-practice through storytelling, learning by doing
Information interpretation	Linear, rule-bound interpretations based on formal techniques, synthesis by senior managers and/or cultural consensus will tend to produce convergent meaning	Recursive and informal interpretations based on intuition and experience may produce divergent meanings
Organizational memory	Lessons from experience are codified in the form of explicit knowledge and/or institutionalized in cultural values whose meaning is relatively unequivocal; access to organizational memory will be consistent either through formal regulation or through systematic socialization; contents of the organizational memory will tend to reinforce current routines and sanctioned interpretations	Lessons from experience remain tacit; they may exist in the form of stories and myths whose meanings remain unclear; access to the organizational memory will be haphazard and informal; contents of the organizational memory will support multiple interpretations; experimentation and 'frame-breaking' creative action may result from trial and error
Skills	Technical and professionally legitimated skills, inscribed in formal roles or skills associated with cultural norms, heroes and myths	On-the-job, hands-on skills, culturally embedded and legitimated, not necessarily part of formal roles
Learning	Incremental refinement of existing knowledge and practice	Radical changes in practice which could easily be 'wrong'
Key parameters	Formal structures and processes, convergent aspects of culture	Sense making, meaning, divergent aspects of culture

Sources: Partially adapted from Daft and Weick, 1984; Ford and ogilvie, 1996

is 'something that admits several possible or plausible interpretations and therefore can be esoteric, subject to misunderstandings, uncertain, complex and recondite'.[86] In other words, to understand technological development, we must explore meaning and, specifically, how fluid meanings become fixed, reified, objectified and institutionalized within the context of a particular culture.

Interpretive views thus link learning, innovation and technological development to meaning. As Dougherty[87] has pointed out, competencies 'do not exist apart from the people' who develop them, 'nor from the social processes of interpretation and construction through which people make their experiences meaningful'. Brown and Duguid[88] point out that whatever is learned is inextricably connected to the conditions under which it is learned:

> Learners do not receive or construct abstract 'objective', individual knowledge: rather, they learn to function in a community ... They learn that particular community's subjective view point and learn to speak its language ... Learners are acquiring not explicit, formal 'expert knowledge' but the embodied ability to behave as community members.

To learn, then, is to:

> use language, to communicate, both at the interpersonal and the intrapersonal level. At the intrapersonal level, language allows for reflection which, along with action or behaviour, is a critical part of learning – all learning occurs through social interaction. Language is both the tool and the repository of learning. It is the critical tool for reflection at both the interpersonal and intrapersonal levels.[89]

Brown and Duguid[90] provide an example of this when they describe an attempt to repair a machine. The explanation of the breakdown was not contained in the explicit knowledge provided in written documentation, nor was it explained by reference to the tacit experience of either the service technician or the technical specialist. The machine was, however, eventually repaired though a long storytelling procedure between the service technician and technical specialist, during which a series of anecdotes were discussed and used to produce a collective, convergent, coherent interpretation of what had gone wrong.

According to the interpretive view then, learning is 'the acquiring, sustaining, and changing, through collective actions, of the meanings embedded in the organization's cultural artefacts',[91] which are accessed through language.[92] Learning resides in relationships and thus the organizational 'memory' or the 'collective mind', insofar as it exists, lies *between* people rather than inside their heads. Weick and Roberts[93] argue that an organization's collective properties emerge from interrelated social practices that are conducted 'mindfully'. Thus the collective mind lies between people rather than within them.

According to this approach, narrative skills are crucial to learning because stories organize know-how, tacit knowledge and multiple causation into a memorable plot that aids learning.[94] Brown and Duguid[95] show how story-telling represented organizational learning in their example above. First, the storytelling constituted of a diagnosis in which the machine was understood causally and this causal map was eventually related to practice, i.e. the fact that the machine did not work. Second, storytelling was an important way to articulate and disseminate some of the tacit knowledge that was needed to fix the machine. Third, during this process, previous stories were amended and previously unintelligible data were given meaning. Conse-quently, the new story was added to the accumulation of organizational knowledge. Fourth, the storytelling was collective – *organizational* learning occurred because the individual service technician could not construct a coherent account alone and looked to others to construct one collectively. In other words, organizational learning took the form of a process of social construction where a shared understanding, meaningful in a particular context, was created collectively.

Recommendations for managerial practice, according to the interpretive view, reside in fostering communities-of-practice (Table 8.10). Communi-ties-of-practice are informal relationships that emerge as people attempt to solve problems, although they may be influenced by formal roles and relationships. Within them, people share tacit knowledge, exchange ideas about work, experiment with new methods and ideas, test and modify theories in use. In so doing, they engage in experiential learning, develop

TABLE 8.10   *Characteristics of communities-of-practice*

- Communities-of-practice are informal relationships that emerge as people attempt to solve problems, although they may be influenced by formal roles and relationships.
- Within them, people share tacit knowledge, exchange ideas about work, experiment with new methods and ideas, test and modify theories in use. In so doing, they engage in experiential learning, develop cognitive structures and engage in the formation of culture.
- They represent relationships and activities which embody shared understandings for participants, access to which is related to language and shared meaning.
- They involve complex social processes centred on the construction, maintenance and change of identities.
- They emerge in a historical, political and social context that affects possibilities for learning.
- They give rise to 'situated learning' in that learning and practice occur in a spatial and temporal context.
- Such learning is associated with a person acting in a cultural setting rather than simply through narrowly defined processes of cognitive assimilation.
- Skills learned in communities-of-practice are socially defined, tacit skills that link formal, technical skills to the particular context.
- Resources for learning are embedded in existing practices, work relations, and other communities of practice.
- By forming and transmitting culture, communities-of-practice also inhibit change.
- Communities-of-practice thus embody tensions between forces that encourage learning and those that impede it.

Source: Adapted from Hendry, 1996

cognitive structures and engage in the formation of culture. However, in these routines lies a paradox in that by forming and transmitting culture do communities-of-practice create new learning or reinforce old learning (Exercise 8.4)? Communities-of-practice thus both impede change through the transmission of cultural conformity and facilitate innovation through organizational learning.[96]

In summary, the interpretive view has quite different implications for management practice than the systems-structural model. Organizational learning is a sense-making process: it concerns learning and constructing appropriate stories and knowing the appropriate occasions for telling them.[97] The interpretive view thus focuses attention on meaning, culture and language as the mechanisms through which organizational learning occurs by facilitating sense making, convergence seeking and identity building. It acknowledges that culturally situated skills and tacit knowledge, acquired from and constituted through conversation, shape behaviour. It places emphasis on socialization processes that facilitate the mutual creation of compatible and shared meaning through communities-of-practice, in which individual and organizational identities are modified and changed. Organizational learning is about '*becoming* a practitioner not learning *about* practice'.[98] It suggests we need a theory of meaning – as well as of identity – rather than a theory of 'truth'.[99]

THE PARADOX OF ORGANIZATIONAL LEARNING

The organizational learning literature is full of contradictions as, indeed, is organizational change.[100] Cook and Yanow[101] frame the challenge of organizational learning as: to 'change without changing'. Learning involves 'learning how to do and make something different without becoming a new and different company'. In their discussion of organizational learning, Weick and Westley[102] juxtapose remembering and forgetting, as well as order and disorder. Hedberg[103] has noted that one of the main problems in organizational learning is unlearning. 'Understanding involves both learning new knowledge and discarding obsolete and misleading knowledge. The discarding activity – unlearning – is as important as is adding new knowledge, and often more difficult to do.'[104] Srikantia and Pasmore[105] juxtapose conviction and doubt. They argue that learning begins with self-doubt that current methods are not as perfect or as effective as they might be, and continues with conviction as risks are taken to introduce new methods. Too much conviction blocks continuation of learning; too much doubt leads to paralysis. Levinthal and March[106] argue that to learn from experience, organizations need to simplify and specialize. This produces bureaucratic pressures to facilitate exploitation. But learning also hinges on experimentation and creativity to enhance exploration. If exploitation dominates, short-run costs and returns will preclude more adventurous moves. If exploration dominates, a frenzy of change and innovation may occur that soak up resources.

EXERCISE 8.4 PROFILING THE LEARNING ORGANIZATION?

- Consider the nature of learning in your organization (or select an organization from the literature).
- Answer the following questions.
- Reflect on the profile that has emerged. What conclusions do you draw?
- What would you change to enhance organizational learning and how would you change it?

Left pole	Category	Scale	Right pole
Reduce uncertainty	Aim of organizational learning	1 2 3 4 5 6 7 8 9 10	Acknowledge ambiguity
Formal scanning	Knowledge acquisition	1 2 3 4 5 6 7 8 9 10	Informal, haphazard, personal
Formal processes/clear norms	Information distribution	1 2 3 4 5 6 7 8 9 10	Informal, storytelling, learning by doing
Techniques/cultural consensus to produce convergent meaning	Information interpretation	1 2 3 4 5 6 7 8 9 10	Intuition and experience to produce multiple meanings
Embedded in codified, explicit knowledge	Organizational memory	1 2 3 4 5 6 7 8 9 10	Embedded in tacit knowledge of communities-of-practice
Technical or those associated with cultural 'heroes'	Valued skills	1 2 3 4 5 6 7 8 9 10	On-the-job, hands-on experience
Refinement of existing processes	Learning aims	1 2 3 4 5 6 7 8 9 10	Radical change
Formal structures, processes, convergent culture	Key parameters	1 2 3 4 5 6 7 8 9 10	Sense making, meaning, divergent culture

These contradictions illuminate the paradoxical nature of learning – learning is as much about maintenance as it is about change; as much about preservation as innovation.[107] From the interpretivist view, it is clear that socialization into communities-of-practice reaffirms the old at the same time as it provides the basis for the new. Organizational learning is socially constructed and dependent upon shared meaning, but this process, in turn, makes learning highly conservative, sustaining the existing belief structures. 'Stable, shared knowledge interferes with the discovery of contrary experience from which valid learning arises, and the exploration of novel ideas interferes with the reliable maintenance of sharing of interpretations.'[108] This paradox also applies to the systems-structural view – how does change occur once experiences and learning are embedded into the organizational mind or memory?[109] In other words, the institutionalization of learning, whether in stories and myths or standard operating procedures and routines, represents a pull towards the old, while learning relies on receptivity towards the new. Consequently, learning is as much about 'reaffirmation, conservation, complication, efficiency, appreciation, community, and sometimes even self-destruction, as it is about change and improvement'.[110] In this section, we examine some of the debates that emerge from this fundamental paradox.

Struggling to converge?

One debate concerns whether organizational learning represents commonality or variety among interpretations. Has an organization learned more if its members interpret information and events the same way or if they interpret them differently?[111] The traditional basis of the interpretive approach has been to emphasize convergence in meaning. The existing literature on organizational innovation and learning has tended to emphasize the importance of a unified culture, bridging discontinuous thought worlds and shared meanings. Many writers emphasize the need for coherence and alignment of organizational cognitive elements,[112] whether referred to as gestalts, worldviews, theories of action or cognitive schemata. Dougherty[113] found that unsuccessful innovation projects were characterized by departments apparently working consensually but where, in fact, each department had a different meaning of the term 'market-oriented'. For employees in R&D, it meant product specifications and technical features – what the product can do. To members of manufacturing, it meant durability and reliability, which translated into fewer features and simpler specifications. For marketing, it meant what customers wanted. Business planning groups thought it meant having the product in the right market niche. The consensus was thus illusory and while traditional integrative mechanisms brought departments together, it failed to identify and reconcile dissimilarities in their frames of reference. According to this approach, learning involves sharing a deep understanding and opening up the possibility of mutual interpretation to enable a new definition of the situation in which all participants share and on which all agree.[114]

Srikantia and Pasmore say that the current literature on organizational learning is too biased 'toward the achievement of consensus and the reduction of doubt' and the need to collapse multiple interpretations into common understanding before learning is said to have taken place. However, 'driving for consensus too soon . . . reduces doubt to levels that threaten learning from continued exploration of the alternatives'.[115] Dougherty[116] emphasizes the importance of tensions between the inside and the outside (technology vs. the market); the old and the new (routine vs. creative problem solving); determined and emergent innovations (monitoring vs. evaluating new projects); and responsibility and freedom (accountability vs. commitment to innovation). She argues that coming down on one side or the other is detrimental to innovation; instead organizations need to juggle these contradictory pressures. Fiol[117] points out that contradiction plays an important role in fostering creativity by juxtaposing 'widely divergent bodies of knowledge and experience'. To harness the creative tensions, she argues it is necessary to embrace a series of stories, rather than a single tale. Rather than merge completely incompatible thought worlds, learning involves interactions among successively overlapping thought worlds. The trick is to balance diversity and consensus.

We see here evidence of possibilities for action borne of struggle. Brown and Duguid (1991) suggest that learning may result from the interplay of separate communities with independent worldviews. Similarly, strong cultures that produce unified organizational and individual identities may circumscribe learning as efforts go into reproducing identity rather than challenging and changing it. Individuals locked into a single subject position have fewer choices for action than individuals who lack identification with a single, stable role. Thus individuals who experience contradictions and antagonism that rupture dominant organizational discourses, cultures and identities experience a 'lack' – rather than a certainty – that open up alternative possibilities for action.[118]

Telling what we know or knowing more than we tell?

A second debate concerns the relative importance of tacit and explicit knowledge. Polanyi[119] argued that we know more than we can tell. The knowledge we cannot easily tell is tacit – based on experience – as opposed to explicit knowledge, which is articulated in management information systems, manuals, routines, etc. Whereas explicit, codified knowledge is transmittable in formal, systematic knowledge, tacit knowledge is rooted in action, commitment and involvement. It resides within people, is acquired through experience and cannot easily be communicated.[120] Of particular importance in the design of the learning organization is the development and circulation of tacit knowledge.[121] Consequently, it has been argued that learning organizations should work towards communication processes 'in which individuals' tacit knowledge is brought to the surface and, mixed with other knowledges . . . learning means a growth in the knowledge that circulates or flows through parts of an organization'.[122]

Nonaka[123] argues that the *interaction* between explicit and tacit knowledge is crucial to organizational learning (Table 8.11). Through socialization, existing tacit knowledge is converted into new tacit knowledge. Different bodies of explicit knowledge held by individuals are combined by reconfiguring existing information through formal information processing channels to form new information systems. As explicit knowledge is internalized, it is transformed into tacit knowledge. The externalization of tacit knowledge changes it into explicit knowledge, making it easier to embed in organizational memory. Knowledge creation is assisted by organizational structures and processes that facilitate all four forms of knowledge conversion. Japanese firms are often held up as models of organizational learning[124] and, although opinions differ as to whether Japanese secrets can be transferred to different cultures,[125] writers argue that they effectively address relationships between tacit and explicit knowledge.[126] They rely on tacit communication internally, which enhances learning, but engage in explicit communication for incoming/outgoing flows (through technical literature and patents). Moreover, the interaction between explicit and tacit knowledge occurs at the group level and not simply the individual (Exercise 8.5). US

TABLE 8.11 *Tacit and explicit knowledge conversion*

	Tacit knowledge is	Explicit knowledge is
Converted into tacit knowledge	Experiences are shared to create mental models and technical skills through socialization	Explicit knowledge is internalized through such methods as 'learning by doing'
Converted into explicit knowledge	Tacit knowledge is externalized through its articulation and expression	Explicit knowledges are combined as they are systematized and converted into a knowledge system

Source: Adapted from Nonaka, 1994: 19

EXERCISE 8.5 BE EXPLICIT?

Consider your organization or select one from the business literature and answer the following questions:

- What is the relative importance of tacit and explicit knowledge? Explain your answer.
- Do different groups view tacit and explicit knowledge differently? Explain your answer.
- What mechanisms exist for converting tacit and explicit knowledge? Refer to Table 8.11 and explain how conversion takes place and/or note those forms of conversion that do not occur.
- What effects does this have on organizational learning?

organizations are argued to be the opposite – external communication is tacit, often through the recruitment of specialists from other companies who bring their tacit knowledge with them while internal communication is explicit.[127]

Many interpretive writers challenge the emphasis on explicit knowledge advocated by Nonaka, as well as the even greater focus in the systems-structural approach. Brown and Duguid argue that the abstractions of work found in explicit knowledge fall short of the complexity of actual practice. Consequently, they argue that organizational members often regard any emphasis on explicit knowledge as unhelpful, impoverished and even demeaning. Explicit knowledge is hard to apply, hard to learn, hard to change. According to this view, organizational learning hinges less on externalizing and combining explicit knowledge and more on encouraging storytelling, apprenticeships, observation and learning-by-doing as ways to access tacit knowledge. Thus interpretive work challenges the view that what is to be learned must be capable of being stated in terms that can be understood by others in the organization.[128] Moreover, structural solutions to transmit explicit knowledge to different parts of the organization, argue interpretivists, will not work because they rigidify and reify knowledge, making it difficult to learn and change. Instead, fluid communities-of-practice[129] enable organizational members to have a legitimate status on the periphery, where they can watch others and develop know-how. Learning is fostered by expanding access to these communities-of-practice, not by explicating abstractions of individual practice or by setting up formal teams.

Organize for disorganizing?

Another debate concerns how to design a learning organization. Systems-structural approaches advocate formality and standardization, while inter-pretive theorists challenge these recommendations. Nonaka[130] attempts to combine the two with his model of the hypertext organization which 'com-bines the efficiency and stability of a hierarchical bureaucratic organization', necessary to deal with explicit knowledge, with 'the dynamism of the flat, cross-functional task-force organization' which is amenable to tacit know-ledge. Other writers question whether this 'best of both worlds' can be enacted in the form of a sustainable organizational design. While authors offer a variety of suggestions regarding ways of increasing both doubt and conviction, order and disorder, learning and unlearning, it still remains unclear as to how organizations can be designed to accommodate both sets of contradictory processes at the same time. 'The relationship between learning and organizing is inherently uncomfortable, a tension, rather than a compatibility.'[131]

Armchair theorizing is somewhat different to management practice and may explain why organizations find it difficult to learn and innovate. 'Stable, shared knowledge interferes with the discovery of contrary experi-ence from which valid learning arises, and the exploration of novel ideas interferes with the reliable maintenance of sharing of interpretations.'[132] Organizing and learning are, then, antithetical processes:

> To learn is to disorganize and increase variety. To organize is to forget and reduce variety. In the rush to embrace learning, organizational theorists often overlook this tension, which explains why they are never sure whether learning is something new or simply warmed over organizational change.[133]

Small wonder, then, that the learning organization may be more difficult to find in practice than it is to describe in theory.

In summary, the paradox of organizational learning engenders debates regarding the design of learning organizations. It is not clear how much divergence is creative and how much convergence is necessary for action. The relationship between explicit and tacit knowledge remains problematic with systems-structural approaches highlighting the former and interpretive approaches emphasizing the latter. Finally, embedding contradictory elements in organization structures, processes and cultures is rather more difficult than theorists would have us believe. These difficulties lead Weick and Westley[134] to suggest that learning occurs in moments in time when order and disorder are juxtaposed, such as moments of humour, improvization and small wins. Humour allows anxiety and competence, doubt and conviction to co-exist. It allows criticisms and makes new connections. It confirms identity and allows it to evolve. Improvization works on the basis of intuition, gut feel and tacit knowledge. It includes a willingness to tolerate errors. Opportunities for small wins produce visible and tangible outcomes whose meaning is not fixed. They are occasions that attract unexpected allies, deter opponents, uncover new opportunities and beach old assumptions. By juxtaposing 'new symbols with old artefacts', small wins[135] 'can churn old routines into new learning'.[136] Through moments like these individuals may learn, but the question remains as to whether such moments can be organizationally orchestrated?

CONCLUSIONS: SO SHOULD ORGANIZATIONS BOTHER TO LEARN?

'To learn then is to dwell in the oxymoron of 'organizational learning' and to be pulled simultaneously in multiple directions, and to have no assurance of success.'[137] Organizational learning would not appear to be a comfortable state. Nor is it clear how to build a learning organization. One writer asks: is the learning organization idyllic? 'Absolutely. Desirable? Without question. But does it provide a framework for action? Hardly.'[138] In fact, depending on the approach to organizational learning, recommendations may be quite different (Table 8.12). Nor are organizations learning as easily as they might. Despite the learning opportunities supposedly provided by cross-national alliances,[139] one study of forty joint ventures between Japanese and North American firms found that learning was either not occurring

TABLE 8.12 *Approaches to organizational learning*

Focus	Individual components	Organizational hardware	Organizational software
Status of organizational learning	'Organizational' learning is really individual learning	'Organizational learning' is really individual learning applied to organizations	Organizational 'learning' is a process quite different to individual learning
Learning process	Individuals learn: they think and act	Organizations learn: they think and act	Meaning is created that enables collective actions: organizations are sum of thoughts and actions
Problems with learning	Learning breaks down because individual components are faulty	Learning breaks down because organizational hardware is faulty	Learning breaks down because organizational software is faulty
Fixing the problems	Ensure that individuals learn more effectively by improving their cognitive processes and by balancing espoused theories and theories-in-use	Ensure that organizations learn more effectively by improving structural and cultural processes and by balancing and absorption of new knowledge with institutionalization of experience	Ensure that organizations learn more effectively by improving meaning creation processes and by balancing convergence and divergence

at all, or not occurring as easily and successfully as had been hoped.[140] (See Exercise 8.6.)

Many writers have argued that we have little evidence that entities defined as learning organizations are any more successful than other organizations.[141] There are considerable problems with measuring learning. A study[142] of a Toyota/General Motors joint venture in California (NUMMI) compared it with a GM plant, on the same site, with the same unions and similar high degrees of standardization based on Taylorist principles of organization, that had collapsed some years earlier. The findings suggested that the difference, which accounted for NUMMI's success, lay in the fact that the new plant was set up in partnership with the unions and included employee empowerment, more job security, and a 'learning orientation'. A later comparison of NUMMI with a Swedish Volvo plant[143] argued that higher productivity at NUMMI indicated greater organizational learning through standardization than through the more humanistic orientation at Volvo. Apparently, it was difficult to disseminate individual learning because of long work cycles and variability in production tasks at the Volvo plant. In contrast, standardization at NUMMI made it easier to transfer learning in one part of the plant to another and short production cycles made ideas easy to identity. These conclusions were, however, challenged by Berggren,[144] who argued that earlier comparisons of productivity had only been taken at one point in time and the rate of improvement had not been measured. He also pointed out that productivity is only one possible outcome of organizational learning and that other aspects were ignored, such as satisfaction, quality, etc. In other words, definitive conclusions regarding the debate between Japanese lean production and Swedish humanism as facilitators of organizational learning remain elusive.[145]

Another problem in the organizational learning literature lies with an

---

EXERCISE 8.6 HOT-WIRING THE ORGANIZATION FOR LEARNING

Compare the three views of organizational learning in Table 8.12 and answer the following questions:

- Which approach do you think is the most useful for understanding what organizational learning is? Explain your answer.
- Which approach do you think is the most useful for designing and implementing a learning organization? Explain your answer.
- If you work for a learning organization, does it manifest any of these approaches? If so, describe how.
- Do you think management practice can combine these approaches or not? If so, which ones? Explain your answer.

emphasis on successful case studies, which may owe more to public relations than to scientific study. Easterby-Smith[146] has criticized studies of Whirlpool and BP for congratulating these companies for 'generative' learning but failing to acknowledge the severe problems caused by these cultural changes. Similarly, he points out that Shell is often cited as an example of a learning organization based primarily on a single account presented by a former senior executive of that company. There is a lack of longitudinal data and case study research. Nor is action research (such as the work of the Organizational Learning Center at MIT, associated with Peter Senge) likely to solve the problem as such researchers are unwilling publicly to parade their failures.[147] Given the lack of performance data and the difficulties in designing sustainable learning organizations, organizational learning may end up as just another fad whose time has come and gone.

NOTES

(See Bibliography at the end of the book for full references)

1 Mirvis, 1996: 13; Pedler, 1995
2 Senge, 1990
3 Crossan and Guatto, 1996
4 Garvin, 1993
5 Inkpen and Crossan, 1995; Levinson and Asahi, 1995
6 Hendry, 1996; Weick and Westley, 1996; see chapter on organizational change.
7 Weick, 1991
8 Fiol and Lyles, 1985
9 Garvin, 1993: 78
10 Senge, 1990: 1
11 Nicolini and Meznar, 1995; Mirvis, 1996
12 Thatchenkery, 1996
13 Dodgson, 1993
14 Dodgson, 1993; Garvin, 1993; Pedler, 1995; Easterby-Smith, 1997
15 Fiol and Lyles, 1985
16 Miller, 1996
17 Easterby-Smith, 1997
18 Fiol and Lyles, 1985
19 Dodgson, 1993
20 Dodgson, 1993
21 Cook and Yanow, 1993; Dodgson, 1993
22 Cook and Yanow, 1993
23 Garvin, 1993; Nevis et al. 1995; Nicolini and Meznar, 1995; Spender, 1996
24 Miller, 1996: 485
25 Nicolini and Meznar, 1995
26 Brown and Duguid, 1991
27 Argyris, 1993
28 Miller, 1996
29 Weick and Westley, 1996
30 Cook and Yanow, 1993; Weick and Westley, 1996
31 Dodgson, 1993: 377; March and Olsen, 1976; Hedberg, 1981
32 Argyris and Schon, 1978
33 Duncan and Weiss, 1979
34 Huber, 1991
35 Hedberg, 1981; Levinthal and March, 1993
36 Sandelands and Stablein, 1987
37 Weick and Westley, 1996
38 Cook and Yanow, 1993: 374
39 Shrivastava, 1983: 8
40 Senge, 1990; Schein, 1993a, b; Beer and Eisenstat, 1996; Lenke and Davies, 1996; Daudelin, 1996
41 Miller, 1996
42 Grandori, 1984; Nonaka, 1988; Senge, 1990
43 Miller, 1996
44 Daudelin, 1996
45 Miller, 1996; Hedberg, 1981; March, 1991
46 Senge, 1990
47 Senge, 1990: 139
48 Argyris and Schon, 1978: 19; Argyris, 1993
49 Argyris and Schon, 1978
50 Argyris, 1990
51 Isaacs, 1993; Schein, 1993a
52 Child, 1994
53 Hedberg, 1981: 6
54 Cohen and Levinthal, 1990; Nevis et al. 1995
55 Huber, 1991; Levinson and Asahi, 1995
56 Schein, 1993a
57 Hedberg, 1981: 6
58 Lipshitz et al. 1996
59 Weick and Westley, 1996
60 Nevis et al. 1995; Lipshitz et al. 1996
61 Galbraith, 1973; Duncan and Weiss, 1979; Shrivastava, 1983

62 Nicolini and Meznar, 1995
63 Hedberg et al. 1976; Fiol and Lyles, 1985
64 Duncan and Weiss, 1979
65 Daft and Huber, 1987
66 Shrivastava, 1983
67 Shrivastava, 1983 argues that mythological learning and information-sharing cultures are evolutionary rather than deliberately planned. However, we would argue that much of the literature on the learning organization has advocated the deliberate implementation of such 'designer-cultures' as a means to facilitate learning.
68 Dodgson, 1993
69 Schein, 1993b (SMR)
70 Senge, 1990; Pedler et al. 1989
71 Wishart et al. 1996
72 Garvin, 1993: 80
73 Garvin, 1993
74 Dougherty and Hardy, 1996
75 Daft and Huber, 1987; Ford and ogilvie, 1996
76 Addleson, 1996
77 Daft and Huber, 1987
78 Addleson, 1996: 33
79 Nevis et al. 1995
80 Geppert, 1996
81 Dougherty, 1992; Cook and Yanow, 1993; Weick and Roberts, 1993; Nicolini and Meznar, 1995; Addleson, 1996; Ford, 1996; Ford and ogilvie, 1996; Geppert, 1996; Weick and Westley, 1996
82 Spender, 1996; Fiol and Lyles, 1985; Daft and Huber, 1987; Addleson, 1996; Ford and ogilvie, 1996
83 Ford and ogilvie, 1996
84 Roberts and Grabowski, 1996
85 Orlikowski, 1992: 406
86 Weick, 1991: 2
87 Dougherty, 1995: 115
88 Brown and Duguid, 1991: 48
89 Weick and Westley, 1996: 446
90 Brown and Duguid, 1991
91 Cook and Yanow, 1993: 384
92 Weick and Westley, 1996
93 Weick and Roberts, 1993
94 Weick and Westley, 1996
95 Brown and Duguid, 1991
96 Hendry, 1996
97 Brown and Duguid, 1991
98 Brown and Duguid, 1991: 48; Cook and Yanow, 1993
99 Spender, 1996
100 See chapter on change.
101 Cook and Yanow, 1993: 383
102 Weick and Westley, 1996
103 Hedberg, 1981: 3; McGill and Slocum, 1993; Dodgson, 1993; Nicolini and Meznar, 1995
104 This debate is similar to the one we explored in the chapter on organizational change and concerning unlearning past frames.
105 Srikantia and Pasmore, 1996
106 Levinthal and March, 1993
107 Cook and Yanow, 1993
108 March et al. 1991: 6
109 Child, 1994; Inkpen and Crossan, 1995
110 Weick and Westley, 1996: 446
111 Huber, 1991: 102
112 Nicolini and Meznar, 1995
113 Dougherty, 1992; Boland and Tenkasi, 1995
114 Boland and Tenkasi, 1996
115 Srikantia and Pasmore, 1996: 45
116 Dougherty, 1996
117 Fiol, 1995: 71; Fiol, 1994
118 Holmer-Nadesan, 1996; Rodrigues, 1996
119 Polanyi, 1966: 4
120 Nonaka, 1994; see also Brown and Duguid, 1991 on canonical and non-canonical practice.
121 Brown and Duguid, 1991
122 Addelson, 1996: 37
123 Nonaka, 1994
124 Pucik, 1988; Marceau, 1992
125 Kidd and Teramoto, 1995; Lillrank, 1995
126 Nonaka and Takeuchi, 1995
127 Hedlund and Nonaka, 1993
128 Cook and Yanow, 1993
129 Brown and Duguid, 1991
130 Nonaka, 1994: 33
131 Weick and Westley, 1996: 44
132 March, 1991: 85
133 Weick and Westley, 1996: 440
134 Weick and Westley, 1996
135 See the change chapter for further discussion on 'small wins'.
136 Weick and Westley, 1996: 454
137 Weick and Westley, 1996: 456
138 Garvin, 1993: 79
139 Levinson and Asahi, 1995
140 Inkpen and Crossan, 1995
141 Addleson, 1996
142 Adler, 1993
143 Adler and Cole, 1993
144 Berggren, 1994
145 Easterby-Smith, 1997
146 Easterby-Smith, 1997
147 Easterby-Smith, 1997

9 MANAGEMENT AND LEADERSHIP IN CONTEXT

Hero, Villain or Myth?

The previous chapters have focused on a range of debates that confront the manager, or aspiring manager. Our assumption is that reducing management to a series of simple solutions reflects neither managers' lived experience of organizations, nor the wealth of academic thought and research about management. Clearly, as the previous chapters show, ambiguity and complexity characterize both the theory and practice of management. Responding to this messiness by sweeping it under the organizational carpet, in the name of producing clean solutions and neat lines of action, is unlikely to be an effective long-term strategy. The effects of ambiguity can rarely be controlled; paradoxes are difficult to resolve and simple solutions have an increasingly short shelf life. So, where does this leave the manager? At some point, readers of this book will want to translate their understanding of different debates into action. Linking debates to leadership provides a mechanism with which to bridge what we think we know about management with the *practice* of management by providing ideas whereby an individual might act.

A second reason for using the theme of leadership as a way to revisit issues raised in earlier chapters concerns the tendency to view leadership in the abstract. Bryman[1] notes that most leadership research has been conducted in isolation from the wider organizational literature, despite the supposed importance of leadership to organizational performance and despite the fact that areas of organizational studies have clear implications for leadership. Accordingly, instead of discussing particular theories of leadership in isolation, this chapter specifically reviews work on leadership in the context of the earlier chapters. Readers who wish to learn more about specific theories of leadership are referred to the supplementary reading material.

This chapter first provides an overview of leadership research and presents some of the contradictory reviews about what leadership is and what it does. It then links leadership to each of the earlier themes covered in this book – structure, people, power, culture, strategy, change and learning. In this way, we use the theme of leadership to revisit debates covered in each of the earlier chapters. By identifying the implications for leadership in relation to each of these areas, we accomplish two objectives. First, we provide

LEADERSHIP: SUPPLEMENTARY READING

- Alvesson, M. (1996) 'Leadership studies: from procedure and abstraction to reflexivity and situation', *Leadership Quarterly* 7 (4): 455–85.
- Barker, R.A. (1997) 'How can we train leaders if we do not know what leadership is?', *Human Relations*, 50 (4): 343–62.
- Bryman, A. (1996) 'Leadership in organizations', in S.C. Clegg, C. Hardy and W.R. Nord (eds), *Handbook of Organizations Studies*. London: Sage: 276–92.
- Conger, J.A. and Kanungo, R.N. (1994) 'Charismatic leadership in organizations: perceived behavioral attributes and their measurement', *Journal of Organizational Behavior*, 15: 439–52.
- Dunphy, D. and Bryant, B. (1996) 'Teams: panaceas or prescriptions for improved performance?', *Human Relations*, 49 (5): 677–99.
- Fiedler, F.E. (1996) 'Research on leadership selection and training: one view of the future', *Administrative Science Quarterly*, 41: 241–50.
- Graeff, C.L. (1997) 'Evolution of situational leadership theory: a critical review', *Leadership Quarterly*, 8 (2): 153–70.
- House, R.J. (1996) 'Path-goal theory of leadership: lessons, legacy, and a reformulated theory', *Leadership Quarterly*, 7 (3): 323–52.
- Neck, C.P. and Manz, C.C. (1996) 'Thought self-leadership: the impact of mental strategies training on employee cognition, behavior, and affect', *Journal of Organizational Behavior*, 17: 445–67.
- Quinn, R.E. (1996) *Deep change: discovering the leader within*, San Francisco: Jossey-Bass.
- Tracey, J.B. and Hinkin, T.R. (1998) 'Transformational leadership or effective managerial practices?', *Group and Organization Management*, 23 (3): 220–36.

the reader with a conceptual framework that integrates different aspects of managing the organization. Second, we contextualize leadership by grounding it in the wider organizational studies literature.

WHAT'S THE MATTER WITH LEADERSHIP?

One debate underpinning the entire field concerns a lack of consensus on definitions and conceptualizations of leadership. A plethora of leadership terms confronts the reader. For example, the term 'post-heroic' leadership is also referred to as servant leadership, distributed leadership and virtual leadership.[2] The charismatic leader is also known as the mythic leader and the heroic leader.[3]

Part of the problem is that often writers do not define the term. Rost[4] found that of 587 articles on leadership, 366 failed to define what was meant by the concept. One reason for this lack of clarity is that researchers seem to assume that everyone knows what leadership is.[5] This assumption would appear to be misplaced since these definitional problems reflect a broader conceptual divergence concerning what constitutes leadership. For some, leadership refers to processes of influencing organized group activities in specific directions; for others, leadership is a sense-making activity that entails symbolic actions and processes that generate meaning.[6] Even the well-worked term of 'democratic' leadership is rarely defined and often misunderstood.[7]

Too many differences?

Different paradigms have dominated leadership research at different times over the last fifty years and each has been criticized by successive generations of researchers (Table 9.1). For example, the popular Hersey and Blanchard[8] model of situational leadership has recently been critiqued[9] on the grounds that there is a lack of consistency in the presentation of the model and that it lacks a rigorous theoretical foundation. From a practitioner's point of view, the model's prescriptions embody conflicting guidelines about the style of leadership that should be used in particular situations. Earlier theories, such as the path–goal theory of leadership effectiveness, have been reassessed[10] in an attempt to escape the paradigm traps of the times in which they were developed.[11] This reworking of old theories leads to countless variations around a theme and has led some to argue that research on leadership 'has become bogged down by the subtle tweaking of old theories that makes it difficult to publish new ideas'.[12]

Can you tell the difference?

These conceptual and definitional problems are further reflected in the debate about the distinction between leadership and management. Some writers favour distinguishing between the two. For example, Barker maintains that the 'function of leadership is to create change while the function of management is to create stability'.[13] In contrast, Hooijberg argues that there is no meaningful dichotomy between management and leadership. He views leadership as a continuum of influence that extends from 'very little incremental influence to substantial influence. Such a conception of leadership is more fruitful, because less and less of current organizational functioning can be called routine. As organizational life becomes less and less routine, what becomes important is the amount of incremental influence managers can exert over their subordinates, peers, and superiors'.[14] It is perhaps for this reason that Tracey and Hinkin[15] found no clear distinction

TABLE 9.1 *Leadership theories – past and present*

Theory	Dominant period	Key assumptions	Examples of authors*	Criticisms of theory
Trait	Up to 1940s	• Leaders have physical traits, individual abilities and personality characteristics which distinguish them from non-leaders	Lord et al. (1986); Lord and Maher (1991)	• Inconsistent evidence concerning importance of cited traits
Style	1940s to 1960s	• Shift from focus on traits to behaviours • Emphasis on training of leaders rather than on the selection of leaders • Two key behaviour styles: **consideration** for subordinates = high morale, but lower performance; **initiating style** tells subordinates what to do and how to do it = poor morale, but higher performance • Later studies argue that better leaders were high on both styles	Ohio State University researchers e.g. Stoghill (1948)	• Inconsistent results • Lack of attention to impact of situation on leadership effectiveness • Difficult to establish causal interpretations • Overly focused on formal leaders rather than informal leadership processes • Problems of measurement
Contingency	Late 1960s to early 1980s	• Situational factors affect leadership effectiveness • Leadership attributes are related to personality • Therefore, to increase leadership effectiveness, need to change work situation to fit leader rather than the reverse	Fiedler (1967; 1993); Fiedler and Garcia (1987)	• Writers unconvinced about measurement of leadership using 'least preferred co-worker' (LPC) scale • Dispute about validity of measuring 'situation' • Exclusion of informal leadership processes
New leadership	1980s+	• Leaders as managers of meaning – leaders as transformational, charismatic and visionary	Bass and Avolio (1990, 1993); Conger (1989); Tichy and Devanna (1986); Bennis and Nanus (1985); Kotter (1990)	• Excessive focus on top leaders; overemphasis on successful leaders • Little focus on informal leadership processes • Little attention to situational factors • Problems of assumed causality
Dispersed leadership	1990s+	• Leadership not 'heroic' or the domain of formally designated leaders but a widely dispersed activity • Nurture leadership capacity in others • Dispersion of leadership throughout teams • Recognition of non-traditional leadership skills, e.g. organizing, networking	Manz and Sims (1991); Sims and Lorenzi (1992); Katzenbach and Smith (1993); Kouzes and Posner (1993); Hosking (1988, 1991); Knights and Willmott (1992)	• Question of whether dispersed leadership – and its implications of responsibility and empowerment – is a political technique for achieving greater employee output

* see Bryman, 1996 for full reference details
Source: Adapted from Bryman, 1996

between purported behaviours of transformational leaders and those associated with mainstream management practices. Cammock et al. arrived at a similar conclusion in finding that, for their respondents, 'management and leadership are not the disparate entities implied by much of the leadership literature'.[16] (See Exercise 9.1.)

Does it make a difference?

The high degree of confusion calls into question whether leadership has any impact on organizational outcomes. If no one is quite clear on what leadership is, how do they know whether it makes any difference? Even Fiedler, the chief architect of situational leadership, a major strand of leadership theory, has voiced reservations. He acknowledges that there 'has been much moaning and groaning in the past that we didn't know anything worthwhile about leadership, that leadership theories and research lacked focus and were chaotic'.[17] Barker is even less equivocal – he argues that the confusion is evidence that 'the study of leadership as an academic discipline is in shambles'.[18] Fiedler notes that other writers, frustrated with the lack of agreement, have questioned the very existence of the term, arguing there is no such thing as leadership.[19]

While acknowledging the problems, proponents of leadership nevertheless continue to argue that leadership does exist and does make a difference.[20] For example, Bryman suggests that 'we view leadership as an important feature of everyday and organizational affairs',[21] which accounts for the long history of research and the continual attraction of this area.

EXERCISE 9.1 WHO'S A LEADER?

Reflect back to your work situation and select five different individuals in leadership positions, or select five individuals from the business literature, and answer the following questions:

- Define what you mean by a leadership position.
- Who would you regard as a manager, but not a leader? What are their key characteristics?
- Who would you regard as a leader, but not a manager? What are their key characteristics?
- Who would you regard as both a leader and a manager? What are their key characteristics?
- What conclusions do you draw about the relationship between leaders and managers?
- If you are in a leadership position, or were to be appointed to one, which would you be – a leader or a manager? Explain your answer.

Leadership skills are deemed to be important to a wide range of organizational initiatives, including the success of strategic alliances,[22] to the effective management of diverse workforces,[23] to the ability to respond to the pressure of customers and the wider environment,[24] and to the reduction of workforce absenteeism.[25]

Regardless of these debates, or perhaps because of them, the centrality of leadership in management discourse is firmly established in both academic and practitioner arenas. Articles on leadership continue to appear in academic journals. The business literature continues to follow and publicize the activities of organizational leaders. Individuals continue to be labelled as leaders and praised – or blamed – for organizational performance. A burgeoning industry aimed at developing leadership skills has evolved. Many of us aspire to be better leaders so, regardless of academic bickering, leadership is here to stay. Much like the term strategy, as we discussed earlier, the term 'leadership' is difficult to escape. As a result, it is a useful lens through which to reflect back on some of the debates discussed in our earlier chapters. Consequently, the remainder of the chapter discusses some of the ways in which leadership converges with structure, people, power, culture, strategy, change and learning. We select particular themes to explore in detail and, by providing a series of exercises, we also invite readers to reflect on the implications of each chapter for leadership.

STRUCTURE

In this section we discuss the debates that surround the adoption of new forms of leadership in the context of new organizational forms. We show that, despite apparent convergence between these 'new' forms, questions remain as to whether we really are witnessing a brave new world which, in turn, has implications for whether the brand of brave new leadership, promulgated by many writers, is appropriate.

Sharing it around?

The argument that we are witnessing a shift from old to new forms of organizing parallels a similar shift in the leadership literature regarding the need to move away from authoritarian to 'dispersed' modes of leadership. Whereas traditional organizational structures are based upon differentiation and domination, new organizational forms celebrate de-differentiation and collaboration. These concepts fit with the tenets of sharing leadership throughout the organization as advocated by dispersed leadership theories.[26] Originally, referred to as 'unleadership', then self-leadership, dispersed leadership is also associated with super-leadership[27] and post-heroic leadership,[28] all of which embody a form of participative leadership where employees share in decision-making and take responsibility for their own work.[29] It occurs when individuals monitor and evaluate their own job performance, set their own goals, reward or discipline themselves in relation to their own performance, set their own expectations, systematically practice required behaviours, and facilitate environmental conditions appropriate to productive behaviour.[30] Leadership in this context is about nurturing the capacity for self-leadership throughout the organization.[31]

The rationale for this form of leadership is that as structures become more flexible in response to customers and the wider business environment, so should leadership permeate all levels of an organization to encourage entrepreneurial behaviour in subordinates.[32] These post-heroic leaders still require 'many of the attributes that have always distinguished the best leaders – intelligence, commitment, energy, courage of conviction, integrity. But here's the big difference: It expects those qualities of just about everyone in the organization. The time when a few rational managers could run everything, it seems, was just an anomaly, or part of an era very different from the fast-paced, continually shifting present.'[33] Ashkenas et al. refer to these people as 'boundaryless leaders'. They are able to manage in the present while creating renewal for the future. They can live with change processes that are ambiguous and uncertain. They are able to lead change without having a clear idea of the destination. They have the capacity to deal with disruption. They know how to reflect upon and enact the personal changes they need to make in order to manage boundaryless organizations.[34] (See Exercise 9.2.)

Another important aspect of new organizational forms is the existence of cross-functional and cross-organizational teams, which are believed to facilitate the breaking down of boundaries. White[35] argues that

---

EXERCISE 9.2 HEROIC OR POST-HEROIC ORGANIZATIONS?

Reflect back to your work situation or select four articles from the business literature on organizational leaders and answer the following questions:

- Does your organization/the business literature celebrate heroic leaders?
- If so, how do they emerge?
- If not, why do you think that this is the case?
- To what extent has your organization/the business literature moved towards a dispersed leadership model? Compare the situation today with five or ten years ago?
- If dispersed leadership is more important today, why do you think this is the case? What factors support the introduction and extension of this model of leadership?
- If not, why do you think that this is the case? What barriers hinder the introduction and extension of this model of leadership?

high-performance workplaces, based upon self-managing teams, do not need the traditional 'command and control' leader, but rather the entrepreneurial, irreverent, action-focused and empowered team leader. While not traditionally authoritarian, this leader is still a leader. Other writers challenge the relevance of such hands-on leadership and prefer to apply the concept of self-leadership in these circumstances. For example, Katzenbach[36] argues that teams are more effective when they assess the task in hand and appropriately shift leadership capacity among its members. Dunphy and Bryant[37] differentiate teams on the basis of their degree of self-management and self-leadership. Self-management occurs when 'members take over many of the operational responsibilities previously performed by managers and supervisors'. Self-leadership arises when 'members participate in problem solving, innovation, and strategic direction'. Self-led teams do not have supervisors because team members have taken over middle management functions such as implementing strategy, planning and budgeting and, in some cases, setting strategic direction.

Proceed with caution?

However, before jettisoning traditional leadership and embracing the tenets of dispersed leadership, three cautionary points must be considered. First, some writers maintain that it is less the structure and more the task to which leadership should be matched. For example, Bowen et al.[38] argue that there is no one leadership type which is best suited to the management of all projects – different types of leadership should be matched with individual projects in an organization. In other words, there should be no dominant leadership style – dispersed or centralized – in the organization, but a range of leadership styles that are matched to particular tasks and projects.

Second, writers caution against the assumption that we are witnessing the replacement of old forms of organizing by new organizational forms. For example, Hilmer and Donaldson maintain that the new forms do not represent fundamental shifts in organizing but rather are ways in which traditional hierarchies are evolving.[39] Hierarchy, then, is not something that is being replaced, as some would argue[40] but rather is being modified to incorporate new structures. Similarly, the prevalence of self-led, self-managed teams has also been questioned.[41] Dunphy and Bryant[42] found no evidence of fully fledged self-leading work teams and have pointed out that the considerable costs of training and developing such teams may restrict their use to a small number of highly specialized and unusual situations. In addition, many organizations, such as airlines and banks, place a premium on 'high reliability'. They institute rules and procedures, monitored by managers, to retain efficiency and reduce risk.[43] In this situation, the outdated directive leader may be crucial to organizational performance. In other words, as Chapter 2 on structure explored, many writers are sceptical of whether new organizational forms are as ubiquitous and as radical as their proponents suggest. If these observations are correct, hierarchical forms of leadership may not be dead either but also evolving in different ways.

Third, Gordon points out that the work on dispersed forms of leadership has failed to address the extent to which deep underlying structures of power inhibit the implementation of dispersed leadership. He suggests:

> While the surface level structural changes implemented by an organization may appear to reinforce the theoretical underpinnings of the dispersed leadership theories (de-differentiate and collaborate), its deeper social structures and embedded discourse patterns may continue to reinforce the theoretical under-pinnings of the traditional leadership theories (differentiate and dominate).[44]

The result is the re-centralization rather than the dispersion of power because dispersed leaders act on what they perceive to be the expectations of senior management, implementing their desires and wishes. While Gordon has yet to verify his arguments empirically, he has nevertheless identified an important omission in the dispersed leadership approaches and raised questions concerning whether new forms of leadership are really possible in new organizational structures (Exercise 9.3).

PEOPLE

When it comes to people in organizations, the aim of leadership is primarily to influence them. Leaders are those who can influence the people in the organization to carry out the behaviours required of them. The leadership literature offers two main strategies for influencing people. The first revolves

---

EXERCISE 9.3 MANAGING STRUCTURE?

Reread Chapter 2 on structure. Reflect on the three most important debates discussed in that chapter for an individual responsible for 'leading' an organization or a unit within an organization. Where appropriate, relate the leadership role back to your position within your organization. Answer the following questions:

- List the three most important debates.
- For each debate, explain why you believe it to be important.
- Elaborate what you have learned from thinking about each debate.
- Describe how you would translate your thoughts into actions for members of your organization to take.
- If you do not have organizational experience, describe how you would translate your thoughts into actions that you will take when you start work.

around adopting leadership styles that are appropriate to the needs of the particular situation. The second emphasizes the use of charisma. In this section, we consider the debates connected with these two strategies.

Changing actors or changing costumes?

Some researchers present a range of leadership 'archetypes' that show how different types of leaders use particular methods to influence people (Table 9.2). The implication of this body of literature is that leaders have particular styles that rely on particular methods of influencing subordinates. Other writers adopt a more contingent view by linking the means of influence to the task, the context and the characteristics of the subordinate or group.

Some contingency theorists argue that leaders should have a dominant approach, which should cater to the demands of the particular contingency. For example, Farkas and Wetlaufer[45] argue that where CEOs lack a dominant stance and draw from different approaches, they lose organizational focus and effectiveness (Table 9.3).[46] Hooijberg[47] challenges this idea by arguing in favour of a theory of behavioural complexity which encompasses two dimensions. First, the behavioural repertoire refers to the range of

TABLE 9.2 *Leadership archetypes and influence styles*

Leadership archetype	Influence behaviours
Authoritarian	• Directive and dictatorial • Punitive measures • Use of position power • Expectation of conformance to leader's directives by subordinates either to avoid sanction or in 'blind' obedience to formal authority
Transactor	• Instrumental exchange relationship between leader and subordinate • Rewards and compensation • Use of reward power • Expectation of calculated compliance with desired behaviour by subordinates in order to secure rewards
Transformational	• Creation of vision • Charismatic relationship with subordinates • Use of personal power • Expectation of compliance with desired behaviour by subordinates through collective vision in which everyone benefits
Empowering	• Emphasizes self-influence and ownership • Facilitative and consultative behaviours • Empowerment of subordinates • Expectation of enactment of desired behaviour by subordinates through the use of empowerment that gets others to lead themselves

Source: Adapted from Salem et al. 1997: 187

TABLE 9.3   ***Contingency approaches to influence***

Leadership approach	Characteristics of situation and nature of influence
Strategic approach	• Formulation and implementation of long-term strategy is main task • External orientation (to business situation) • Delegate work to employees with planning and analytical skills • Appropriate situation: high level of organizational complexity (e.g. technology, geography, structure); unstable environments; where large decisions are required
Human assets approach	• Strategy formulation at business unit level is main task • Nurturing and developing individuals using values and commitment • Employees committed to the 'company way' are most valued – 'mavericks' are not valued • Appropriate situation: where success depends upon the talent of employees to defeat competition through the way they make decisions, interact, and design new products
Expertise approach	• Creating competitive advantage by providing expertise (technology, competitor analysis, etc.) is main task • Focus on systems and procedures • Individuals selected and rewarded who are knowledgeable in area of expertise • Appropriate situation: where specific capabilities are viewed as the way to achieve success by differentiating the organization from its competitors
Box approach	• Creating consistent experience for both employees and customers is main task • Focus on control and monitoring devices (e.g. cultural or financial controls, etc.) • Seniority and internal promotion valued • Appropriate situation: highly regulated industries; industry where safety and reliability are important (e.g. banks, airlines)
Change approach	• Continual reinvention of organization is the most important task • Focus on process for achieving this – especially a variety of communication devices to help employees to embrace change • Values independent people who see opportunities to be seized and who embrace ambiguity • Appropriate situation: where organizational success is achieved only through constant change and entrenched ways will produce failure

Source: Adapted from Farkas and Wetlaufer, 1996

leadership behaviours that an individual can perform. Second, behavioural differentiation encompasses the extent to which the individual can enact these behaviours in response to the demands of a particular organizational situation, and not perform them when the situation does not call for them. In other words, if leaders are to influence people effectively, they must have a range of behaviours on which they can draw, can assess the situation and identify the appropriate behaviours, enact those behaviours and not enact those that are not called for (Exercise 9.4).

Another contingency for leaders to consider relates to the time orientation

EXERCISE 9.4 WHAT'S IN AN APPROACH?

Reflect on Table 9.3 and answer the following questions:

- Do you have a dominant style that matches one of these approaches or do you feel that you have a dominant style that is not described in Table 9.3? Explain your answer.
- Are you in a position where your style matches the situation that you are required to lead?
- Select up to five people in your organization whom you regard as a leader. Can you classify their approach in terms of the styles outlined in Table 9.3?
- Farkas and Wetlaufer found that 20 per cent of CEOs adopted the strategy or the human assets approach, 15 per cent relied on the expertise or change approach, and 30 per cent used the box approach. Does this distribution match your experience in your organization?
- To what extent do these leaders work better in some situations than others and to what extent are their styles matched to appropriate situations?
- What would happen if these individuals were moved to different positions that provided a better match? Explain your answer.
- Alternatively, can you imagine these individuals adopting a different style?
- Farkas and Wetlaufer argue that where CEOs lack a dominant approach and draw from each of these approaches at once they lose organizational focus and effectiveness. Do you agree or do you feel the leaders in your organization would be more effective if they drew on different styles? Explain your answer.

If you do not have organizational experience, select five organizational leaders covered in the business literature and answer the following questions:

- Can you classify their approaches in terms of the styles outlined in Table 9.3?
- Farkas and Wetlaufer found that 20 per cent of CEOs adopted the strategy or the human-assets approach, 15 per cent relied on the expertise or change approach, and 30 percent used the box approach. How does this distribution compare with your analysis of the five leaders you have chosen?
- To what extent do you think that these leaders' styles are matched to appropriate situations?
- Can you imagine these individuals adopting a different style? Explain your answer.

> • Farkas and Wetlaufer argue that where CEOs lack a dominant approach and draw from each of these approaches at once they lose organizational focus and effectiveness. Do you agree or do you feel the leaders would be more effective if they drew on different styles? Explain your answer.

Source: Adapted from Farkas and Wetlaufer, 1996

of leaders – the extent to which they use a past-time orientation, a present-time orientation, or a future-time orientation.[48] Each orientation draws on different temporal skills to influence individuals, including time warping, which integrates the future with the present; visioning – dreaming and planning – a future; time chunking to create different time units, such as the time of a project; predicting the future; and recapturing the past to determine what will work in future circumstances. The use of these temporal skills must be attuned to the situation if leaders are to carry out their leadership responsibilities and influence people.[49]

Other writers are more sceptical of the claim that individuals can swap easily between different sets of leadership skills, roles or archetypes. Fiedler suggests that a leader's performance is related to the stress level of the situation and the leader's control over it. He concludes that it may be easier to adapt the situation so that leaders can make the best use of their strengths, rather than force them to use different styles with which they are less comfortable (and which may increase stress). 'We cannot make leaders more intelligent or more creative, but we can design situations that allow leaders to utilize their intellectual abilities, expertise, and experience more effectively.'[50] In other words, it may be easier for leaders to change the context in which they operate than it is to change their leadership style.

Commanding charisma?

A continuing fascination exists in both the academic and popular management literatures with the charismatic or transformational leader. Behling and McFillen[51] suggest that leadership research focused mainly on incremental improvements until the late 1970s, when perceptions of a more competitive business environment started to generate interest in the abilities of individual managers to motivate employees to extraordinary levels of effort and commitment. But by the 1980s many writers had already become disillusioned with the inability of research on leadership to deal with large-scale organizational change.[52] It was in this context that Max Weber's theory of the charismatic leader was resurrected and linked to transformational leadership, with some writers arguing that the two were indistinguishable[53] and others claiming that they could be differentiated.[54] While these writers disagree over the exact definition of charismatic leadership, they nonetheless agree that individual leaders are crucial to managing change and they continue to promote the view that charismatic and transformational leadership is a set of learnable, teachable behaviours that enhance organizational performance.[55]

Other writers have challenged the focus on charismatic leaders and their apparent importance to organizational performance. They point out that it is difficult to clarify exactly what constitutes charismatic leadership and note that most research evidence attributing positive outcomes to such leaders is based upon speculation and anecdotal evidence.[56] This heroic paradigm of leadership has also been disputed by writers who adhere to a more dispersed view of leadership. Mintzberg[57] argues against the leadership cult approach, which suggests that the leader is a hero who will provide the correct solution for any and all organizational problems and inadequacies. He criticizes the business press for reducing organizations as complex as ABB, General Motors and General Electric to a single person at the top, such as Percy Barnevik, Jack Smith or Jack Welch. He suggests that great organizations are composed not of great leaders, but rather of many unsung, devoted and competent leaders.

Collins and Porras[58] also challenge the myth that visionary companies need great ideas and charismatic leaders. They found that great ideas brought forth by charismatic leaders can be negatively correlated with building a visionary company and that both visionary and non-visionary companies were associated with solid leadership in their early years. These authors reject the notion that great leaders are needed to build visionary companies and suggest that the reason why we see the continuity of great leaders at the helm of great companies may have more to do with the latter rather than the former. In other words great companies produce great leaders – not the other way round. As evidence, they point to Jack Welch who, they argue, was a product of General Electric.

Other writers concede that charismatic leaders exist but, rather than extol their virtues, they point out the potential dark side of this form of leadership. Bass and Avolio[59] distinguish between ethical and unethical charismatic leaders. Unethical charismatic leaders are those who demand adherence from others to their own personal vision, are intolerant of criticism, lack a sensitivity to the needs of others and use their power to further their own personal gain. Sankowsky[60] depicts such people as narcissistic and pathological, approaching 'ventures with sureness of self based on their own pathology rather than on their command of information or clarity of insight'. By contrast, ethical charismatic leaders align their personal vision with those of the followers, are committed to the development of their followers and use their power to the benefit of those with whom they interact.[61] Only those individuals who create positive transformations for their organizations should be labelled ethical charismatic leaders.[62]

Nadler[63] argues that charismatic or mythic leaders create problems for those around them in a variety of ways. First, these leaders often do not wish to be seen as ineffective or fallible and therefore stifle dissent. Second, they often paint over-optimistic pictures of the future which, when they fail to emerge, cause people to feel betrayed. Third, organizational members may place unrealistic expectations on the powers and capabilities of these leaders and project escalating expectations on to future accomplishments. Fourth, individuals may transfer their positive or negative psychological feelings about leaders to particular individuals, creating either dependency on particular leaders or resistance to them. Finally, other managers may feel sidelined and relegated to the perpetual shadow of their more charismatic counterparts (Exercise 9.5).

Other writers have also considered the problems faced by new leaders who must deal with the charismatic 'shadow' of their predecessor. Memories of a former charismatic leader may continue to shape perceptions, emotions and behaviour of organizational members well beyond what might be expected from a straightforward comparison.[64] This charismatic shadow makes it difficult for a new leader because they are continually deemed to fall short compared to the former leader. In the popular management literature, *Fortune* recently published a short survey that managers could fill out to determine if they were 'charismatically impaired'.[65] (Exercise 9.6)

EXERCISE 9.5 TRAPPING THE CHARISMATIC LEADER?

Reflect on a charismatic leader in your organization or from the business literature and answer the following questions:

- Briefly explain why you consider this leader to be charismatic.
- What problems have arisen or might arise from such a leader?
- Divide these problems into those that emanate from the activities of the leader; those that result from the actions of followers; those that are associated with the reactions of other managers; and those that are linked to leaders who succeed the leader.
- Provide recommendation to counteract these problems.

POWER

The role of leaders in influencing people alerts us to issues concerning the use of power by leaders. In this section we consider two aspects related to leaders' use of power – the power to motivate and the management of meaning.

Leading motivationally?

As indicated in the previous section, leaders try to influence people in the organization and use different power bases to do so. Part of influencing an

---

EXERCISE 9.6 MANAGING PEOPLE?

Reread Chapter 3 on people. Reflect on the three most important debates discussed in that chapter for an individual responsible for 'leading' an organization or a unit within an organization. Where appropriate, relate the leadership role back to your position within your organization. Answer the following questions:

- List the three most important debates.
- For each debate, explain why you believe it to be important.
- Elaborate what you have learned from thinking about each debate.
- Describe how you would translate your thoughts into actions for members of your organization to take.
- If you do not have organizational experience, describe how you would translate your thoughts into actions that you will take when you start work.

---

individual involves motivating them. Valikangas and Okumura[66] argue that people follow leaders for three different rationales. Where the rationale is compliance, motivation is based upon utility – obtaining certain rewards or avoiding punishment. Where the rationale is identification, motivation is based upon identification of the follower with the leader – people relate to the behaviours of the leader. Where the rationale is internalization, the follower shares the values of the leader and a sense of trust is established through which motivation is engaged.

Effective leaders are those who are able to use different power sources appropriate to different followers' motivational rationales. For example, coercive power and controlling behaviour is appropriate to utility-related motivation. Referent and expert power bases are appropriate to identity-related motivation because they help to establish social identity. Power based upon charisma and perceived legitimacy, which appeal to common values, is appropriate to value-related motivation.

The consequence of this argument is that effective leaders are those who are able to use appropriate power bases that tap into different contexts and motivations. It assumes that leaders can find out which motivations their followers have. In touching on an issue that will be dealt with in more depth in the following section, it also suggests that different motivations are culturally grounded. For example, the authors suggest that the US context is one grounded in compliance, while the Japanese context may be better suited to leaders who appeal to social identification, although these cultural differences may change over time and generation.[67]

Making an impression?

At a number of points in this book we have referred to the management of meaning as one of the activities in which managers engage. Gardner and Avolio[68] have extended this concept by drawing on Goffman's[69] work to apply a dramaturgical model to impression management between charismatic leaders and their followers. Gardner and Avolio[70] suggest that charismatic leaders engage in impression management using framing to shape a general perspective, scripting to provide guidelines for actions and interactions, staging through the management of symbols and props and performing through the enactment of specific behaviours. Work on charismatic leaders regularly mentions their skill in managing meaning (Exercise 9.7).

There is, however, a debate about whether impression management is an expression of deceit or simply a means of conveying information. Most writers in the leadership field tend to view it as neutral and rarely consider its ethical implications. However, more critical writers would see such activities as the sophisticated use of power.[71] Neither position denies that activities designed to manage meaning occur, in this case enacted by the leader and targeted at the follower.[72] The difference lies in the ethical connotations attributed to these actions. The more common approach is the ethical-neutral one. Researchers explore the activities associated with the management of meaning with a view to helping leaders hone their skills by, for example, coaching them in presentation skills (including framing, scripting,

---

EXERCISE 9.7 IMPRESSIVE IMPRESSION MANAGEMENT?

Reflect on leaders in your organization or featured in the business literature and answer the following questions:

- To what extent can you apply the dramaturgical model to these leaders? Specifically, in what ways do they engage in the following activities?
  - Framing – shaping the general perspective and vision within the organization
  - Scripting – providing people with guidelines for action and interaction
  - Staging – using symbols and props to reinforce the message they wish to convey
  - Performing – enacting specific behaviours and encouraging others to do likewise
- Provide a concrete example of each activity.
- How successful are these leaders in getting followers to respond in the desired way? Explain your answer.

staging and performance), as well as in sensitivity to how followers receive and respond to their messages.[73] Critical writers highlight these activities in order to 'expose' them and to reveal the dynamics of power. Their aim is to warn the targets of these activities – followers – that meaning is being managed by leaders for their own benefit (Exercise 9.8).

CULTURE

In this section we focus on two specific issues that connect culture and leadership – cultural perspectives on leadership and the debate about the universality of leadership skills.

Leading through a lens?

The relationship between culture and leadership varies depending upon the particular perspective on culture through which leadership is viewed.[74] First, the integration lens views leadership as akin to value engineering. This occurs either through leaders creating and/or changing organizational cultures, or through the transmission of cultural values throughout the organization. Second, the differentiation perspective emphasizes the role of the group and informal leadership, through which meaning is conveyed in different sub-cultures. Viewed from this perspective, organizations are no longer seen as being integrated and, therefore, organizational leaders are not seen as sources of organizational consensus or integration.[75] However, the differentiation perspective may provide a way of bringing together super

---

EXERCISE 9.8 MANAGING POWER?

Reread Chapter 4 on power. Reflect on the three most important debates discussed in that chapter for an individual responsible for 'leading' an organization or a unit within an organization. Where appropriate, relate the leadership role back to your position within your organization. Answer the following questions:

- List the three most important debates.
- For each debate, explain why you believe it to be important.
- Elaborate what you have learned from thinking about each debate.
- Describe how you would translate your thoughts into actions for members of your organization to take.
- If you do not have organizational experience, describe how you would translate your thoughts into actions that you will take when you start work.

leadership and culture – as leaders dispersed throughout the organization 'engineer' particular sub-cultures.

Third, the fragmentation perspective, which views organizations as arenas of confusion and ambiguity, argues that 'the attempt to impose a coherent culture by dint of one's organizational vision is futile and dishonest because it fails to acknowledge the diversity, ambiguity and fluidity of modern cultures'.[76] According to this view, leadership is problematic and may constitute a source of ambiguity because leaders convey different, and inconsistent, symbols throughout the organization. So one conclusion from the fragmentation approach is that leaders send contradictory and confusing signals through the organization and, as such, contribute to the existence of fragmented organizational cultures.

An alternative interpretation from the fragmentation approach is one that arrives at rather different conclusions. It diverts attention away from the role of the leader in creating culture and focuses on the followers. It suggests that organizational members are active and imaginative consumers of culture. Followers do not passively receive leaders' visions and attempts at meaning construction but contribute to them. These writers accord a large role to followers in the construction of meaning.[77] Bryman, however, cautions against the idea that organizational members can construct any meaning that they wish. He argues that only messages which are already present can be consumed. In other words, he promotes the idea that leaders must send the messages out in the first place, although followers may consume them in different and unpredictable ways. He argues in favour of a midway position that assumes 'neither that people are cultural dopes to passively imbibe cultural messages emanating from leaders, nor that the manipulation of organizational culture is constantly being undermined through imaginative consumption on the part of organizational members'.[78] (See Exercise 9.9.)

EXERCISE 9.9 CONTRIBUTING TO CULTURE?

Reflect on an organization with which you are familiar, either through experience or from the business literature, and answer the following questions:

- Briefly describe the culture of this organization.
- Describe the extent to which the organization has a single, pervasive organizational culture, separate sub-cultures, a fragmented ambiguous culture or an absence of culture.
- How does the organizational leader contribute to this culture (these cultures or lack of culture)?
- How do other leaders contribute to this culture (these cultures or lack of culture)?
- How do followers – organizational members – contribute to this culture (these cultures or lack of culture)?
- What conclusions do you draw?

National dress?

From a national perspective, a debate exists about whether cultural differences in terms of language, beliefs and values necessitate different styles of leadership in different nations, or whether leadership consists of universal skills that remain the same across cultures.

In a study of leadership in Japan, Taiwan, Mexico, South Korea and the USA, Dorfman et al.[79] concluded that both sides of the debate are valid. Their results suggested that leader supportiveness, contingency reward and charisma were universal behaviours appropriate to each of these nations, whereas participativeness, directiveness and contingent punishment were only relevant to two of these five nations. Similar conclusions were found by Yeung and Ready[80] who identified six leadership capabilities that crossed national boundaries – articulating tangible vision, values and strategy, facilitating strategic change, a results orientation, empowerment, facilitating cultural change and a strong customer orientation – although other leadership capabilities varied across countries. They explained these results by suggesting that certain leadership capabilities are context-specific but, as new environmental pressures are experienced in different countries, there is a shift in what is perceived to be important leadership capabilities.

Other writers question the importance of national cultural perspectives to leadership. Shenkar et al. used data from China to investigate the extent to which Confucian principles such as harmony, hierarchy, personal relations and collectivism affect leadership. They conclude that these principles do affect the value that is placed upon leadership behaviour, but also argue that 'culture, while important, is not the sole contingency affecting the managerial role; political, economic, social, and enterprise-level variables, adjoin cultural influences in producing the role structure of the Chinese manager'.[81] In other words, the relationship between national culture and effective leadership activities is rather more complex than previously thought (Exercise 9.10).

STRATEGY

Our concern with the relationship between leadership and strategy is twofold. First, we explore arguments concerning the relationship between leadership style and choice of strategy. Second, we track the nature of the relationship between these two concepts.

Getting personal?

Recognizing the complex relationship that exists between strategy and leadership, some researchers have argued that the choice of organizational strategy is affected by the style of the leader[82] or the core personality of the CEO.[83] For example, Kets de Vries et al. argue 'that strategies very much reflect the idiosyncrasies of the decision maker'.[84] What characterizes these approaches (Table 9.4) is their assumption that the CEO has strategic choice, that the CEO does affect an organization's strategy, but that they do

---

EXERCISE 9.10 MANAGING CULTURE?

Reread Chapter 5 on culture. Reflect on the three most important debates discussed in that chapter for an individual responsible for 'leading' an organization or a unit within an organization. Where appropriate, relate the leadership role back to your position within your organization. Answer the following questions:

- List the three most important debates.
- For each debate, explain why you believe it to be important.
- Elaborate what you have learned from thinking about each debate.
- Describe how you would translate your thoughts into actions for members of your organization to take.
- If you do not have organizational experience, describe how you would translate your thoughts into actions that you will take when you start work.

---

not have full control over this process as their actions are constrained by personality factors (Exercise 9.11).

Crafty, huh?

Leavy[85] points out that the strategy field is some thirty years old and, for much of its history, has treated leadership and strategy as synonymous. The field was dominated by a rational-economic model, which saw the organization's future as dependent upon 'management by analysis' and emphasized technical and economic factors. Consequently, interest in leadership was limited since it was not seen as an important strategic variable although, at the same time, leadership was implicit in the top-down approach embodied in the rational models of strategy making. Other approaches to strategy downplayed the role of leadership even more, particularly population ecology and contingency theory, but also resource dependency and attribution theory. Such deterministic approaches assumed that leaders had little impact on either strategy making or organizational performance.[86]

The emergence of a process orientation, associated with the work of writers such as Pettigrew and Mintzberg, represented a major shift insofar as it saw strategy as something leaders 'crafted' out of the actions of a divergent range of people. In moving from a rational instrumental orientation to processual, context specific and socially constructed perspectives, the importance of leadership to strategy was reaffirmed through concepts such as strategic vision.[87] In this way, the actions of the leader in making strategy cannot be taken out of context – he or she must be sufficiently adept to

TABLE 9.4 *Matching CEO personality to strategy*

Core wish of CEO	Appropriate strategy
To be in control	• Modest risk taking • Desire for much information • Cost control, budgets, planning • Focused cost leadership • Defender strategy
To be domineering	• Broad score (low focus) • Takeovers • Risk taking • Marketing differentiation
To be open to others	• Collaborative structures • Participative decision-making • Prospector strategy
To be organized	• Diversification • Acquisitions

Source: Adapted from Kets de Vries et al. 1993: 14

EXERCISE 9.11 IDIOSYNCRATIC STRATEGIES?

Reflect on the categories described in Table 9.4 and on the personality of a CEO, either the one in your organization or one described in the business literature. Answer the following questions:

• To what extent do the categories match the personality of your CEO?
• Is there a relationship between your CEO's personality and the strategies being pursued by his/her organization?
• To what extent are the strategic actions of your CEO affected by factors other than his/her personality? Describe these factors and evaluate the relative importance of personality in influencing strategy when compared with these factors.

---

work with and through the expectations, perceptions and aspirations of people throughout the organization.

In building upon the process orientation perspective, Leavy argues that the leader is an 'historical actor, wrestling dynamically with the forces of history and context in the shaping of strategy, rather than simply commanding it'.[88] He recognizes that leaders do not lead under conditions of their own choosing but suggests that exceptional leaders are nevertheless able to influence both the mission and vision of an organization to varying degrees. He also acknowledges that leadership has a symbolic dimension that is part of the drama of everyday organizational life and that outcomes are often attributed to leadership after the event such that the concept of leadership becomes romanticized (Exercise 9.12).

CHANGE

In this section we examine two approaches to leadership and change. The first advocates transformational leadership as a series of steps in which leaders should engage in order to produce successful organization-wide change. The second explores writers who suggest that leaders should use different styles relative to the type of change they wish to introduce and to their position in the organization.

Step by step?

Kotter's work accords a strong role to leaders in conducting transformational organizational change which 'by definition, requires creating a new system, which in turn always demands leadership'.[89] This is one of the most popular approaches to leading change based upon a phased sequence of steps. Change typically goes nowhere until enough 'real' leaders are promoted or hired into senior positions. Leaders also are required to be active supporters of change, ensure that coalitions of support for change are established, guide and communicate vision, encourage self-leadership in employees within the parameters of the vision, structure short-term wins into the change process and anchor the changes into the corporate culture. In this model, it is clear that leaders are crucial to establishing and driving transformational changes by carrying out a set of specific tasks that, together, comprise a change process.

EXERCISE 9.12 MANAGING STRATEGY?

Reread Chapter 6 on strategy. Reflect on the three most important debates discussed in that chapter for an individual responsible for 'leading' an organization or a unit within an organization. Where appropriate, relate the leadership role back to your position within your organization. Answer the following questions:

- List the three most important debates.
- For each debate, explain why you believe it to be important.
- Elaborate what you have learned from thinking about each debate.
- Describe how you would translate your thoughts into actions for members of your organization to take.
- If you do not have organizational experience, describe how you would translate your thoughts into actions that you will take when you start work.

A bit of this and a bit of that?

Dunphy and Stace[90] focus on leadership style, position in the organization and the stage of change. They point out that different theorists promote different types of leaders – organization development theorists argue in favour of an involvement style of leadership in achieving change, while theorists who adopt a pluralist power perspective argue for authoritarian and directive approaches to achieve change in the face of competing interests. Dunphy and Stace challenge both the 'tender-minded' organization development view and the 'tough-minded' pluralist power perspective. 'Rather than evolution and transformation being incompatible strategies, and collaboration and tuition being incompatible modes, they are in fact complementary, the usefulness depending on the particular circumstances.'[91] They argue that in a transformational change situation, while a directive leadership style may be needed to initiate the change, a consultative style may be needed at the business level in order for change to be fully implemented over time.[92] Eggleston and Bhagat[93] adopt a similar position in arguing that leadership roles are dependent upon, or contingent to, the situations in which they are exercised. However, as Burke argues, there is a continuing difficulty in knowing exactly what constitutes 'the right match between the culture change that is required and the leader's style and personality to ensure that the change will indeed be successful – that is, in the proper direction and fast enough'.[94] (See Exercises 9.13 and 9.14.)

LEARNING

In this section we examine debates regarding whether leaders are born to lead or can learn how to lead, as well as what it is, exactly, that leaders should learn.

Nature or nurture?

Can you learn to be a leader? This is a question that has occupied the literature for many years. The trait perspective assumed that leadership is something innate – you've either got it or you haven't! On the other hand, many writers believe that even charisma can be taught.[95] If leadership is not a trait but rather a style, a debate exists concerning whether it is easier to change styles or to change the circumstances to suit an individual's dominant style. In the latter case, the implication is that it is difficult to learn and use new styles. Other approaches, such as 'values-based' leadership, found in companies such as Hewlett-Packard, Microsoft and GE, link leadership to learning about the values of the organization. 'If values-based leadership in fact is replacing autocratic and charismatic leadership, then the old argument about whether leaders are born or made loses some pertinence' because values can be taught and reinforced by reward mechanisms,[96] regardless of the nature and calibre of organizational leaders.

EXERCISE 9.13 STYLING CHANGE?

Reflect on an organizational change initiative with which you are familiar, either through experience or from the business literature, and answer the following questions:

- Were different styles of leadership applied at different stages of the change process? (See Tables 9.2 and 9.3) What were the styles? Did each style match the particular stage? Explain your answer.
- Were different styles of leadership applied by leaders at different points or positions in the organization? Did each style match the particular position? Explain your answer.
- Was the change initiative a success or not? Can you link the outcome to your analysis of matching leadership styles to the particular stages and positions?
- What conclusions do you draw about leadership, the particular stage of a change process, and the position occupied by the change leader?

EXERCISE 9.14 MANAGING CHANGE?

Reread Chapter 7 on change. Reflect on the three most important debates discussed in that chapter for an individual responsible for 'leading' an organization or a unit within an organization. Where appropriate, relate the leadership role back to your position within your organization. Answer the following questions:

- List the three most important debates.
- For each debate, explain why you believe it to be important.
- Elaborate what you have learned from thinking about each debate.
- Describe how you would translate your thoughts into actions for members of your organization to take.
- If you do not have organizational experience, describe how you would translate your thoughts into actions that you will take when you start work.

One recent development in the 'leadership training' field is the concept of 'thought self-leadership'. Self-leadership is 'the process of influencing oneself to establish the self-direction and self-motivation needed to perform'.[97] Thought self-leadership 'proposes that employees in organizations can influence or lead themselves by using specific cognitive strategies'. These strategies include: the self-management of individual self-dialogue, which is what we overtly tell ourselves; using mental imagery by which we create and symbolically experience the results of our behaviour before we actually perform it; and the questioning of beliefs and assumptions since distorted individual beliefs may be the basis of dysfunctional thought processes. Together these strategies contribute to the creation of constructive thought patterns or habitual ways of thinking. The concept of thought self-leadership assumes both that leadership can be taught and that it will improve performance.

An extension of the view that leadership can be learned is the perspective that leadership is a lifelong learning process, something that is argued to be integral to the achievement of learning organizations. According to this view, leaders learn by taking risks, by taking themselves outside of their comfort zones, by engaging in humble self-reflection of their successes and failures, by seeking opinions and ideas from others, by engaging in careful listening of others' advice and by remaining open to new ideas.[98] Hierarchical leadership is dismissed out of hand on the grounds that it is unable to harness a range of people and engage them in continual building and knowledge sharing. Organizations are conceived of as knowledge creating communities in which front-line leaders and top-level managers rely not just upon each other but upon everyone in the organization, but must manage these relationships with no recourse to formal authority that might undermine commitment.[99] (See Exercise 9.15.)

EXERCISE 9.15 LEARNING TO LEAD?

Reflect on your answer to Exercise 9.1 and the characteristics of leaders. Answer the following questions:

- List the characteristics and activities that you associate with leadership.
- For each one, explain whether an individual can learn to enact the characteristic or activity.
- If you do not believe that individuals can learn it, explain why not.
- If you believe that individuals can learn it, explain how they would do so.
- What conclusions do you draw for selecting and training effective leaders?

What's the subject today, teacher?

If one accepts that leadership is trainable, a debate emerges concerning which behaviours should individuals be trained in if they are to end up as effective leaders. Table 9.5 provides two different views on what leaders need to learn. Moreover, even if agreement can be secured regarding appropriate behaviours, they may not translate well into practice because of a gap between simplistic steps and the complexities of social and organizational processes.[100]

Of course, the highly developed industry associated with leadership training has a vested interest in maintaining that leadership is something that can be learned. However, Barker[101] argues that the leadership training industry panders 'to the egos of corporate executives by equipping them with the secret formulas for achieving saviourhood. Not to mention that it is relatively easy to develop the seven steps of this or the ten ways of that, and to present these ways and steps very effectively'. (See Exercise 9.16.)

CONCLUSIONS: ALL THINGS TO ALL PEOPLE?

Our aim in this chapter has been to contextualize the complexities associated with leading organizations in relation to the areas examined in earlier chapters. Presenting leadership debates in this way provides a conceptual map for thinking about and integrating the various activities associated with 'leadership'. The debates facing managers are many and the choices they confront are varied. The creative challenge is how to move through these debates, recognize that there are rarely simple answers, and that embracing complexity and paradox is a fundamental aspect of managing contemporary organizations.

Some writers on leadership are wrestling with this complexity. Hart and Quinn[102] and Quinn[103] argue that there are many models of leadership,

TABLE 9.5 *Defining characteristics of effective leaders*

Covey	Bennis
• Be proactive	• Create compelling visions
• Begin with the end in mind	• Admit to mistakes
• Put first things first	• Encourage reflective talkback
• Think win/win	• Encourage dissent
• Seek first to understand, then to be understood	• Express optimism and faith
• Synergize	• Stretch people's expectations, but don't strain them
• Sharpen the saw (create physical, emotional, spiritual and mental balance in life)	• Maintain a sense of where the organization is going
	• Take the long view
	• Balance competing groups and claims
	• Create partnerships

Sources: Adapted from Covey, 1989; Bennis, 1989

most of which dichotomize leadership activities. On the one hand, successful leaders are portrayed as 'visionary, innovative, dynamic, charismatic, transformational, participative, empowering, and motivating'. On the other hand, they are also seen as 'powerful, assertive, decisive, expert, analytical, stable, consistent, and demanding'.[104] These dichotomies are, in fact, dilemmas that must be addressed (Table 9.6) if the literature is not to remain deeply divided regarding the behaviours of effective leaders. Dunphy and Stace also suggest that traditional dichotomies should be combined. 'Rather than evolution and transformation being incompatible strategies, and collaboration and tuition being incompatible modes, they are in fact complementary, the usefulness depending on the particular circumstances.'[105] In the case of transformational change, a directive leadership style may be needed to initiate the change while a consultative style is essential if the change is to be successfully implemented. Similarly, from a theoretical perspective,

---

EXERCISE 9.16 MANAGING LEARNING?

Reread Chapter 8 on learning. Reflect on the three most important debates discussed in that chapter for an individual responsible for 'leading' an organization or a unit within an organization. Where appropriate, relate the leadership role back to your position within your organization. Answer the following questions:

- List the three most important debates.
- For each debate, explain why you believe it to be important.
- Elaborate what you have learned from thinking about each debate.
- Describe how you would translate your thoughts into actions for members of your organization to take.
- If you do not have organizational experience, describe how you would translate your thoughts into actions that you will take when you start work.

TABLE 9.6 *Leadership dilemmas*

- Independence vs. inter-dependence
- Long term vs. short term
- Creativity vs. discipline
- Bureaucracy busting vs. economies of scale
- People vs. productivity
- Revenue growth vs. cost containment
- Task oriented leadership vs. socio-emotional leadership
- Participative vs. autocratic leadership
- Transactional vs. transformational leadership

Source: Adapted from Stewart, 1996

Leavy attempts to move beyond dichotomies such as voluntarism vs. determinism and rationality vs. interpretation, suggesting that each has a part to play in understanding leadership.[106]

Quinn and his colleagues prefer a more paradoxical and complex view of leadership, suggesting that effective leaders think and act multi-dimensionally. They identify four leadership roles (Table 9.7). The Vision Setter deals with demands for innovation to position the organization strategically in relation to markets, competitors and customers. The Motivator deals with demands to foster commitment and ensures that staff are motivated, challenging people to aspire to new levels of performance. The Analyser deals with the demands for efficiency within the organization by ensuring the integration of the overall systems of the company with the achievement of strategic goals. The Task Master deals with the problem of overall firm performance in the marketplace and ensures that actions are appropriately prioritized to meet stakeholder demands.[107]

According to Quinn, leaders must be able to act out a cognitively complex strategy by playing multiple, competing roles in a highly integrated and complementary way. In other words, leaders must be both reflective and decisive. They are capable of paying attention to detail as well as having a broad vision. They have the skills to attend to both people and performance. It is precisely 'this behavioral complexity – the ability to deal with the competing demands through the mastery of seemingly contradictory or paradoxical roles – which distinguishes the highest performing executives from their more mediocre counterparts'.[108] Effective leaders are those who are perceived to have a greater degree of behavioural complexity,[109] enabling them to address both sides of the leadership dilemmas they face (Exercise 9.17).

Clearly, leadership is a complex matter. Some writers argue that it does not exist; others suggest that it exists but does not make a difference to organizational performance; still others say that it exists, can make a difference, but is complex, ambiguous and paradoxical. This chapter assumes the latter and attempts to integrate it with the themes discussed in earlier chapters, thereby doubtless adding to complexity, ambiguity and paradox.

TABLE 9.7   *Leadership roles*

Vision setter	• Focus on organization direction and future • Searching for trends • Communicating sense of where the organization is going
Motivator	• Encouraging commitment • Forging company values • Engendering a sense of excitement
Analyser	• Evaluating efficiency of projects • Prioritizing conflicting needs
Task master	• Focusing on performance and results • Problem solving

---

EXERCISE 9.17 PULLING IT ALL TOGETHER?

Reflect on the four roles described in Table 9.7 and in the text. Quinn argues that effective CEOs simultaneously occupy four, sometimes conflicting, leadership roles. If you are in a leadership role, think about the way you currently spend your time. If not, select a leader with whom you are familiar, either through experience or from the business literature. Answer the following questions:

- How much of your (the leader's) time is allocated to each of the four roles. Out of 100 per cent, how much would you allocate to each of the roles?
- Do you (does the leader) spend a disproportionate amount of time on one or two of the roles?
- Does this timing depend on the business cycle or other factors which change over the year?
- How should you (or the leader) change the distribution of time in relation to these four roles? Explain your answer.
- What barriers might you (or the leader) face in making these changes?
- What benefits would you see in redistributing time in this way?

Source: Adapted from Quinn, 1996: 153–4

NOTES

(See Bibliography at the end of the book for full references)

1 Bryman, 1996
2 Huey, 1994
3 Nadler, 1998
4 Rost,1991, cited in Barker, 1997: 344–5
5 Barker, 1997
6 Bryman, 1996
7 Gastil, 1994
8 Hershey and Blanchard, 1977
9 Graeff, 1997
10 Jermier, 1996; Schriesheim and Neider, 1996
11 House, 1996: 346
12 Thomas and Greenberger, 1995: 290
13 Barker, 1997: 349
14 Hooijberg, 1996: 944
15 Tracey and Hinkin, 1998
16 Cammock et al. 1995: 465
17 Fiedler, 1996: 241
18 Barker, 1997: 346
19 Fiedler, 1996
20 Fiedler, 1996
21 Bryman, 1996: 276
22 Ellis, 1996
23 Thomas and Ely, 1996
24 Ehrlich, 1994
25 Tharenou, 1993
26 Gordon, 1998
27 Schnake et al. 1993
28 Huey, 1994: 28
29 Schnake et al. 1993
30 Schnake et al. 1993
31 Bryman, 1996
32 Limerick and Cunnington, 1993; Ghoshal and Bartlett, 1995
33 Huey, 1994: 28
34 Ashkenas et al. 1995: 325–32
35 White, 1994
36 Katzenbach, 1997
37 Dunphy and Bryant, 1996: 681
38 Bowen et al. 1994; DiTomaso and Hooijberg 1996
39 Hilmer and Donaldson, 1996

40 Halal, 1994
41 Cohen et al. 1996
42 Dunphy and Bryant, 1996
43 Roberts and Lihuser, 1993
44 Gordon, 1998: 11
45 Farkas and Wetlaufer, 1996: 122
46 Kerr and Jermier, 1978; Howell, 1997
47 Hooijberg, 1996
48 Thomas and Greenberger, 1995
49 Thomas and Greenberger, 1995: 287
50 Fiedler, 1996: 249
51 Behling and McFillen, 1996
52 Conger and Kanungo,1994
53 Avolio and Gibbons, 1988; see also Conger and Kanungo, 1994
54 Bass, 1985; see also Conger and Kanungo, 1994
55 Behling and McFillen, 1996; Collins and Porras, 1995
56 Behling and McFillen, 1996: 164
57 Mintzberg, 1996
58 Collins and Porras, 1995
59 Howell and Avolio, 1995
60 Sankowsky, 1995: 65
61 Howell and Avolio, 1995
62 Howell and Avolio, 1992
63 Nadler, 1998
64 Gilmore and Ronchi, 1995
65 Sellers, 1996
66 Valikangas and Okumura, 1997
67 Valikangas and Okumura, 1997: 325
68 Gardner and Avolio, 1998
69 Goffman, 1959
70 Gardner and Avolio, 1998
71 Willmott, 1993
72 Gardner and Avolio, 1998
73 Gardner and Avolio, 1998
74 Bryman, 1996
75 Bryman, 1996
76 Bryman, 1996: 285
77 Linstead and Grafton-Small, 1992
78 Bryman, 1996: 287
79 Dorfman et al. 1997
80 Yeung and Ready, 1995
81 Shenkar et al. 1998: 68
82 Nahavandi and Malekzadeh, 1993
83 Kets de Vries et al. 1993
84 Kets de Vries et al. 1993: 6-7
85 Leavy, 1996
86 Kets de Vries et al. 1993; Nahavandi and Malekzadeh, 1993
87 Leavy, 1996
88 Leavy, 1996: 448
89 Kotter, 1995: 60
90 Dunphy and Stace, 1990, 1993
91 Dunphy and Stace, 1993: 916
92 Dunphy and Stace, 1993: 917
93 Eggleston and Bhagat, 1993
94 Burke, 1995: 163
95 Behling and McFillen, 1996
96 Wind and Main, 1998: 105
97 Neck and Manz, 1996: 446
98 Kotter, 1996
99 Senge, 1997
100 Barker, 1997
101 Barker, 1997: 348
102 Hart and Quinn, 1993
103 Quinn, 1996
104 Hart and Quinn, 1993: 543–4
105 Dunphy and Stace, 1993: 916
106 Leavy, 1996
107 Hart and Quinn, 1993: 548–53
108 Hart and Quinn, 1993: 556
109 Denison et al. 1995

10 MANAGEMENT AND POSTMODERNISM

Bonfire of the Certainties?[1]

So far in this book we have argued that debate is central to both management thought and management practice because it helps to make assumptions explicit, to review logics, to explore implications and to assess directions. The challenge is to translate debates embedded in academic discourse in ways that make them accessible and relevant to management practice. To that end, we have assessed a variety of debates centred on particular management issues under the rubric of such themes as structure, power, strategy, etc. In the previous chapter, we used the theme of leadership to revisit and integrate some of these debates by focusing on what a manager or leader might do or how they might act. In this chapter, we adopt a somewhat different focus. Instead of examining debates as they pertain to particular issues, we engage in a broader debate – one that challenges more fundamental assumptions that underpin not only management practice but also management research and theory. To do so, we draw on postmodern approaches to the study of organizations.

Accessing this literature is important because the writers adopting postmodern perspectives have shaken some of the fundamental tenets associated with traditional, 'modernist' management. Postmodern approaches raise a number of important challenges to more conventional ways of thinking and, as such, provide a number of valuable insights to our understanding of and engagement in management practices, as well as the process of management education itself. At the same time, accessing this literature is problematic – in this case, building a bridge between management thought and management practice is particularly difficult. Postmodern approaches are relatively new to management theory and have not been applied to management practice to any significant degree. Moreover, this body of work is 'slippery' – there is no single postmodern theory or approach, but theor*ies* and approach*es* (see Supplementary Reading box). The challenges facing a successful translation are, then, considerable. Nevertheless, in this chapter, we attempt to explain what postmodernism is, to explore how it leads us to rethink organizational debates at a more fundamental level, and to present its insights and implications for management practice.

We first introduce postmodernism as, itself, a matter of intense debate.

POSTMODERNISM: SUPPLEMENTARY READING

- Alvesson, M. (1995) 'The meaning and meaninglessness of postmodernism: some ironic remarks', *Organization Studies*, 16 (6): 1047–75.

- Brown, R.H. (1994) 'Reconstructing social theory after the postmodern critique', in H.W. Simons and M. Billig, *After Postmodernism: Reconstructing Ideology Critique*. London: Sage.

- Chia, R. (1996) 'Teaching paradigm shifting in management education: university business schools and the entrepreneurial imagination', *Journal of Management Studies*, 33 (4): 409–28.

- Cooper, R. and G. Burrell (1988) 'Modernism, postmodernism and organizational analysis: an introduction', *Organization Studies*, 9 (1): 91–112.

- Hassard, J. (1994) 'Postmodern organizational analysis: toward a conceptual framework', *Journal of Management Studies*, 31 (3): 303–24.

- Knights, D. (1992) 'Changing spaces: the disruptive impact of a new epistemological location for the study of management', *Academy of Management Review*, 17 (3): 514–36.

- Parker, M. (1992) 'Post-modern organizations or postmodern organization theory?', *Organization Studies*, 13 (1): 1–17.

- Rosenau, P.M. (1992) *Post-Modernism and the Social Sciences: Insights, Inroads, and Intrusions*. Princeton, NJ: Princeton University Press.

- Thompson, P. (1993) 'Postmodernism: fatal distraction', in J. Hassard and M. Parker, *Postmodernism and Organizations*. London: Sage.

We then provide an overview of postmodern approaches. We review the challenges that postmodern approaches pose to two areas that are fundamental to management theory and practice – the organization and the individual. This discussion is followed by an examination of what might constitute postmodern organizational practice and how one might teach from a postmodern perspective. We conclude with a summary of critiques of postmodernist thinking.

CONTESTED TERRAIN?

The nature of postmodernism is a highly ambiguous and contested debate for a variety of reasons. First, writers disagree over what is postmodern and who is a postmodernist. So, for example, some theorists would cite the work of Michel Foucault, the French philosopher and historian, in a discussion of postmodernism[2] while others[3] would dispute such a categorization, arguing he is simply a 'modernist' writing about 'postmodernism'. Similarly, some commentators[4] refer to the work of Henry Mintzberg and Karl Weick in the context of postmodernism, while others would strongly resist any such idea. Second, in challenging the very idea of a definitive or overarching theory, practice or experience of organizations, many postmodern writers explicitly avoid simplicity and clarity in their writing. Their aim is to expose multiple interpretations and meanings through confusion, nuance and irony and not, as we seek to do, to make things more accessible and transparent.[5] Third, many postmodernists reject the idea of education, especially from a managerial perspective. They consider it to be 'violence' and have called business schools 'factories of the mind' because of the search for convergent explanations and 'right' answers.[6] Such writers have also repudiated any practical application of postmodernism on the grounds that it 'neuters', 'tames' and 'harnesses' it simply for the benefit of consultants.[7] Fourth, there is also a complex debate about the difference and overlap between 'postmodernism' and 'poststructuralism' with which we will not concern ourselves here; as well as considerable animation concerning whether a hyphen should be absent or present (i.e. postmodern or post-modern), which we also ignore.[8]

As a result of these factors, many management and organization theorists not converted to the postmodern cause have expressed increasing disillusionment, if not to say irritation with it.[9] Some writers have gone to considerable lengths to dispute its claims.[10] They argue that it is too vague a term to be useful and invites muddled thinking and sweeping statements.[11] They suggest it has outlived its usefulness and, instead of stimulating new ways of thinking, now simply produces a new kind of conformity. Some have argued that postmodernism serves simply as a brand identity to promote a certain kind of academic approach and have gone so far as to suggest that it merely represents therapy for disillusioned, self-indulgent academic elites.[12]

While this book has focused specifically on the debates associated with a number of different areas in organization and management theory, these are phlegmatic when compared to the debates associated with postmodernism.[13] Postmodernism is a subject fraught with a degree of disagreement and emotion rarely found elsewhere. These problems notwithstanding, our aim in writing this chapter is straightforward. We hope to provide readers with a clearer idea of what postmodern approaches involve and how they might be used to reflect on management practice.

MORE MODERN THAN MODERN?

Postmodernism is, as one might expect, linked to modernism. Modernism, or modernity as it is sometimes known, refers to the period that commenced when 'modern' science attacked the authority of church and monarch emphasizing, instead, rigorous, objective methods of inquiry.[14] Modernism has been portrayed as the moment when 'man [sic] invented himself, rather than seeing himself as a reflection of God or Nature, and Reason was elevated to the highest of human attributes'.[15] Modernism has since come to be associated with the various attributes of 'modern' industrial society. Postmodernism, a term first coined in the 1960s by literary critics,[16] was a reflection of a growing dissatisfaction and unease concerning the lack of progress of modern society and the fallibility of modern science (Table 10.1). Modernism had been conceived of as a progressive force but, in the eyes of many, was failing to live up to expectations; postmodernism represented a concerted effort to question the defining belief of modernism – the superiority of the present over the past.[17]

Postmodernism gained wider currency in the 1970s and 1980s in architecture, the arts and the social sciences and more recently in management and organization theory. Key individuals in the growing coverage and acceptance of postmodernism were French philosophers such as Jean-François Lyotard, Jacques Derrida, Michel Foucault and Jean Baudrillard, who were in turn inspired by German philosophers like Nietzsche and Heidegger. Writers on organizations have subsequently taken up this work, where it has evolved into a plethora of different approaches.

Some writers have concentrated on postmodernism as a *period* in which society is characterized by newly emerging features, different from those associated with modern industrial society; while others have adopted postmodern *perspectives* in which new ways of studying social phenomena are proposed. In the context of management and organization theory, these translate into what has been termed the postmodern organization, often juxtaposed against the traditional bureaucracy, and postmodern 'theorizing' which embodies a series of ideas concerning the nature of our world and our ability to study it. Different approaches have also led to a distinction between *hard* and *soft* versions of postmodernism. We examine these different postmodern strands.

The postmodern organization

The idea of the postmodern organization has emerged in the broader context of post-industrial society. Writers have drawn attention to changes regarding

TABLE 10.1 *Reasons for disillusionment with modern science*

- The failure of modern science to produce the promised results
- The misuse and abuse of modern science
- The discrepancy between modern science in theory and in practice
- The ill-founded belief that science could solve all problems
- The neglect of the mystical and metaphysical
- The neglect of the normative and the ethical

Source: Adapted from Rosenau, 1992: 10

globalization, telecommunications, the mass media, consumerism, mass consumption and information technology, as well as the increasing popularity of simulations (or simulacra) like Disneyland, MTV, IMAX and the like.[18] Whether these changes have occurred to a significant degree and had the predicted effects can be verified, somewhat ironically, through the empirical methods associated with modern science. These 'facts' are a source of considerable debate and some writers contest strongly whether society has indeed changed.[19] Nevertheless, as far as organizations are concerned, postmodernism as a period suggests a 'postbureaucratic' organizational form, which we discuss in more detail later in this chapter. These organizations are loosely coupled, fluid, organic and adhocratic instead of the static bureaucratic structures that have traditionally preoccupied much of the organization literature.[20]

Postmodern perspectives

Other writers have taken postmodernism several steps further, using it to challenge the conventional wisdom that characterizes the way in which we study organizations.[21] This work tries to draw attention to and undermine the assumptions we take for granted in how we view the world. In this regard, postmodernism can be considered as a theory of knowledge which, briefly and somewhat simplistically, amounts to the belief that the 'real' is not out there awaiting discovery, but rather is created out of the language that we use and the power relations in which we are entwined. Accordingly, there is no singular reality but multiple ones, none of which should be given a privileged or special status over others. Because we often accept certain views, ideas, experiences and images without thinking, we must strive to critique continually our assumptions; but not in the hope of finding an ultimate truth but, rather, in the hope of finding new and different 'truths' not previously considered.[22]

To explore these ideas, a new 'language' of postmodernism has emerged, some of which we translate in Table 10.2. We provide examples of a number of postmodern terms along with our attempt to clarify what they mean in the context of our overview of postmodernism. The table highlights the breadth of ideas associated with postmodernism and provides a common basis for the discussion of specific postmodern themes (Exercise 10.1).

EXERCISE 10.1 LEARNING THE LINGO?

Take each of the terms in Table 10.2. Make sure you understand what each term means and find an organizational example of it from your experience or from the business literature. What conclusions do you draw about the relevance of these terms?

TABLE 10.2 *Key terms used by postmodern writers*

• The linguistic turn	The language that we use does not reflect 'reality' but rather it defines what we know and how we know it. Language produces the objects of which it speaks.
• Hyper-reality	Reality does not exist; it is simply an image created by the language we use; there are multiple 'realities' none of which are more or less real than the others; hyper-reality is a reproduction of a reality, a 'real' illusion.
• Representation	Since there is no single reality, any situation is open to multiple interpretations and, therefore, multiple representations.
• Decentring the subject	Individuals are not distinct, identifiable, autonomous actors that possess specific characteristics, but are embedded in webs of relationships that produce multiple, fluid identities for them, as well as constrain and enable the actions they take.
• Discourse	Discourse refers to the statements, texts activities, practices and interactions that surround and constitute a phenomenon which often create an image of inevitability and naturalness that invisibly and pervasively reinforces their existence.
• Local narratives and lost voices	No single 'grand' theory explains the world; instead situations must be studied and understood at a local level, with particular attention to diversity, and to those voices at the periphery.
• Différance	Our understanding of current situations and problems is a product of taken for granted categories that rely on or defer to comparisons with other, different situations and past experiences. For example, 'organization' only makes sense with reference to 'disorganization'; the continuing tension between the two means that what constitutes 'the' organization is under constant review.
• Confronting dualism	The tension of différance requires us: to recognize the inevitable interdependence between apparently polar opposites; to challenge boundaries between supposedly discrete categories; and to acknowledge the importance of ongoing tensions and paradoxes.
• Power/knowledge	Power is not a finite resource but a web of relationships in which all individuals are enmeshed. While some are advantaged within this web, no one is 'in control' of it. What passes for knowledge (and truth) is not neutral but emerges from these relationships.
• Privileged	Nothing can be 'naturally' privileged; all privilege is the product of power/knowledge effects.
• Reflexivity	The importance of reflecting on the assumptions that we make in producing what we regard as knowledge.

Source: Hardy and Palmer, 1999

Insofar as organizations are concerned, postmodernists argue that one view which has been inappropriately privileged is that of 'the organization' rather than the processes of organiz*ing*.[23] One goal of postmodern theorizing, then, is to explore the more ephemeral aspects of organizing in terms of the implications for both the entity known as 'the organization', as well as the entities called 'individuals' who work in and around them. Thus, many postmodern writers suggest a concern with 'becoming' rather than 'being' and suggest that 'the organization' and 'the individual' are always open to question.[24] In other words, an organization is not one thing but many; they do not have clearly defined insides and outsides and, because the boundaries are uncertain and reversible, no organization, no description of it can ever be complete.[25]

Hard or soft postmodernism?

Hard, sceptical, or pessimistic postmodernism takes these ideas to their limit. This form of postmodernism is anti-intellectual because no statements may be privileged, not even those of postmodern critics.[26] By dwelling on the powerlessness of so-called 'individuals,' the ephemeral nature of supposed 'institutions' and the transitory quality of 'truth', adherents of such views can only dismiss scholarly work.[27] Such an approach, or anything close to it, presents difficulties in management and organization theory because, according to this view, 'postmodern organization' is a contradiction in terms. Not surprisingly, the field has proven resistant to such intrusions.[28] Consequently, many postmodern writers on organizations have limited their role to one of critique. Rather than abandon modernity and reason altogether, they often advocate a soft or optimistic version of postmodernism, which recognizes the ontological existence of the social world, however precarious and fluid, and focuses on the location of alternative interpretations, marginalized voices and different readings.[29]

By summarizing and simplifying postmodernism and by seeking to apply it to practice, we inevitably fall into the 'soft' camp. We attempt to show that certain implications for practice are to be found in this literature. We want to 'take advantage of what postmodernism has to offer without becoming casualties of its excesses'.[30] We believe that the time is ripe to explore the contribution of postmodernism as traditional certainties are becoming unstitched through globalization, new organizational forms, information technology and cyberspace. In fact, some of the popular management approaches already show signs of postmodern rhetoric, with titles embracing chaos and unreason.[31]

AND IN THIS CORNER . . . THE CHALLENGER?

As indicated in our overview, postmodernism challenges existing ways of thinking and studying our world. Here we identify two arenas where postmodernism offers a critique of taken for granted assumptions and conventional wisdom. Specifically, we show how postmodern approaches take us beyond the organization and how they cast doubt on the self-contained individual. Readers should note that, in this discussion, we treat postmodernism as one theoretical strand among many within the context of organization and management theory: we do not treat it as a privileged, distinct theoretical entity but, instead, emphasize its links to related work that falls outside the postmodern camp. Consequently, we not only refer to writers considered to be postmodern but also to more 'traditional' work.

Beyond the organization chart

This work can be separated into two streams. The first, which focuses on the blurring of organizational boundaries, draws on the idea of a post-modern period. It differentiates the postmodern organization, as a new form of organizing, from the modern or bureaucratic organization.[32] The second stream uses many of the ideas of postmodern perspectives to conceptualize the organization as a spiderless web. Table 10.3 summarizes the implications for practice of each, which are discussed in more detail below.

Blurred boundaries and fragile boxes

In general terms, the postmodern organization is one whose external bound-aries are far from fixed and within which traditional divisions of labour and hierarchy are breaking down. Interpretivist work on the social construction of organization and the processes of organizing has already warned us against reifying the organization[33] or, for that matter, the environment.[34] These phenomena only exist insofar as they consist of and are perceived by people. The entity that constitutes an organization is simply a location at a crossroads of multiple, dynamic relationships. In other words, traditionally distinctive organizational boundaries that 'separate' it from other organiz-ations are becoming increasingly fluid and transient as they are permeated by a variety of interorganizational relationships, some of which have already been described in Chapter 2 on organizational structure.[35]

Internally, flexibility and fast response times are argued to break down the barriers between formerly discrete levels and departments. Activities that

TABLE 10.3 *Beyond the organization chart*

• Blurred boundaries and fragile boxes	The postmodern organization involves different forms of organizing, in which the internal and external boundaries of the organization are far less fixed than in the past. It shifts its boundaries, its internal structure, and the reach and span of its operations in terms of both time and space in response to new environmental pressures. In so doing, it is capable of creating a new environment. Previous attention on distinct, recognizable organizations that operate in deterministic, analysable environments must be supplemented with a stronger appreciation of the more ephemeral and fluid aspects of organizing so that 'the organization' can be changed, adapted and modified as the need arises.
• Spiderless webs	The design of organizations is not the result of the ideas and actions of particular individuals, regardless of how powerful they might seem. Instead, organizations emerge as part of a larger picture in which certain forms emerge and become legitimized and institutionalized. Everyone is enmeshed in the practices, procedures, rules and regulations that comprise an organization: even senior managers are unable to transform the organization because of the pervasive effects of history and society. This web of power works on the body as well as the mind.

would have been centralized at corporate headquarters or divided into clear divisional or departmental responsibilities in the modern organization are, instead, 'distributed' among an evolving internal network of divisions or units.

> Businesses have to move from single profit centres to multiple profit-measurable units. As the control of quality at the point of origin, and delivery of service at the point of customer contact require decisions to be moved to lower levels and decision power to be moved to teams, hierarchy and bureaucracy decline.[36]

Other traditional boundaries are also argued to be evaporating. Organizations have traditionally been seen as specific to a particular point in time, space and history. With the advent of electronic mail, cyberspace and telecommunications technology, however, these certainties are breaking down. So, we have the advent of the 'global village', 24-hour operations; and the multiple uses of office space (where companies rent out their offices to another organization at night). Postmodern work contributes to the recognition that space and time are not natural phenomena but disciplinary practices that are imposed on us and which we accept without thinking.[37]

These changes offer more diverse and creative ways to enhance competitive advantage by, for example, improving innovation, spreading risk and increasing product life cycles. They represent a chance of breaking out from existing regimes[38] and denying traditional contradictions by deriving the advantages of being big and small simultaneously.[39] By maintaining, modifying and transforming multifaceted interorganizational relationships, organizations can reconstruct their environments in radical ways, allowing them to 'reinvent' their futures.[40] In other words, as the organization's 'solidity' is suspended, so too are the environments in which it operates.

In summary, literature on the postmodern organization draws attention to radically different forms of organizing compared to the traditional modern organization (Table 10.4), in which 'the organization' is far less stable and solid than in the past. Its boundaries, internal structure, the reach of its operations in terms of both time and space shift in response to new environmental pressures and, in so doing, conjure up a new environment. Previous certainties concerning distinct, recognizable organizations that operated in deterministic, analysable environments are breaking down. Postmodernist emphasis on the processes of organizing is argued to lend itself to a more fruitful study of these changes than more traditional approaches. Postmodern writers 'seek alternative modes of expression that can allow the ephemeral aspects of process to be more adequately expressed. Modernist thinking turns verbs into nouns, process into structure, relationships into things, presence into re-present-ation (i.e. making the absent present) and constructs in concrete (reified) objects. At the same time, these relationships are inverted and "forgotten" so as to give cognitive priority to outcome and effects'.[41] (See Exercise 10.2.)

Owing to the interest in new forms of organizing, this strand of postmodern literature makes important contributions. It is not, however,

TABLE 10.4 *Modern vs. postmodern organization*

Modern	Postmodern
Organization	*Organization*
• Mechanistic	• Organic
• Technical	• Social
• Objective	• Subjective
• Bureaucratic	• Democratic
• Disempowered	• Empowered
Environment	*Environment*
• Laissez-faire policy	• Industry policy
Goals	*Goals*
• Specialized mission	• Diffuse mission
• Short-term planning	• Long-term planning
• Authority driven	• Market driven
Emphasis on outcomes	*Emphasis on processes*
• Specialized	• Holistic
• Predictable	• Spontaneous
• Stable	• Creative
• Analytical	• Intuitive
Interpersonal emphasis	*Interpersonal emphasis*
• Roles	• Relationships
• Hierarchy	• Networks
• Obedience	• Individuality
• Orders	• Inspiration
• Direction	• Support
• Contracts	• Community
• Utility	• Empathy
• Individualized rewards	• Collective rewards
• Mistrust	• Trust
Intrapersonal emphasis	*Intrapersonal emphasis*
• Role	• Person
• Inflexible skills	• Flexible skills
• Performance	• Happiness
• Cognition	• Affect
• Compliance	• Commitment

Sources: Adapted from Clegg, 1990; Ostell, 1996

without debate since many writers question whether these 'new' postmodern forms of organizing are as pervasive as is often suggested.[42]

Spiderless webs
Ironically, while the concept of the postmodern organization challenges the certainty of organization and environment in ways consistent with postmodern perspectives, it assumes a degree of agency or control over the processes of organization that is antithetical to postmodern thinking. Consequently, other postmodern writers have challenged the idea that the organization, and the systems and practices that comprise it, can be designed

---

EXERCISE 10.2 BUT IS IT REALISTIC?

Examine the concepts and descriptions in Tables 10.3 and 10.4. How
well do they apply to contemporary organizations? Can you find an
example, either from the business literature or from your experience,
of a postmodern organization? What conclusions do you draw
regarding the prevalence of postmodern organizations in today's
society?

---

and modified in such a deliberate way. Instead, these writers see the organization as a web of power but without a spider at its centre. This web is not
singlemindedly constructed to achieve particular forms of control over its
environment; rather it is a web that grows out of a past, changes in response
to accidental events and emerges to entrap the very people who are advantaged by it.[43] It is a discursive web where pre-existing ideas, vocabularies
and techniques culminate, in conjunction with events in the past and outside
the organization, in a particular form of organizing.

The term discourse refers to the texts, activities, practices and interactions
that surround a phenomenon and, in so doing, bring it into being.
Foucault,[44] whose ideas are particularly important here, describes how, as
psychology emerged as a profession, its discourse led to new ways of defining and understanding madness which, in turn, became associated with
particular forms of institutions and treatments. These events were not
orchestrated by psychiatrists and psychologists, although these professionals have become privileged by the way sanity and insanity have been
defined and in how treatment has been organized. Similarly, our discussion
of discursive approaches to strategy in Chapter 6 show how we have been
'captured' by the term.

Postmodern writers caution us against the image of inevitability and nat-
uralness that discourses often create and which often, invisibly and per-
vasively, reinforce their existence. So, for example, postmodern critiques
of accounting reveal that techniques like standard cost accounting and
budgeting are not 'natural' but evolved in a historical context in which
notions of efficiency were of paramount concern. The principles of scientific
management had standardized the shop floor to produce efficient workers;
and standard costing embodied practices that had the potential to embrace
everyone in the firm. Accounting conventions take on a very different light
if they are seen as concerning the 'active engineering of the organizationally
useful person' by enmeshing them within norms of efficiency.[45]

These views suggest that the reasons behind particular forms of organizing are to be found not in the minds and plans of managers, but in the
broader society. So, for example, organizing practices and the discourses

developed to identify and legitimize them 'are the medium and outcome of a larger picture'. To understand them, we must appreciate how contradictory efforts to 'maintain and expand capital accumulation while simultaneously retaining a viable degree of legitimacy'[46] produce new organizational forms. Similarly, Knights and Willmott[47] show how organizations in the UK have been shaped by the growth of Thatcherism and the 'New Right'. Other work has noted the infiltration of corporatist principles of organizing in the public sector, such as universities.[48] Other organizations have adopted the discourses and practices of 'downsizing' through institutional pressures rather than necessarily through conscious, rational design.[49] Similarly, 'best' practice is that which has already been institutionalized in a community of organizations or experts. Postmodern insights suggest that best practice emerges outside anyone's control because of local conditions, differences and ambiguities. Once established, isomorphic pressures may mean that people adopt best practice as the easiest way to signal that they are effective, successful or excellent.[50] Consequently, according to postmodern theorists, there is no such thing as best practice. What passes for best practice changes over time; so the discourse of best practice itself is on shifting sands.

The structures, systems and practices of an organization do not just discipline the mind, they also discipline the body. Employees have both discursive and bodily capabilities that challenge, potentially at least, the control of their employers. Consequently, the body has to be trained to be a productive force.[51] Through this bio-power, or control of the body, organizations organize people both 'inside' and 'outside' them. This interest in the body stems from Foucault's work on panoptic control.[52] The panopticon was an idea of Jeremy Bentham for a nineteenth-century prison. Its architecture provided omnipresent but invisible surveillance. Since inmates might be under surveillance at any point in time, they policed – or disciplined – themselves. Thus these micro-practices of bio-power produce docile bodies. Writers have equated these ideas with the technological surveillance of computers, communication satellites and telecommunications, as well as with new management practices like team-building and empowerment which make it possible to monitor large populations without a cumbersome architectural construction: 1984 has arrived but without Big Brother at the helm.

The ideas behind the spiderless web raise a number of important points. First, 'the organization' is part of a larger picture that encompasses the past and present and, because it is incomplete, is also part of the future. Second, organizations require the co-operation of the body as well as the mind. Organizations are sites of normalizing discourses and disciplinary practices or 'bio-power' that affect the body. The individual is managed through a series of interventions that take hold of 'his or her physiology, in order to experiment with it and to improve its productive capabilities'.[53] Third, everyone is trapped in this web of practices: it is beyond the power of even senior managers to transform the organization and start over again from scratch because of the pervasive effects of history and society (Exercise 10.3).

EXERCISE 10.3 DISCIPLINE AND SURVEILLANCE?

Read the following summary of the findings of a survey conducted by the American Management Association survey and answer the questions below.

> Nearly two-thirds of employers record employee voice mail, e-mail or phone calls, review computer files or videotape workers. . . . Moreover . . . up to a quarter of companies that spy don't tell their employees. In almost all cases it's perfectly legal. Employers can secretly record and review almost anything a worker does, short of, say, videotaping the bathroom stalls. The survey looked at 900 midsize and large AMA member companies. The findings – 63 per cent of companies use some surveillance or monitoring, and up to 23 per cent don't tell workers . . . The most common forms of surveillance are: the tallying of phone numbers called and duration of calls (37 per cent of companies); video-taping of employees' work (16 per cent); storing and reviewing of e-mail (15 per cent); and storing and reviewing computer files (14 per cent). Eric Rolfe Greenberg, who directed the study for the AMA, a non-profit management training group also argued that monitoring 'can work to the customers' benefit.'

Questions

- What does the case tell you about forms of surveillance in organiz-ations? Explain how these forms of surveillance work. Do they discipline the mind, the body or both?
- What other 'disciplinary' processes exist at different levels? Are managers also subject to 'disciplinary' controls? If so, in what form? What impact do they have?
- How do organizations use time (e.g. clocking on/off, flexi-time, telecommuting), space (e.g. office space, meeting rooms, management 'retreats') and speech (e.g. the use of first names, titles, acronyms and terminology) to control members?
- Is it possible to resist these various forms of surveillance? How? What forms of resistance have you observed or heard about? How effective were they?

Sources: Adapted from Jackson, 1997: D8; Hardy and Palmer, 1999

In summary, many of these insights contradict the idea of the deliberately engineered postmodern organization. Instead, they identify how the prac-tices associated with new forms of organizing arise somewhat arbitrarily at the confluence of a number of different, complex factors and then become legitimated and institutionalized.

Beyond the self-contained individual

Individuals are often the focal point in organization and management theory: how to motivate them; how to reward them; how to control, direct or focus them; how to overcome their resistance to change. Postmodern approaches challenge our notion of 'the individual' in a number of, often contradictory, ways. First, some writers decentre the subject to cast doubt on the existence of distinct identifiable autonomous actors who can take action and make a difference. Instead, individuals are constrained by the web of relationships that envelops them. The fact that what passes for truth is shaped by these relationships means that we cannot stand outside them but are, inevitably, part of them. So, the potential for breaking free of conventional norms, transforming organizations or breaking new frontiers is extremely limited. These writers downplay the role of the subject altogether.

Second, other writers, especially those who have used postmodernism in the context of feminist theory, have used it to highlight particular subjects, notably the role of women and minorities in the organization.[54] They draw attention to the multiplicity of identities that make up an individual. They point out that these identities are not something which the individual possesses but, rather, they represent signs – attributes, actions, characteristics, and scripts – that are recognized as relevant in particular settings. Thus the individual is a far more complex phenomenon than is traditionally acknowledged.

Third, continuing further along these lines is the work that emphasizes the passionate and emotional aspects of the person. Resisting the notion of a two-dimensional, rational human being, these writers have urged us to be more aware of the whole person. Finally, we consider the role of postmodernism in the 'death' of the expert (Table 10.5).

Constrained actors

This work continues the line of thinking behind the organization as a spiderless web by reminding us of the limits to individual potential. As we have already discussed in Chapter 4 on power, Foucault's work[55] repudiates the idea of an isolated agent who possesses a battery of power sources that can be mobilized to produce particular outcomes. Instead, power is a network of relations and discourses that capture advantaged and disadvantaged alike in its web. Actors may have intentions concerning desired outcomes, and may act with the idea of achieving them; but pulling these 'strings' of power does not necessarily produce them. According to this view, power is no longer a convenient, manipulable resource under the control of autonomous actors. Instead, all actors are subjected to prevailing webs of power relations that reside in every perception, judgement and act, and from which it is impossible to escape.[56] This view has also been discussed in some detail in Chapter 4.

The approach to the individual invites an 'anti-actor' stance that has relevance for a number of areas of organizational practice including, for

TABLE 10.5 *Beyond the self-contained individual*

• Constrained actors	'Leaders' arise out of interactions with 'followers'; they are specific to a time and place; stories of success and failure often emphasize the role of leadership because it is privileged within Western European and North American cultures. As such, it leads to organization theory and business practice predicated on the great 'man', which serves to downplay other aspects of organizational life, e.g. the role of 'followers' and the irrelevance of 'leaders'.
• Complicated identities	The diversity and fragility of individuals is part of any organization whose contribution to and self-fulfilment in their work may be enhanced by nurturing this diversity and exploring its nuances, ambiguities and variations rather than by categorizing and standardizing it. By seeing individuals as capable of having multiple identities attention is focused on the many different aspects of the person. It suggests a more personalized and finely grained approach to management; and it may offer scope for encouraging organizational action.
• Passionate individuals	Emotions are an integral part of the individual and cannot be excised. They are multi-faceted, unpredictable and contradictory. Moreover there are cultural differences in how, when and why emotions are displayed and recognized. While we can become more sensitive to, tolerant of, and receptive to emotional displays, we cannot police or manage them in 'cookbook' fashion. They demand both a greater emphasis on an individual approach and an appreciation of the 'whole' person. Emotions, as experienced by individuals, can generate a momentum for action and change in organizational settings.
• The 'death' of the expert	Experts are products of their own training and employment. Therefore they will tend to perceive 'problems' and produce 'solutions' consistent with their experience. They will make sense of the organization in ways that have meaning for them. They will find what they are looking for but the meaning they find may be meaningless to others.

example, the issue of leadership. Postmodern insights question whether leadership is simply a matter of possessing the relevant traits or demonstrating the relevant leadership skills. Instead, what is taken to be leadership and who is accepted to be a leader is socially constituted in the interaction between 'leaders' and 'followers'. Postmodern writers have noted the 'consumption' of leadership by organizational members who, in actively consuming it, shape and modify it. So, for example, a review of strategic change by the president of a large US university found that the 'outcome of the president's influence ultimately rested with others' interpretations and the effect these interpretations had on cultural assumptions and expectations. In this light, it is worthwhile questioning whether the president was as central to the initiation effort or the organizational culture, as he first appeared to be'.[57] In this way, postmodernism challenges the traditional top-down approach to leadership and the preoccupation with heroic leaders. It also encourages researchers to adopt a reflexive approach to leadership studies and to problematize conventional assumptions such as what is leadership, what is objective reality, what type of information is gained from questionnaires and interviews, and how texts on leadership are produced. In this approach the active construction of the researcher in the production of leadership data is an important reflexive aspect of studying leadership.[58]

Writers outside the postmodern fold have also drawn attention to the limits of leadership as both concept and practice. For example, research has found that even charisma, usually closely linked to individual behaviour, has limits to its durability and evaporates if the individual is moved to another position or if the context changes significantly.[59] Similarly, Tsoukas[60] has discussed the work of Mintzberg in the context of postmodernism, arguing that he has 'given us valuable insights into the decentred process of strategy-making. He replaced the traditional focus on the omniscient strategists, with an investigation of the relatively impersonal patterns of decisions which emerge, disappear, mutate and get realized in a manner that is beyond a person's rational control'. Additionally, the interest noted in the previous chapter on the idea of emergent, dispersed and multidimensional leadership – where greater attention is paid to leadership processes and practices, regardless of whether or not they are carried out by formally designated leaders and traditional dichotomies are broken down – is not dissimilar to postmodern claims.[61]

In other words, writers both with and without postmodern credentials have mounted a serious challenge to the fixation on great leaders and on leader attributes and behaviour. In so doing, they require us to review the preoccupation with 'great' leaders, which is common in North American and Western Europeans in terms of both research and practice. They also remind us of the fallibility of leadership and force us to contemplate its irrelevance to organizational change (Exercise 10.4).

Complicated identities

While some postmodern writers have downplayed the person, others have used postmodern insights to refocus attention on a more fragile, complex, fluid individual comprised of multiple and fragmented identities.[62] Individuals have identities only insofar as they are recognized by those with whom they interact. We recognize some aspects of identity, but not others, and the aspects we do recognize change over time. So, as we have pointed out in Chapter 3 on people, identities connected to race and gender are far more salient today in organizations and organization theory than they were twenty or thirty years ago when they were often 'invisible'.

There is, according to this view, no 'true' self. People do not exhibit personal characteristics; rather they perform them for and in a particular time and place, as Goffman[63] pointed out some years ago. However, warn the postmodern writers, we must be careful not to assume that these performances speak for themselves, regardless of who witnesses them. Instead we

---

EXERCISE 10.4 LEADING FROM BEHIND?

Select a book about or by a business leader.

- How does the text produce an individual who is considered to be a 'leader'?
- How do the activities and events discussed in the book produce an individual who is considered to be a 'leader'?
- Who are the 'followers'? What role do they play in constructing this leader?
- What gaps in our understanding are created by the focus on this leader?
- What alternative stories might there be that are not written about in this book?

---

should consider identity to be 'a continuous process of narration where both the narrator and audience formulate, edit, applaud and refuse various elements of the constantly-produced narrative'.[64] There is not one autobiography but many autobiographical acts – formal and informal – which reinforce and contradict each other. 'It is not sufficient to select an attractive identity and then present it. The . . . identity must be accepted by other actors involved.'[65] Moreover, the power relationships that provide individuals with a sense of identity are difficult to change. In providing feelings of self-worth, any repudiation of them involves significant personal costs. According to this view, then, identity is fragile and not completely controlled by the individual who 'possesses' it. This fragmentary and multiple nature of identity has a number of implications for our understanding of, and work in, organizations.

First, these insights suggest that we should see people in the organization rather than of the organization. The organization carries only some parts of the individual and, within that, often recognizes only particular taken for granted aspects – age, service, job classification – while other facets of the individual are ignored by the organizational bureaucracy. One arena where considerable change has occurred in this regard concerns the attention now being placed on 'diversity', i.e. the recognition that gender and race are identities with which organizational members should concern themselves.[66] Consequently, the place of women and minorities in the organization has been placed centre stage through harassment policies and equal opportunity legislation; while organization theory – traditionally and invisibly codified as white and male – is being reassessed to take into account voices that were previously excluded.

Second, postmodernism warns us of the dangers of imposing mutually exclusive categories, such as white/black, male/female, on the organization and replacing one binary language – racism/sexism – with another – reverse discrimination. Attempts to address inequality that are themselves constituted in gendered, coloured terms may be ineffective because of a backlash from those adversely affected by such actions, whose anger generates more racism and sexism. They may also be ineffective because those who benefit from equal opportunity are labelled as 'token' and their contribution is marginalized and presence stigmatized. Moreover, those who no longer warrant the privilege of bureaucratic categorization simply provide new fodder for society's wastebaskets. So, for example, as our interest in class-based inequalities has been supplanted by those associated with (female) gender and (non-white) race, what are the consequences for working-class white males? Postmodern approaches help us to repudiate the certainty of political correctness and to reflect on how we might nurture multiplicity while, at the same time, remembering the multiple and complex sources of disadvantages in our society and its institutions.

Third, postmodern approaches draw our attention to the irrelevance of cutting up the world into distinctions that may no longer be meaningful. One arena where this may be particularly important concerns the traditional dichotomy of non-managers and managers, which postmodern interest in multiple, fragmented identities as well as its refutation of dualities cautions us against. So, for example, as the practices associated with empowerment become more widespread, there is more self and peer management[67] to be found in organizations. Differentiating organizational members in terms of 'management' and 'non-management' may, then, be an outmoded way to conceptualize individuals in contemporary organizations.

A fourth matter drawn to our attention by postmodern approaches to identity concerns the division between work and non-work spheres. Our organizational identities cannot be divorced from our non-work identities. Over time, organizations have realized this by, for example, supplying crèches, counselling for alcoholics, job sharing, teleworking, paternity leave, etc. By so doing, organizations have started to remove the duality that demarcates work from non-work. Instead work and non-work are enfolded into each other as we recognize the complex and interdependent nature of this relationship. Brown and McCartney[68] note that the contemporary schism between work and family and between the public and the private is relatively new, dating from the industrial revolution. Nor is it typical of all industrial sectors, let alone all countries. Moreover, while some changes reinforce the distinction, such as the trend towards larger organizations and smaller families, modern technology that allows telecommuting may blur these distinctions once more.

The emphasis on team building and collegiality in some organizations can provide a 'home away from home' by introducing a family atmosphere into the workplace. Ironically, telecommuting is often 'work away from work' since it deprives the individual of social contact and is often devalued by family members who do not consider it 'real' work precisely because it is carried out at home.[69] This alerts us to the privileged position of 'the family' in our society. The picture of work as a family not only 'makes sense' to us but is something to be strived for. It helps to explain why so much dissatisfaction and alienation is associated with the layoffs, management practices and technology that make work seem less like a family than it used to. There are, then, clear overlaps and links between work and family that defy conventional dualities and bear closer examination in terms of both practice and research.

Finally, in emphasizing the socially constructed nature of identities, postmodern work draws our attention to the link between individual and collective identity. In this regard, postmodern work is not unique but, rather, it supports other work on identity. For example, Collins[70] argues that individual identities are created out of individual interactions as other people talk about and with an individual, thereby constituting her or his reputation. Thus, one acquires an identity through the minutiae of being on the innovation team, a member of the management committee, sending out memos, sitting in on meetings, etc. With continued conversations, the identity extends beyond the individual and his or her immediate experience. If there is a link between individual identity (by which we refer to the way in which the individual recognizes him or herself and is recognized by others) and how that individual behaves, there may also be a link between collective identity and organizational action. Some writers argue that organizational identity is a key factor in influencing whether and how strategic issues are noticed, considered legitimate and, hence, acted upon;[71] and in whether organizational members are willing to innovate and carry out new ideas.[72] This is not to say that collective identity is an overarching attribute to which all organizational members subscribe, or that it rules out the existence of conflicting and contradictory identities of individuals and groups within the organization. It does, however, suggest that understanding of the ways in which identity is socially constructed, as well as the different collective and individual identities that may be constructed, offers routes to help us think about and engender organizational action (Exercise 10.5).

Passionate individuals

A discussion of identity leads us to the consideration of emotion. As Dutton and Duckerich[73] point out, identity involves an emotional component: some identities – both individual and collective – are energizing;[74] while others are restrictive and demoralizing.[75] Fineman[76] defines emotions as personal displays of 'moved' and 'agitated' states, such as joy, love, fear, anger, sadness, shame, embarrassment. Writers have traditionally depicted organizations as composed of 'emotion-less', 'rational' individuals whose non-rational selves have been suppressed or sidelined, while postmodern writers would draw attention to the emotional, aesthetic side of life.[77]

Some writers, using a critical lens of emotional 'labour', have examined the exploitation and commodification of employee emotion by management.[78] Organizations often control emotion by neutralizing it and preventing it from emerging; by relegating emotional displays to 'backstage'

EXERCISE 10.5 WHO'S THERE?

Select two annual reports from a major company, one from the 1960s
and one from the 1990s. Examine the photographs and pictures in
these reports and answer the following questions:

- What types of people are present in these pictures?
- What types of people who you would expect to be working in the
  organization are absent from these pictures? Why?
- What prominent messages are conveyed in these pictures?
- One role of annual reports is the presentation of organizational
  successes. What organizational identities are associated with
  'success'? How do definitions of success change?
- How do these pictures categorize individuals? What do they tell
  us about the categories of people in the organization? Do they, for
  example, demarcate managers and non-managers? Do they
  create other identities for people working in the organizations? Do
  they tell us anything about these people's lives outside the
  organization?

Source: Palmer and Hardy, 1999

and 'behind the scenes' arenas where they can be expressed out of earshot;
by prescribing and specifying the range, intensity and duration of 'appropriate' emotional responses; and by normalizing emotion, perhaps by diffusing it through humour or stigmatizing the 'offender'.[79] Such work focuses
on the surface emotions demanded by the manager that mask the feelings
of frustration, disappointment, alienation or anger experienced by the
employee. Deetz[80] provides an example of how a shop steward, in believing an emotional response to layoffs would indicate a 'bad attitude' on his
part, controls his anger and consequently never challenges the management
decision to lay off workers irrespective of seniority. Interestingly, this brings
us back to the earlier discussion of constrained people: by not getting angry,
the shop steward is co-opted into a managerial framing of the problem but,
had he got angry, his anger and his objections might well have been marginalized and dismissed because he was emotional.

Interestingly, many researchers also suppress emotion. Even when
research does address emotion, unemotional terminology is often preferred.
So, instead of joy or anger, organizational members are attributed with satisfaction or alienation; instead of passions and desires, they have preferences,
attitudes or interests. Thus researchers present managers with the apparently easier task of 'changing attitudes', rather than 'instilling passion': of
'reducing alienation' instead of 'confronting anger': of 'protecting interests'
as a substitute for 'pursuing desires'.[81]

Emotion often drives action. Fineman[82] argues that shame, embarrassment and guilt are important to the self-regulation which allows social enterprises to function. But more positive emotions are equally important: they explain why people toil away at their work, take risks, come up with new ideas, challenge the status quo. Gabriel[83] argues that all organizations contain a terrain where emotions prevail over rationality and pleasure dominates reality. He argues that this terrain cannot be managed but, by refashioning official events and stories, it represents a source of creativity; a way to manage contradiction and tension; a means of relieving boredom, in other words a way of making sense of and contributing to the experience of work.[84] It is commonplace to accept that work in aesthetic occupations such as dancing, designing, decorating, painting and pottery is intrinsically pleasurable;[85] and it would be strange if apparently more prosaic occupations did not afford positive experiences and emotions too.

Emotion may be far more important than rational calculation in provoking action.[86] In this regard, passion has started to make the agenda of more popular writers, who have pointed out the potential of unleashing passion. For example, Peters[87] talks about the need for passionate individuals as a core competence in an organization. In other words, 'positive' emotions such as joy, pleasure, passion in one's work drive individuals to action in ways that enhance their own self-worth as well as benefiting organizational goals. However, postmodernism counsels us against separating emotion into good or bad, positive or negative. For example, changes are made that enable some people to experience a better life because people get angry and sad about perceived injustices. Anxiety and the heightened activity it engenders often enable individuals to escape from dangerous situations. Guilt may inhibit us from engaging in hurtful behaviour that adversely affects others.[88]

The literature is noticeably quiet on the practicalities of managing emotion.[89] Ostell[90] offers some prescriptions to address the emotional reactions of organizational members. First, he argues that it is important to recognize a strong emotional reaction. Usually this is relatively easy since emotion manifests itself in clear visible signals but sometimes, for example, anger may be repressed; depression may be hidden; apparent joy may hide distress. The next step is to clarify the nature and source of emotion, assess its organizational implications and, where appropriate, indicate a willingness to help. At this point, Ostell offers a number of tactics (Table 10.6) to prevent exacerbating an already emotional situation. If employed appropriately, these tactics buy time for a strategic resolution of the 'problem', which involves a number of stages.

Ostell's work seems like a theory for managing emotion, antithetical to the notions of postmodernism and certainly his work would not readily be seen as a postmodern approach. Nevertheless, the focus on emotion and on 'solutions' to 'dysfunctional' emotions highlights postmodern complexities, ambiguities and contradictions. Emotions both bring the whole person into focus and differentiate one person from another. Emotions cannot be managed en masse since different emotions require different responses.

TABLE 10.6   *Tactics to manage emotion*

Tactics	Appropriate use	Inappropriate use
Reflection on underlying emotional content, e.g. 'You seem upset, happy, annoyed that . . .'	To indicate awareness of emotion and to provide an opportunity to express emotion and talk through underlying problems	When used judgementally, reproachfully, disparagingly
Apology, e.g. 'I'm sorry I didn't realize that . . .'	When used confidently and constructively to facilitate discussion	When the apology is patronizing, insincere or inappropriate
Permission, e.g. 'Feel free; go ahead; it's all right to . . .'	When a person needs to give vent to their emotions	When the person is behaving self-piteously or is trying to intimidate
Silence, e.g. sitting quietly and attentively	To encourage someone who is reticent; to give time for someone to compose themselves	When the person is using silence to control or when the person needs help to start talking
Conditional assistance, e.g. 'I will try to help . . . but you will need to . . . If you stop . . . I'll be able to . . .'	To focus the attention of someone who is emotional and to engage them in solving the problem	When it is used to control rather than help
Normalizing, e.g. 'It is usual to find . . .; People often . . .'	To encourage talking and to avoid judging	When used patronizingly or when the behaviour cannot or should not be normalized
Challenging, e.g. You say . . . [one thing] but act as if . . . [another]; 'On one hand . . . on the other . . .'	To surface contradictions based on concrete examples	When the challenge is judgemental and the motive is to embarrass or punish rather than help
Asserting boundaries, e.g. 'Let me point out that . . . Before you go any further . . .'	To indicate negative effects of expressing emotion	When used too early to allow the person to work through their emotions
Time-out, e.g. 'Let's take a break; Perhaps if we take a step back . . .'	When emotions are running too high to allow discussion to be effective	When tactic is to avoid dealing with either the person or the issue

Source: Adapted from Ostell, 1996: 542–3

Furthermore, the same emotion can confer very different experiences and have very different effects in different situations. For example, anger can galvanize people into action beyond the call of duty or it can disable them though fury. The line that divides anxiety and stress from challenge and thrill is thin indeed. Fear excites some and paralyses others. Emotion thus brings our attention to bear on the contradictions in dealing with people in organizations (Exercise 10.6).

The 'death' of the expert

Postmodernism undermines the whole conception of an expert, consultant or teacher as someone with privileged insight.[91] Instead, experts are conjured into existence because of a need for their presence. No postmodernist would

EXERCISE 10.6 IN TOUCH WITH YOUR FEELINGS?

From your organizational experiences, think of an emotional outburst (joy, anger, fear, love, sadness, shame, embarrassment, etc.) which you either witnessed or in which you were involved. Reflect upon the situation and answer the following questions:

- What emotions were expressed?
- Why were they expressed?
- What were the reactions of others to the display of emotions?
- What general conclusions do you draw from this experience (or combination of experiences) regarding the expression and management of individual emotions?
- To what extent did your example of an emotional outburst contribute positively or negatively to organizational outcomes? Why?

believe they have the right answers, only that they are subjects whose knowledge and identity have been constituted as privileged in a particular setting by their actions and by those around them. Such insights are not confined to postmodern writers. For example, Silverman[92] has pointed out that experts treat their engagements as a 'thing' to be transferred between people like a package. They distance themselves by treating the client's role as one of passive acceptance. The superiority of the expert is partially the result of the social acceptability of the use of scientific methods. Postmodernists would take these insights further by emphasizing the societal and historical context in which these activities and actions have meaning, and the role of the 'consumer' in attributing meaning to, and reading meaning into, particular interactions and texts.

A postmodernist analysis suggests that 'experts' offer pre-packaged solutions as a result of disciplinary and linguistic practices. Because they are socialized into a career with norms, rules, policies, language and procedures, the solutions they offer are inevitably shaped by the discourses and practices to which they have been subjected, a process of which they may be more or less unaware. Postmodernism shows us that experts have no monopoly on the 'truth', but simply produce knowledge in the context of particular power relationships which privilege certain knowledge, thereby socially constituting some information and some people as 'expert'. In other words, the status of being an expert has less to do with any special knowledge or skills, and more to do with being perceived as consistent with ideas of what an expert should be and do. In this regard, the solutions offered by experts are, inevitably limited.

Experts often impose one-dimensional meanings on the situations which they face; otherwise their status as expert may be endangered. If multiple definitions of problems exist and multiple ways can be used to solve them, why would you bother to hire an expert? The role of experts is to oust ambiguity in favour of certainty and they may, as a result, be unable to see or tolerate the different 'stories' that make up the organization. In fact, their privileged status may derive from their ability to impose meaning on a situation. But there is nothing about the expert's voice that is definitive or natural. It is simply one voice among many in a contested arena, which has managed to drown out other voices that may be equally 'expert'. According to this view, 'experts' may be scattered throughout the organization, but are marginalized and excluded because they do not subscribe or adhere to dominant discourses. So, we might say there is either no expert or we are all experts. This work suggests that we need to think reflexively about why someone is deemed to be an expert. Otherwise we lock ourselves into a predetermined way of proceeding, while delegitimizing and excluding other ways of proceeding and other forms of knowledge. In this regard, the presence of experts in an organization may have more to do with political reasons than anything else. Moreover, their success may stem from their ability to impose meaning on a situation, regardless of whether it makes much sense to other 'non-expert' members (Exercise 10.7).

In summary, then, the contribution of postmodernism in understanding the individual helps us to appreciate a number of nuances about 'the individual'. First, there are limits to the ability of individuals to wield power. Second, identities are tenuous, fragmentary and overlapping but, at the same time, passionate and emotional. Third, the identity of the so-called expert warrants careful scrutiny.

EXERCISE 10.7 CONSULT THE EXPERTS?

Watch one of two films — *Being There* or *Dave* — and answer the following questions:

- How did the lead character come to be an expert?
- Who perceived the lead character as an expert and why?
- What actions or events reinforced their status as experts?
- Did their positions as experts break down? Why/not?

Source: Palmer and Hardy, 1999

WHAT IS POSTMODERN PRACTICE?

Given what we know about postmodernism, is there anything we can call postmodern practice? Much of the mainstream management literature assumes a logic associated with one best way of managing or of organizing. Most of this work remains convinced of some degree of certainty and seeks to avoid or reduce ambiguity. Postmodern approaches suggest, on the other hand, that there are multiple ways to read any situation and we should not privilege one above another. Nonetheless, in this section, we attempt to provide some ideas for practices informed by, if not totally consistent with, postmodern insights.

Play with paradox

Postmodern approaches emphasize the importance of recognizing that what one knows is constituted by other alternatives which often remain unrecognized or unknown. Things are not 'natural' but exist only through comparisons with opposites. So, 'organization' only makes sense in the light of 'disorganization'. Moreover, the tension between the two is never resolved and, in fact, this continuing tension focuses our attention on the precarious and fluid nature of organiz*ing*. Thus we can conceive of organizations as continually adapting, changing, adding and dropping activities and actions as they evolve. In this regard, we develop a far more dynamic sense of organization, or organizing, which is probably far more akin to individuals' experiences of work lives rather than the concretized, static hierarchy. As anyone who has been asked to explain an organization chart knows, even in a stereotypical bureaucracy, filling in the gaps requires a description of history, context, exceptions and deviations that bear little relation to the original blueprint.

The aim here is not to resolve the tensions between what appear to be binary opposites and privilege one over the other, but to acknowledge the existence of both and to work with the ongoing tension that is created. So, as we discuss in Chapter 8 on organizational learning, Dougherty[93] suggests that organizations are more likely to innovate if they embrace tensions between the needs of 'inside' innovators and 'outside' customers; between new ideas and old routines; between determining strategies and allowing them to emerge; and between allowing innovators freedom and demanding responsibility from them. She argues that successful innovation lies not in privileging one over the other, but in recognizing the difference between the conflicting demands and managing, balancing and juggling the creative tension between them on a continuous basis. Similarly, Weick and Westley[94] argue that organizational learning occurs when order is juxtaposed against disorder; when individuals both forget and remember; when organization is contrasted against disorganization through mechanisms such as humour and improvization. In other words, the 'answer' lies not in privileging one duality, one side of the coin, over the other but in bringing them together. Chapters 7 and 8 on change and learning both highlight the existence of paradox.

Tell (and listen to) stories

Postmodernism suggests that we tell and listen to stories – lots of them.[95] Individuals process information by looking for a story and in so doing they ignore the pieces that fail to fit the story and infer causality to make the story work.[96] Regardless of how 'true' it is, many writers argue that it is the coherence of a story that leads to a decision – generating commitment by binding disparate organizational members together. If this is the case, then what may generate action is not an accurate story but a plausible one. On the other hand, postmodernism would also suggest that we encourage multiple stories, which generate insight precisely because they contradict each other, helping organizational members to diagnose problems and promote change, as we discussed in Chapter 8 on organizational learning.

Postmodern approaches also remind us that, while one story may dominate, it is never the only story and not everyone gets to hear all stories.[97] It is important not to place oneself ahead of others in the storytelling. By understanding and admitting what one is doing and why, organizational members are more likely to reflect on what they hear and fail to hear, as well as the meaning they make of what they hear.[98] We must also be careful not to dismiss people as having stories that do not count; who are too emotional to tell stories; who have no story. We need to recognize and embrace the silent voices of those marked by gender, race, colour, physical differences, etc. to ensure that they retain a place centre-stage rather than being shunted off at the periphery. As Cobb and Rifkin[99] note, those individuals with less coherent stories tend to be marginalized. Moreover, as stories are elaborated, persons are co-opted into identities they do not author and cannot transform. So, stories establish positions from which persons must speak and from which material consequences flow. In this way, while a collective story may produce commitment, it risks excluding other stories; and multiple stories may produce more creativity and insight precisely because they contradict each other.

Rattle the cage

In many respects, then, postmodern practice can be seen as rattling the cage – resisting attempts to reach closure and certainty by deliberately being confusing, opening up meanings and interpretations and up-ending and undermining taken for granted assumptions. In some respects, rattling the cage has been advocated before; for example, Janis[100] advises the assignation of the role of devil's advocate in order to prevent groupthink. Postmodernism does, however, offer a more ongoing and complete approach by seeing all sides of all stories, continually critiquing assumptions, acknowledging individuals' experiences and recognizing the limits to agency (Table 10.7; Exercise 10.8).

POSTMODERN PEDAGOGY: TEACHING IGNORANCE?[101]

Postmodernism presents teachers with a dilemma – it highlights the tension between education as empowerment and education as indoctrination. Those seeking to promote the former often end up in an untenable position because

TABLE 10.7 *Interpretations of the postmodern organization*

Dream	Nightmare
• Individuals are valued as ends, for their unique contributions; playfulness and quality of life are central.	• Individuals are valued as a means to serve organizational goals; team processes and group tyranny dominate.
• Hierarchical controls are eschewed as inconsistent with shared power; emphasis is on egalitarian relationships.	• Unobtrusive controls substitute for bureaucratic controls. Meanings negotiated within teams enforce conformity.
• Change is expected and celebrated. It is a source of renewal and creativity for organizational members.	• Constant change robs individuals of feelings of security and stability, producing alienation and frustration.
• Diversity is valued, everyone has a voice and all the voices are heard. Difference is sought after as a valued attribute. Diversity of all types – gender, age, ethnicity, and culture – abounds. Difference of opinion is expected; emotions are encouraged.	• A cacophony of voices erupts as political correctness stymies open discussion and supplants purposeful work. Contention is pervasive and members are on the defensive. Noise dominates and individuals are frustrated at not being heard.
• Leadership is diffuse and distributed among all those who seek it. Collaboration and consensus are put into practice and trust and confidence soar. All members help to construct and implement a vision into which diverse realities from inside and outside the organization are integrated.	• Leadership is absent or manipulative. Either no one is in charge, everyone feels abandoned, and there are no answers without experts or leaders practice manipulative and subtle forms of seduction. Form dominates substance and deviant views are censored or co-opted.
• Needs govern the choice of technology instead of efficiency. Technological determinism is challenged, as is the idea that people serve technology.	• 'New' technologies are used to control. E-mail becomes a means of surveillance and tele-commuting a source of isolation and powerlessness.
• Members have holistic and global views of the organization, the business, social, and physical environment. They are comfortable with the idea that the organization has multiple identities and yet represents a holistic entity of which they are an architect/designer.	• Local meanings and multiple identities confuse members. The picture is so fragmented that they are unable to make sense of it. Incompatible messages confuse and different identities from different parts of the organization cannot communicate.
• Individuals experience a sense of fulfilment: their work provides different challenges and allows them sufficient autonomy to reconcile them; personal life is enhanced by and enhances work life.	• Individuals are torn apart: their work life makes incompatible demands of them which they find difficult to reconcile and their personal life intrudes uncomfortably into their work.

Source: Adapted from Gillespie and Meyer, 1995: 33–4

they seek to facilitate participation and liberation but they do so by perpetuating existing classroom power relations. So, students may be encouraged to speak out but certain comments, such as those read as non-rational or 'disruptive', will be censored; while others that fail to meet the instructor's expectations will be explained away. There is, then, no postmodern pedagogy on which professors can rely and, even if there were, the bureaucratic and evaluative practices associated with universities would soon undermine it.[102]

Chia[103] argues that teachers can make some headway against traditional 'downstream' thinking, where past patterns of thought constrain and shape

---

EXERCISE 10.8 DID I DREAM IT?

Divide into three groups: one group is given a copy of the 'dream' column in Table 10.7 and a second group a copy of the 'nightmare' column. These two groups prepare for a debate entitled: 'The post-modern organization will liberate all'. The third group acts as the audience and decides which group 'won' the debate.

- Each group prepares for the debate by using examples and justifications for their arguments.
- Run the debate.
- Allow the third group time to deliberate and to decide on a 'winner' and then to explain their decision. Ask this group to lead a discussion on how they experienced the multiple perspectives with which they were confronted.
- Ask all participants to consider both columns and to debate the tensions and paradoxes that link the two views and to consider whether they can be reconciled and, if so, how.
- Can we move beyond the 'dualism' associated with these differing perspectives?

Source: Palmer and Hardy, 1999

future thinking in the way that a river carves out a convergent groove as it flows downstream. Education typically promotes this type of 'strong' thinking in which 'facts' achieve a concrete and objective status by closing off other possibilities. In so doing, it creates a 'convergent, consequential mental attitude that privileges consensus and univocality', and which marginalizes and silences 'controversies that challenge the generally held axioms and truths' of a particular community. For example, the emphasis on organizations as consciously co-ordinated, with identifiable boundaries, designed to achieve particular goals is, effectively, a ploy of teachers and writers to redirect attention away from controversial issues about the social and incomplete nature of organizing towards its consequences. But it also gives priority to the solidity of 'individuals', 'organization', 'society', 'decision' and 'strategic advantage', etc., which in turn distorts our understanding, leading us to think of action, movement and relationships as peripheral rather than central to social life.

'Weak' thinking, on the other hand, 'sensitizes us to the precarious nature of conventional social practices and therefore the limitations of conventional knowledge and wisdom'.[104] This is 'upstream' thinking where the river becomes more complex, more fragmented and less discernible as one confronts multiple tributaries branching out in different directions. Teaching upstream thinking means taking ignorance for granted. Ignorance is no longer a gap in knowledge; it is inevitable. Only by forgetting what we know and tolerating ambiguity and confusion can we 'teach' postmodern precepts. At a more fundamental level, postmodernism suggests that asking the question of how we can teach postmodern management is irrelevant: the real question is whether business schools and management education are still relevant to society and, if not, what will replace them?[105] (See Exercise 10.9.)

CONCLUSIONS: ATTRACTION OR DISTRACTION?

While postmodern approaches have attracted increasing attention in organization and management theory, some writers still remain highly dubious of their contribution. Some critics charge that postmodern writers are not saying anything that has not been said before. 'Threads of postmodern arguments weave in and out of those advanced by more conventional critics of modern social science, and so postmodernism is not always as entirely original as it first appears.'[106] Certainly, in our discussion, we have also pointed out that antecedents of postmodern arguments are to be found in other literatures. In many respects, that should not be surprising. Academic theorizing does not occur in a vacuum and it would be unusual if postmodernism did not owe something to the past, despite the claims of some writers that it represents a qualitative break.

Some critics are concerned that the repudiation of autonomy and agency leads to a politically conservative agenda.[107] The lack of agency and absence of privilege mean that postmodernists can get away without doing anything to change things for 'the better'. Critics are concerned that 'anything goes' leads to relativism where no judgements can be made about what is 'right' or 'good'. Postmodernism can, then, end up as a political retreat, where researchers hide behind word games and ignore both the positive and negative results of organizations and organizing in the contemporary world.[108] Another charge levelled at postmodernism is that its 'solipsistic concern with language does not yield knowledge about the world. If you choose to see organizations as clouds you may be able to discover some similarities, and you may rejoice in the poetic awe and the linguistic tension that you have created, but it is unlikely that you will be able to intervene in, or explain, concrete organizational phenomena'.[109] However, we would argue that postmodernism has introduced interesting new metaphors which, while perhaps more prosaic than clouds, nonetheless offer new insights as researchers and practitioners broaden and multiply their vision by using different lenses.

Critics also point to contradictory findings. For example, Alvesson[110] notes that when two authors examine Sweden in terms of modernism and postmodern, one calls it a museum of modernist management while the other sees it as an intriguing set of postmodern possibilities. We would argue, however, that such ambiguity serves to open our eyes to the fact that

Exercise 10.9 Downstream or Upstream?

Issue	Answer the questions below on each issue	For each issue, identify changes to bring this course more in line with the insights provided by postmodernism
Course outline	• How was the course outline presented? • What criteria were used to include and exclude topics? • To what extent were the topics presented as a coherent package? • What means were used to order the presentation of the topics, e.g. topics were presented in a linear fashion, theory and practice were compared, competing perspectives were contrasted? • To what extent did the presentation of the topics suggest a 'natural' progression? • What were the goals of the course?	
Teaching style	• How was the course taught? • Were techniques used to integrate the different topics? • Was there a dominant mode of presenting the course material, for example: one best way; mastery of a body of knowledge; raising debates; multiple frames/metaphors; widening horizons; challenging assumptions. • How was the relevance and utility of the course demonstrated?	
Learning environment	• Describe the learning environment (e.g. classroom, internet, etc.). • What was the relationship between the instructor and the students? • What was acceptable and what was unacceptable behaviour? • Which emotions could be legitimately displayed and which could not, e.g. anger, joy, despair, terror?	
Evaluation	• What learning outcomes were considered legitimate and testable and what were not? • How did the assessment process construct classroom knowledge and identities, e.g. 'experts'.	
Larger context	• How does this course interact with the larger context? • What webs of power relations influence the way in which this course is designed, taught and evaluated such as faculty and university policy; the training and career progression of the professor; business school accreditation processes; the expectations of government, business, the public; broader changes in demographics, politics, norms and behaviours.	

other stories do exist. Postmodern approaches are useful because they draw attention to the uncertainties, ambiguities and paradoxes of organizational life. They remind us to think about how the entities which we think of as discrete, fixed and tangible are, rather, a product of our language and thinking (Exercise 10.10).

Postmodernism is, then, an important contributor to debate because it forces us to reflect on the way in which we think about organizations and the practice of management. If we realize how trapped we are by existing ways of thinking and acting, we may be able to think differently about work and act in more meaningful ways. Postmodernism frees up our preconceptions of fixed entities in favour of processual modes of organizing. It reminds us of the 'whole' individual and the importance of individual experience which is itself ambiguous and ambivalent, contentious and contradictory. There is no underlying 'truth' concerning the postmodern 'experience'. It can be either heaven or hell, depending on person, place and period, as these authors have found out for themselves (Table 10.8).

EXERCISE 10.10 BUT WHAT'S THE *RIGHT* ANSWER?

Read *Modern Organizations* by S. Clegg (Sage, 1990: 221–2) and 'Modernism and the dominating firm – on the managerial mentality of the Swedish model', P. Guillett de Montheux (*Scandinavian Journal of Management*, 1991, 7: 27–40).

- Compare the two accounts of Sweden.
- Why do you think the two authors came up with contradictory conclusions?
- Which is 'correct'? Why?
- What do we learn from the contradictions?

TABLE 10.8 *Wrestling with the postmodern*

Postmodernism	Exasperation
What's really angering about instructions of this sort is that they imply there's only one way to put this rotisserie together – *their* way. And that presumption wipes out all the creativity. Actually, there are hundreds of ways to put the rotisserie together and when they make you follow the one way . . . you lose feeling for the work.	I've spent all bloody morning trying to put together desks for the kids because they came with no instructions. And I've still only managed to get one of them done. (One of the authors in 1996, shortly after purchasing two self-assembly desks)
(Robert Pirsig, *Zen and the Art of Motorcycle Maintenance*, 1974: 160)	

NOTES

(See Bibliography at the end of the book for full references)

1 Law, 1994
2 Cooper and Burrell, 1988; Brown, 1994
3 Letiche, 1992
4 Tsoukas, 1992
5 Rosenau, 1992; Legge, 1995
6 Letiche, 1992; White and Jacques, 1995: 65
7 Burrell, 1994: 82
8 Rosenau, 1992
9 Parker, 1992; Alvesson, 1995
10 Thompson, 1993
11 Alvesson, 1995
12 Alvesson, 1995
13 Kilduff and Mehra, 1997
14 Rosenau, 1992
15 Cooper and Burrell, 1988
16 Brown, 1994
17 Rosenau, 1992
18 Lash and Urry, 1987
19 Thompson, 1993
20 Also see the chapter on structure.
21 Cooper and Burrell, 1988
22 Legge, 1995: 306–7
23 Cooper and Burrell, 1988; Chia, 1995
24 Cooper and Burrell, 1988; Chia, 1995
25 Law, 1994
26 Rosenau, 1992: 131
27 Rosenau, 1992: 143
28 Linstead et al. 1996
29 Tsoukas, 1992; Parker, 1992
30 Rosenau, 1992: 12
31 Peters, 1987; Handy, 1989; see also Parker, 1992
32 Clegg, 1990; Berg, 1989; see also the chapter on organizational structure.
33 Glaser and Strauss, 1967; Silverman, 1970; Ranson et al. 1980; Eccles and Nohria, 1992
34 Daft and Weick, 1984
35 Powell, 1990; Alter and Hage, 1993; Tully, 1993; Winkleman, 1993; Byrne, 1993
36 Galbraith and Lawler, 1993: 285-6; see also Clegg and Hardy, 1996
37 Hassard, 1996
38 Rothwell, 1992: 234
39 Amara, 1990: 145; Fairtlough, 1994
40 Hamel and Prahalad, 1994
41 Chia, 1995: 589
42 Thompson, 1993
43 Deetz, 1992a, b; Parry and Morris, 1975
44 Foucault, 1965
45 Miller and O'Leary, 1987: 261; Hoskin and Macve, 1988; Arrington and Francis, 1989
46 Willmott, 1995: 46
47 Knights and Willmott, 1992
48 Hardy, 1991
49 See chapter on organizational structure.
50 Meyer and Rowan, 1977
51 Clegg, 1989; Hetrick and Boje, 1992
52 Hetrick and Boje, 1992
53 Miller and O'Leary, 1987: 261
54 See chapter on power.
55 Foucault, 1977, 1980, 1982, 1984; Dreyfus and Rabinow, 1982; Smart, 1985, 1986; Turner, 1990; see also Clegg, 1989; Knights and Willmott, 1989; Knights and Morgan, 1991; Alvesson and Willmott, 1992a, b; Deetz, 1992a, b; Knights, 1992; Kerfoot and Knights, 1993; Townley, 1993
56 Clegg, 1989; Knights and Willmott, 1989; Knights and Morgan, 1991
57 Bryman, 1996
58 Alvesson, 1995
59 Roberts and Bradley, 1988; Westley and Mintzberg, 1988
60 Tsoukas, 1992: 647-8
61 Hosking, 1988, 1991; Knights and Willmott, 1992
62 Rosenau, 1992: 50; Laclau and Mouffe, 1987; Lash, 1990; Willmott, 1993
63 Goffman, 1959
64 Czarniawska-Joerges, 1996: 160
65 Czarniawska-Joerges, 1996: 169
66 See chapter on power.
67 Barker, 1993
68 Brown Berman and McCartney, 1996
69 Brown Berman and McCartney, 1996: 249
70 Collins, 1981
71 Dutton and Dukerich, 1991
72 Dougherty, 1996
73 Dutton and Duckerich, 1991; Collins, 1981; Westley, 1990
74 Collins, 1981; Dutton and Dukerich, 1991; Westley, 1990
75 Cobb and Rifkin, 1991
76 Fineman, 1996
77 Fineman, 1993, 1996; Gagliardi, 1996
78 Hochschild, 1983; Wharton, 1993
79 Ashforth and Humphrey, 1995
80 Deetz, 1994: 195
81 Fineman, 1993: 9
82 Fineman, 1996
83 Gabriel, 1995
84 Fine, 1988; Pogrebin and Poole, 1988
85 Sandelands and Buckner, 1989
86 Collins, 1981; Fine, 1988; Abramis, 1990; Kahn, 1990, 1992
87 Peters, 1987
88 Ostell, 1996
89 Fineman, 1993, 1996; Ashforth and Humphrey, 1995

90 Ostell, 1996
91 Legge, 1995
92 Silverman, 1985; White and Taket, 1994
93 Dougherty, 1996
94 Weick and Westley, 1996; Chia, 1995
95 Boje, 1995
96 de Koning, 1996
97 Boje, 1991, 1995
98 Jeffcutt, 1994
99 Cobb and Rifkin, 1991
100 Janis, 1982
101 Chia, 1995
102 Lather, 1994; Simons, 1994; White and
Jacques, 1995
103 Chia, 1995
104 Chia, 1995
105 White and Jacques, 1995
106 Rosenau, 1992: 5; Tsoukas, 1992
107 Parker, 1992; Thompson, 1993; Alvesson, 1995
108 Thompson, 1993
109 Tsoukas, 1992: 645
110 Alvesson, 1995: 1070, comparing Clegg, 1990: 221–2 and Guillet de Montheux, 1991: 38–40

APPENDIX

A WORD TO MANAGEMENT EDUCATORS ON HOW TO USE THIS BOOK

As noted in Chapter 1, this book has been designed to enable individual readers to choose between using all the chapters to provide a broad overview of management or to select a small number to explore particular issues in more depth. It has also been designed for use within more traditional educational settings such as universities. With this in mind, we provide below some ideas on how management educators can use this book to design tailored courses with audiences that have different levels of experience of organizations.

Advanced and experienced audiences

With an audience that has experience of working in organizations or that has already taken subjects and courses in the various components, the entire book can be used, and a selection of the supplementary reading can serve as preparation. In the case of highly experienced or advanced readers, the reading lists may not be necessary at all and, instead, each of the chapters can be used to frame one or two classes. Educators can get readers to work through the exercises with reference to their experience. In the case of readers who lack experience, the exercises can be tied to a project on an organization either relying on interviews or using the business literature.

Focused approaches

A sub-set of the chapters can be used to go into somewhat more depth on particular issues. Some useful configurations of chapters include the following:

- A focus on general management: structure, people, culture, strategy, change, learning and leadership chapters.
- A focus on organizational change: change, learning and leadership chapters.
- A focus on the 'postmodern' organization: structure, strategy and postmodern chapters.
- A focus on leadership: strategy, change and leadership chapters.
- A focus on critical approaches to management: power, culture and postmodern chapters.

In this case, educators may suggest that readers use the supplementary reading to ensure that they are familiar with the subject in question. Two or three classes can then be devoted to each chapter.

In-depth approaches

In this case, one chapter is used to form the basis of an entire course. The orientation can be either academic or managerial.

- An academic orientation towards a particular chapter can be used to document the development of a field of study. In this case, the supplementary reading list is used extensively to explore particular issues and the more recent debates are tracked back to the history of the field. The particular chapter forms the overview; the various sections are then expanded with the use of supplementary reading (as well as materials from the bibliography, which is broken down by chapter at the end of the book) and readers work through the exercises in detail.
- Another possibility is to work through a management situation using a particular organization, for example, a project to manage culture, a strategic planning exercise, a reorganization, etc. An individual chapter can be used either in conjunction with readers' own organizations if they are working or as part of a project to analyse an organization through interviews or the business literature, in the case of less experienced readers. In this case, some supplementary reading may be used but the main aim is to apply and use the debates in each of the sections of a particular chapter to the organization. Exercises would be completed with reference to the organization under study and either be worked through in class, completed as part of a written project, or a combination of both.

BIBLIOGRAPHIES

1 MANAGEMENT AND ORGANIZATIONAL DEBATES

Barley, S.R., Meyer, G.W. and Gash, D.C. (1988) 'Cultures of culture: academics, practitioners and the pragmatics of normative control', *Administrative Science Quarterly*, 33 (1): 24–60.

Bolman, L. and Deal, T. (1997) *Reframing Organizations*, 2nd edn. San Francisco: Jossey-Bass.

Clegg, S.R. and Hardy, C. (1996) 'Organizations, organization and organizing', in S. Clegg, C. Hardy and W. Nord (eds), *Handbook of Organization Studies*. London: Sage. pp. 1–27.

Hardy, C. and Clegg, S.R. (1997) 'Relativity without relativism: reflexivity in post paradigm organization studies', *British Journal of Management*, 8 (special issue): 5–17.

Hatch, M.J. (1997) *Organization Theory: Modern, Symbolic and Postmodern Perspectives*. Oxford: Oxford University Press.

Martin, J. (1992) *Cultures in Organizations: Three Perspectives*. New York: Oxford University Press.

Morgan, G. (1986) *Images of Organization*. Newbury Park, CA: Sage.

Morgan, G. (1993) *Imaginization: The Art of Creative Management*. Newbury Park, CA: Sage.

Reed, M. (1996) 'Organization theorizing: a historically contested terrain', in S. Clegg, C. Hardy and W. Nord (eds), *Handbook of Organization Studies*. London: Sage. pp. 31–56.

Rittel, H.W.J. and Webber, M. (1973) 'Dilemmas in a general theory of planning', *Policy Sciences*, 4 (2): 155–69.

Roberts, J. (1996) 'Management education and the limits of technical rationality: the conditions and consequences of management practice', in R. French and C. Grey (eds), *Rethinking Management Education*. London: Sage. pp. 54–75.

Thomas, A.B. and Anthony, P.D. (1996) 'Can management education be educational?', in R. French and C. Grey (eds), *Rethinking Management Education*. London: Sage. pp. 17–35.

Van Maanen, J. (1995) 'Fear and loathing in organization studies', *Organization Science*, 6 (6): 687–92.

Zald, M.N. (1994) 'Organization studies as a scientific and humanistic enterprise: towards a reconceptualization of the foundations of the field', *Organization Studies*, 4 (4): 513–28.

2 MANAGING STRUCTURE

Adler, P.S. and Borys, B. (1996) 'Two types of bureaucracy: enabling and coercive', *Administrative Science Quarterly*, 41: 61–89.

Amburgey, T.L. and Dacin, T. (1994) 'As the left foot follows the right? The dynamics of strategic and structural change', *Academy of Management Journal*, 37 (6): 1427–52.

Arthur, M.B., Claman, P.H. and DeFillippi, R.J. (1995) 'Intelligent enterprise, intelligent careers', *Academy of Management Executive*, 9 (4): 7–22.

Ashkenas, R., Ulrich, D., Jick, T. and Kerr, S. (1995) *The Boundaryless Organization: Breaking the Chains of Organizational Structure*. San Francisco: Jossey-Bass.

Aughton, P. (1996) 'Participative design within a strategic context', *Journal for Quality and Participation*, 19 (2): 68–75.

Beniger, J.R. (1986) *The Control Revolution: Technological and Economic Origins of the Information Society*. Cambridge, MA: Harvard University Press.

Beniger, J.R. (1990) 'Conceptualizing information technology as organization, and vice versa', in J. Fulk and C. Steinfeld (eds), *Organizations and Communication Technology*. Newbury Park, CA: Sage. pp. 29–45.

Bergstrom, R.Y. (1994) 'The prophet of lean principle', *Production*, 106 (10): 44–8.

Berquist, W. (1993) *The Postmodern Organization: Mastering the Art of Irreversible Change*. San Francisco: Jossey-Bass.

Bettis, R.A., Bradley, S.P. and Hamel, G. (1992) 'Outsourcing and industrial decline', *Academy of Management Executive*, 6 (1): 7–22.

Bleeke, J. and Ernst, D. (1995) 'Is your strategic alliance really a sale?', *Harvard Business Review* (Jan–Feb): 97–105.

Bohl, D.L., Luthans, F., Slocum, J.W.J. and Hodgettes, R.M. (1996) 'Ideas that will shape the future of management practice', *Organizational Dynamics*, 25 (1): 7–14.

Bolman, L.G. and Deal, T.E. (1991) *Reframing Organizations: Artistry, Choice, and Leadership*. San Francisco: Jossey-Bass.

Boyd, B.K., Dess, G.G. and Rasheed, A.M.A. (1993) 'Divergence between archival and perceptual measures of the environment: causes and consequences', *Academy of Management Review*, 18 (2): 204–26.

Bruton, G.D., Keels, J.K. and Shook, C.L. (1996) 'Downsizing the firm: answering the strategic questions', *Academy of Management Executive*, 10 (2): 38–45.

Cameron, K.S., Freeman, S.J. and Mishra, A.K. (1991) 'Best practices in white collar downsizing: managing contradictions', *Academy of Management Executive*, 5 (3): 57–73.

Cascio, W.F. (1993) 'Downsizing: what do we know? What have we learned?', *Academy of Management Executive*, 7 (1): 95–104.

Chandler, A.D. (1962) *Strategy and Structure: Chapters in the History of the Industrial Enterprise*. Cambridge, MA: MIT Press.

Chesbrough, H.W. and Teece, D.J. (1996) 'When is virtual virtuous? Organizing for innovation', *Harvard Business Review* (Jan–Feb): 65–73.

Crossan, M.M., Lane, H.W., White, R.E. and Klus, L. (1996) 'The improvising organization: where planning meets opportunity', *Organizational Dynamics*, 24 (4): 20–35.

Daft, R.L. and Lewin, A.Y. (1993) 'Where are the theories for the "new" organizational forms? An editorial essay', *Organization Science*, 4 (4): i–vi.

Davis, G.F., Diekmann, K.A. and Tinsley, C.H. (1994) 'The decline and fall of the conglomerate firm in the 1980s: the deinstitutionalization of an organizational form', *American Sociological Review*, 59: 547–70.

DeMeuse, K.P. and McDaris, K.K. (1994) 'An exercise in managing change', *Training and Development*, 48 (2): 55–7.

Desmarescaux, F. (1998) 'Exploding the merger myth', *Asian Business*, 34 (7): 44–6.

Donaldson, L. (1996) 'The normal science of structural contingency theory', in S.R. Clegg, C. Hardy and W.R. Nord (eds), *Handbook of Organization Studies*. London: Sage. pp. 57–76.

Dougherty, D. and Bowman, E.H. (1995) 'The effects of organizational downsizing on product innovation', *California Management Review*, 37 (4): 28–44.

Dunford, R. and Palmer, I. (1996) 'Metaphors in popular management discourse: the case of corporate restructuring', in D. Grant and C. Oswick (eds), *Metaphor and Organizations*. London: Sage. pp. 95–109.

Eccles, R.G. and Nohria, N. (1992) *Beyond the Hype: Rediscovering the Essence of Management*. Boston: Harvard Business School Press.

Fox, A. (1974) *Beyond Contract: Work, Power and Trust Relations*. London: Faber and Faber.

Fulk, J. and DeSanctis, G. (1995) 'Electronic communication and changing organizational forms', *Organization Science*, 6 (4): 337–49.

Ghoshal, S. and Bartlett, C.A. (1995) 'Changing the role of top management: beyond structure to processes', *Harvard Business Review* (Jan–Feb): 86–96.

Gin, E. (1995) 'Business collaboration key to success', *Computerworld*, 29: 78.

Goold, M. and Luchs, K. (1993) 'Why diversify? Four decades of management thinking', *Academy of Management Executive*, 7 (3): 7–25.

Granovetter, M. (1985) 'Economic action and social structure: the problem of embeddedness', *American Journal of Sociology*, 88: 489–515.

Gross, N. (1995) 'New patent office pending', *Business Week*, 23 October: 130.

Halal, W.E. (1994) 'From hierarchy to enterprise: internal markets are the new foundation of management', *Academy of Management Executive*, 8 (4): 69–83.

Hamel, G. and Prahalad, C.K. (1994) *Competing for the Future*. Boston: Harvard Business School Press.

Handy, C. (1995) 'Trust and the virtual organization', *Harvard Business Review*, 73 (3): 4–50.

Hardy, C. and Phillips, N. (1998) 'Strategies of engagement: lessons from the critical examination of collaboration and conflict in an interorganizational domain', *Organization Science*, 9 (2): 217–30.

Jacob, R. (1995) 'The struggle to create an organization for the 21st century', *Fortune*, 131: 90–99.

Jaques, E. (1990) 'In praise of hierarchy', *Harvard Business Review*, 68 (1): 127–33.

Jarillo, J.C. (1993) *Strategic Networks: Creating the Borderless Organization*. Oxford: Butterworth-Heinemann.

Kanter, R.M. (1994) 'Collaborative advantage: the art of alliances', *Harvard Business Review* (July–August): 96–108.

Keidel, R.W. (1994) 'Rethinking organizational design', *Academy of Management Executive*, 8 (4): 12–30.

Kiernan, M. (1993) 'The new strategic architecture: learning to compete in the twenty-first century', *Academy of Management Executive*, 7 (1): 7–21.

Lawler, E.E.I. (1994) 'Total quality management and employee involvement: are they compatible?', *Academy of Management Executive*, 8 (1): 68–76.

Leiba, S. and Hardy, C. (1994) 'Employee empowerment: a seductive misnomer?', in C. Hardy (ed.), *Managing Strategic Action: Mobilizing Change*. London: Sage. pp. 256–71.

Lubatkin, M.H. and Lane, P.J. (1996) 'Psst . . . the merger mavens still have it wrong!' *Academy of Management Executive*, 10 (1): 21–39.

Lucas, H. (1996) *The T-Form Organization*. San Francisco: Jossey-Bass.

Lucas Jr, H.C. and Baroudi, J. (1994) 'The role of information technology in organization design', *Journal of Management Information Systems*, 10 (4): 9–23.

McCaffrey, D.P., Faerman, S.R. and Hart, D.W. (1995) 'The appeal and difficulties of participative systems', *Organization Science*, 6 (6): 603–27.

McKinley, W. (1992) 'Decreasing organizational size: to untangle or not to untangle?', *Academy of Management Review*, 17 (1): 112–23.

McKinley, W., Mone, M.A. and Barker III, V.L. (1998) 'Some ideological foundations of organizational downsizing', *Journal of Management Inquiry*, 7 (3): 198–212.

McKinley, W., Sanchez, C.M. and Schick, A.G. (1995) 'Organizational downsizing: constraining, cloning, learning', *Academy of Management Executive*, 9 (3): 32–44.

Marsden, P.V., Cook, C.R. and Knoke, D. (1994) 'Measuring organizational structures and environments', *American Behavioral Scientist*, 37: 891–910.

Miles, R.E. and Snow, C.C. (1992) 'Causes of failure in network organizations', *California Management Review*, 34 (4): 53–72.

Mills, D.Q. (1993) *Rebirth of the Corporation*. New York: John Wiley.

Mintzberg, H., Dougherty, D., Jorgensen, J. and Westley, F. (1996) 'Some surprising things about collaboration – knowing how people connect makes it work better', *Organizational Dynamics*, 25 (1): 60–71.

Morgan, G. (1993) *Imaginization: The Art of Creative Management*. Newbury Park, London: Sage.

Mulvey, P.W., Veiga, J.F. and Elsass, P.M. (1996) 'When teammates raise a white flag', *Academy of Management Executive*, 10 (1): 40–49.

Neal, J.A. and Tromley, C.L. (1995) 'From incremental change to retrofil: creating high-performance work systems', *Academy of Management Executive*, 9 (1): 42–54.

Nilson, C. (1993) *Team Games for Trainers*. New York: McGraw-Hill.

O'Neill, H.M. and Lenn, D.J. (1995) 'Voices of survivors: words that downsizing CEOs should hear', *Academy of Management Executive*, 9 (4): 23–34.

Palmer, I. and Dunford, R. (1997) 'Organising for hyper-competition: new organisational forms for a new age?', *New Zealand Strategic Management*, 2 (4): 38–45.

Peters, T. (1992) *Liberation Management: Necessary Disorganization for the Nanosecond Nineties*. New York: Alfred A. Knopf.

Peters, T. (1996) 'We hold these truths to be self-evident (more or less)', *Organizational Dynamics*, 25 (1): 27–32.

Peters, T.J. and Waterman Jr, R.H. (1982) *In Search of Excellence: Lessons from America's Best-Run Companies*. Sydney: Harper & Row.

Quinn, J.B., Anderson, P. and Finkelstein, S. (1996) 'New forms of organizing', in H. Mintzberg and J.B. Quinn (eds), *The Strategy Process*. Upper Saddle River, NJ: Prentice-Hall. pp. 350–62.

Robbins, S.P. (1983) *Organization Theory*. Englewood Cliffs, NJ: Prentice-Hall.

Roberts, K.H. and Grabowski, M. (1996) 'Organizations, technology and structuring', in S.R. Clegg, C. Hardy and W.R. Nord (eds), *Handbook of Organization Studies*. London: Sage. pp. 409–23.

Roberts, K.H. and Libuser, C. (1993) 'From Bhopal to banking: organizational design can mitigate risk', *Organizational Dynamics*, 21 (4): 15–26.

Romme, G. (1996) 'Making organizational learning work: consent and double linking between circles', *European Management Journal*, 14 (1): 69–75.

Scase, R. and Goffee, R. (1987) *The Real World of the Small Business Owner*. London: Croom Helm.

Schneier, C.E., Shaw, D.G. and Beatty, R.W. (1992) 'Companies' attempts to improve performance while containing costs: quick fix versus lasting change', *Human Resource Planning*, 15 (3): 1–25.

Seabright, M.A. and Delacroix, J. (1996) 'The minimalist organization as a post-bureaucratic form: the example of alcoholics anonymous', *Journal of Management Inquiry*, 5 (2): 140–54.

Semler, R. (1994) 'Why my former employees still work for me', *Harvard Business Review* (Jan–Feb): 64–74.

Smircich, L. and Stubbart, C. (1985) 'Strategic management in an enacted world', *Academy of Management Review*, 10 (4): 724–36.

Solomon, C.M. (1998) 'Corporate pioneers navigate global mergers', *Workforce*, 3 (5): 12–17.

Stevenson, M. (1993) 'Virtual mergers', *Canadian Business*, 23 September.

Taylor, A. (1994) 'Will success spoil Chrysler?', *Fortune*, 129: 88–92.

Victor, B. and Stephens, C. (1994) 'The dark side of the new organizational forms: an editorial essay', *Organization Science*, 5 (4): 479–82.

Vinton, D.E. (1992) 'A new look at time, speed, and the manager', *Academy of Management Executive*, 6 (4): 7–16.

Walker, K. (1998) 'Meshing cultures in a consolidation', *Training and Development*, 52 (5): 83–90.

3 MANAGING PEOPLE

Adler, N.J. and Bartholomew, S. (1992) 'Managing globally competent people', *Academy of Management Executive*, 6 (3): 52–65.

Allred, B.B., Snow, C.C. and Miles, R.E. (1996) 'Characteristics of managerial careers in the 21st century', *Academy of Management Executive*, 10 (4): 17–27.

Amabile, T.M. (1997) 'Motivating creativity in organizations – on doing what you love and loving what you do', *California Management Review*, 40 (1): 39 ff.

Antonioni, D. (1996) 'Designing an effective 360-degree appraisal feedback process', *Organizational Dynamics*, 25 (2): 24–38.

Arthur, M.B., Claman, P.H. and DeFillippi, R.J. (1995) 'Intelligent enterprise, intelligent careers', *Academy of Management Executive*, 9 (4): 7–20.

Arthur, M.B. and Rousseau, D.M. (1996) 'A career lexicon for the 21st century', *Academy of Management Executive*, 10 (4): 28–39.

Atchison, T.J. (1991) 'The employment relationship: un-tied or re-tied', *Academy of Management Executive*, 5 (4): 52–62.

Bacon, N., Ackers, P., Storey, J. and Coates, D. (1996) 'It's a small world: managing human resources in small businesses', *International Journal of Human Resource Management*, 7 (1): 82–100.

Bailyn, L., Fletcher, J.K. and Kolb, D. (1997) 'Unexpected connections – considering employees' personal lives can revitalize your business', *Sloan Management Review*, 38 (4): 11 ff.

Barney, J.B. and Wright, P.M. (1998) 'On becoming a strategic partner – the role of human resources in gaining competitive advantage', *Human Resource Management*, 37 (1): 31–46.

Bartlett, C.A. and Ghoshal, S. (1997) 'The myth of the generic manager – new personal competencies for new management roles', *California Management Review*, 40 (1): 92–116.

Becker, T.E., Billings, R.S., Eveleth, D.M. and Gilbert, N.L. (1996) 'Foci and bases of employee commitment – implications for job performance', *Academy of Management Journal*, 39 (2): 464–82.

Becker, B. and Gerhart, B. (1996) 'The impact of human resource management on organizational performance – progress and prospects', *Academy of Management Journal*, 39 (4): 779–801.

Bedeian, A.G. (1995) 'Workplace envy', *Organizational Dynamics*, 23 (4): 49–56.

Blackburn, R. and Rosen, B. (1993) 'Total quality and human resources management: lessons learned from Baldridge award-winning companies', *Academy of Management Executive*, 7 (3): 49–66.

Blackler, F. (1995) 'Knowledge, knowledge work and organizations – an overview and interpretation', *Organization Studies*, 16 (6): 1021–46.

Brett, J.F., Cron, W.L. and Slocum, J.W. (1995) 'Economic dependency on work – a moderator of the relationship between organizational commitment and performance', *Academy of Management Journal*, 38 (1): 261–71.

Bridges, W. (1994) 'The end of the job', *Fortune*, 130 (6): 62–74.

Broderick, R. and Boudreau, J.W. (1992) 'Human resource management, information technology, and the competitive edge', *Academy of Management Executive*, 6 (2): 7–17.

Brousseau, K.H., Driver, M.J., Eneroth, K. and Larsson, R. (1996) 'Career pandemonium: realigning organizations and individuals', *Academy of Management Executive*, 10 (4): 52–66.

Burack, E.H. and Singh, R.P. (1995) 'The new employment relations compact', *Human Resource Planning*, 18 (1): 12–19.

Caggiano, J. (1995) 'Executive commentary', *Academy of Management Executive*, 9 (1): 39–41.

Cappelli, P. and Crocker-Hefter, A. (1996) 'Distinctive human resources are firms' core competencies', *Organizational Dynamics*, 24 (3): 7–22.

Carson, K.D. and Carson, P.P. (1997) 'Career entrenchment: a quiet march toward occupational death?', *Academy of Management Executive*, 11 (1): 62–75.

Coff, R.W. (1997) 'Human assets and management dilemmas – coping with hazards on the road to resource-based theory', *Academy of Management Review*, 22 (2): 374–402.

Collins, D. (1997) 'The ethical superiority and inevitability of participatory management as an organizational system [review]', *Organization Science*, 8 (5): 489–507.

Cooksey, R.W. and Gates, G.R. (1995) 'HRM: a management science in need of discipline', *Journal of the Australian and New Zealand Academy of Management*, 1 (1): 1–16.

Cox, T.H. and Blake, S. (1991) 'Managing cultural diversity: implications for organizational competitiveness', *Academy of Management Executive*, 5 (3): 45–56.

Coyle, J. and Schnarr, N. (1995) 'The soft-side challenges of the "virtual corporation"', *Human Resource Planning*, 18 (1): 41–2.

Cummings, A. and Oldham, G.R. (1997) 'Enhancing creativity – managing work contexts for the high potential employee', *California Management Review*, 40 (1): 22 ff.

Cutcher-Gershenfeld, J., Kosseck, E.E. and Sandling, H. (1997) 'Managing concurrent change initiatives: integrating quality and work/family strategies', *Organizational Dynamics*, 25 (3): 21–37.

Davis, E. (1997) 'Towards improved people management: an analysis', *Journal of the Australian and New Zealand Academy of Management*, 3 (2): 28–33.

Davis, T.R.V. (1997) 'Open-book management: its promise and pitfalls', *Organizational Dynamics*, 25 (3): 7–20.

Davis-Blake, A. and Uzzi, B. (1993) 'Determinants of employment externalization: a study of temporary workers and independent contractors', *Administrative Science Quarterly*, 38 (2): 195–223.

de-Forest, M.E. (1994) 'Thinking of a plant in Mexico', *Academy of Management Executive*, 8 (1): 33–40.

Delery, J.E. and Doty, D.H. (1996) 'Modes of theorizing in strategic human resource management: tests of universalistic, contingency, and configurational performance predictions', *Academy of Management Journal*, 39 (4): 802–35.

DeVries, M.F.R.K. (1998) 'Charisma in action: the tranformational abilities of Virgin's Richard Branson and ABB's Percy Barnevik', *Organizational Dynamics*, 26 (3): 7–21.

Dunford, R. (1995) '"You want loyalty, get a dog!": tensions and paradox in the lean organization'. Paper presented at the 6th APROS International Colloquium, Mexico, 11–14 December.

Editors (1995) 'More on the folly', *Academy of Management Executive*, 9 (1): 15–16.

Eisenstat, R.A. (1996) 'What corporate human resources brings to the picnic: four models for functional management', *Organizational Dynamics*, 25 (2): 7–22.

Feldman, D.C. (1996) 'Managing careers in downsizing firms', *Human Resource Management Journal*, 35 (2): 154–61.

Feldman, D.C., Doerpinghaus, H.I. and Turnley, W.H. (1994) 'Managing temporary workers: a permanent HRM challenge. *Organizational Dynamics*, autumn: 49–63.

Forster, N. (1997) 'The persistent myth of high expatriate failure rates: a re-appraisal', *International Journal of Human Resource Management*, 8 (4): 414–33.

Ghorpade, J. and Chen, M.M. (1995) 'Creating quality-driven performance apraisal systems', *Academy of Management Executive*, 9 (1): 32–9.

Goodstein, J.D. (1994) 'Institutional pressures and strategic responsiveness: employer involvement in work-family', *Academy of Management Journal*, 37 (2): 350–82.

Guest, D.E. (1997) 'Human resource management and performance: a review and research agenda', *International Journal of Human Resource Management*, 8 (3): 263–76.

Hall, D.T. and Moss, J.E. (1998) 'The new protean career contract: helping organizations and employees adapt', *Organizational Dynamics*, 26 (3): 22–37.

Hallier, J. and James, P. (1997) 'Middle managers and the employee psychological contract: agency, protection and advancement', *Journal of Management Studies*, 34 (5): 727.

Handy, C. (1990) *The Age of Unreason*. Boston, MA: Harvard Business School Press.

Hannon, J.M. and Milkovich, G.T. (1996) 'The effect of human resource reputation signals on share prices: an event study', *Human Resource Management*, 35 (3): 405–24.

Harzing, A.-W. (1995) 'The persistent myth of high expatriate failure rates', *International Journal of Human Resource Management*, 6 (2): 457–74.

Hilmer, F.G. and Donaldson, L. (1996) *Management Redeemed: Debunking the Fads that Undermine Corporate Performance*. Sydney: Free Press.

Hirsch, P. (1988) *Pack Your Own Parachute*. Boston: Addison-Wesley.

Hochschild, A.R. (1997) 'When work becomes home and home becomes work', *California Management Review*, 39 (4): 79–97.

Huselid, M.A., Jackson, S.E. and Schuler, R.S. (1997) 'Technical and strategic human resource management effectiveness as determinants of firm performance', *Academy of Management Journal*, 40 (1): 171–88.

Jain, H.C., Lawler, J.J. and Morishmima, M. (1998) 'Multinational corporations, human resource management and host-country nationals', *International Journal of Human Resource Management*, 9 (4): 553–66.

Jones, C. and De Fillippi, R.J. (1996) 'Back to the future in film: combining industry and self-knowledge to meet career challenges of the 21st century', *Academy of Management Executive*, 10 (4): 89–103.

Joplin, J.R.W. and Daus, C.S. (1997) 'Challenges of leading a diverse workforce', *Academy of Management Executive*, 11 (3): 32–47.

Kamoche, K. (1997) 'Knowledge creation and learning in international HRM', *International Journal of Human Resource Management*, 8 (3): 213–25.

Kane, R. (1996) 'HRM: changing concepts in a changing environment', *International Journal of Employment Studies*, 4 (2): 115–77.

Kerr, S. (1975) 'On the folly of rewarding A, while hoping for B', *Academy of Management Journal*, 18: 769–83.

Kiedel, R.W. (1994) 'Rethinking organizational design', *Academy of Management Executive*, 8 (4): 12–28.

Kochanski, J.T. and Ruse, D.H. (1996) 'Designing a competency-based human resources organization', *Human Resource Management*, 35 (1): 19–33.

Konrad, A.M. and Linnehan, F. (1995) 'Formalized HRM structures: coordinating equal employment opportunity or concealing organizational practices?', *Academy of Management Journal*, 38 (3): 787–820.

Kossek, E.E., Huber-Yoder, M., Castellino, D. and Lerner, J. (1997) 'The working poor: locked out of careers and the organizational mainstream?', *Academy of Management Executive*, 11 (1): 76–92.

Krefting, L.A., Kirby, S.L. and Kryzstofiak, F.J. (1997) 'Managing diversity as a proxy for requisite variety: risks in identify-conscious inclusion and pressure to conform', *Journal of Management Inquiry*, 6 (4): 376–89.

Lado, A.A. and Wilson, M.C. (1994) 'Human resource systems and sustained competitive advantage: a competency-based perspective', *Academy of Management Review*, 19 (4): 699–727.

Lawler, E.E. (1994) 'From job-based to competency-based organizations', *Journal of Organizational Behaviour*, 15: 3–15.

Legge, K. (1995) *Human Resource Management: Rhetorics and Realities*. London: Macmillan.

Lever, S. (1997) 'An analysis of managerial motivations behind outsourcing practices in human resources', *Human Resource Planning*, 20 (2): 37–47.

Lewis, K.J. (1994) 'Executive commentary', *Academy of Management Executive*, 8 (4): 29–30.

Limerick, D.C. and Cunnington, B. (1993) *Managing the New Organisation: A Blueprint for Networks and Strategic Alliances*. Wheeler Heights: Business and Professional Publishing.

Lu, Y. and Bjorkman, I. (1997) 'HRM practices in China-Western joint ventures: MNC standardization versus localization', *International Journal of Human Resource Management*, 8 (5): 614–28.

Lundberg, C.C. (1991) 'Creating and managing a vanguard organization: design and human resource lessons from Jossey-Bass', *Human Resource Management*, 30 (1): 89–112.

McDaniel, R.R. and Walls, M.E. (1997) 'Diversity as a management strategy for organizations: a view through the lenses of chaos and quantum theories', *Journal of Management Inquiry*, 6 (4): 363–75.

McGraw, P. (1997) 'International human resource management', in R. Kramar, P. McGraw and R. Schuler (eds), *Human Resource Management in Australia*. Melbourne: Addison Wesley Longman. pp. 538–86.

Mansfield, R.S. (1996) 'Building competency models: approaches for HR professionals', *Human Resource Management*, 35 (1): 7–18.

Medcof, J.W. and Needham, B. (1998) 'The supra-organizational HRM systems', *Business Horizons*, 41 (1): 43–50.

Milliken, F.J. and Martins, L.L. (1996) 'Searching for common threads: understanding the multiple effects of diversity in organizational groups', *Academy of Management Review*, 21 (2): 402–33.

Mirvis, P.H. (1997) 'Human resource management: leaders, laggards and followers', *Academy of Management Executive*, 11 (2): 43–56.

Morrison, D.E. (1994) 'Psychological contracts and change', *Human Resource Management*, 33 (3): 353–72.

Morrison, E.W. and Robinson, S.L. (1997) 'When employees feel betrayed: a model of how psychological contract violation develops', *Academy of Management Review*, 22 (1): 226–56.

Nicholson, N. (1996) 'Career systems in crisis: change and opportunity in the information age', *Academy of Management Executive*, 10 (4): 40–51.

Nonaka, I. and Takeuchi, H. (1995) *The Knowledge-creating Company: How Japanese Companies Create Dynamics of Innovation*. New York: Oxford University Press.

Osterman, P. (1995) 'Work/family programs and the employment relationship', *Administrative Science Quarterly*, 40 (4): 681–700.

Paul, R.J. and Townsend, J.B. (1993) 'Managing the older worker – don't just rinse away the grey', *Academy of Management Executive*, 7 (3): 67–74.

Peiperl, M. and Baruch, Y. (1997) 'Back to square zero: the post-corporate career', *Organizational Dynamics*, Spring: 7–22.

Pfeffer, J. (1995) 'Producing sustainable advantage through the effective management of people', *Academy of Management Executive*, 9 (1): 55–69.

Pfeffer, J. (1998) 'Seven practices of successful organizations', *California Management Review*, 40 (2): 96–124.

Quinn, J.B., Anderson, P. and Finkelstein, S. (1996) 'Leveraging intellect', *Academy of Management Executive*, 10 (3): 7–27.

Reed, M.I. (1996) 'Rediscovering Hegel: the "new historicism" in organization and management studies', *Journal of Management Studies*, 33 (2): 139–58.

Robinson, S.L., Kraatz, M.S. and Rousseau, D.M. (1994) 'Changing obligations and the psychological contract: a longitudinal study', *Academy of Management Journal*, 37 (1): 137–52.

Robinson, G. and Dechant, K. (1997) 'Building a business case for diversity', *Academy of Management Executive*, 11 (3): 21–31.

Rousseau, D.M. (1996) 'Changing the deal while keeping the people', *Academy of Management Executive*, 10 (1): 50–59.

Sanchez, J.I. and Brock, P. (1996) 'Outcomes of perceived discrimination among hispanic employees: is diversity management a luxury or a necessity', *Academy of Management Journal*, 39 (3): 704–19.

Semler, R. (1994) 'Why my former employees still work for me', *Harvard Business Review* (Jan–Feb): 64–74.

Sisson, K. (1990) 'Introducing the *Human Resource Management Journal*', *Human Resource Management Journal*, 1 (1).

Stevens, G. and Greer, C.R. (1998) 'Doing business in Mexico: understanding cultural differences', in F. Luthans (ed.), *The People Side of Successful Global Alliances*. New York: American Management Association. pp. 43–59.

Stewart, T.A. (1998) 'Is this job really necessary?', *Fortune*, 12: 82–3.

Stroh, L.K. and Reilly, A.H. (1997) 'Loyalty in the age of downsizing', *Sloan Management Review*, 38 (4): 83–8.

Sugalski, T.D., Manzo, L.S. and Meadows, J.L. (1995) 'Resource link: re-establishing the employment relationship in an era of downsizing', *Human Resource Management*, 34 (3): 389–403.

Swiercz, P.M. (1995) 'Strategic HRM', *Human Resource Planning*, 18 (3): 53–9.

Tayeb, M. (1998) 'Transfer of HRM practices across cultures: an American company in Scotland', *International Journal of Human Resource Management*, 9 (2): 332–58.

Taylor, M.S., Audia, G. and Gupta, A.K. (1996) 'The effect of lengthening job tenure on managers' organizational commitment and turnover', *Organization Science*, 7 (6): 632–48.

Townley, B. (1993) 'Foucault, power/knowledge, and its relevance for human resource management', *Academy of Management Review*, 18 (3): 518–45.

Townley, B. (1994) *Reframing Human Resource Management: Power, Ethics and the Subject at Work*. London: Sage.

Truss, C., Gratton, L., Hope-Haley, V., McGovern, P. and Styles, P. (1997) 'Soft and hard models of human resource management: a reappraisal', *Journal of Management Studies*, 34 (1): 53–73.

Tsui, A.S., Pierce, J.L., Porter, L.W. and Tripoli, A.M. (1997) 'Alternative approaches to the employee–organization relationship: does investment in employees pay off?', *Academy of Management Journal*, 40 (5): 1089–121.

Ulrich, D. (1998) 'Intellectual capital = competence times [?] commitment', *Sloan Management Review*, 39 (2): 15–26.

von-Hippel, C., Mangum, S.L., Greenberger, D.B., Heneman, R.L. and Skoglind, J.D. (1997) 'Temporary employment: can organizations and employees both win?', *Academy of Management Executive*, 11 (1): 93–104.

Wallace, J.E. (1995) 'Organizational and professional committment in professional and non-professional organizations', *Administrative Science Quarterly*, 40 (2): 228–55.

Welbourne, T.M. and Andrews, A.O. (1996) 'Predicting the performance of initial public offerings: should human resource management be in the equation?', *Academy of Management Journal*, 39 (4): 891–919.

Welch, D. (1994) 'Determinants of international human resource management approaches and activities: a suggested framework', *Journal of Management Studies*, 1 (2): 139–64.

Williams, K.J. and Alliger, G.M. (1994) 'Role stressors, mood spillover, and perceptions of work–family conflict in employed parents', *Academy of Management Journal*, 37 (4): 837–68.

Wood, S. (1995) 'The four pillars of HRM: are they connected?', *Human Resource Management Journal*, 5 (5): 49–59.

Wright, P., Ferris, S., Hiller, J.S. and Kroll, M. (1995) 'Competitiveness through management of diversity: effects on stock price valuation', *Academy of Management Journal*, 30 (1): 272–87.

Wright, P.M. and McMahan, G.C. (1992) 'Theoretical perspectives for strategic human resource management', *Journal of Management*, 18 (2): 295–320.

Yeung, I.Y.M. and Tung, R.L. (1998) 'Achieving business success in Confucian societies: the importance of GUANXI (connections)', in F. Luthans (ed.), *The People Side of Successful Global Alliances*. New York: American Management Association. pp. 72–83.

4 MANAGING POWER

Acker, J. (1990) 'Hierarchies, jobs, bodies: a theory of gendered organizations', *Gender and Society*, 4 (2): 139–58.

Acker, J. and Van Houton, D. (1974) 'Differential recruitment and control: the sex structuring of organizations', *Administrative Science Quarterly*, 19 (2): 152–63.

Alcoff, L. (1988) 'Cultural feminism versus post-structuralism: the identity crisis in feminist theory', *Signs*, 13 (31): 405–36.

Alvesson, M. and Billig, Y.D. (1992) 'Gender and organization: towards a differentiated understanding', *Organization Studies*, 13: 73–103.

Alvesson, M. and Deetz, S. (1996) 'Critical theory and postmodernism approaches to organizational studies', in S. Clegg, C. Hardy and W. Nord (eds), *Handbook of Organization Studies*. London: Sage. pp. 191–217.

Alvesson, M. and Willmott, H. (1984) 'Questioning rationality and ideology: on critical organization theory', *International Studies of Management and Organizations*, 14 (1): 61–79.

Alvesson, M. and Willmott, H. (1992a) 'On the idea of emancipation in management and organization studies', *Academy of Management Review*, 17 (3): 432–64.

Alvesson, M. and Willmott, H. (eds) (1992b) *Critical Management Studies*. London: Sage.

Anonymous (1991) 'Advice and dissent: rating the corporate governance compact', *Harvard Business Review*, 69 (9): 136–43.

Arnold, G. (1995) 'Dilemmas of feminist coalitions: collective identity and strategic effectiveness in the battered women's movement', in M.M. Ferree and P.Y. Martin (eds), *Feminist Organizations: Harvest of the New Women's Movement*. Philadelphia: Temple University Press. pp. 276–90.

Ashkenas, R., Ulrich, D., Jick, T. and Kerr, S. (1995) *The Boundaryless Organiz-ation: Breaking the Chains of Organizational Structure.* San Francisco: Jossey-Bass.

Astley, W.G. and Sachdeva, S.P. (1984) 'Structural sources of intraorganizational power: a theoretical synthesis', *Academy of Management Review,* 9 (1): 104–13.

Bacchi, C.L. (1990) *Same Difference.* London: Allen and Unwin.

Bailey, D. (1988) *Directors and Officers Liability Loss Prevention.* Columbus, OH: Arter and Hadden for Chubb and Son Inc.

Bailey, D. (1993) *Canadian Director and Officer Liability and Insurance.* Colum-bus, OH: Arter and Hadden.

Barker, J. (1993) 'Tightening the iron cage: concertive control in self-managing teams', *Administrative Science Quarterly,* 38, 408–37.

Bass, B.M. and Avolio, B.J. (1994) 'Shatter the glass ceiling: women may make better managers', *Human Resource Management,* 33 (4): 549–60.

Bazerman, M.H. and Schoorman, F.D. (1983) 'A limited rationality model of inter-locking directorates', *Academy of Management Review,* 4: 497–506.

Beatty, R.W. and Ulrich, D.O. (1991) 'Re-energizing the mature organization', *Organizational Dynamics,* 20 (1): 16–30.

Belasco, J.A. (1989) 'Masters of empowerment', *Executive Excellence,* 6 (3): 11–12.

Bell, C. and Zemke, R. (1988) 'Do service procedures tie employees hands?', *Per-sonnel Journal,* 67 (9): 77–83.

Bernstein, A.J. (1992) 'Why empowerment programs often fail', *Executive Excel-lence,* 9 (7): 5.

Billig, Y.D. and Alvesson, M. (eds) (1994) *Gender, Managers, and Organizations.* Berlin: Walter de Gruyter.

Bird, F. and Gandz, J. (1991) *Good Management.* Englewood Cliffs, NJ: Prentice-Hall.

Bird, F. and Hardy, C. (1994) 'Power and ethical action', in C. Hardy (ed.), *Man-aging Strategic Action.* London: Sage. pp. 272–84.

Block, P. (1990) 'How to be the new kind of manager', *Working Woman,* 15 (7): 51–6.

Bowen, D.E. and Lawler, E.E. (1992) 'The empowerment of service workers: what, why, how, and when', *Sloan Management Review,* 33 (3): 31–9.

Bradshaw-Camball, P. and Murray, V. (1991) 'Illusions and other games: a theor-etical view of organizational politics', *Organization Science,* 2 (4): 379–98.

Brown, D. (1992) 'Why participative management won't work here', *Management Review,* 81 (16): 42–6.

Bryan, J.H. (1995) 'Allegiance to a diverse board', *Directors and Boards,* 19 (3): 6–8.

Brymer, R.A. (1991) 'Employee empowerment: a guest-driven leadership strategy', *Cornell Hotel and Restaurant Administration Quarterly,* 32 (1): 58–68.

Burke, R.J. (1997) 'Women on corporate boards of directors: a needed resource', *Women in Management,* 8: 4–5.

Burke, W.W. (1986) 'Leadership as empowering others', in S. Srivastva and Associ-ates (eds), *Executive Power.* San Francisco: Jossey-Bass. pp. 51–77.

Burrell, G. (1984) 'Sex and organizational analysis', *Organization Studies,* 5 (2): 97–118.

Burrell, G. and Hearn, J. (1989) 'The sexuality of organization', in J. Hearn, D.L. Sheppard, P. Tancred-Sheriff and G. Burrell (eds), *The Sexuality of Organization.* London: Sage. pp. 1–28.

Calás, M.B., and Smircich, L. (1991) 'Using the "F" word: feminist theories and the social consequences of organizational research', in A. Mills and P. Tancred (eds), *Gendering Organizational Analysis* . London: Sage. pp. 222–34.

Calás, M.B. and Smircich, L. (1992) 'Re-writing gender into organizational theoriz-ing: directions from feminist perspective', in M. Reed and M. Hughes (eds),

Rethinking Organization: New Directions in Organization Theory and Analysis. Newbury Park, CA: Sage. pp. 227–53.

Calás, M.B. and Smircich, L. (1996) 'From the "woman's" point of view: feminist approaches to organization studies', in S. Clegg, C. Hardy and W. Nord (eds), *Handbook of Organization Studies.* London: Sage. pp. 218–57.

Cannella, A.A.J. (1995) 'Executives and shareholders: a shift in the relationship', *Human Resource Management,* 34 (1): 165–84.

Carr, C. (1991) 'Managing self-managed workers', *Training and Development,* 45 (9), 36–42.

Caudron, S. (1998) 'Diversity watch', *Black Enterprise,* 29 (2): 91–4.

Cavanagh, G.F., Moberg, D.J. and Velasquez, M. (1981) 'The ethics of organizational politics', *Academy of Management Review,* 6 (3): 363–74.

Clarkson, M.B.E. (1995) 'A stakeholder framework for analyzing and evaluating corporate social performance', *Academy of Management Review,* 20 (1): 92–117.

Clegg, S.R. (1975) *Power, Rule and Domination.* London: Routledge and Kegan Paul.

Clegg, S.R. (1989) *Frameworks of Power.* London: Sage.

Collinson, D. (1988) ' "Engineering humor": masculinity, joking and conflict in shop-floor relations', *Organization Studies,* 9: 181–99.

Collinson, D.L. and Collinson, M. (1989) 'Sexuality in the workplace: the domination of men's sexuality', in J. Hearn, D.L. Sheppard, P. Tancred-Sheriff and G. Burrell (eds), *The Sexuality of Organization.* London: Sage. pp. 91–109.

Collinson, D. and Hearn, J. (1994) 'Naming men as men: implications for work, organization and management', *Gender, Work and Organization,* 1 (1): 2–22.

Conger, J. (1989). 'Leadership: the art of empowering others', *The Academy of Management Executive,* 3 (1): 17–24.

Conger, J.A. and Kanungo, R.N. (1988) 'The empowerment process: integrating theory and practice', *Academy of Management Review,* 13 (3): 471–82.

Connell, R.W. (1994) 'The state, gender, and sexual politics: theory and appraisal', in H.L. Radtke and H.J. Stam (eds), *Power/Gender.* London: Sage. pp. 136–73.

Conner, C. (1995) *Canadian Directorship Practices 1995 – A New Era in Corporate Governance:* Conference Board of Canada.

Coote, A. and Campbell, B. (1982) *Sweet Freedom.* London: Pan.

Crozier, M. (1964) *The Bureaucratic Phenomenon.* Chicago: University of Chicago Press.

Culbert, S. and McDonough, J. (1980) *The Invisible War: Pursuing Self Interests at Work.* New York: John Wiley.

Cullen, D. and Townley, B. (1994) 'Autonomy and empowerment: new wine in old bottles'. Paper presented at the Western Academy of Management, Santa Fe, NM.

Czarniawska-Joerges, B. (1994) 'Gender, power, organizations: an interruptive interpretation', in J. Hassard and M. Parker (eds), *Towards a New Theory of Organizations.* London: Routledge. pp. 227–47.

Daily, C.M. and Dalton, D.R. (1997) 'CEO and board chair roles held jointly or separately: much ado about nothing?', *Academy of Management Executive,* 11 (3): 11–20.

Daily, C.M. and Schwenk, C. (1996) 'Chief executive officers, top management teams, and boards of directors: congruent or countervailing forces?', *Journal of Management,* 22 (2): 185–208.

Daniels, R.J. and Waitzer, E.J. (1994) 'Challenges to the citadel: a brief overview of recent trends in Canadian corporate governance', *Canadian Business Law Journal,* 23: 23–44.

Daniels, R.J. and Morck, R. (1995) 'Canadian corporate governance: policy options', in R.J. Daniels and R. Morck (eds), *Corporate Decision-Making in Canada.* Calgary: University of Calgary Press. pp. 661–96.

Davis, G.F. and Thompson, T.A. (1994) 'A social movement perspective on corporate control', *Administrative Science Quarterly,* 39 (1): 141–73.

Davis, J.H., Schoorman, F.D. and Donaldson, L. (1997) 'Toward a stewardship theory of management', *The Academy of Management Review*, 22 (1): 20–47.

Dean, J.W. and Bowen, D.E. (1994) 'Management theory and total quality: improving research and practice through theory development', *Academy of Management Review*, 19 (3): 392–418.

Deetz, S. (1992a) *Democracy in an Age of Corporate Colonization: Developments in Communication and the Politics of Everyday Life*. Albany, NY: State University of New York.

Deetz, S. (1992b) 'Disciplinary power in the modern corporation', in M. Alvesson and H. Willmott (eds), *Critical Management Studies*. London: Sage. pp. 21–45.

Delorme, J.-C. (1993) 'Corporate governance: the need for a shareholders' charter', *Canadian Business Review*, autumn: 42–3, 48.

Donaldson, L. and Davis, J.H. (1994) 'Boards and company performance – research challenges the conventional wisdom', *Corporate Governance: An International View*, 2 (3): 151–60.

Donaldson, T. and Preston, L.E. (1995) 'The stakeholder theory of the corporation: concepts, evidence, and implications', *Academy of Management Review*, 20 (1): 65–91.

Doyle, F.P. (1990) 'Peope-power: the global human resource challenge for the 90's', *Columbia Journal of World Business* (spring–summer): 36–45.

Dreyfus, H.L. and Rabinow, P. (1982) *Michel Foucault: Beyond Structuralism and Hermeneutics*. Brighton: Harvester.

Early, V. (1991) 'Empowering organizations', *Executive Excellence*, 8 (2): 13–14.

Eccles, T. (1993) 'The deceptive allure of empowerment', *Long Range Planning*, 26 (6): 13–21.

Eccles, R.G. and Nohria, N. (1993) *Beyond the Hype: Rediscovering the Essence of Management*. Boston: Harvard Business School Press.

Eisman, R. (1991) 'Power to the people', *Incentive*, 165 (10): 116.

Eubanks, P. (1991) 'Employee empowerment key to culture change', *Hospitals*, 65 (24): 40.

Faludi, S. (1991) *Backlash: The Undeclared War Against American Women*. New York: Crown.

Feldman, D.C. and Leana, C.R. (1994) 'Better practices in managing layoffs', *Human Resource Management*, 33 (2): 239–60.

Feldman, S. (1991) 'Keeping the customer satisfied – inside and out', *Management Review*, 80 (11): 58–60.

Ferguson, K.E. (1984) *The Feminist Case Against Bureaucracy*. Philadelphia: Temple University Press.

Ferlie, E. and Pettigrew, A. (1996) 'The nature and transformation of corporate headquarters: a review of recent literature and a research agenda', *Journal of Management Studies*, 33 (4): 495–522.

Ferree, M.M. and Martin, P.Y. (eds) (1995) *Feminist Organizations: Harvest of the New Women's Movement*. Philadelphia: Temple University Press.

Fierman, J. (1990) 'Do women manage differently?', *Fortune*, 122 (15): 115–18.

Fincham, R. (1992) 'Perspectives on power: processual, institutional and "internal" forms of organizational power', *Journal of Management Studies*, 29 (6): 741–59.

Flax, J. (1987) 'Postmodernism and gender relations in feminist theory', *Signs*, 12 (4): 621–43.

Fleming, P.C. (1991) 'Empowerment strengthens the rock', *Management Review*, 80 (12): 34–7.

Foerster, S. (1995) 'Institutional activism by public pension funds the CalPERS model in Canada?', in R.J. Daniels and R. Morck (eds), *Corporate Decision-Making in Canada*. Calgary: University of Calgary Press. p. 379.

Follett, M.P. (1924) *Creative Experience*. New York: Peter Smith.

Ford, R.C. and Fottler, M.D. (1995) 'Empowerment: a matter of degree', *Academy of Management Executive*, 9 (3): 21–31.

Forester, J. (1989) *Planning in the Face of Power*. Berkeley: University of California Press.

Foucault, M. (1979) *Discipline and Punish: The Birth of the Prison*. New York: Vintage Books.

Foucault, M. (ed.) (1980) *Power/Knowledge: Selected Interviews and Other Writings 1972–1977*. Brighton: Harvester.

Foucault, M. (1982) 'The subject and power', in H.L. Dreyfus and P. Rabinow (eds), *Michel Foucault: Beyond Structuralism and Hermeneutics*. Brighton: Harvester. pp. 208–26.

Foucault, M. (1984) *The History of Sexuality: An Introduction*. Harmondsworth: Penguin.

Fraser, N. and Nicholson, L.J. (1988) 'Social criticism without philosophy: an encounter between feminism and postmodernism', *Theory Culture and Society*, 5 (2/3): 373–94.

Freeman, R.E. (1984) *Strategic Management: A Stakeholder Approach*. Boston: Pitman.

Freeman, R.E. and Gilbert, D.R. (1988) *Corporate Strategy and the Search for Ethics*. Englewood Cliffs, NJ: Prentice-Hall.

Freeman, S.J. (1994) 'Organizational downsizing as convergence and reorientation: implications for human resource management', *Human Resource Management*, 33 (2): 213–38.

French, J.R.P. and Raven, B. (1968) 'The bases of social power', in D. Cartwright and A. Zander (eds), *Group Dynamics*. New York: Harper & Row.

Frost, P.J. (1987) 'Power, politics and influence', in F.M. Jablin, L.L. Putnam, K.H. Roberts and L.W. Porter (eds), *Handbook of Organizational Communications: An Interdisciplinary Perspective*. London: Sage.

Gandz, J. (1990) 'The employee empowerment era', *Business Quarterly*, 55 (2): 74–9.

Gandz, J. and Murray, V.V. (1980) 'The experience of workplace politics', *Academy of Management Journal*, 23 (2): 237–51.

Gaventa, J. (1980) *Power and Powerlessness: Quiescence and Rebellion in an Appalachian Valley*. Oxford: Clarendon Press.

Gonring, M.P. (1991) 'Communication makes employee involvement work', *Public Relations Journal*, 47 (11): 38–40.

Gopinath, C., Siciliano, J.I. and Murray, R.L. (1994) 'Changing role of the board of directors: in search of a new strategic identity?', *Mid-Atlantic Journal of Business*, 30 (2): 175–85.

Goski, K.L. and Belfry, M. (1991) 'Achieving competitive advantage through employee empowerment', *Employee Relations Today*, 18 (2): 213–20.

Granovetter, M.S. (1973) 'The strength of weak ties', *American Journal of Sociology*, 78: 1360–80.

Granovetter, M.S. (1985) 'Economic action and social structure: the problem of embeddedness', *American Journal of Sociology*, 91: 481–510.

Gray, B. (1994) 'A feminist critique of collaborating', *Journal of Management Inquiry*, 3 (3): 286–93.

Gray, B. and Ariss, S.S. (1985) 'Politics and strategic change across organizational life cycles', *Academy of Management Review*, 10 (4): 707–23.

Gutek, B.A. (1989) 'Sexuality in the workplace: key issues in social research and organizational practice', in J. Hearn, D.L. Sheppard, P. Tancred-Sheriff and G. Burrell (eds), *The Sexuality of Organization*. London: Sage. pp. 56–70.

Hall, M. (1989) 'Private experiences in the public domain: lesbians in organizations', in J. Hearn, D.L. Sheppard, P. Tancred-Sheriff and G. Burrell (eds), *The Sexuality of Organization*. London: Sage. pp. 125–38.

Hardy, C. (1985a) 'The nature of unobtrusive power', *Journal of Management Studies*, 22 (4): 384–99.

Hardy, C. (1985b) *Managing Organizational Closure*. Aldershot: Gower.

Hardy, C. (1994) *Managing Strategic Action: Mobilizing Change.* London: Sage.

Hardy, C. (1995) 'Managing strategic change: power, paralysis and perspective', *Advances in Strategic Management,* 12 (B): 3–31.

Hardy, C. and Clegg, S. (1996) 'Some dare call it power', in S. Clegg, C. Hardy and W. Nord (eds), *Handbook of Organization Studies.* London: Sage.

Hardy, C. and Leiba, S. (1998) 'The power behind empowerment: implications for research and practice', *Human Relations,* 51 (4): 451–83.

Hardy, C. and Phillips, N. (1998) 'Strategies of engagement: lessons from the critical examination of collaboration and conflict in an interorganizational domain', *Organization Science,* 9 (2): 217–30.

Hearn, J. and Parkin, P.W. (1987) *'Sex' at 'Work'.* New York: St. Martin's Press.

Hickson, D.J., Butler, R.J., Cray, D., Mallory, G.R. and Wilson, D.C. (1986) *Top Decisions: Strategic Decision-Making in Organizations.* San Francisco: Jossey-Bass.

Hickson, D.J., Hinings, C.R., Lee, C.A., Schneck, R.E. and Pennings, J.M. (1971) 'A strategic contingencies theory of intraorganizational power', *Administrative Science Quarterly,* 16 (2): 216–29.

Hill, C.W.L. and Jones, T.M. (1992) 'Stakeholder-agency theory', *Journal of Management Studies,* 29: 131–54.

Hills, R.M. (1994) 'Boards can work!', *Directors and Boards,* 18 (3): 4–7.

Hilmer, F.G. and Donaldson, L. (1996) 'The board of directors as watchdog', *Management Redeemed.* New York: Free Press. pp. 141–64.

hooks, b. (1984) *Feminist Theory: From Margin to Center.* Boston, MA: South End Press.

Howlett, K. (1993) 'A question of governance', *The Globe and Mail,* 19 July: B1.

Hoy, D.C. (1986) 'Power, repression, progress: Foucault, Lukes, and the Frankfurt School', in D.C. Hoy (ed.), *Foucault: A Critical Leader.* Oxford: Basil Blackwell. pp. 123–47.

Humphrey, J.W. (1991) 'A time of 10,000 leaders', *Executive Excellence,* 8 (6): 17–18.

Huse, M. and Eide, D. (1996) 'Stakeholder management and the avoidance of corporate control', *Business and Society,* 35 (2): 211–43.

Iannello, K.P. (1993) *Decisions without Hierarchy: Feminist Interventions in Organization Theory and Practice.* London: Routledge.

Jackall, R. (1988) *Moral Mazes: The World of Corporate Managers.* New York: Oxford University Press.

Kanungo, R.N. (1992) 'Alienation and empowerment: some ethical imperatives in business', *Journal of Business Ethics,* 11 (5/6): 413–22.

Keller, T. and Dansereau, F. (1995) 'Leadership and empowerment: a social exchange perspective', *Human Relations,* 48 (2): 127–47.

Kenneally, J.J. (1981) *Women and American Trade Unions.* Montreal: Eden Press Women's Publications.

Kesner, I.F., Victor, B. and Lamont, B.T. (1986) 'Board composition and the commission of illegal acts: an investigation of Fortune 500 companies', *Academy of Management Journal,* 29 (4): 789–99.

Kirby, J. (1996) 'Shareholder lobby sets sights on banks', *Weekend Australian,* 13–14 January: 35.

Kitzinger, C. (1994) 'Problematizing pleasure: radical feminist deconstruction of sexuality and power', in H.L. Radtke and H.J. Stam (eds), *Power/Gender.* London: Sage. pp. 194–209.

Kizilos, P. (1990) 'Crazy about empowerment?', *Training,* 27 (12): 47–56.

Knights, D. and Morgan, G. (1991) 'Strategic discourse and subjectivity: towards a critical analysis of corporate strategy in organisations', *Organisation Studies,* 12 (3): 251–73.

Knights, D. and Willmott, H. (1989) 'Power and subjectivity at work: from degradation to subjugation in social relations', *Sociology,* 23 (4): 535–58.

Kotter, J. and Heskett, J. (1992) *Corporate Culture and Performance*. New York: Free Press.

Latham, G.P., Erez, M. and Locke, E.A. (1988) 'Resolving scientific disputes by the joint design of crucial experiments by the antagonists: application of the Erez-Latham dispute regarding participation in goal-setting', *Journal of Applied Psychology Monograph*, 73: 753–72.

Lawler, E.E. (1992) *The Ultimate Advantage: Creating the High-Involvement Organization*. San Francisco: Jossey-Bass.

Lawler, E., Mohrman, S. and Ledford, G. (1992) *Employee Involvement and Total Quality Management*. San Francisco, CA: Jossey-Bass.

Lawrence, B.C. and Engleman, S.P. (1993) 'Bolstering the board's environmental focus', *Directors & Board*, 18 (1): 23–26.

Leana, C.R. (1987) 'Power relinquishment versus power sharing: theoretical clarification and empirical comparison of delegation and participation', *Journal of Applied Psychology*, 72: 228–33.

Leana, C.R., Ahlbrandt, R.S. and Murrel, A.J. (1992) 'The effects of employee involvement on unionized workers' attitudes, perceptions, and preferences in decision making', *Academy of Management Journal*, 35 (4): 861–73.

Ledford, G.E.J. and Lawler, E.E.I. (1994) 'Research on employee participation: beating a dead horse?', *Academy of Management Review*, 19 (4): 633–6.

Leiba, S. and Hardy, C. (1994) 'Employee empowerment: a seductive misnomer?', in C. Hardy (ed.), *Managing Strategic Action: Mobilizing Change*. London: Sage.

Leighton, D.S.R. and Thain, D.H. (1993) 'Selecting new directors', *Business Quarterly*, summer: 17–25.

Liff, S. and Wajcman, J. (1996) ' "sameness" and "difference" revisited: which way forward for equal opportunity initiatives?', *Journal of Management Studies*, 33 (1): 79–94.

Lorsch, J.W. (1995) 'Empowering the board', *Harvard Business Review* (January–February): 107–17.

Lukes, S. (1974) *Power: A Radical View*. London: Macmillan.

McCaffrey, D.P., Faerman, S.R. and Hart, D.W. (1995) 'The appeal and difficulties of participative systems', *Organization Science*, 6 (6): 603–27.

MacIntosh, J.G. and Schwartz, L.P. (1995) 'Do institutional and controlling shareholders increase corporate value?', in R.J. Daniels and R. Morck (eds), *Corporate Decision-Making in Canada*. Calgary: University of Calgary Press.

McKenna, J.F. (1990) 'Smart scarecrows: the wizardry of empowerment', *Industry Week*, 239 (14): 8–19.

McKenna, J.F. (1991a) 'America's best plants: SPX', *Industry Week*, 240 (20): 49–50.

McKenna, J.F. (1991b) 'Failure: managing the last taboo', *Industry Week*, 240 (5): 12–16.

MacLeod, L. (1989) *The City for Women: No Safe Place*. Ottawa: Secretary of State.

MacMillan, I.C. (1978) *Strategy Formulation: Political Concepts*. St. Paul, MN: West.

Mann, S. (1995) 'Politics and power in organizations: why women lose out', *Leadership and Organization Development Journal*, 16 (2): 9–15.

Manz, C.C. (1990) 'Beyond self-managing work teams: toward self-leading teams in the workplace', in W.A. Pasmore and R.W. Woodman (eds), *Research in Organizational Change and Development*. Greenwich, CT: JAI Press. pp. 273–99.

Marshall, J. (1995a) 'Gender and management: a critical review of research', *British Journal of Management*, 6 (special issue): S53–62.

Marshall, J. (1995b) 'Working at senior management and board levels: some of the issues for women', *Women in Management Review*, 10: 21–5.

Martin, J. (1990) 'Deconstructing organizational taboos: the suppression of gender conflict in organizations', *Organization Science*, 1 (4): 339–59.

Mathias, P. (1995) 'Just how fat are these cats?', *The Financial Post,* 4 November: 10–11.

Matthes, K. (1992) 'Empowerment: fact or fiction?', *HR Focus,* 69 (3): 1–6.

Mayes, B.T. and Allen, R.W. (1977) 'Toward a definition of organizational politics', *Academy of Management Review,* 2: 674–8.

Miles, R. and Cameron, K. (1982) *Coffin Nails and Corporate Strategies.* Englewood Cliffs, NJ: Prentice-Hall.

Mills, A.J. (1989) 'Gender, sexuality and organization theory', in J. Hearn, D.L. Sheppard, P. Tancred-Smith and G. Burrell (eds), *The Sexuality of Organizations.* London: Sage. pp. 29–44.

Mills, A. and Tancred, P. (1992) *Gendering Organization Analysis.* London: Sage.

Mintzberg, H. (1983) *Power In and Around Organizations.* Englewood Cliffs, NJ: Prentice-Hall.

Molz, R. (1995) 'The theory of pluralism in corporate governance: a conceptual framework and empirical test', *Journal of Business Ethics,* 14 (10): 789–804.

Monks, R.A.G. and Minow, N. (1995) *Corporate Governance.* Cambridge: Blackwell.

Montgomery, K.E. and Leighton, D.S.R. (1993) 'The unseen revolution is here', *Ivey Business Quarterly,* autumn: 39–48.

Morgen, S. (1994) 'Personalizing personnel decisions in feminist organizational theory and practice', *Human Relations,* 47 (6): 665–84.

Mumby, D. (1996) 'Feminism, postmodernism, and organizational communication studies', *Management Communication Quarterly,* 9 (3): 259–95.

Mumby, D.K. and Putnam, L.L. (1992) 'The politics of emotion: a feminist reading of bounded rationality', *Academy of Management Review,* 17 (3): 465–86.

Narayanan, V.K. and Fahey, L. (1982) 'The micro-politics of strategy formulation', *Academy of Management Review,* 7 (1): 25–34.

Nieva, V.F. and Gutek, B.A. (1985) 'Sex effects on evaluation', in B.A. Stead (ed.), *Women in Management.* Englewood Cliffs: Prentice-Hall.

Nkomo, S. (1992) 'The emperor has no clothes: rewriting "Race in Organizations"', *Academy of Management Review,* 17: 487–513.

Nkomo, S.M. and Cox, T.J. (1996) 'Diverse identities in organizations', in S. Clegg, C. Hardy and W. Nord (eds), *Handbook of Organization Studies.* London: Sage. pp. 338–56.

Nord, W.R. and Jermier, J.M. (1992) 'Critical social science for managers? Promising and perverse possibilities', in A. Mats and W. Hugh (eds), *Critical Management Studies.* London: Sage.

O'Connor, E.S. (1995) 'Paradoxes of participation: textual analysis and organizational change', *Organization Studies,* 16 (5): 769–803.

Odiorne, G.S. (1991) 'Competence versus passion', *Training and Development,* 45 (5): 61–4.

Ohlott, P., Ruderman, M. and McCauley, C. (1994) 'Gender difference in managers' developmental job experiences', *Academy of Management Journal,* 37: 46–67.

Parker, B. (1996) 'Evolution and revolution: from international business to globalization', in S.R. Clegg, C. Hardy and W. Nord (eds), *Handbook of Organization Studies.* London: Sage. pp. 484–506.

Parker, M. (1993) 'Industrial relations myth and shop-floor reality: the "Team concept: in the auto industry"', in N. Lichtenstein and J.H. Howell (eds), *Industrial Democracy in America.* Cambridge: Cambridge University Press.

Parker, M. and Slaughter, J. (1988) 'Managing by stress: the dark side of team concept', *ILR Report,* 26 (1): 19–23.

Parkin, W. (1989) 'Private experiences in the public domain: sexuality and residential care organizations', in J. Hearn, D.L. Sheppard, P. Tancred-Sheriff and G. Burrell (eds), *The Sexuality of Organization.* London: Sage. pp. 110–24.

Parry, G. and Morris, P. (1975) 'When is a decision not a decision?', in L. Crewe (ed.), *British Political Sociology Yearbook,* vol. 1. London: Croom Helm.

Peitchinis, S.G. (1989) *Women at Work*. Toronto: McClelland and Stewart.

Penzer, E. (1991) 'The power of empowerment', *Incentive*, 165 (5): 97–8, 138.

Pettigrew, A.M. (1973) *The Politics of Organizational Decision Making*. London: Tavistock.

Pettigrew, A.M. (1979) 'On studying organizational cultures', *Administrative Science Quarterly*, 24: 570–81.

Pettigrew, A. (1985) *The Awakening Giant: Continuity and Change in Imperial Chemical Industries*. Oxford: Blackwell.

Pfeffer, J. (1981) *Power in Organizations*. Marshfield, MA: Pitman.

Pfeffer, J. (1992a) 'Understanding power in organizations', *California Management Review*, 34 (2): 29–50.

Pfeffer, J. (1992b) *Managing with Power*. Boston, MA: Harvard Business School Press.

Pfeffer, J. and Salancik, G. (1974) 'Organizational decision making as a political process: the case of a university budget', *Administrative Science Quarterly*, 19: 135–51.

Pfeffer, J. and Salancik, G. (1978) *The External Control of Organizations: A Resource Dependence Perspective*. New York: Harper & Row.

Piercy, M. (1973) *To Be of Use*. Garden City, NY: Doubleday.

Preston, L.E. and Sapienza, H.J. (1990) 'Stakeholder management and corporate performance', *Journal of Behavioural Economics*, 19: 361–75.

Priest, M., Mecredy-Williams, R., Barbara, R.C. and O'Reilly, J.W. (1995) *Directors' Duties in Canada: Managing Risk*. North York: CCH Canadian.

Radtke, L.H. and Stam, H.J. (eds) (1994) *Power/Gender*. London: Sage.

Ranson, S., Hinings, R. and Greenwood, R. (1980) 'The structuring of organizational structure', *Administrative Science Quarterly*, 25 (1): 1–14.

Rees, T. (1994) 'Feminising the mainstream: women and the European Union's training policies', *Equal Opportunities Review*, 13 (3–5): 9–28.

Rosenau, P.M. (1992) *Post-Modernism and the Social Sciences: Insights, Inroads, and Intrusions*. Princeton, NJ: Princeton University Press.

Rosener, J.B. (1990) 'Ways women lead', *Harvard Business Review* (Nov–Dec): 119–25.

Rousseau, D.M. and Aquino, K. (1992) 'Fairness and implied contract obligations in job terminations: the role of contributions, promises and performance', *Journal of Organizational Behavior*, 15: 1–43.

Rousseau, D.M. and Parks, J.M. (1993) 'The contracts of individuals and organizations', *Research in Organizational Behaviour*, 15: 1–43.

Samuels, J.M., Greenfield, S. and Piper, A. (1996) 'The role of non-executive directors post-Cadbury', *Journal of General Management*, 21 (4): 1–14.

Sanday, P.R. (1981) *Female Power and Male Dominance*. Cambridge: Cambridge University Press.

Sawicki, J. (1991) *Disciplining Foucault: Feminism, Power and the Body*. New York: Routledge.

Schaeffer, O. (1991) 'Empowerment as a business strategy', *Executive Excellence*, 8 (10): 9–10.

Schlossberg, H. (1991) 'Authors blast those who make excuses for poor business', *Marketing News*, 25 (15): 5.

Schwenk, C.R. (1989) 'Linking cognitive, organizational and political factors in explaining strategic change', *Journal of Management Studies*, 26 (2): 177–88.

Sexty, R.W. (1995) *Canadian Business and Society: Understanding Social and Ethical Challenges*. Scarborough: Prentice-Hall.

Shelton, K. (1991) 'People power', *Executive Excellence*, 8 (12): 7–8.

Sheridan, J.N. (1991a) 'America's best plants: Tennessee Eastman', *Industry Week*, 240 (20): 59–60.

Sheridan, J.N. (1991b) 'A philosophy for commitment', *Industry Week*, 240 (3): 11–13.

Sherwood, J.J. (1988) 'Creating work cultures with competitive advantage', *Organizational Dynamics*, 17: 4–27.

Skaggs, B.C. and Labianca, G. (1993) *Redefining Empowerment: From a Management-Centered Construct to Economic Democracy.* Paper presented at the Academy of Management, Atlanta.

Smart, B. (1985) *Michel Foucault.* London: Tavistock.

Spencer, B.A. (1994) 'Models of organization and total quality management: a comparison and critical evaluation', *Academy of Management Review*, 19 (3): 446–71.

Stead, W.E., Worrel, D.L. and Stead, J.G. (1990) 'An integrative model for understanding and managing ethical behaviour in business organizations', *Journal of Business Ethics*, 9 (3): 233–42.

Stewart, T.A. (1989) 'New ways to exercise power', *Fortune*, 120: 52–7.

Stewart, T.A. (1993) 'The king is dead', *Fortune*, 127: 34–9.

Stone, D.L. and Colella, A. (1996) 'A model of factors affecting the treatment of disabled individuals in organizations', *Academy of Management Review*, 21 (2): 352–401.

Stopford, J. and Baden-Fuller, C. (1990) 'Corporate rejuvenation', *Journal of Management Studies*, 27: 399–415.

Thain, D.H., Leighton, D.S.R. and Kovacheff, J.D. (1994) 'Effective director dissent', *Business Quarterly*, summer: 35–48.

Thomas, K.W. and Velthouse, B.A. (1990) 'Cognitive elements of empowerment: an "interpretive" model of intrinsic task motivation', *Academy of Management Review*, 15 (4): 666–81.

Topaz, L. (1989/90) 'Empowerment: human resource management in the 90's', *Management Quarterly*, 30 (4): 3–8.

Turner, B.S. (ed.) (1990) *Theories of Modernity and Post Modernity.* London: Sage.

Vance, S.C. (1983) *Corporate Leadership: Boards, Directors and Strategy.* New York: McGraw-Hill.

Velasquez, M. et.al. (1983) 'Organizational statesmanship and dirty politics: ethical guidelines for the organizational politician', *Organizational Dynamics*, 12: 65–80.

Velthouse, B.A. (1990) 'Creativity and empowerment: a complementary relationship', *Review of Business*, 12 (2): 13–18.

Vianello, M. and Siemienska, R. (1990) *Gender Inequality.* London: Sage.

Von der Embse, T.J. (1989) 'Transforming power into empowerment', *Manage*, 41 (3): 25–8.

Vroom, V.H. and Jago, A.G. (1988) *The New Leadership: Managing Participation in Organizations.* Englewood Cliffs: Prentice-Hall.

Walby, S. (1990) *Theorizing Patriarchy.* Oxford: Blackwell.

Waldman, D.A. (1994) 'The contributions of total quality management to a theory of work performance', *Academy of Management Review*, 19 (3): 312–30.

Waters, J. (1978) 'Catch 20.2', *Organizational Dynamics*, spring: 3–19.

Welter, T.R. (1991a) 'A winning team begins with you', *Industry Week*, 240 (9): 35–42.

Welter, T.R. (1991b) 'America's best plants: Lord Corp.', *Industry Week*, 240 (20): 44–6.

Werther Jr, W.B., Kerr, J.L. and Wright, R.G. (1995) 'Strengthening corporate governance through board-level consultants', *Journal of Organisation Change Management*, 8 (3): 63–74.

White, J. (1980) *Women in Unions.* Ottawa: Minister of Supply and Services Canada.

Wilson, F. (1996) 'Research note: blind and deaf to gender?', *Organization Studies*, 17 (5): 825–42.

5 MANAGING CULTURE

Abrahamson, E. and Fombrun, C.J. (1994) 'Macrocultures: determinants and consequences', *Academy of Management Review*, 19 (4): 728–55.

Adler, N.J. and Jelinek, M. (1986) 'Is organization culture "Culture Bound?"', *Human Resource Management*, 25 (2): 73–90.

Alvesson, M. (1993) *Cultural Perspectives on Organizations*. Cambridge: Cambridge University Press.

Ashforth, B.E. (1985) 'Climate formations: issues and extensions', *Academy of Management Review*, 10 (4): 837–47.

Barley, S.R., Meyer, G.W. and Gash, D.C. (1988) 'Cultures of culture: academics, practitioners and the pragmatics of normative control', *Administrative Science Quarterly*, 33 (1): 24–60.

Barrett, F.J. (1995) 'Creating appreciative learning cultures', *Organizational Dynamics*, 24 (2): 36–49.

Bate, P. (1990) 'Using the culture concept in an organization development setting', *Journal of Applied Behavioral Science*, 26 (1): 83–106.

Boje, D.M. (1991) 'The storytelling organization: a study of story performance in an office-supply firm', *Administrative Science Quarterly*, 36 (1): 106–26.

Boje, D.M. (1995) 'Stories of the storytelling organization: a postmodern analysis of Disney as "Tamara-Land"', *Academy of Management Journal*, 38 (4): 997–1035.

Boyce, M.E. (1996) 'Organizational story and storytelling: a critical review', *Journal of Organizational Change Management*, 9 (5): 5–26.

Cartwright, S. and Cooper, C.L. (1993) 'The role of culture compatibility in successful organizational marriage', *Academy of Management Executive*, 7 (2): 57–70.

Champy, F. (1995) *Reengineering Management: The Mandate for New Leadership*. New York: Harper Business.

Chatman, J.A. and Barsade, S.G. (1995) 'Personality, organizational culture, and cooperation: evidence from a business simulation', *Administrative Science Quarterly*, 40: 423–43.

Chatman, J.A. and Jehn, K.A. (1994) 'Assessing the relationship between industry characteristics and organizational culture: how different can you be?', *Academy of Management Journal*, 37 (3): 522–53.

Collins, J.C. and Porras, J.I. (1994) *Built to Last: Successful Habits of Visionary Companies*. London: Century.

Cook, S.D.N. and Yanow, D. (1993) 'Culture and organizational learning', *Journal of Management Inquiry*, 2 (4): 373–90.

Cooke, R.A. and Rousseau, D.M. (1988) 'Behavioral norms and expectations: a quantitative approach to the assessment of organizational culture', *Group and Organization Studies*, 13: 245–73.

Deal, T. and Kennedy, A.E. (1982) *Corporate Cultures*. Reading, MA: Addison-Wesley.

De Lisi, P. (1990) 'Lessons from the steel axe: culture, technology and organizational change', *Sloan Management Review*, 32 (1): 83–93.

Denison, D.R. (1996) 'What is the difference between organizational culture and organizational climate? A native's point of view on a decade of paradigm wars', *Academy of Management Review*, 21 (3): 619–54.

Dougherty, D. (1996) 'Organizing for innovation', in S.R. Clegg, C. Hardy and W.R. Nord (eds), *Handbook of Organization Studies*. London: Sage. pp. 424–39.

Ebers, M. (1995) 'The framing of organizational cultures', *Research in the Sociology of Organizations*, 13: 129–70.

Fedor, K.J. and Werther, W.B. (1996) 'The fourth dimension: creating culturally responsive international alliances', *Organizational Dynamics*, 25 (2): 39–53.

Feldman, S.P. (1990) 'Stories as cultural creativity: on the relation between symbolism and politics in organizational change', *Human Relations*, 43 (9): 809–28.

Fitzgerald, T.H. (1988) 'Can change in organizational culture really be managed?', *Organizational Dynamics*, 17 (2): 5–15.

Fletcher, B.C. and Jones, F. (1992) 'Measuring organizational culture: the cultural audit', *Managerial Auditing Journal*, 7 (6): 30–36.

Goodall, H.L. (1992) 'Empowerment, culture, and postmodern: organizing deconstructing the Nordstrom employee handbook', *Journal of Organizational Change Management*, 5 (2): 25–30.

Gordon, G.G. (1991) 'Industry determinants of organisational culture', *Academy of Management Review*, 16 (2): 396–415.

Green, S. (1988) 'Strategy, organizational culture and symbolism', *Long Range Planning*, 21 (4): 121–9.

Grint, K (1995). *Management: A Sociological Introduction*. Cambridge: Polity Press.

Handy, C. (1993) *Understanding Organizations*. Oxford: Oxford Polity Press.

Harrison, J.R. and Carroll, G.R. (1991) 'Keeping the faith: a model of cultural transmission in formal organizations', *Administrative Science Quarterly*, 36 (4): 552–82.

Harrison, R. and Stokes, H. (1992) *Diagnosing Organizational Culture*. San Diego: Pfeiffer.

Hatch, M.J. (1993) 'The dynamics of organizational culture', *Academy of Management Review*, 18 (4): 657–93.

Hilmer, F.G. and Donaldson, L. (1996) *Management Redeemed: Debunking the Fads that Undermine Corporate Performance*. New York: Free Press.

Hofstede, G. (1993) 'Cultural constraints in management theories', *Academy of Management Executive*, 7 (1): 81–94.

Hofstede, G., Neuijen, B., Ohayv, D.D. and Sanders, G. (1990) 'Measuring organizational cultures: a qualitative and quantitative study across twenty cases', *Administrative Science Quarterly*, 35: 286–316.

Klein, A.S., Masi, R.J. and Weidner, C.K. (1995) 'Organizational culture, distribution and amount of control, and perceptions of quality', *Group and Organization Management*, 20 (2): 122–48.

Kotter, J.P. and Heskett, J.L. (1992) *Corporate Culture and Performance*. New York: Free Press.

Kroeber, A.L. and Kluckholn, C. (1952) *Culture: A Critical Review of Concepts and Definitions*. Cambridge, MA: Harvard University Press.

Kunda, G. (1995) 'Engineering culture: control and commitment in a high-tech corporation', *Organization Science*, 6 (2): 228–30.

Lahiry, S. (1994) 'Building commitment through organizational culture', *Training and Development*, 48 (4): 50–2.

Linstead, S. and Grafton-Small, R. (1992) 'On reading organizational culture', *Organization Studies*, 13 (3): 331–55.

Lundberg, C.C. (1990) 'Surfacing organisational culture', *Journal of Managerial Psychology*, 5 (4): 19–26.

McEnery, J. and DesHarnais, G. (1990) 'Culture shock', *Training and Development Journal*, 44 (4): 43–7.

Martin, J. (1992) *Cultures in Organizations: Three Perspectives*. New York: Oxford University Press.

Martin, J. and Frost, P. (1996) 'The organizational culture war games: a struggle for intellectual dominance', in S.R. Clegg, C. Hardy and W.R. Nord (eds), *Handbook of Organization Studies*. London: Sage. pp. 599–621.

Mason, E.S. (1994) 'Symbolism in managerial decision making: manipulation or inspiration?', *Journal of Managerial Psychology*, 9 (6): 27–34.

Meyerson, D. (1991) 'Acknowledging and uncovering ambiguities', in P. Frost, L. Moore, M. Louis, C. Lundberg and J.E. Martin (eds), *Reframing Organizational Culture*. Beverly Hills, CA: Sage.

Meyerson, D. and Martin, J. (1987) 'Cultural change: an integration of three different views', *Journal of Management Studies*, 24 (6): 623–47.

Morgan, G. (1986) *Images of Organization*. Beverly Hills, CA: Sage.

Morgan, G. (1989) *Creative Organization Theory: A Resourcebook*. Newbury Park, CA: Sage.

Morgan, G. (1993) *Imaginization: The Art of Creative Management*. Newbury Park, CA: Sage.

O'Connor, J.T. (1988) 'Architecture: building corporate symbols', *Harvard Business Review*, 66 (5): 131–3.

O'Reilly, C.A., Chatman, J. and Caldwell, D.F. (1991) 'People and organizational culture: a profile comparison approach to assessing person-organization fit', *Academy of Management Journal*, 23 (3): 487–516.

Ouchi, W.G. (1981) *Theory Z*. New York: Avon Books.

Peters, J. (1993) 'On culture', *Management Decision*, 31 (6): 34–8.

Peters, T.J. and Waterman, R.H. (1982) *In Search of Excellence: Lessons From America's Best-Run Companies*. New York: Harper & Row.

Phillips, M.E. (1994) 'Industry mindsets: exploring the cultures of two macro-organizational settings', *Organization Science*, 5 (3): 384–402.

Preston, D. (1993) 'Management development structures as symbols of organizational culture', *Personnel Review*, 22 (1): 18–30.

Price Waterhouse Change Integration Team (1996) *The Paradox Principles: How High-Performance Companies Manage Chaos, Complexity, and Contradiction to Achieve Superior Results*. Chicago: Irwin Professional Publishing.

Ricks, D.A. (1993) *Blunders in International Business*. Cambridge, MA: Blackwell.

Rose, R.A. (1988) 'Organizations as multiple cultures: a rules theory analysis', *Human Relations*, 41 (2): 139–70.

Rousseau, D.M. (1990) 'Assessing organizational culture: the case for multiple methods', in B. Schneider (ed.), *Organizational Climate and Culture*. San Francisco: Jossey-Bass. pp. 153–92.

Sackmann, S.A. (1992) 'Culture and subcultures: an analysis of organizational knowledge', *Administrative Science Quarterly*, 37: 140–61.

Salama, A. and Easterby-Smith, M. (1994) 'Cultural change and managerial careers', *Personnel Review*, 23 (3): 21–33.

Sathe, V. (1983) 'Implications of corporate culture: a manager's guide to action', *Organizational Dynamics*, 12 (2): 5–23.

Schein, E.H. (1985) *Organizational Culture and Leadership*. San Francisco: Jossey-Bass.

Schein, E.H. (1996) 'Culture: the missing concept in organization studies', *Administrative Science Quarterly*, 41 (2): 229–40.

Schneider, B., Brief, A.P. and Guzzo, R.A. (1996) 'Creating a climate and culture for sustainable organizational change', *Organizational Dynamics*, 24 (4): 7–19.

Schriber, J.B. and Gutek, B.A. (1987) 'Some time dimensions of work: measurement of an underlying aspect of organization culture', *Journal of Applied Psychology*, 72 (4): 642–50.

Siehl, C. and Martin, J. (1990) 'Organizational culture: a key to financial performance?', in B. Schneider (ed.), *Organizational Climate and Change*. San Francisco: Jossey-Bass. pp. 241–81.

Smircich, L. (1983) 'Concepts of culture and organizational analysis', *Administrative Science Quarterly*, 28: 339–58.

Smircich, L. (1995) 'Writing organizational tales: reflections on three books on organizational culture', *Organization Science*, 6 (2): 232–8.

Spradley, J.P. and McCurdy, D.W. (1972) *The Cultural Experience: Ethnography in Complex Society*. Prospect Heights, IL: Waveland Press.

Trice, H.M. and Beyer, J.M. (1984) 'Studying organizational cultures through rites and ceremonials', *Academy of Management Review*, 9 (4): 653–69.

Trice, H.M. and Beyer, J.M. (1995) 'Writing organizational tales: the cultures of work organizations', *Organization Science*, 6 (2): 226–8.

Tucker, R.W., McCoy, W.J. and Evans, L.C. (1990) 'Can questionnaires objectively assess organisational culture', *Journal of Managerial Psychology*, 5 (4): 4–11.

Van Buskirk, W. and McGrath, D. (1992) 'Organizational stories as a window on affect in organizations', *Journal of Organizational Change Management*, 5 (2): 9–24.

Van Maanen, J. (1976) 'Breaking in: socialization to work', in R. Dobin (ed.), *Handbook of Work, Organization, and Society*. Chicago: Rand McNally. pp. 67–130.

Weick, K.E. and Westley, F. (1996) 'Organizational learning: affirming an oxymoron', in S.R. Clegg, C. Hardy and W. Nord (eds), *Handbook of Organization Studies*. London: Sage. pp. 440–58.

Westley, F. (1990) 'The eye of the needle: cultural and personal transformation in a traditional organization', *Human Relations*, 43 (3): 273–93.

Wilkins, A.L. (1983) 'The culture audit: a tool for understanding organizations', *Organizational Dynamics*, 12 (2): 24–38.

Wilkinson, M., Fogarty, M. and Melville, D. (1996) 'Organizational culture change through training and cultural immersion', *Journal of Organizational Change Management*, 9 (4): 69–81.

Yanow, D. (1993) 'Review: controlling cultural engineering?', *Journal of Management Inquiry*, 2 (2): 206–13.

Young, E. (1989) 'On the naming of the rose: interests and multiple meanings as elements of organizational culture', *Organization Studies*, 10 (2): 187–206.

6 MANAGING STRATEGY

Abegglen, J.C. and Stalk, G.J. (1985) *Kaisha: The Japanese Corporation*. New York: Basic Books.

Aldrich, H.E. and Pfeffer, J. (1976) 'Environments of organization', *Annual Review of Sociology*, 2: 79–105.

Andrews, K.R. (1980) *The Concept of Corporate Strategy*. Homewood, IL: Dow-Jones Irwin.

Ansoff, H.I. (1965) *Corporate Strategy*. New York: McGraw-Hill.

Ansoff, H.I. (1984) *Implanting Strategic Management*. Englewood Cliffs, NJ: Prentice-Hall.

Ansoff, H.I. (1988) *The New Corporate Strategy*. New York: John Wiley.

Aoki, M. (1990) *The Firm as a Nexus of Treatise*. London: Sage.

Barney, J.B. (1986) 'Organizational culture: can it be a source of sustained advantage?', *Academy of Management Review*, 11: 656–65.

Barney, J.B. (1991) 'Firm resources and sustained competitive advantage', *Journal of Management*, 17 (1): 99–120.

Barney, J.B. (1996) 'Strategic factor markets: expectations, luck and business strategy', *Management Science*, 42: 1231–41.

Barry, D. and Elmes, M. (1997) 'Strategy retold: towards a narrative view of strategic discourse', *Academy of Management Review*, 22 (2): 429–52.

Bartlett, C.A. and Ghoshal, S. (1989) *Managing Across Borders: The Transnational Solution*. Boston, MA: Harvard Business School Press.

Bates, D.L. and Dillard, J.E. (1993) 'Generating strategic thinking through multilevel teams', *Long Range Planning*, 26 (5): 103–10.

Bennis, W.G. and Nanus, B. (1985) *Leaders: The Strategies for Taking Charge*. New York: Harper & Row.

Bourgeois, L.J. (1984) 'Strategic management and determinism', *Academy of Management Review*, 9: 586–96.

Bowman, C. and Johnson, G. (1992) 'Surfacing competitive strategies', *European Management Journal*, 10 (2): 315–24.

Bresser, R.K. and Harl, J.E. (1986) 'Collective strategy: vice or virtue?', *Academy of Management Review*, 11: 408–27.

Brodwin, D.R. and Bourgeois, L.J. (1984) 'Five steps to strategic action', *California Management Review*, 26 (3): 176–90.

Burns, T. and Stalker, M. (1961) *The Management of Innovation*. London: Tavistock.

Chaffee, E.E. (1985) 'Three models of strategy', *Academy of Management Review*, 10 (1): 89–98.

Chandler, A.D. (1962) *Strategy and Structure: Chapters in the History of the Industrial Enterprises*. Cambridge: MIT Press.

Child, J. (1997) 'Strategic choice in the analysis of action, structure, organizations and environment: retrospect and prospect', *Organization Studies*, 18 (1): 43–76.

Christensen, C.R., Andrews, K.R., Bower, J.L., Hammermesh, R.G. and Porter, M.E. (1982) *Business Policy: Text and Cases*, 5th edn. Homewood, IL: Richard D. Irwin.

Clegg, S. (1990) *Modern Organizations: Organization Studies for the Postmodern World*. London: Sage.

Collis, D. (1991). 'A resource-based analysis of global competition', *Strategic Management Journal*, 12 (special issue): 49–68.

Daft, R.L. and Weick, K.E. (1984) 'Toward a model of organizations as interpretation systems', *Academy of Management Review*, 9 (2): 284–95.

Deal, T. and Kennedy, A.E. (1982) *Corporate Cultures*. Reading, MA: Addison-Wesley.

DiMaggio, P.J. and Powell, W.W. (1983) 'The iron cage revisited: institutional isomorphism and collective rationality in organization fields', *American Sociological Review*, 35: 147–60.

Donaldson, L. (1996) 'The normal science of structural contingency theory', in S.R. Clegg, C. Hardy and W.R. Nord (eds), *Handbook of Organization Studies*. London: Sage.

Dougherty, D. (1995) 'Managing your core incompetencies for corporate venturing', *Entrepreneurship Theory and Practice*, 19 (3): 113–35.

Dutton, J.E. and Dukerich, J.M. (1991) 'Keeping an eye on the mirror: image and identity in organizational adaptation', *Academy of Management Journal*, 34 (3): 517–54.

Dutton, J.E. and Penner, W.J. (1993) 'The importance of organizational identity for strategic agenda building', in J. Hendry, G. Johnson and J. Newton (eds), *Strategic Thinking: Leadership and Management of Change*. New York: John Wiley and Sons. pp. 89–113.

Eccles, R. and Nohria, N. (1993) *Beyond the Hype*. Cambridge, MA: Harvard Business School Press.

Fairclough, N. (1992) *Discourse and Social Change*. Cambridge: Polity Press.

Fineman, S. (1996) 'Emotional subtexts in corporate greening', *Organization Studies*, 17 (1): 479–500.

Floyd, S.W. and Wooldridge, B. (1992) 'Managing strategic consensus: the foundation of effective implementation', *Academy of Management Executive*, 6 (4): 27–39.

Foss, N.J. (1996) 'Research in strategy, economics, and Michael Porter', *Journal of Management Studies*, 33 (1): 1–24.

Ghemawat, P. (1991) *Commitment: The Dynamic of Strategy*. New York: Free Press.

Giddens, A. (1981) *A Contemporary Critique of Historical Materialism*. London: Macmillan.

Gioia, D.A. and Chittipeddi, K. (1991) 'Sensemaking and sensegiving in strategic change initiation', *Strategic Management Journal*, 12: 433–48.

Graetz, F. (1996) 'Leading strategic change at Ericsson', *Long Range Planning*, 29 (3): 304–13.

Grant, R.M. (1991) The resource-based theory of competitive advantage: implications for strategy formulation', *California Management Review*, spring: 114–35.

Gratton, L. (1996) 'Implementing a strategic vision – key factors for success', *Long Range Planning*, 29 (3): 290–303.

Greenwood, R. and Hinings, C. (1988) 'Organizational design types, tracks and the dynamics of strategic change', *Organization Studies*, 9 (3): 293–316.

Greiner, L. (1972) 'Evolution and revolution as organizations grow', *Harvard Business Review*, 50 (4): 37–46.

Hall, D.J. and Saias, M.A. (1980) 'Strategy follows structure', *Strategic Management Journal*, 1: 149–63.

Hambrick, D.C. and Mason, P.A. (1984) 'Upper echelons: the organization as a reflection of its top managers', *Academy of Management Review*, 9: 193–206.

Hamel, G. and Prahalad, C.K. (1989) 'Strategic intent', *Harvard Business Review* (May–June): 63–76.

Hamel, G. and Prahalad, C.K. (1993) 'Strategy as stretch and leverage', *Harvard Business Review*, 71 (2): 75–84.

Hamel, G. and Prahalad, C.K. (1994) *Competing for the Future*. Boston: Harvard Business School Press.

Hamilton, G.C. and Biggard, N.W. (1988) 'Market, cultures and authority: a comparative analysis of management and organisation in the Far East', *American Journal of Sociology*, 94 (supplement): 52–94.

Hannan, M.T. and Freeman, J. (1977) *Organizational Ecology*. Cambridge, MA: Harvard University Press.

Hardy, C. (1994) *Managing Strategic Action: Mobilizing Change*. London: Sage.

Hardy, C., Lawrence, T.B. and Phillips, N. (1998) 'Talk and action: conversations and narrative in interorganizational collaboration', in D. Grant, T. Keenoy and C. Oswick (eds), *Discourse and Organization*. London: Sage. pp. 65–83.

Hayes, R.H. and Abernathy, W. (1980) 'Managing our way to economic decline', *Harvard Business Review* (July–August): 67–75.

Henderson, R. and Cockburn, I. (1994) 'Measuring competence? Exploring firm effects in pharmaceutical research', *Strategic Management Journal*, 15: 63–84.

Hendry, J., Johnson, G. and Newton, J. (eds) (1994) *Strategic Thinking: Leadership and the Management of Change*. Chichester: John Wiley.

Hinings, B. and Greenwood, R. (1988) 'The normative prescription of organizations', in L.G. Zucker (ed.), *Institutional Patterns and Organizations: Culture and Environment*. Cambridge, MA: Ballinger. pp. 53–70.

Hodgson, G. (1988) *Economics and Institutions: A Manifesto for a Modern Institutional Economics*. Cambridge, MA: Polity Press.

Hofer, C.W. (1975) 'Toward a contingency theory of business strategy', *Academy of Management Journal*, 18: 784–810.

Horowitz, J.H. (1980) *Top Management Control in Europe*. London: Macmillan.

Huff, A.S. (ed.) (1990) *Managing Strategic Thought*. Chichester: John Wiley.

Inkpen, A. and Choudhury, N. (1995) 'The seeking of strategy where it is not: towards a theory of strategy absence', *Strategic Management Journal*, 16: 313–23.

Johnson, G. (1987) *Strategic Change and the Management Process*. Oxford: Blackwell.

Johnson, G. (1992) 'Managing strategic change – strategy, culture and action', *Long Range Planning*, 25 (1): 28–36.

Johnson, G. (1994) *Strategic Thinking, Leadership and the Management of Change*. New York: John Wiley.

Knights, D. and Morgan, G. (1991) 'Strategic discourse and subjectivity: towards a critical analysis of corporate strategy in organisations', *Organisation Studies*, 12 (3): 251–73.

Langley, A. (1988) 'The role of formal strategic planning', *Long Range Planning*, 21 (3): 40–50.

Langley, A. (1991) 'Formal analysis and strategic decision-making', *OMEGA*, 19 (213): 79–99.

Langlois, R.N. (ed.) (1986) *Economics as a Process: Essays in the New Institutional Economics*. Cambridge: Cambridge University Press.

Lavers, C. (1996) *The Strategic Thinking Process – Using The Literature to Develop a Conceptual Framework for Conducting Field Research*. Working Paper 4. Sydney: University of Technology.

Leonard-Barton, D. (1992) 'Core capabilities and core rigidities: a paradox in managing new product development', *Strategic Management Journal*, 13: 111–25.

Lorsch, J.W. (1986) 'Managing culture: the invisible barrier to strategic change', *California Management Review*, 28 (2): 95–109.

Lubatkin, M.H. and Lane, P.J. (1996) 'Psst . . . the merger mavens still have it wrong!', *Academy of Management Executive*, 10 (1): 21–39.

Lyles, M.A. (1990) 'A research agenda for strategic management in the 1990s', *Journal of Management Studies*, 27 (4): 363–75.

Marino, K.E. (1996) 'Developing consensus on firm competencies and capabilities', *Academy of Management Executive*, 10 (3): 40–51.

Meyer, J.W. and Rowan, B. (1977) 'Institutionalized organizations: formal structure as myth and ceremony', *American Journal of Sociology*, 83: 340–63.

Meyer, A., Tsui, A. and Hinings, R. (1993) 'Configural approaches to organizational analysis', *Academy of Management Journal*, 36: 1175–95.

Miles, R.E. and Snow, C.C. (1978) *Organizational Strategy, Structure, and Process*. New York: McGraw-Hill.

Miller, D. (1982) 'Evolution and revolution: a quantum view of structural change in organizations', *Journal of Management Studies*, 19 (2): 131–51.

Miller, D. (1986) 'Configurations of strategy and structure: towards a synthesis', *Strategic Management Journal*, 7: 233–49.

Miller, D. (1987) 'The structural and environmental correlates of business strategy', *Strategic Management Journal*, 8: 55–76.

Miller, D. (1990) *The Icarus Paradox*. New York: Harper Business.

Miller, D. (1993) 'The architecture of simplicity', *Academy of Management Review*, 18: 116–38.

Miller, D. (1996) 'Configurations revisited', *Strategic Management Journal*, 17 (7): 505–12.

Miller, D. and Friesen, P. (1977) 'Strategy making in context: ten empirical archetypes', *Journal of Management Studies*, 14: 259–80.

Miller, D. and Friesen, P. (1980) 'Momentum and revolution in organizational adaptation', *Academy of Management Journal*, 23: 867–92.

Miller, D. and Friesen, P. (1984) *Organizations: A Quantum View*. Englewood Cliffs, NJ: Prentice-Hall.

Mintzberg, H. (1979) *The Structuring of Organizations*. Englewood Cliffs, NJ: Prentice-Hall.

Mintzberg, H. (1983) *Structure in Fives: Designing Effective Organizations*. Englewood Cliffs, NJ: Prentice-Hall.

Mintzberg, H. (1987) 'Crafting strategy', *Harvard Business Review*, 65 (4): 66–75.

Mintzberg, H. (1990a) 'Strategy formation schools of thought', in J.W. Fredrickson (ed.), *Perspectives on Strategic Management*, vol. 5. Greenwich, CT: JAI Press. pp. 1–67.

Mintzberg, H. (1990b). 'The design school: reconsidering the basic premises of Strategic Management', *Strategic Management Journal*, 11: 171–95.

Mintzberg, H. (1994) *The Rise and Fall of Strategic Planning*. Hemel Hempstead: Prentice-Hall.

Mintzberg, H. and Waters, J.A. (1982) 'Tracking strategy in an entrepreneurial firm', *Academy of Management Journal*, 25: 465–99.

Mintzberg, H. and Waters, J.A. (1985) 'Of strategies, deliberate and emergent', *Strategic Management Journal*, 6: 257–72.

Orr, R.M. (1990) 'Sharing knowledge, celebrating identity: war stories and community memory in a service culture', in D.S. Middleton and D. Edwards (eds), *Collective Remembering: Memory in Society*. Beverley Hills, CA: Sage.

Ouchi, W.G. (1981) *Theory Z*. New York: Avon Books.

Palmer, I. and Dunford, R. (1995) 'Reframing and organizational action'. Paper presented at the 6th International Colloquium of the APROS (Asian-Pacific Researchers on Organization Studies), Cuernavaca, Mexico.

Parker, B. (1996) 'Evolution and revolution: from international business to globalization', in S.R. Clegg, C. Hardy and W. Nord (eds), *Handbook of Organization Studies*. London: Sage. pp. 484–506.

Pekar Jr, P. and Abraham, S. (1995) 'Is strategic management living up to its promise?', *Long Range Planning*, 28 (5): 32–44.

Peters, T.J. and Waterman, R.H. (1982) *In Search of Excellence*. New York: Harper & Row.

Pettigrew, A. (1985) *The Awakening Giant: Continuity and Change in Imperial Chemical Industries*. Oxford: Blackwell.

Pettigrew, A.M. (1977) 'Strategy formulation as a political process', *International Studies of Management and Organization*, 7 (2): 78–87.

Porter, M. (1980) *Competitive Strategy*. New York: Free Press.

Porter, M. (1985) *Competitive Advantage: Creating and Sustaining Superior Performance*. New York: Free Press.

Porter, M. (1990) *The Competitive Advantage of Nations*. New York: Free Press.

Prahalad, C.K. and Hamel, G. (1990) 'The core competence of the corporation', *Harvard Business Review*, 68 (3): 79–91.

Prahalad, C.K. and Hamel, G. (1994) 'Strategy as a field of study: why search for a new paradigm?', *Strategic Manageement Journal*, 15: 5–16.

Quinn, J.B. (1978) 'Logical incrementalism', *Sloan Management Review*, 20: 7–21.

Quinn, J.B. (1980) *Strategies for Change: Logical Incrementalism*. Homewood, IL: Irwin.

Reger, R.K. and Huff, A.S. (1993) 'Strategic groups: a cognitive perspective', *Strategic Management Journal*, 14 (2): 103–23.

Roberts, P.W. and Greenwood, R. (1997) 'Integrating transaction cost and institutional theories: toward a constrained-efficiency framework for understanding organizational design adoption', *Academy of Management Review*, 22 (2): 346–73.

Rouleau, L. and Seguin, F. (1995) 'Strategy and organization theories: common forms of discourse', *Journal of Management Studies*, 32 (1): 101–17.

Rumelt, R.P. (1984) 'Towards a strategic theory of the firm', in R. Lamb (ed.), *Competitive Strategic Management*. Englewood Cliffs, NJ: Prentice-Hall. pp. 556–70.

Rumelt, R.P., Schendel, D. and Teece, D. (1991) 'Strategic management and economics', *Strategic Management Journal*, 12: 5–29.

Schotter, A. (1981) *The Economic Theory of Social Institutions*. Cambridge: Cambridge University Press.

Schwenk, C.R. (1984) 'Cognitive simplification processes in strategic decision making', *Strategic Management Journal*, 5: 111–28.

Shrivastava, P. (1986) 'Is strategic management ideological?', *Journal of Management*, 12 (3): 363–77.

Smircich, L. and Stubbart, C. (1985) 'Strategic management in an enacted world', *Academy of Management Review*, 10 (4): 724–36.

Spender, J.C. (1989) *Industry Recipes, and Enquiry into the Nature and Sources of Managerial Judgement*. Oxford: Blackwell.

Stalk, G., Evans, P. and Shulman, L.E. (1992) 'Competing on capabilities: the new rules of corporate strategy', *Harvard Business Review* (March–April): 57–69.

Taylor, B. (1995) 'The new strategic leadership – driving change, getting results', *Long Range Planning*, 28 (5): 71–81.

Tolbert, P.S. and Zucker, L.G. (1996) 'The institutionalization of institutional theory', in S.R. Clegg, C. Hardy and W.R. Nord (eds), *Handbook of Organization Studies*. London: Sage. pp. 175–90.

Tung, R.L. (1994) 'Strategic management thought in East Asia', *Organizational Dynamics*, 22 (4): 55–65.

Waldersee, R. and Sheather, S. (1996) 'The effects of strategy type on strategy implementation actions', *Human Relations*, 49 (1): 105–22.

Waterman, R.H., Peters, T.J. and Phillips, J.R. (1980) 'Structure is not organization', *Business Horizons*, 23 (3): 14–26.

Webster, J.L., Reif, W.E. and Bracker, J.S. (1989) 'The manager's guide to strategic planning tools and techniques', *Planning Review*, 17 (6): 4–13.

Weick, K.E. (1995) *Sensemaking in Organizations*. Thousand Oaks: Sage.

Weick, K.E. and Westley, F. (1996) 'Organizational learning: affirming an oxymoron', in S.R. Clegg, C. Hardy and W.R. Nord (eds), *Handbook of Organization Studies*. London: Sage. pp. 440–58.

Wernerfelt, B. (1984) 'A resource-based view of the firm', *Strategic Management Journal*, 5 (2): 171–80.

Westley, F. (1990) 'Middle managers and strategy: microdynamics of inclusion', *Strategic Management Journal*, 11: 337–51.

Westley, F. and Mintzberg, H. (1988) 'Profiles of strategic vision: Levesque and Iacocca', in J. Conger, R.N. Kanungo and Associates (eds), *Charismatic Leadership: The Elusive Factor in Organizational Effectiveness*. San Francisco: Jossey-Bass.

Westley, F. and Mintzberg, H. (1989) 'Visionary leadership and strategic management', *Strategic Management Journal*, 10: 17–32.

Whipp, R. (1996) 'Creative deconstruction: strategy and organizations', in S.R. Clegg, C. Hardy and W.R. Nord (eds), *Handbook of Organization Studies*. London: Sage. pp. 261–75.

Whitley, R.D. (1990) 'East Asian entrepreneurial structures and the comparative analysis of forms of business organization', *Organization Studies*, 11 (1): 47–74.

Whitley, R.D. (1991) 'The social construction of business systems in East Asia', *Organization Studies*, 12 (1): 1–28.

Whittington, R. (1993) *What is Strategy and Does it Matter?* London: Routledge.

Williamson, O.E. (1975) *Markets and Hierarchies: Analysis and Antitrust Implications*. New York: Free Press.

Williamson, O.E. (1985) *The Economic Institutions of Capitalism: Firms, Markets and Relational Contracting*. New York: Free Press.

Wortzel, L. (1991) 'Global strategies: standardization versus flexibility', in H. Vernon-Wortzel and L. Wortzel (eds), *Global Strategic Management: The Essentials*. New York: John Wiley. pp. 135–49.

Zabriskie, N.B. and Huellmantel, A.B. (1991) 'Developing strategic thinking in senior management', *Long Range Planning*, 24 (6): 25–32.

Zan, L. (1990) 'Looking for theories in strategy studies', *Scandinavian Journal of Management*, 6 (2): 89–108.

7 MANAGING CHANGE

Abrahamson, E. (1996) 'Management fashion, academic fashion, and enduring truths', *Academy of Management Review*, 21 (3): 616–18.

Bartunek, J.M. and Moch, M.K. (1994) 'Third-order organizational change and the western mystical tradition', *Journal of Organizational Change Management*, 7 (1): 24–41.

Bolman, L. and Deal, T. (1997) *Reframing Organizations*, 2nd edn. San Francisco: Jossey-Bass.

Brown, S.L. and Eisenhardt, K.M. (1997) 'The art of continuous change: linking complexity theory and time-paced evolution in relentlessly shifting organizations', *Administrative Science Quarterly*, 42 (1): 1–34.

Bunker, B.B. and Alban, B.T. (1996) *Large Group Interventions: Engaging the Whole System for Rapid Change*. San Francisco: Jossey-Bass.

Burke, W.W. (1995) 'Organization change: what we know, what we need to know', *Journal of Management Inquiry*, 4 (2): 158–71.

Carini, G.R., Livingstone, L.P. and Palich, L.E. (1995) 'Trialectics: a questionable logic for organization change research', *Academy of Management Review*, 20 (3): 503–9.

Child, J. (1972) 'Organizational structure, environment, and performance: the role of strategic choice', *Sociology*, 6: 1–22.

Cummings, T.G. and Worley, C.G. (1993) *Organization Development and Change*, 5th edn. Minneapolis/St. Paul: West.

DeMeuse, K.P. and McDaris, K.K. (1994) 'An exercise in managing change', *Training and Development*, 48 (2): 55–7.

Doerr, J.E. (1996) 'Uncommon common sense', *Management Review*, 85 (8): 5.

Dubinskas, F.A. (1994) 'On the edge of chaos: a metaphor for transformative change', *Journal of Management Inquiry*, 3 (4): 355–66.

Dunbar, R.L.M., Garud, R. and Raghuram, S. (1996a) 'A frame for deframing in strategic analysis', *Journal of Management Inquiry*, 5 (1): 23–34.

Dunbar, R.L.M., Garud, R. and Raghuram, S. (1996b) 'Run, rabbit run! But, can you survive?', *Journal of Management Inquiry*, 5 (2): 168–75.

Dunford, R. and Palmer, I. (1996) 'Metaphors in popular management discourse: the case of corporate restructuring', in D. Grant and C. Oswick (eds), *Metaphor and Organizations*. London: Sage.

Dunphy, D. and Stace, D. (1990) *Under New Management: Australian Organizations in Transition*. Sydney: McGraw-Hill.

Ford, J.D. and Ford, L.W. (1994) 'Logics of identity, contradiction, and attraction in change', *Academy of Management Review*, 19 (4): 756–85.

Ford, J.D. and Ford, L.W. (1995) 'The role of conversations in producing intentional change in organizations', *Academy of Management Review*, 20 (3): 541–70.

French, W.L. and Bell, C.H. (1995) *Organization Development: Behavioral Science Interventions for Organization Improvement*. Englewood Cliffs, NJ: Prentice-Hall.

French, E. and Delahaye, B. (1996) 'Individual change transition: moving in circles can be good for you', *Leadership and Organization Development Journal*, 17 (7): 22.

Ghoshal, S. and Bartlett, C.A. (1996) 'Rebuilding behavioral context: a blueprint for corporate renewal', *Sloan Management Review*, 37 (2): 23–36.

Greenberg, D.A. (1995) 'Blue versus gray: a metaphor constraining sensemaking around a restructuring', *Group and Organization Management*, 20 (2): 183–209.

Greenwood, R. and Hinings, C.R. (1993) 'Understanding strategic change: the contribution of archetypes', *Academy of Management Journal*, 36 (5): 1052–81.

Greenwood, R. and Hinings, C.R. (1996) 'Understanding radical organizational change: bringing together the old and the new institutionalism', *Academy of Management Review*, 21 (4): 1022–54.

Greiner, L.E. (1992) 'Resistance to change during restructuring', *Journal of Management Inquiry*, 1 (1): 61–5.

Hall, R.H. (1996) *Organizations: Structures, Processes, and Outcomes*, 6th edn. Englewood Cliffs, NJ: Prentice-Hall.

Haveman, H.A. (1992) 'Between a rock and a hard place: organizational change and performance under conditions of fundamental environmental transformation', *Administrative Science Quarterly*, 37: 48–75.

Hendry, C. (1996) 'Understanding and creating whole organizational change through learning theory', *Human Relations*, 49 (5): 621–41.

Hirsch, P.M. and Lonsbury, M. (1997) 'Putting the organization back into organization theory: action, change, and the "New" institutionalism', *Journal of Management Inquiry*, 6 (1): 79–88.

Hutt, M.D., Walker, B.A. and Frankwick, G.L. (1995) 'Hurdle the cross-functional barriers to strategic change', *Sloan Management Review*, 36 (3): 22–30.

Huy, N. (1998) 'Change navigation styles and corporate revitalization'. Paper presented at the Academy of Management Conference, San Diego.

Iskat, G.J. and Liebowitz, J. (1996) 'What to do when employees resist change', *Supervision*, 57 (8): 3–5.

Jick, T.D. (1995) 'Accelerating change for competitive advantage', *Organizational Dynamics*, 24 (1): 77–82.

Kabanoff, B., Waldersee, R. and Cohen, M. (1995) 'Espoused values and organizational change themes', *Academy of Management Journal*, 38 (4): 1075–104.

Kanter, R.M., Stein, B.A. and Jick, T.D. (1992) *The Challenge of Organizational Change: How Companies Experience It and Leaders Guide It*. New York: Free Press.

Kilcourse, T. (1995) 'Keep the small change', *Leadership and Organization Development Journal*, 16 (8): 40.

Klein, S.M. (1996) 'A management communication strategy for change', *Journal of Organizational Change Management*, 9 (2): 32–46.

Kotter, J.P. (1996) *Leading Change*. Boston, MA: Harvard Business School Press.

Large, M. (1996) 'The chaotic passages of developing companies: tools for organizational transitions', *Leadership and Organization Development Journal*, 17 (7): 44.

Lawrence, P.R. and Lorsch, J.W. (1967) *Organization and Environment*. Boston, MA: Harvard Business School Press.

Lewin, K. (1947) 'Frontiers in group dynamics', *Human Relations*, 1: 5–41.

Lippitt, R., Watson, J. and Westley, B. (1958) *The Dynamics of Planned Change: A Comparative Study of Principles and Techniques*. New York: Harcourt, Brace and World.

Macdonald, S. (1995) 'Learning to change: an information perspective on learning in the organization', *Organization Science*, 6 (5): 557–68.

McWhinney, W., McCulley, W.J.B., Smith, D.M. and Novokowsky, B.J. (1993) *Creating Paths of Change: Revitalization, Renaissance and Work*. Venice, CA: Enthision.

March, J.G. and Simon, H.A. (1958) *Organizations*. New York: John Wiley.

Marshak, R.J. (1993a) 'Managing the metaphors of change', *Organizational Dynamics*, 22 (1): 44–56.

Marshak, R.J. (1993b) 'Lewin meets Confucius: a re-view of the OD model of change', *Journal of Applied Behavioral Science*, 24 (4): 393–415.

Mason, R.O. (1996) 'Commentary on varieties of dialectic change processes', *Journal of Management Inquiry*, 5 (3): 293–9.

Meyerson, D.E. and Scully, M.A. (1995) 'Tempered radicalism and the politics of ambivalence and change', *Organization Science*, 6 (5): 585–600.

Miller, D., Greenwood, R. and Hinings, B. (1997) 'Creative chaos versus munificent momentum: the schism between normative and academic views of organizational change', *Journal of Management Inquiry*, 6 (1): 71–8.

Mink, O.G., Esterhuysen, P.W., Mink, B.P. and Owen, K.Q. (1993) *Change at Work: A Comprehensive Management Process for Transforming Organizations*. San Francisco: Jossey-Bass.

Morgan, G. (1986) *Images of Organization*. Newbury Park, CA: Sage.

Morgan, G. (1993) *Imaginization: the Art of Creative Management*. Newbury Park, CA: Sage.

Morris, K.F. and Raben, C.S. (1995) 'The fundamentals of change management', in D.A. Nadler, R.B. Shaw, A.E. Walton and Associates (eds), *Discontinuous Change: Leading Organizational Transformation*. San Francisco: Jossey-Bass. pp. 47–65.

Nadler, D.A. and Tushman, M.L. (1995) 'Types of organizational change: from incremental improvement to discontinuous transformation', in D.A. Nadler, R.B. Shaw, A.E. Walton and Associates (eds), *Discontinuous Change: Leading Organizational Transformation*. San Francisco: Jossey-Bass. pp. 15–34.

Nielsen, R.P. (1996) 'Varieties of dialectic change processes', *Journal of Management Inquiry*, 5 (3): 276–92.

Old, D.R. (1995) 'Consulting for real transformation, sustainability, and organic form', *Journal of Organizational Change Management*, 8 (3): 6–17.

Orlikowski, W.J. and Hofman, J.D. (1997) 'An improvisational model for change management: the case of groupware technologies', *Sloan Management Review*, 38 (2): 11–21.

Porac, J. and Rosa, J.A. (1996) 'In praise of managerial narrow-mindedness', *Journal of Management Inquiry*, 5 (1): 35–42.

Price Waterhouse Change Integration Team (1996) *The Paradox Principles: How High-Performance Companies Manage Chaos, Complexity, and Contradiction to Achieve Superior Results*. Chicago: Irwin.

Reger, R.K., Gustafson, L.T., DeMarie, S.M. and Mullane, J.V. (1994) 'Reframing the organization: why implementing total quality is easier said than done', *Academy of Management Review*, 19 (3): 565–84.

Robertson, P.J., Roberts, D.R. and Porras, J.I. (1993) 'Dynamics of planned organizational change: assessing empirical support for a theoretical model', *Academy of Management Journal*, 36 (3): 619–34.

Romano, C. (1995) 'Managing change, diversity and emotions', *Management Review*, 84 (7): 6–7.

Schein, E. H. (1987) *Process Consultation, Volume 2: Lessons for Managers and Consultants*. Reading, MA: Addison-Wesley.

Schneider, B., Brief, A.P. and Guzzo, R.A. (1996) 'Creating a climate and culture for sustainable organizational change', *Organizational Dynamics*, spring: 7–19.

Selznick, P. (1957) *Leadership in Administration: A Sociological Interpretation*. New York: Harper & Row.

Siegal, W.E.A. (1996) 'Understanding the management of change: an overview of managers' perspectives and assumptions in the 1990s', *Journal of Organizational Change Management*, 9 (6): 54–80.

Sinclair, J. (1994) 'Reacting to what?', *Journal of Organizational Change Management*, 7 (5): 32–40.

Spencer, K.L. (1996) 'Book review: beyond the wall of resistance: unconventional strategies that build support for change', *Academy of Management Executive*, 10 (1): 90–2.

Spiker, B.K. and Lesser, E. (1995) 'We have met the enemy . . .', *Journal of Business Strategy*, 16 (2): 17–21.

Thietart, R.A. and Forgues, B. (1995) 'Chaos theory and organization', *Organization Science*, 6 (1): 19–31.

Thompson, J.D. (1967) *Organizations in Action*. New York: McGraw-Hill.

Van de Ven, A.H. and Poole, M.S. (1995) 'Explaining development and change in organizations', *Academy of Management Review*, 20 (3): 510–40.

Vince, R. and Broussine, M. (1996) 'Paradox, defense and attachment: accessing and working with emotions and relations underlying organizational change', *Organization Studies*, 17 (1): 1–21.

Vrakking, W.J. (1995) 'The implementation game', *Journal of Organizational Change Management*, 8 (3): 31–46.

Watzlawick, P., Weakland, J. and Fisch, R. (1974) *Change: Principles of Problem Formation and Problem Resolution*. New York: W.W. Norton.

Weick, K. (1979) *The Social Psychology of Organizing*. Reading, MA: Addison-Wesley.

Weick, K.E. (1984) 'Small wins: redefining the scale of social problems', *American Psychologist*, 39 (1): 40–49.

Worley, C.G., Hitchin, D.E. and Ross, W.L. (1996) *Integrated Strategic Change: How OD Builds Competitive Advantage*. Reading, MA: Addison-Wesley.

Zimmerman, J.H. (1995) 'The principles of managing change', *HR Focus*, 72 (2): 15–16.

8 MANAGING ORGANIZATIONAL LEARNING

Addleson, M. (1996) 'Resolving the spirit and substance of organizational learning', *Journal of Organizational Change Management*, 9 (1): 32–41.

Adler, P. (1993) 'The "learning bureaucracy": new United Motors Manufacturing Incorporated', in B.M. Staw and L.L. Cummings (eds), *Research in Organizational Behavior*, vol. 15. Greenwich, CT: JAI Press. pp. 111–94.

Adler, P. and Cole, R. (1993) 'Designing for learning: a tale of two auto plants', *Sloan Management Review*, 34 (3): 85–95.

Argyris, C. (1986) 'Reinforcing organizational defensive routines: an unintended human resources activity', *Human Resource Management*, 25 (4): 541–55.

Argyris, C. (1990) *Overcoming Organizational Defenses: Facilitating Organizational Learning*. Boston: Allyn and Bacon.

Argyris, C. (1993) 'Education for leading-learning', *Organizational Dynamics*, 21 (3): 5–17.

Argyris, C. and Schon, D. (1978) *Organizational Learning: A Theory of Action Perspective*. Reading, MA: Addison-Wesley.

Beer, M. and Eisenstat, R.A. (1996) 'Developing an organization capable of implementing strategy and learning', *Human Relations*, 49 (5): 597–619.

Berggren, C. (1994) 'NUMMI vs. Uddevalla; rejoinder', *Sloan Management Review*, 35 (2): 37–49.

Boland, R.J. and Tenkasi, R.V. (1996) 'Perspective making and perspective taking in communities of knowing', *Organization Science*, 4 (6): 350–72.

Brown, J.S. and Duguid, P. (1991) 'Organizational learning and communities-of-practice: toward a unified view of working, learning and innovation', *Organization Science*, 2 (1): 40–57.

Child, J. (1994) 'On organisational learning', *Journal of Management Studies*, 31 (3): 448–51.

Cohen, W.M. and Levinthal, D. (1990) 'Absorptive capacity: a new perspective on learning and innovation', *Administrative Science Quarterly*, 35 (1): 128–52.

Cook, S.D.N. and Yanow, D. (1993) 'Culture and organizational learning', *Journal of Management Inquiry*, 2: 373–90.

Crossan, M. and Guatto, T. (1996) *The Evolution of Organizational Learning* Western Business School Working Paper Series (95–07). London, ON: University of Western Ontario.

Daft, R.L. and Huber, G.P. (1987) 'How organizations learn: a communication framework', *Research in the Sociology of Organizations*, 5: 1–36.

Daft, R.L. and Weick, K.E. (1984) 'Toward a model of organizations as interpretation systems', *Academy of Management Review*, 9: 284–95.

Daudelin, M.W. (1996) 'Learning from experience through reflection', *Organizational Dynamics*, 24 (3): 36–48.

Dodgson, M. (1993) 'Organizational learning: a review of some literatures', *Organization Studies*, 14 (3): 375–94.

Dougherty, D. (1992) 'A practice-centered model of organizational renewal through product innovation', *Strategic Management Journal*, 13: 77–92.

Dougherty, D. (1995) 'Managing your core competencies for corporate venturing', *Entrepreneurship Theory and Practice*, 19 (3): 113–35.

Dougherty, D. (1996) 'Organizing for innovation', in S.R. Clegg, C. Hardy and W.R. Nord (eds), *Handbook of Organization Studies*. London: Sage. pp. 424–39.

Dougherty, D. and Hardy, C. (1996) 'Sustained product innovation in large, mature organizations: overcoming innovation-to-organization problems', *Academy of Management Journal*, 39 (5): 1120–53.

Duncan, R.B. and Weiss, A. (1979) 'Organizational learning: implications for organizational design', in B. Staw (ed.), *Research in Organizational Behavior*. Greenwich, CT: JAI Press. pp. 75–123.

Easterby-Smith, M. (1997) 'Disciplines of organizational learning: contributions and critiques', *Human Relations*, 50 (9): 1085–113.

Elmes, M.B. and Kassouf, C.J. (1995) 'Knowledge workers and organizational learning: narratives from biotechnology', *Management Learning*, 26 (4): 403–22.

Fiol, C.M. (1994) 'Consensus, diversity, and learning in organizations', *Organization Science*, 5: 403–37.

Fiol, C.M. (1995) 'Corporate communications: comparing executives' private and public statements', *Academy of Management Journal*, 38 (2): 522–36.

Fiol, C. and Lyles, M. (1985) 'Organizational learning', *Academy of Management Review*, 10: 803–13.

Ford, C.M. (1996) 'A theory of individual creative action in multiple social domains', *Academy of Management Review*, 21 (4): 1112–42.

Ford, C.M. and ogilvie, d. (1996) 'The role of creative action in organizational learning and change', *Journal of Organizational Change Management*, 9 (1): 54–62.

Galbraith, J. (1973) *Designing Complex Organizations*. Reading, MA: Addison-Wesley.

Garvin, D.A. (1993) 'Building a learning organization', *Harvard Business Review* (July–August): 78–91.

Geppert, M. (1996) 'Paths of managerial learning in the East German context', *Organization Studies*, 17 (2): 249–68.

Grandori, A. (1984) 'A prescriptive contingency view of organizational decision making', *Administrative Science Quarterly*, 29: 192–209.

Hardy, C. and Dougherty, D. (1997) 'Powering product innovation', *European Management Journal*, 15 (1): 16–27.

Hedberg, B.L.T. (1981) 'How organizations learn and unlearn', in P.C. Nystrom and W.H. Starbuck (eds), *Handbook of Organizational Design*. Oxford: Oxford University Press. pp. 8–27.

Hedberg, B.L.T., Nystrom, P.C. and Starbuck, W.H. (1976) 'Camping on seesaws: prescriptions for a self-designing organization', *Administrative Science Quarterly*, 21: 41–65.

Hedlund, G. and Nonaka, I. (1993) 'Models of knowledge management in the west and Japan', in P. Lorange (ed.), *Implementing Strategic Processes*. Oxford: Blackwell. pp. 117–44.

Hendry, C. (1996) 'Understanding and creating whole organizational change through learning theory', *Human Relations*, 49 (5): 621–41.

Holmer-Nadesan, M. (1996) 'Organizational identity and space of action', *Organization Studies*, 17 (1): 49–81.

Huber, G. (1991) 'Organizational learning: the contributing process and the literatures', *Organization Science*, 2: 88–115.

Inkpen, A.C. and Crossan, M.M. (1995) 'Believing is seeing: joint ventures and organization learning', *Journal of Management Studies*, 32 (5): 595–618.

Isaacs, W.N. (1993) 'Taking flight: dialogue, collective thinking and organizational learning', *Organizational Dynamics*, 22 (2): 24–39.

Kidd, J.B. and Teramoto, Y. (1995) 'The learning organization: the case of the Japanese RHQs in Europe', *Management International Review*, 35 (2): 39–56.

Lenke, S. and Davies, G. (1996) 'A contextual approach to management learning: the Hungarian case', *Organization Studies*, 17 (2): 269–89.

Levinson, N. and Asahi, M. (1995) 'Cross-national alliances and interorganizational learning', *Organizational Dynamics*, 24 (2): 50–63.

Levinthal, D.A. and March, J.G. (1993) 'Exploration and exploitation in organizational learning', *Strategic Management Journal*, 14: 95–112.

Lillrank, P. (1995) 'The transfer of management innovations from Japan', *Organization Studies*, 16 (6): 971–89.

Lipshitz, R., Popper, M. and Oz, S. (1996) 'Building learning organizations: the design and implementation of organizational learning mechanisms', *Journal of Applied Behavioral Science*, 32 (3): 292–305.

McGill, M.E. and Slocum, J.W.J. (1993) 'Unlearning the organization', *Organizational Dynamics*, 22 (2): 67–79.

Marceau, J. (1992) *Reworking the World: Organization, Technologies and Cultures in Comparative Perspective*. Berlin: Walter de Gruyter.

March, J. (1991) 'Exploration and exploitation in organizational learning', *Organization Science*, 2 (1): 71–87.

March, J.G. and Olsen, J. (1976) *Ambiguity and Choice in Organizations*. Bergen: Universitetsforlaget.

March, J.G., Sproull, L.S. and Tamuz, M. (1991) 'Learning from samples of one or fewer', *Organization Science*, 2: 1–13.

Miller, D. (1996) 'A preliminary typology of organizational learning: synthesizing the literature', *Journal of Management*, 22 (3): 485–505.

Mirvis, P.H. (1996) 'Historical foundations of organization learning', *Journal of Organizational Change Management*, 9 (1): 13–31.

Moorman, C. (1995) 'Organizational market information processes: cultural antecedents and new product outcomes', *Journal of Marketing Research*, 32: 318–35.

Nevis, E.C., Dibella, A.J. and Gould, J.M. (1995) 'Understanding organizations as learning systems', *Sloan Management Review*, winter: 73–85.

Nicolini, D. and Meznar, M.B. (1995) 'The social construction of organizational learning: conceptual and practical issues in the field', *Human Relations*, 48 (7): 727–46.

Nonaka, I. (1988) 'Towards middle-up-down management: accelerating information creation', *Sloan Management Review*, spring: 9–18.

Nonaka, I. (1994). 'A dynamic theory of organizational knowledge creation', *Organization Science*, 5 (1): 15–37.

Nonaka, I. and Takeuchi, H. (1995) *The Knowledge-Creating Company*. Oxford: Oxford University Press.

Orlikowski, W.J. (1992) 'The duality of technology: rethinking the concept of technology in organizations', *Organization Science*, 3 (3): 398–427.

Pedler, M. (1995) 'A guide to the learning organization', *Industrial and Commercial Training*, 27 (4): 21–5.

Pedler, M., Boydell, T. and Burgoyne, J. (1989) 'Towards the learning company', *Management Education and Development*, 20 (1): 1–8.

Pennings, J.M., Barkema, H. and Douma, S. (1994) 'Organizational learning and diversification', *Academy of Management Journal*, 37 (3): 608–40.

Polanyi, M. (1966) *The Tacit Dimension*. Garden City, NY: Doubleday.

Pucik, V. (1988) 'Strategic alliances with the Japanese: implications for human resource management', in F. Contractor and P. Lorange (eds), *Cooperative Strategies in International Business*. Lexington, MA: Lexington Books. pp. 487–98.

Roberts, K.H. and Grabowski, M. (1996) 'Organizations, technology and structuring', in S.R. Clegg, C. Hardy and W.R. Nord (eds), *Handbook of Organization Studies*. London: Sage. pp. 409–23.

Rodrigues. (1996) 'Corporate culture and de-institutionalization: implications for identity in a Brazilian telecommunications company', in S. Clegg and G. Palmer (eds), *Constituting Management: Markets, Meaning and Identities*. Berlin: De Gruyter. pp. 115–37.

Sandelands, L.E. and Stablein, R. (1987) 'The concept of organization mind', in S. Bachrach and N. DiTomaso (eds), *Research in the Sociology of Organizations*, vol. 5. Greenwich, CT: JAI Press. pp. 135–62.

Schein, E. (1985) *Organizational Culture and Leadership*. San Francisco: Jossey-Bass.

Schein, E.H. (1993a) 'On dialogue, culture and organizational learning', *Organization Dynamics*, 22 (2): 40–51.

Schein, E.H. (1993b) 'How can organizations learn faster? The challenge of entering the green room', *Sloan Management Review*, 34 (2): 85–92.

Senge, P. (1990) *The Fifth Discipline*. New York: Doubleday.

Shrivastava, P. (1983) 'A typology of organizational learning systems', *Journal of Management Studies*, 20 (1): 7–28.

Spender, J. (1996) 'Making knowledge the basis of a dynamic theory of the firm', *Strategic Management Journal*, 17: 45–62.

Srikantia, P. and Pasmore, W. (1996) 'Conviction and doubt in organizational learning', *Journal of Organizational Change Management*, 9 (1): 42–53.

Swidler, A. (1986) 'Culture in action: symbols and strategies', *American Sociological Review*, 51: 273–86.

Tenkasi, R.V. and Boland Jr, R.J. (1996) 'Exploring knowledge diversity in knowledge intensive firms: a new role for information systems', *Journal of Organizational Change Management*, 9 (1): 79–91.

Thatchenkery, T. (1996) *Postmodern Management and Organization Theory*. Thousand Oaks, CA: Sage.

Ulrich, D., von Glinow, M.A. and Jick, T. (1993) 'High impact learning: building and diffusing learning capability', *Organizational Dynamics*, 22 (1): 52–79.

Watkins, K. and Marsick, V. (1993) *Sculpting the Learning Organization*. San Francisco: Jossey-Bass.

Weick, K.E. (1991) 'The nontraditional quality of organizational learning', *Organization Science*, 2 (1): 116–24.

Weick, K.E. and Roberts, K.H. (1993) 'Collective mind in organizations: heedful interrelating on flight decks', *Administrative Science Quarterly*, 38 (3): 357–81.

Weick, K.E. and Westley, F. (1996) 'Organizational learning: affirming an oxymoron', in S.R. Clegg, C. Hardy and W. Nord (eds), *Handbook of Organization Studies*. London: Sage. pp. 440–58.

Wheelright, S. and Clark, K. (1992) *Revolutionizing Product Development*. New York: Free Press.

Wishart, N.A., Elam, J.J. and Robey, D. (1996) 'Redrawing the portrait of a learning organization: inside Knight-Ridder, Inc.', *Academy of Management Executive*, 10 (1): 7–20.

9 MANAGEMENT AND LEADERSHIP IN CONTEXT

Altman, B.W. (1995) 'Trends in executive transition: a conversation with John Isaacson', *Human Resource Management*, 34 (1): 203–13.

Alvesson, M. (1996) 'Leadership studies: from procedure and abstraction to reflexivity and situation', *Leadership Quarterly*, 7 (4): 455–85.

Ashforth, B. (1994) 'Petty tyranny in organizations', *Human Relations*, 47 (7): 755–78.

Ashkenas, R., Ulrich, D., Jick, T. and Kerr, S. (1995) *The Boundaryless Organization: Breaking the Chains of Organizational Structure*. San Francisco: Jossey-Bass.

Avolio, B.J. and Gibbons, T. (1988) 'Developing transformational leaders: a lifespan approach', in J.A. Conger and R.N. Kanungo (eds), *Charismatic Leadership: The Elusive Factor in Organizational Effectiveness*. San Francisco: Jossey-Bass. pp. 276–308.

Barker, R.A. (1997) 'How can we train leaders if we do not know what leadership is?', *Human Relations*, 50 (4): 343–62.

Bass, B.M. (1985) *Leadership and Performance Beyond Expectations*. New York: Free Press.

Bass, B.M. and Avolio, B.J. (1994) 'Shatter the glass ceiling: women may make better managers', *Human Resource Management*, 33 (4): 549–60.

Behling, O. and McFillen, J.M. (1996) 'A syncretical model of charismatic/transformational leadership', *Group and Organization Management*, 21 (2): 163–91.

Bennis, W. (1989) *On Becoming a Leader*. Reading, MA: Addison-Wesley.

Bowen, H.K., Clark, K.B., Holloway, C.A. and Wheelwright, S.C. (1994) 'Development projects: the engine of renewal', *Harvard Business Review*, 72 (5): 110–20.

Bryman, A. (1996) 'Leadership in organizations', in S.C. Clegg, C. Hardy and W.R. Nord (eds), *Handbook of Organization Studies*. London: Sage. pp. 276–92.

Burke, W.W. (1995) 'Organization change: what we know, what we need to know', *Journal of Management Inquiry*, 4 (2): 158–71.

Cammock, P., Nilakant, V. and Dakin, S. (1995) 'Developing a lay model of managerial effectiveness: a social constructionist perspective', *Journal of Management Studies*, 32 (4): 443–74.

Chen, C.C. and Velsor, E.V. (1996) 'New directions for research and practice in diversity leadership', *Leadership Quarterly*, 7 (2): 285–302.

Cohen, S.G., Ledford, G.E.J. and Spreitzer, G.M. (1996) 'A predictive model of self-managing work team effectiveness', *Human Relations*, 49 (5): 643–76.

Collins, J.C. and Porras, J.I. (1995) 'Building a visionary company', *California Management Review*, 37 (2): 80–100.

Conger, J.A. and Kanungo, R.N. (1994) 'Charismatic leadership in organizations: perceived behavioral attributes and their measurement', *Journal of Organizational Behaviour*, 15: 439–52.

Covey, S.R. (1989) *The Seven Habits of Highly Effective People: Restoring the Character Ethic*. New York: Simon & Schuster.

Denison, D.R., Hooijberg, R. and Quinn, R.E. (1995) 'Paradox and performance: toward a theory of behavioral complexity in managerial leadership', *Organization Science*, 6 (5): 524–40.

DiTomaso, N. and Hooijberg, R. (1996) 'Diversity and the demands of leadership', *Leadership Quarterly*, 7 (2): 163–87.

Dorfman, P., Howell, J.P., Hibino, S., Lee, J.K., Tate, U. and Bautista, A. (1997) 'Leadership in western and Asian countries: commonalities and differences in effective leadership processes and across cultures', *Leadership Quarterly*, 8 (3): 233–74.

Dunphy, D. and Bryant, B. (1996) 'Teams: panaceas or prescriptions for improved performance', *Human Relations*, 49 (5): 677–99.

Dunphy, D. and Stace, D. (1990) *Under New Management: Australian Organizations in Transition*. Sydney: McGraw-Hill.

Dunphy, D. and Stace, D. (1993) 'The strategic management of corporate change', *Human Relations*, 46 (8): 905–20.

Eggleston, K.K. and Bhagat, R.S. (1993) 'Organizational contexts and continent leadership roles: a theoretical exploration', *Human Relations*, 46 (10): 1177–92.

Ehrlich, C.J. (1994) 'Creating an employer-employee relationship for the future', *Human Resource Mangement*, 33 (3): 491–501.

Eisler, R. (1994) 'From domination to partnership: the hidden subtext for sustainable change', *Journal of Organizational Change Management*, 7 (4): 32–46.

Ellis, C. (1996) 'Making strategic alliances succeed: the importance of trust', *Harvard Business Review* (July–August): 8–9.

330 *Thinking about management*

Farkas, C.M. and Wetlaufer, S. (1996) 'The ways chief executive officers lead', *Harvard Business Review* (May–June): 110–22.

Farquar, K.W. (1995) 'Not just understudies: the dynamics of short-term leadership', *Human Resource Management*, 34 (1): 51–70.

Fiedler, F.E. (1996) 'Research on leadership selection and training: one view of the future', *Administrative Science Quarterly*, 41: 241–50.

Friedman, S.D. and Olk, P. (1995) 'Four ways to choose a CEO: crown heir, course race, coup d'état, and comprehensive search', *Human Resource Management*, 34 (1): 141–64.

Gardner, W.L. and Avolio, B.J. (1998) 'The charismatic relationship: a dramaturgical perspective', *Academy of Management Review*, 23 (1): 32–58.

Gastil, J. (1994) 'A definition and illustration of democratic leadership', *Human Relations*, 47 (8): 953–75.

Ghoshal, S. and Bartlett, C.A. (1995) 'Changing the role of top management: beyond structure to processes', *Harvard Business Review* (Jan–Feb): 86–96.

Gilmore, T.N. and Ronchi, D. (1995) 'Managing predecessors' shadows in executive transitions', *Human Resource Management*, 34 (1): 11–26.

Goffman, E. (1959) *The Presentation of Self in Everyday Life*. Garden City, NY: Doubleday Anchor.

Gordon, R.D. (1998) 'The re-conceptualization of leadership for new organizational forms'. Unpublished paper.

Graeff, C.L. (1997) 'Evolution of situational leadership theory: a critical review', *Leadership Quarterly*, 8 (2): 153–70.

Halal, W.E. (1994) 'From hierarchy to enterprise: internal markets are the new foundation of management', *Academy of Management Executive*, 8 (4): 69–83.

Hall, D.H. (1995) 'Unplanned executive transitions and the dance of the subidentities', *Human Resource Management*, 34 (1): 71–92.

Hart, S.L. and Quinn, R.E. (1993) 'Roles executives play: CEOs, behavioral complexity, and firm performance', *Human Relations*, 46 (5): 543–74.

Hershey, P. and Blanchard, K.H. (1977) *Management of Organization Behavior: Utilizing Human Resources*, 3rd edn. Englewood Cliffs, NJ: Prentice-Hall.

Hilmer, F.G. and Donaldson, L. (1996) *Management Redeemed: Debunking the Fads that Undermine Corporate Performance*. Sydney: Free Press.

Hooijberg, R. (1996) 'A multidirectional approach toward leadership: an extension of the concept of behavioral complexity', *Human Relations*, 49 (7): 917–46.

House, R.J. (1996) 'Path-goal theory of leadership: lessons, legacy, and a reformulated theory', *Leadership Quarterly*, 7 (3): 323–52.

Howell, J.M. and Avolio, B.J. (1992) 'The ethics of charismatic leadership: submission or liberation?', *Academy of Management Executive*, 6 (2): 43–54.

Howell, J.M., and Avolio, B.J. (1995) 'Charismatic leadership: submission or liberation?', *Business Quarterly*, autumn: 62–70.

Howell, J.P. (1997) 'Substitutes for leadership: their meaning and measurement – an a historical assessment', *Leadership Quarterly*, 8 (2): 113–16.

Huey, J. (1994) 'The new post-heroic leadership', *Fortune*, 21: 24–8.

Javidan, M., Bemmels, B., Stratton Devine, K. and Dastmalchian, A. (1995) 'Superior and subordinate gender and the acceptance of superiors as role models', *Human Relations*, 48 (11): 1271–84.

Jermier, J.M. (1996) 'The path-goal theory of leadership: a subtextual analysis', *Leadership Quarterly*, 7 (3): 311–16.

Katzenbach, J.R. (1997) 'The myth of the top management team', *Harvard Business Review* (Nov–Dec): 83–91.

Keller, T. and Dansereau, F. (1995) 'Leadership and empowerment: a social exchange perspective', *Human Relations*, 48 (2): 127–36.

Kerr, S. and Jermier, J. (1978) 'Substitutes for leadership: some implications for organizational design', *Organizations and Administrative Sciences*, 8: 135–46.

Kets de Vries, M.F.R., Miller, D. and Noel, A. (1993) 'Understanding the leader-strategy interface: application of the strategic relationship interview method', *Human Relations*, 46 (1): 5–22.

Kotter, J.P. (1995) 'Leading change: why transformations efforts fail', *Harvard Business Review* (March–April): 59–67.

Kotter, J.P. (1996) *Leading Change*. Boston, MA: Harvard Business School Press.

Leavy, B. (1996) 'On studying leadership in the strategy field', *Leadership Quarterly*, 7 (4): 435–54.

Limerick, D.C. and Cunnington, B. (1993) *Managing the New Organisation: A Blueprint for Networks and Strategic Alliances*. San Francisco: Jossey-Bass.

Linstead, S. and Grafton-Small, R. (1992) 'On reading organizational culture', *Organization Studies*, 13 (3): 331–55.

Mintzberg, H. (1996) 'Musings on management', *Harvard Business Review* (July–August): 61–7.

Moss, S.E. and Martinko, M.J. (1998) 'The effects of performance attributions and outcome dependence on leader feedback behavior following poor subordinate performance', *Journal of Organizational Behavior*, 19: 259–74.

Nadler, D.A. (1998) *Champions of Change: How CEOs and their Companies are Mastering the Skills of Radical Change*. San Francisco: Jossey-Bass.

Nadler, D.A. and Tushman, M.L. (1997) *Competing by Design: The Power of Organizational Architecture*. Oxford: Oxford University Press.

Nahavandi, A. and Malekzadeh, A.R. (1993) 'Leader style in strategy and organizational performance: an integrative framework', *Journal of Management Studies*, 30 (3): 406–25.

Neck, C.P. and Manz, C.C. (1996) 'Thought self-leadership: the impact of mental strategies training on employee cognition, behavior, and affect', *Journal of Organizational Behavior*, 17: 445–67.

Neck, C.P. and Moorhead, G. (1995) 'Groupthink remodeled: the importance of leadership, time pressure, and mythological decision-making procedures', *Human Relations*, 48 (5): 537–57.

Parry, K.W. (1998) 'Grounded theory and social processes: a new direction for leadership research', *Leadership Quarterly*, 9 (1): 85–105.

Quinn, R.E. (1996) *Deep Change: Discovering the Leader Within*. San Francisco: Jossey-Bass.

Roberts, K.H. and Lihuser, C. (1993) 'From Bhopal to banking: organizational design can mitigate risk', *Organizational Dynamics*, 21 (4): 15–26.

Rost, J.C. (1991) *Leadership for the Twenty-first Century*. New York: Praeger.

Salam, S., Cox, J.F. and Sims, H.P.J. (1997) 'In the eye of the beholder: how leadership relates to 360-degree performance ratings', *Group and Organization Management*, 22 (2): 185–209.

Sankowsky, D. (1995) 'The charismatic leader as narcissist: understanding the abuse of power', *Organizational Dynamics*, 23 (4): 57–71.

Schnake, M., Dumler, M.P. and Cochran, D.S. (1993) 'The relationship between "traditional" leadership, "super" leadership and organizational citizenship behavior', *Group and Organization Management*, 18 (3): 352–65.

Schriesheim, C.A. and Neider, L.L. (1996) 'Path-goal leadership theory: the long and winding road', *Leadership Quarterly*, 7 (3): 317–21.

Sellers, P. (1996) 'What exactly is charisma?', *Fortune*, 15: 68–70.

Senge, P.M. (1997) 'Communities of leaders and learners', *Harvard Business Review*, (Sept–Oct): 31–2.

Shenkar, O., Ronen, S., Shefy, E. and Chow, I.H. (1998) 'The role structure of Chinese managers', *Human Relations*, 51 (1): 51–72.

Stewart, G.L. and Manz, C.C. (1995) 'Leadership for self-managing work teams: a typology and integrative model', *Human Relations*, 48 (7): 747–70.

Stewart, T.A. (1996) 'The nine dilemmas leaders face', *Fortune*, 133 (5): 112–13. (18 March 1996).

Tharenou, P. (1993) 'A test of reciprocal causality for absenteeism', *Journal of Organizational Behavior*, 14: 269–90.

Theus, K.T. (1995) 'Communication in a power vacuum: sense-making and enactment during crisis-induced departures', *Human Resource Management*, 34 (1): 27–49.

Thomas, D.A. and Ely, R.J. (1996) 'Making differences matter: a new paradigm for managing diversity', *Harvard Business Review* (Sept–Oct): 79–90.

Thomas, P. and Greenberger, D.B. (1995) 'The relationship between leadership and time orientation', *Journal of Management Inquiry*, 4 (3): 272–92.

Tierney, W.G. (1996) 'Leadership and postmodernist: on voice and the qualitative method', *Leadership Quarterly*, 7 (3): 371–83.

Tracey, J.B. and Hinkin, T.R. (1998) 'Transformational leadership or effective managerial practices', *Group and Organization Management*, 23 (3): 220–36.

Valikangas, L. and Okumura, A. (1997) 'Why do people follow leaders? A study of a U.S. and a Japanese change program', *Leadership Quarterly*, 8 (3): 313–37.

White, B.J. (1994) 'Developing leaders for the high-performance workplace', *Human Resource Management*, 33 (1): 161–8.

Willmott, H. (1993) 'Strength is ignorance: managing culture in modern organizations', *Journal of Management Studies*, 30: 515–52.

Wind, J.Y. and Main, J. (1998) *Driving Change: How the Best Companies are Preparing for the 21st Century*. New York: Free Press.

Yeung, A.K. and Ready, D.A. (1995) 'Developing leadership capabilities of global corporations: a comparative study in eight nations', *Human Resource Management*, 34 (1): 529–47.

10 MANAGEMENT AND POSTMODERNISM

Abramis, D.J. (1990) 'Play in work: childish hedonism or adult enthusiasm?', *American Behavioral Scientist*, 33: 353–73.

Alter, C. and Hage, J. (1993) *Organizations Working Together*. Newbury Park, CA: Sage.

Alvesson, M. (1995) 'The Meaning and Meaninglessness of Postmodernism: Some Ironic Remarks', *Organization Studies*, 16 (6): 1047–75.

Alvesson, M. and Willmott, H. (1992a) 'On the idea of emancipation in management and organization studies', *Academy of Management Review*, 17 (3): 432–64.

Alvesson, M. and Willmott, H. (eds) (1992b) *Critical Management Studies*. London: Sage.

Amara, R. (1990) 'New directions for innovation', *Futures*, 22 (2): 142–52.

Arrington, C.E. and Francis, J.R. (1989) 'Letting the chat out of the bag: deconstruction, privilege and accounting research', *Accounting, Organizations and Society*, 14 (1/2): 1–28.

Ashforth, B.E. and Humphrey, R.H. (1995) 'Emotion in the workplace: a reappraisal', *Human Relations*, 48 (2): 97–125.

Barker, J. (1993) 'Tightening the iron cage: concertive control in self-managing teams', *Administrative Science Quarterly*, 38: 408–37.

Berg, P.O. (1989) 'Postmodern management? From facts to fiction in theory and practice', *Scandinavian Journal of Management*, 5: 201–17.

Boje, D.M. (1991) 'The storytelling organization: a study of story performance in an office-supply firm', *Administrative Science Quarterly*, 36: 106–12.

Boje, D.M. (1995) 'Stories of the storytelling organization: a postmodern analysis of Disney as "Tamara-Land"', *Academy of Management Journal*, 38 (4): 997–1035.

Brown, J.S. and Duguid, P. (1991) 'Organizational learning and communities-of-practice: toward a unified view of working, learning and innovation', *Organization Science*, 2 (1): 40–57.

Brown, R.H. (1994) 'Reconstructing social theory after the postmodern critique', in H.W. Simons and M. Billig (eds), *After Postmodernism: Reconstructing Ideology Critique*. London: Sage.

Brown Berman, R. and McCartney, S. (1996) 'A home from home: the organization as family', *Studies in Cultures, Organizations and Societies*, 2 (2): 241–55.

Bryman, A. (1996) 'Leadership in organizations', in S.R. Clegg, C. Hardy and W. Nord (eds), *Handbook of Organization Studies*. London: Sage. pp. 276–92.

Burrell, G. (1994) 'Echo and the bunnymen', in J. Hassard and M. Parker (eds), *Postmodernism and Organizations*. London: Sage.

Byrne, J.A. (1993) 'The virtual corporation', *Business Week*, 8 February: 98–103.

Chia, R. (1995) 'Teaching paradigm shifting in management education: university business schools and the entrepreneurial imagination', *Journal of Management Studies*, 33 (4): 409–28.

Clegg, S. (1989) *Frameworks of Power*. London: Sage.

Clegg, S.R. (1990) *Modern Organizations: Organization Studies in the Postmodern World*. London: Sage.

Clegg, S.R. and Hardy, C. (1996) 'Introduction: organizations, organization and organizing', in S.R. Clegg, C. Hardy and W.R. Nord (eds), *Handbook of Organization Studies*. London: Sage. pp. 1–28.

Cobb, S. and Rifkin, J. (1991) 'Neutrality as a discursive practice: the construction and transformation of narratives in community mediation', *Studies in Law, Politics, and Society*, 11: 69–91.

Collins, R. (1981) 'On the microfoundations of macrosociology', *American Journal of Sociology*, 86 (5): 984–1013.

Conger, J. (1989) 'Leadership: the art of empowering others', *The Academy of Management Executive*, 3 (1): 17–24.

Cooper, R. and Burrell, G. (1988) 'Modernism, postmodernism and organizational analysis: an introduction', *Organization Studies*, 9 (1): 91–112.

Czarniawska-Joerges, B. (1996) 'Autobiographical acts and organizational identities', in S. Linstead, R. Grafton Small and P. Jeffcutt (eds), *Understanding Management*. London: Sage.

Daft, R.L. and Weick, K.E. (1984) 'Toward a model of organizations as interpretation systems', *Academy of Management Review*, 9 (2): 284–95.

Deetz, S. (1992a) *Democracy in an Age of Corporate Colonization: Developments in Communication and the Politics of Everyday Life*. Albany, NY: State University of New York.

Deetz, S. (1992b) 'Disciplinary power in the modern corporation', in M. Alvesson and H. Willmott (eds), *Critical Management Studies*. London: Sage. pp. 21–45.

Deetz, S. (1994) 'The new politics of the workplace: ideology and other unobtrusive controls', in H.W. Simons and M. Billig (eds), *After Postmodernism*. London: Sage. pp. 172–99.

de Koning, A. (1996) 'Top management decision making: a framework based on the story model'. Paper presented at the annual meeting of the Academy of Management, Cincinnati, Ohio.

Derrida, J. (1978) *Writing and Difference*. Chicago: University of Chicago Press.

Dougherty, D. (1996) 'Organizing for innovation', in S.R. Clegg, C. Hardy and W.R. Nord (eds), *Handbook of Organization Studies*. London: Sage. pp. 424–39.

Dreyfus, H.L. and Rabinow, P. (1982) *Michel Foucault: Beyond Structuralism and Hermeneutics*. Brighton: Harvester.

Dutton, J.E. and Dukerich, J.M. (1991) 'Keeping an eye on the mirror: image and identity in organizational adaptation', *Academy of Management Journal*, 34 (3): 517–54.

Eccles, R. and Nohria, N. (1992) *Beyond the Hype*. Cambridge, MA: Harvard Business School Press.

Fairtlough, G. (1994) *Creative Compartments: A Design for Future Organisations*. London: Adamantine Press.

Fine, G.A. (1988) 'Letting off steam? Redefining a restaurant's work environment', in M.D. Moore and R.C. Snyder (eds), *Inside Organizations: Understanding the Human Dimension*. Newbury Park, CA: Sage. pp. 119–28.

Fineman, S. (ed.) (1993) *Emotions in Organizations*. London: Sage.

Fineman, S. (1996) 'Emotion and organizing', in S.R. Clegg, C. Hardy and W.R. Nord (eds), *Handbook of Organization Studies*. London: Sage. pp. 543–64.

Fineman, S. and Gabriel, Y. (1996) *Experiencing Organizations*. London: Sage.

Foucault, M. (1965) *The Archeology of Knowledge*. London: Routledge.

Foucault, M. (1977) *Discipline and Punish: The Birth of the Prison*. Harmondsworth: Penguin.

Foucault, M. (ed.) (1980) *Power/Knowledge: Selected Interviews and Other Writings 1972–1977*. Brighton: Harvester.

Foucault, M. (1982) 'The subject and power', in H.L. Dreyfus and P. Rabinow (eds), *Michel Foucault: Beyond Structuralism and Hermeneutics*. Brighton: Harvester. pp. 208–26.

Foucault, M. (1984) *The History of Sexuality: An Introduction*. Harmondsworth: Penguin.

Gabriel, Y. (1995) 'The unmanaged organization: stories, fantasies and subjectivity', *Organization Studies*, 16 (3): 477–501.

Gagliardi, P. (1996) 'Exploring the aesthetic side of organizational life', in S.R. Clegg, C. Hardy and W.R. Nord (eds), *Handbook of Organization Studies*. London: Sage. pp. 565–80.

Galbraith, J.R., Lawler, E.E. and Associates (1993) *Organizing for the Future: The New Logic for Managing Complex Organizations*. San Francisco: Jossey-Bass.

Gillespie, J. and Meyer, G. (1995) 'Gender, voice, electronic communication and postmodern values', *Journal of Organizational Change Management*, 8 (2): 29–44.

Glaser, B. and Strauss, A. (1967) *Discovery of Grounded Theory: Strategies for Qualitative Research*. Chicago: Aldine.

Goffman, E. (1959) *The Presentation of Self in Everyday Life*. Garden City, NJ: Doubleday.

Guillet de Montheux, P. (1991) 'Modernism and the dominating firm – on the managerial mentality of the Swedish model', *Scandinavian Journal of Management*, 7 (1): 27–40.

Hamel, G. and Prahalad, C.K. (1994) *Competing for the Future*. Boston: Harvard Business School Press.

Handy, C. (1989) *The Age of Unreason*. Boston, MA: Harvard Business School Press.

Hardy, C. (1991) 'Pluralism, power and collegiality in universities', *Financial Accountability and Management*, 7 (3): 127–42.

Hardy, C. and Leiba-O'Sullivan, S. (1998) 'The power behind empowerment: implications for research and practice', *Human Relations*, 51 (4): 451–83.

Hardy, C. and Palmer, I. (1999) 'Pedagogical practice and postmodernist ideas', *Journal of Management Education*, 23 (4): 377–95.

Hassard, J. (1994) 'Postmodern organizational analysis: toward a conceptual framework', *Journal of Management Studies*, 31 (3): 303–24.

Hassard, J. (1996) 'Images of time in work and organization', in S.R. Clegg, C. Hardy and W.R. Nord (eds), *Handbook of Organization Studies*. London: Sage. pp. 581–98.

Hatch, M.J. (1997) *Organization Theory: Modern, Symbolic and Postmodern Perspectives*. Oxford: Oxford University Press.

Hetrick, W.P. and Boje, D.M. (1992) 'Organization and the body: post-Fordist dimensions', *Journal of Organizational Change Management*, 5 (1): 48–57.

Hochschild, A. (1983) *The Managed Heart*. Berkeley, CA: University of California.

Hoskin, K. and Macve, R. (1988) 'The genesis of accountability: the West Point connections', *Accounting, Organizations and Society*, 12: 37–73.

Hosking, D.M. (1988) 'Organizing, leadership and skilful process', *Journal of Management Studies*, 25: 147–66.

Hosking, D.M. (1991) 'Chief executives, organising processes, and skill', *European Journal of Applied Psychology*, 41: 95–103.

Jackson, M. (1997) 'Spying on staff: survey', *The Montreal Gazette*, 23 May: D8.

Janis, I.L. (1982) *Groupthink: Psychological Studies of Policy Decisions and Fiascoes*, 2nd edn. Boston: Houghton Mifflin.

Jeffcutt, P. (1994) 'From interpretation to representation in organizational analysis: postmodernism, ethnography and organizational symbolism', *Organization Studies*, 15 (2): 241–74.

Kahn, W.A. (1990) 'Psychological conditions of personal engagement and disengagement at work', *Academy of Management Journal*, 33: 692–724.

Kahn, W.A. (1992) 'To be fully there: psychological presence at work', *Human Relations*, 45: 321–49.

Kerfoot, D. and Knights, D. (1993) 'Management, masculinity and manipulation: from paternalism to corporate strategy in financial services in Britain', *Journal of Management Studies*, 30 (4): 659–77.

Kilduff, M. and Mehra, A. (1997) 'Postmodernism and organizational research', *Academy of Management Review*, 22 (2): 543–81.

Knights, D. (1992) 'Changing spaces: the disruptive impact of a new epistemological location for the study of management', *Academy of Management Review*, 17 (3): 514–36.

Knights, D. and Morgan, G. (1991) 'Strategic discourse and subjectivity: towards a critical analysis of corporate strategy in organisations', *Organisation Studies*, 12 (3): 251–73.

Knights, D. and Willmott, H. (1989) 'Power and subjectivity at work: from degradation to subjugation in social relations', *Sociology*, 23 (4): 535–58.

Knights, D. and Willmott, H. (1992) 'Conceptualizing leadership process: a study of senior managers in a financial services company', *Journal of Management Studies*, 29 (6): 761–82.

Laclau, E. and Mouffe, C. (1987) *Hegemony and Socialist Strategy: Towards a Radical Democratic Politics*. London: Verso.

Lash, S. (1990) *Sociology of Postmodernism*. London: Routledge.

Lash, S. and Urry, J. (1987) *The End of Organised Capitalism*. Oxford: Polity Press.

Lather, P. (1994) 'Staying dumb? Feminist research and pedagogy with/in the postmodern', in W.H. Simons and M. Billig (eds), *After Postmodernism: Reconstructing Ideology Critique*. London: Sage.

Law, J. (1994) 'Organization, narrative and strategy', in J. Hassard and M. Parker (eds), *Towards a New Theory of Organizations*. London: Routledge. pp. 248–68.

Legge, K. (1995) *Human Resource Management: Rhetorics and Realities*. London: Macmillan.

Letiche, H. (1992) 'Having taught postmodernists', *International Studies of Management and Organization*, 22 (3): 46–70.

Linstead, S., Grafton Small, R. and Jeffcutt, P. (eds) (1996) *Understanding Management*. London: Sage.

Meyer, J.W. and Rowan, B. (1977) 'Institutionalized organizations: formal structure as myth and ceremony', *American Journal of Sociology*, 83 (2): 340–63.

Miller, P. and O'Leary, T. (1987) 'Accounting and the deconstruction of the governable person', *Accounting, Organizations and Society*, 12 (3): 235–65.

Ostell, A. (1996) 'Managing dysfunctional emotions in organizations', *Journal of Management Studies*, 33 (4): 525–56.

Parker, M. (1992) 'Post-modern organizations or postmodern organization theory?', *Organization Studies*, 13 (1): 1–17.

Parry, G. and Morris, P. (1975) 'When is a decision not a decision?', in L. Crewe (ed.), *British Political Sociology Yearbook*, vol. 1. London: Croom Helm.

Peters, T.J. (1987) *Thriving on Chaos: Handbook for a Management Revolution.* New York: Knopf.

Phillips, N. and Hardy, C. (1997) 'Managing multiple identities: discourse legitimacy and resources in the UK refugee system', *Organization*, 4 (2): 159–85.

Pirsig, R. (1974) *Zen and the Art of Motorcycle Maintenance.* London: Bodley Head.

Pogrebin, M.R. and Poole, E.D. (1988) 'Humor in the briefing room: a study of the strategic uses of humor among police', *Journal of Contemporary Ethnography*, 17: 183–210.

Powell, W.W. (1990) 'Neither market nor hierarchy: network forms of organization', in B.M. Staw and L.L. Cummings (eds), *Research in Organizational Behaviour.* Greenwich, CT: JAI Press.

Ranson, S., Hinings, R. and Greenwood, R. (1980) 'The structuring of organizational structure', *Administrative Science Quarterly*, 25 (1): 1–14.

Roberts, N.C. and Bradley, R.T. (1988) 'Limits of charisma', in J.A. Conger and R.N. Kanungo (eds), *Charismatic Leadership.* San Francisco: Jossey-Bass. pp. 253–75.

Rosenau, P.M. (1992) *Post-Modernism and the Social Sciences: Insights, Inroads, and Intrusions.* Princeton, NJ: Princeton University Press.

Rothwell, R. (1992) 'Successful industrial innovation: critical factors for the 1990s', *R and D Management*, 22 (3): 221–39.

Sandelands, L.E. and Buckner, G.C. (1989) 'Of art and work: aesthetic experience and the psychology of work feelings', in L.L. Cummings and B.M. Staw (eds), *Research in Organizational Behaviour*, vol. 11. Greenwich, CT: JAI Press. pp. 105–31.

Silverman, D. (1970) *The Theory of Organizations.* New York: Basic Books.

Silverman, D. (1985) *Qualitative Methodology and Sociology: Describing the Social World.* Aldershot: Gower.

Simons, H. W. (1994) 'Teaching the pedagogies: a dialectical approach to an ideological dilemma', in H.W. Simons and M. Billig (eds), *After Postmodernism: Reconstructing Ideology Critique.* London: Sage. pp. 133–49.

Smart, B. (1985) *Michel Foucault.* London: Tavistock.

Smart, B. (1986) 'The politics of truth and the problem of hegemony', in D.C. Hoy (ed.), *Foucault: A Critical Reader.* Oxford: Blackwell. pp. 157–73.

Thompson, P. (1993) 'Postmodernism: fatal distraction', in J. Hassard and M. Parker (eds), *Postmodernism and Organizations.* London: Sage.

Townley, B. (1993) 'Foucault, power/knowledge, and its relevance for human resource management', *Academy of Management Review*, 18 (3): 518–45.

Tsoukas, H. (1992) 'Panoptic reason and the search for totality: a critical assessment of the critical systems perspective', *Human Relations*, 45 (7): 637–57.

Tully, S. (1993) 'The modular corporation', *Fortune*, 8: 106–15.

Turner, B.S. (ed.) (1990) *Theories of Modernity and Post Modernity.* London: Sage.

Weick, K. (1969) *The Social Psychology of Organizing.* Reading, MA: Addison-Wesley.

Weick, K.E. and Westley, F. (1996) 'Organizational learning: affirming an oxymoron', in S.R. Clegg, C. Hardy and W.R. Nord (eds), *Handbook of Organization Studies.* London: Sage. pp. 148–74.

Westley, F. (1990) 'The eye of the needle: cultural and personal transformation in a traditional organization', *Human Relations*, 43 (3): 273–93.

Westley, F. and Mintzberg, H. (1988) 'Profiles of strategic vision: Levesque and Iacocca', in J.A. Conger and R.N. Kanungo (eds), *Charismatic Leadership: The Elusive Factor in Organizational Effectiveness.* San Francisco: Jossey-Bass. pp. 161–212.

Wharton, A.S. (1993) 'The affective consequences of service work: managing emotions on the job', *Work and Occupations*, 20 (2): 205–32.

White, L. and Taket, A. (1994) 'The death of the expert', *Journal of Operational Research Society*, 45 (7): 733–48.

White, R.F. and Jacques, R. (1995) 'Operationalizing the postmodernity construct for efficient organizational change management', *Journal of Organizational Change Management*, 8 (2): 45–71.

Willmott, H. (1993) 'Strength is ignorance: slavery is freedom: managing culture in modern organizations', *Journal of Management Studies*, 30 (4): 515–52.

Willmott, H. (1995) 'What has been happening in organization theory and does it matter?', *Personnel Review*, 24 (8): 33–53.

Winkleman, M. (1993) 'The outsourcing source book', *Journal of Business Strategy*, 15 (3): 52–8.

INDEX

Page numbers in *italics* refer to tables, those in **bold** refer to exercises.